ким # VOICE AND SPEECH PROCESSING

McGraw-Hill Series in Electrical Engineering

Consulting Editor

Stephen W. Director, *Carnegie-Mellon University*

CIRCUITS AND SYSTEMS
COMMUNICATIONS AND SIGNAL PROCESSING
CONTROL THEORY
ELECTRONICS AND ELECTRONIC CIRCUITS
POWER AND ENERGY
ELECTROMAGNETICS
COMPUTER ENGINEERING
INTRODUCTORY
RADAR AND ANTENNAS
VLSI

Previous Consulting Editors

Ronald N. Bracewell, Colin Cherry, James F. Gibbons,
Willis W. Harman, Hubert Heffner, Edward W. Herold, John G. Linvill,
Simon Ramo, Ronald A. Rohrer, Anthony E. Siegman, Charles Susskind,
Frederick E. Terman, John G. Truxal, Ernst Weber, and John R. Whinnery

CAD/CAM, Robotics, and Computer Vision

Consulting Editor

Herbert Freeman, *Rutgers University*

Fu, Gonzalez, and Lee: *Robotics: Control, Sensing, Vision, and Intelligence*
Groover, Weiss, Nagel, and Odrey: *Industrial Robotics: Technology, Programming, and Applications*
Parsons: *Voice and Speech Processing*
Levine: *Vision in Man and Machine*

Communications and Signal Processing

Consulting Editor
Stephen W. Director, *Carnegie-Mellon University*

Antoniou: *Digital Filters: Analysis and Design*
Candy: *Signal Processing: The Modet-Based Approach*
Carlson: *Communications Systems: An Introduction to Signals and Noise in Electrical Communication*
Cherin: *An Introduction to Optical Fibers*
Cooper and McGillem: *Modern Communications and Spread Spectrum*
Davenport: *Probability and Random Processes: An Introduction for Applied Scientists and Engineers*
Drake: *Fundamentals of Applied Probability Theory*
Guiasu: *Information Theory with New Applications*
Keiser: *Optical Fiber Communications*
Melsa and Cohn: *Decision and Estimation Theory*
Papoulis: *Probability, Random Variables, and Stochastic Processes*
Papoulis: *Signal Analysis*
Papoulis: *The Fourier Integral and Its Applications*
Peebles: *Probability, Random Variables, and Random Signal Principles*
Proakis: *Digital Communications*
Schwartz: *Information Transmission, Modulation, and Noise*
Schwartz and Shaw: *Signal Processing*
Shooman: *Probabilistic Reliability: An Engineering Approach*
Smith: *Modern Communication Circuits*
Taub and Schilling: *Principles of Communication Systems*
Viterbi and Omura: *Principles of Digital Communication and Coding*

VOICE AND SPEECH PROCESSING

Thomas W. Parsons
Associate Professor of Computer Science
Hofstra University

McGraw-Hill Book Company

New York   St. Louis   San Francisco   Auckland   Bogotá   Hamburg
Johannesburg   London   Madrid   Mexico   Montreal   New Delhi
Panama   Paris   São Paulo   Singapore   Sydney   Tokyo   Toronto

*To my Mother
and to the memory of
my Father*

This book was set in Times Roman by Santype International Limited.
The editor was Sanjeev Rao; the production supervisor was Diane Renda;
the cover was designed by Rafael Hernandez.
Project supervision was done by Santype International Limited.
R. R. Donnelley & Sons Company was printer and binder.

VOICE AND SPEECH PROCESSING

Copyright © 1987 by McGraw-Hill, Inc. All rights reserved. Printed in the United States of America. Except as permitted under the United States Copyright Act of 1976, no part of this publication may be reproduced or distributed in any form or by any means, or stored in a data base or retrieval system, without the prior written permission of the publisher.

1 2 3 4 5 6 7 8 9 0 DOCDOC 8 9 8 7 6

ISBN 0-07-048541-0

Library of Congress Cataloging-in-Publication Data

Parsons, Thomas W.
    Voice and speech processing.

    (McGraw-Hill series in electrical engineering.
Communications and signal processing)
    Bibliography: p.
    1. Speech processing systems. I. Title. II. Series.
TK882.S65P37   1986   006.4′54   85-23669
ISBN 0-07-048541-0

ABOUT THE AUTHOR

Thomas W. Parsons is an associate professor of computer science at Hofstra University. He received the B.A. degree in classical Greek in 1952 and the B.S. degree in electrical engineering in 1959, from the University of Wisconsin. He received the M.S. degree in electrical engineering from Columbia University in 1965, and the Ph.D. degree in electrical engineering from the Polytechnic Institute of New York in 1975, where he has taught on and off since 1974. From 1962 to 1975 he was a member of the staff of the Federal Scientific Corporation (now the Wavetek Corporation), doing research in speech recognition and enhancement with the Acoustics and Speech Research Group, and from 1979 to 1981 he was with the Defense Communications Division of ITT. His research interests include digital processing and speech enhancement. Dr. Parsons is a member of the Acoustical Society of America, the Association for Computing Machinery, and the Institute of Electrical and Electronics Engineers.

CONTENTS

Preface ... xii

Part One Review Materials

Chapter 1 Linear Systems and Transforms ... 3

1-1 Sampled-Data Systems; The Sampling Theorem ... 4
1-2 Analysis of Linear Systems ... 6
1-3 Transforms ... 12
1-4 The Z Transform ... 13
1-5 The Discrete Fourier Transform (DFT) ... 21
1-6 Practical Considerations in Using the DFT ... 29

Chapter 2 Probability Theory ... 42

2-1 Events; Axioms of Probability ... 42
2-2 Conditional Probability; Independence ... 43
2-3 Random Variables; Probability Density; Moments ... 44
2-4 Two or More Random Variables ... 47
2-5 Random Functions; Autocorrelation and Power Spectrum ... 50
2-6 Random Signals in Linear Systems ... 53

Part Two Linguistic and Technical Fundamentals

Chapter 3 Speech Generation and Perception ... 59

3-1 Organs of Speech ... 59
3-2 Speech Production ... 64
3-3 Hearing and Perception ... 67

Chapter 4 Articulatory Phonetics and Phonemics — 84
- 4-1 Articulatory Phonetics — 84
- 4-2 Phonemics — 92
- 4-3 Distinctive Features — 94
- 4-4 Syllables, Juncture, and Prosodics — 96

Chapter 5 Acoustic Phonetics — 100
- 5-1 Acoustics of the Vocal Tract — 103
- 5-2 Analysis of the Acoustics of Vocoids — 106
- 5-3 Properties of Vowel Waveforms — 114
- 5-4 Acoustic Characteristics of Nasals — 117
- 5-5 Acoustic Characteristics of Stops and Fricatives — 119
- 5-6 Model of Speech Production — 124
- 5-7 Statistics of Speech Signals — 125
- 5-8 Examination of a Sample Utterance — 128

Chapter 6 Linear Prediction — 136
- 6-1 Introduction — 137
- 6-2 Types of System Model — 137
- 6-3 Derivation of the Linear Prediction Equations — 138
- 6-4 Solving the Autocorrelation Equations — 141
- 6-5 The Reverse Predictor; Recurrence Relations — 145
- 6-6 Applications: Filtering and Modeling — 147
- 6-7 Solution of the Covariance Equations — 156
- 6-8 Special Techniques: The Methods of Schur and Burg — 159
- 6-9 Practical Considerations — 163

Chapter 7 Recognition: Features and Distances — 170
- 7-1 Introduction to Pattern Recognition — 170
- 7-2 Decision Rules and Distance Measures — 171
- 7-3 Features Selection — 175
- 7-4 Feature Evaluation — 176
- 7-5 Clustering — 188

Part Three Applications

Chapter 8 Pitch and Formant Estimation — 197
- 8-1 Fundamental Frequency Estimation — 197
- 8-2 Formant Frequency Estimation — 210
- 8-3 Tracking and Smoothing — 219

Chapter 9 Speech Compression — 225
- 9-1 Pulse-Code Modulation (PCM) — 226
- 9-2 Waveform Encoders: Basic Techniques — 228
- 9-3 Application of Linear Prediction: Adaptive DPCM — 234

9-4	Delta Modulation	244
9-5	Filter-Bank Coders	246
9-6	Adaptive Transform Coding	257

Chapter 10 Voice Encoding and Synthesis 262

10-1	Linear-Prediction Vocoders	263
10-2	Vector Quantization	269
10-3	Speech Synthesis	277

Chapter 11 Speech Recognition 291

11-1	Isolated-Word Recognition	293
11-2	Word Spotting	317
11-3	Continuous-Speech Recognition	318
11-4	Speech-Understanding Systems	326

Chapter 12 Speaker Recognition 332

12-1	Selection of Features	335
12-2	Examples of Use of Various Features	335

Chapter 13 Enhancing Noisy Speech 345

13-1	Periodic Noise	346
13-2	Wideband Noise	349
13-3	Interfering Speech	358
13-4	Measures of Intelligibility	360

Appendices 365

A	The Orthogonality Principle	365
B	Program Listings	368

Index 383

PREFACE

This book is intended for a course in voice processing at the senior or first-year graduate level. It is also intended for professionals who are newcomers to the field and need to acquire the background necessary to follow the current technical literature. As voice processing emerges from the laboratory and begins to appear in commercial or military products, many people are finding themselves involved in this area for the first time.

The standard textbooks, at this writing, are Flanagan's *Speech Analysis, Synthesis, and Perception,* Rabiner and Schafer's *Digital Processing of Speech Signals,* and Markel and Gray's *Linear Prediction of Speech.* These works have deservedly become classics, but they are beyond the reach of the average engineering or computer science graduate who is new to the field, and it has been my observation that beginners find them intimidating. This book is written at a significantly less demanding level than these works.

I assume that the reader is at home with calculus and matrix algebra and is, as they say, mathematically mature. Some of my intended readers, students and professionals alike, may have a computer science background in which familiarity with the necessary engineering concepts may be sketchy or nonexistent. For this reason I have started the book with a brief review of elementary topics. Workers experienced in the field will find this material unnecessary and even tedious, but I believe that the newcomer will find it useful, or at least reassuring. Even engineers may not have been exposed to the variety of disciplines on which the field of voice processing draws and may find such a review helpful.

In presenting advanced material, I have emphasized clarity and motivation, and have been at pains to show the many cases where a number of concepts have evolved from a common starting point. For the benefit of electrical engineers, I have occasionally pointed out similarities to material with which they may be familiar (for example, the association between the Kelly-Lochbaum equations and the scattering matrix).

In places I have gone fairly deeply into the mathematics, but overall the style is informal and rather casual. If a proof or a derivation is useful for understanding the logic behind a process, or if it lays the groundwork for topics to be discussed later, I have included it; otherwise the proof is omitted and the reader is referred to a book or paper where it may be found. If a proof can be made to make more sense by sacrificing rigor, rigor has been sacrificed. I have also occasionally sacrificed strict accuracy if doing so clarifies the presentation. This does not mean that the material is easy; many of the approaches in this field are unfamiliar and require getting used to.

As regards the chapters on applications, the stated purpose of the book is to enable the student to read the current literature; if the first sections have done their job, the reader can learn about applications from that literature. The section on applications is therefore limited to brief descriptions of representative efforts in the various subject areas. There seems little point in trying to repeat in detail material which has, for the most part, been adequately covered in the literature. The only exceptions to this have been those places where I have felt it would be helpful to explain a technique which has found extensive use—for example, time-warping in the case of speech and talker recognition, or the hidden Markov model. Hence the reader should regard this section as a survey painted in rather broad strokes and not intended to be exhaustive. This is particularly true in the field of speech recognition, where the literature is vast. For the best introduction to this subject, I recommend Reddy's encyclopaedic survey in the April, 1976, *Proceedings of the IEEE*; after ten years, this paper is still a classic.

Acknowledgements: I suppose my greatest indebtedness is to all the researchers who have given us such a splendid body of literature. The IEEE *Transactions on Acoustics, Speech, and Signal Processing*, along with the *Journal of the Acoustical Society of America* and the *Bell System Technical Journal* (now renamed the *AT & T Technical Journal*), are the principal vehicles in English for technical communications in the field. Open any issue and you will find papers of the highest merit on every aspect of voice processing; taken together, the last ten years' issues are an education in themselves.

I am also obliged to my students at the Polytechnic Institute of New York and in the Continuing Education Program of the George Washington University, where courses based on the material presented here were given, who helped me by their evaluations of the material and of the way in which it was presented. George Feeney and Nathaniel Polish, at The Dun and Bradstreet Corporation, have also offered many valuable suggestions and criticisms. I am grateful to the staff of McGraw-Hill for their assistance and encouragement, and to their reviewers for their many helpful criticisms. I owe, here as in so many other things, a particular debt of gratitude to my wife, for her support, encouragement, and patience while this manuscript was being prepared.

Thomas W. Parsons

Man knows that there are in the soul tints more bewildering, more numberless, and more nameless than the colours of an autumn forest; he knows that there are abroad in the world and doing strange and terrible service in it crimes that have never been condemned and virtues that have never been christened. Yet he seriously believes that these things can, every one of them, in all their tones and semi-tones, in all their blends and unions, be accurately represented by an arbitrary system of grunts and squeals. He believes that an ordinary civilized stockbroker can really produce out of his own inside noises which denote all the mysteries of memory and all the agonies of desire.

G. K. Chesterton, *G. F. Watts* (1904), p. 43f

PART ONE

REVIEW MATERIALS

Speech processing is an interdisciplinary technology. It draws on acoustics, probability theory, linear system theory, physiology, psychology, linear algebra, digital signal processing, computer science, and linguistics, to mention only a few fields. It is unreasonable to expect the reader to be at home in all of these fields, while on the other hand the scope of this book cannot possibly include adequate coverage of everything that might be needed. The review notes provided here and in the appendix are offered as a compromise: they are intended to include just enough material to render the subsequent chapters comprehensible, without pretending to be complete surveys. For readers who are already familiar with these subjects, these chapters will serve to establish a common language and notation. For further background on these topics, references to standard texts are given at the end of each chapter.

CHAPTER
ONE

LINEAR SYSTEMS AND TRANSFORMS

A *system* is a conceptual means for modeling processes, natural or artificial, which we wish to study. A system is usually represented as a featureless enclosure ("black box") to which one or more time functions are applied and which in turn emits one or more time functions. Since these functions are usually information-bearing we call them *signals*. The signals entering the box are called *inputs* and those leaving are called *outputs* (Fig. 1-1). (We will be interested mostly in systems with only one input and one output.)

As this representation implies, our chief interest is in relations between inputs and outputs of systems, and in particular in predicting the output resulting from any given input. We may or may not know the contents of the black box. If we do, we may be able to determine the input/output relations by analyzing its contents. If we do not, we can, under certain circumstances, determine its input/output relations experimentally. We may then wish to use these empirical results as the basis for a system *model*—i.e., a plausible guess as to the contents of the box.

The power of viewing processes as systems lies in the fact that for most natural systems we can find simple systems whose behavior suitably approximates that of the phenomenon under consideration. We will find it convenient to use $H[\ ]$ to represent how the system transforms its input. ($H[\ ]$ is called the *system function*.) Then the principal simplifications are as follows:

1. *Time-invariant* (or *shift-invariant*) *system*. One for which $H[\ ]$ is independent of time. Suppose $y(t) = H[x(t)]$; then if the input is shifted by some time T, the output is $H[x(t - T)] = y(t - T)$.

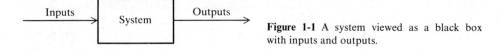

Figure 1-1 A system viewed as a black box with inputs and outputs.

2. *Linear system.* One whose response to inputs is additive. More precisely, let $x_1(t)$ and $x_2(t)$ be two input signals for which $y_1(t) = H[x_1(t)]$ and $y_2(t) = H[x_2(t)]$. Then if a and b are constants and $x(t) = ax_1(t) + bx_2(t)$, then in a linear system,

$$y(t) = aH[x_1(t)] + bH[x_2(t)]$$
$$= ay_1(t) + by_2(t)$$

The application of linearity when analyzing compound inputs is known as the *superposition principle*, because we can analyze the response to x_1 alone and to x_2 alone and sum (superpose) the results to find the response to the combined inputs.

3. *Lumped system.* One in which the parameters are in some sense physically isolated or separable. For our purposes, we can say that if the motion of waves (e.g., sound waves) through the system must be taken into account, it is a distributed system. A shock absorber can be modeled as a simple, lumped mechanical resistance; but an organ pipe must be analyzed as a distributed-parameter system, since its behavior depends on the motion of sound waves along its length.

When we speak of a linear system, we will mean a linear, lumped, time-invariant system. The vocal organs, viewed as a system, are approximately linear; but they are also a time-varying and distributed-parameter system. As we speak, we move the speech organs and change their acoustics and hence the motion of sound waves through them. Since the rate of time variations is slow, however, we can treat the system as time-invariant over short intervals (typically 50 ms or less). This approximation is virtually always used. We handle the distributed-parameter nature of the vocal tract by modeling it as a lumped-parameter system with many parameters.

1-1 SAMPLED-DATA SYSTEMS; THE SAMPLING THEOREM

We can also distinguish among *continuous*, *discrete-time*, and *sampled-data* systems. In a continuous system, all inputs, outputs, and other variables are defined for all t and are considered as capable of changing at any instant of time. In a discrete-time system, variables are assumed capable of taking on new values only at discrete instants and are in fact defined only for discrete times t_k (where $k = \ldots, -1, 0, 1, 2, \ldots$).

Because of the discrete-time nature of digital computers, they are poorly adapted to modeling continuous-time systems; hence the signals must be sampled at discrete times and the system treated as if it were a discrete-time system. Such a system is called a *sampled-data system*. The signals are sampled and converted to numerical values ("digitized"), and these numerical samples are what the computer processes. This process is known as *analog-to-digital (A/D) conversion*. The inverse process is called *digital-to-analog (D/A) conversion*.

Signals in sampled-data systems are sometimes termed *sequences*; one speaks of input sequences and output sequences. They are also called vectors and are frequently treated as vectors for analysis purposes. The fact that signals are generally of indefinite length is no deterrent; it is permissible for vectors to have infinite length, and in practical implementations means can be found to break the vectors up into a sequence of finite-length vectors.

We should mention at this point that these numerical representations of signals are always of finite precision because of word-length limitations both in and out of the computer. Such finite-precision representation is called *quantized* data and the resultant errors *quantization errors*. The existence of quantization errors is one of the chief sources of noise and nonlinearity in practical digital signal-processing systems. In this book we will ignore quantization errors as far as possible. For analyses of quantization error, see any good book on digital signal processing, e.g., Oppenheim and Schafer (1975) or Rabiner and Gold (1975).

In all cases of interest to us, the times t_k are equally spaced; then $t_k = kT$ and instead of writing x as $x(t_k)$ we write either $x(k)$ or x_k. The sampling rate f_s is equal to $1/T$.

The risk in approximating a continuous process or function by a set of discrete samples is that there may be something important going on in between sampling times which we do not see. There is a related problem if it should be necessary later to reconstruct a continuous function from its samples. Both problems disappear if the sampling rate is high enough. The *sampling theorem*, due to C. Shannon, states that any continuous-time function is exactly determined by equally spaced samples provided f_s is at least two times as high as the highest frequency component present in the function. This minimum acceptable sampling rate is commonly known as the *Nyquist rate*. (The rate was determined by Nyquist, 1928, although the general proof was published by Shannon, 1949.) Our knowledge of the signal at hand usually allows us to estimate what this rate should be. For example, the minimum bandwidth for intelligible speech is between 3 and 4 kHz, and sampling rates for most applications range from 8 to 10 kHz.

Functions sampled at a frequency less than the Nyquist rate are said to be *undersampled*. In an undersampled signal, any frequency component at a frequency $f > f_s/2$ will appear to be at a lower frequency $f' = f - f_s$. This phenomenon is known as *aliasing*. An example of an aliased signal is shown in Fig. 1-2.

6 REVIEW MATERIALS

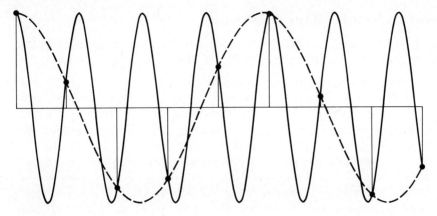

Figure 1-2 An example of aliasing. The dots indicate the sample points; the true frequency (solid curve) is indistinguishable as sampled from the aliased frequency (dotted curve).

The signal is a 795-Hz sine wave sampled at 1 kHz. The solid curve is the input signal and the dots indicate the sample points. As a result of this undersampling, the sequence of samples obtained is indistinguishable from samples of a 205-Hz sinusoid, as indicated by the dashed curve.

If a signal is sampled at a rate well above its Nyquist rate, it is said to be *oversampled*. If the sampling rate is some multiple of the Nyquist rate, the rate can be reduced by discarding the redundant samples. For example, if the original rate is three times the Nyquist rate, then every third sample can be retained and the rest discarded. This process is known as *downsampling*; it may be desirable if the original signal's bandwidth has been further reduced, after sampling, by a low-pass digital filter.

When data are sampled and digitized for computer processing or analysis, it is a standard precaution to precede the sampling device with an *antialiasing filter*. This is a filter which rejects any frequency components higher than $f_s/2$. The user must of course take care to make the sampling frequency high enough that no essential information will be destroyed by the antialiasing filter. When calculating the filter's cutoff frequency and the sampling rate, the user must bear in mind that filters do not cut off abruptly, and some leeway must be left to allow for the gradual rolloff of the filter's response.

1-2 ANALYSIS OF LINEAR SYSTEMS

There are two lines of attack open to us in analyzing a discrete-time linear system, depending on whether or not we have access to the inside of the black box. If we can look at the parts inside the box, we can in principle write equations describing their interactions; otherwise we can characterize the system only in terms of its inputs and outputs.

Difference Equations and Block Diagrams

If we can get inside the black box and examine its workings, we can describe the system in terms of linear, constant coefficient difference equations of the form:

$$y(n) + a_1 y(n-1) + a_2 y(n-2) + \cdots + a_p y(n-p)$$
$$= b_0 x(n) + b_1 x(n-1) + b_2 x(n-2) + \cdots + b_q x(n-q) \quad (1\text{-}1)$$

The coefficients are determined by an analysis of the contents of the box. The resulting equation relates a linear combination of current and past inputs (on the right-hand side) to a linear combination of current and past outputs (on the left-hand side).

We will frequently wish to represent systems by their block diagrams. Equation (1-1) can be made a little less abstract with the aid of its block diagram, shown in Fig. 1-3. In this block diagram, the boxes labeled Δ are delay elements; they hold the applied input exactly one sample time so that the output is a delayed version of the input. These cascaded delay elements make $x(n)$, $x(n-1)$, $x(n-2)$, ..., $y(n)$, $y(n-1)$, $y(n-2)$, ... all available to us at the same time, as shown in the figure. The triangles represent multiplication by constants and the circles represent addition. The equivalence of Fig. 1-3 to Eq. (1-1) can be seen if we rewrite the latter as follows:

$$y(n) = B - A \quad (1\text{-}2)$$

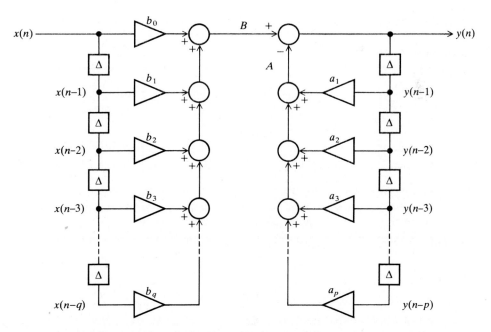

Figure 1-3 The block diagram corresponding to Eq. (1-1). The circles represent addition, the triangles, multiplication by constants, and the boxes, delay elements.

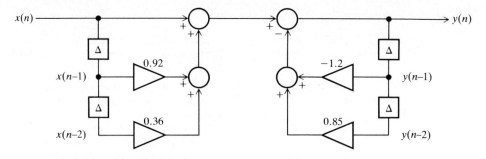

Figure 1-4 A second-order linear system.

where $\quad A = a_1 y(n-1) + a_2 y(n-2) + \cdots + a_p y(n-p)$

and $\quad B = b_0 x(n) + b_1 x(n-1) + b_2 x(n-2) + \cdots + b_q x(n-q)$

The signals A and B are indicated at the appropriate points on the block diagram.

Example 1-1 Consider the system:

$$y(n) - 1.2y(n-1) + 0.85y(n-2) = x(n) + 0.92x(n-1) + 0.36x(n-2)$$

This system has the block diagram shown in Fig. 1-4.

The Impulse Response; Convolution

In many cases, we do not know enough about the inside of the box to write a difference equation. In that case, the linearity of the system enables us to characterize it by its response to a standard input.

We define the *unit impulse function* $\delta(n)$ as follows:

$$\delta(n) = \begin{cases} 1, & n = 0 \\ 0, & \text{otherwise} \end{cases}$$

Then the *impulse response* $h(n)$ is the response to the system to an input $\delta(n)$. That is, if $x(n) = \delta(n)$, then $y(n) = h(n)$. Since we assume systems to be time-invariant, the response to a delayed impulse $\delta(n-k)$ will be simply $h(n-k)$.

The significance of the impulse response is this: any other input signal $x(n)$ can be written as

$$x(n) = \sum_{k=-\infty}^{\infty} x(k)\delta(n-k) \qquad (1\text{-}3)$$

(this follows from the definition of the impulse function). However, by the principle of superposition we can express $y(n)$ as the weighted sum of the responses of the system to all the deltas of Eq. (1-3). This means simply substituting $h(n-k)$

for $\delta(n-k)$ in (1-3). Hence:

$$y(n) = \sum_{k=-\infty}^{\infty} x(k)h(n-k) \qquad (1\text{-}4)$$

If we know the impulse response of a linear system, we can compute its response to any other input whatever. The system's impulse response is thus sufficient to characterize its input/output behavior completely.

The operation

$$\sum_{k=-\infty}^{\infty} x(k)h(n-k)$$

is known as the *convolution* of $x(n)$ and $h(n)$, usually written $x(n) * h(n)$. (The verb is "to convolve.") The operation of convolution has the following properties of interest to us:

1. *Commutativity.* For any h and x,

$$x(n) * h(n) = h(n) * x(n) \qquad (1\text{-}5)$$

This can be seen by substituting $n-j$ for k in the definition.

2. *Associativity.* For any h_1, h_2, and h_3,

$$[h_1(n) * h_2(n)] * h_3(n) = h_1(n) * [h_2(n) * h_3(n)] \qquad (1\text{-}6)$$

3. *Linearity.* If a and b are constants, then

$$h(n) * [ax_1(n) + bx_2(n)] = a[h(n) * x_1(n)] + b[h(n) * x_2(n)] \qquad (1\text{-}7a)$$

This can be seen by substituting $[ax_1(n) + bx_2(n)]$ for $x(n)$ in the defining equation. Note that a corollary of this is that

$$h(n) * \sum_i x_i(n) = \sum_i h(n) * x_i(n) \qquad (1\text{-}7b)$$

That is, we can interchange the operations of convolution and summing.

4. *Time reversal.* If $y(n) = x(n) * h(n)$, then

$$y(-n) = x(-n) * h(-n) \qquad (1\text{-}8)$$

5. If two systems, h_1 and h_2, are cascaded, as in Fig. 1-5a, then:

   a. The overall impulse response of the combined system is the convolution of the individual impulse responses:

   $$h(t) = h_1(t) * h_2(t)$$

   b. The overall impulse response is independent of the order in which the systems are connected. That is, Fig. 1-5b has the same response as Fig. 1-5a. Note, however, that this ignores real-world effects such as system noise and limitations on dynamic range. When these effects are taken into account, the order in which systems are cascaded can be critical.

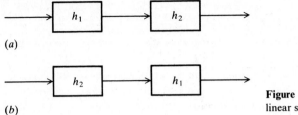

(a)

(b)

Figure 1-5 Commutativity of cascaded linear systems.

Another corollary of linearity is that a transfer function can be "factored" out of a system. That is, a system such as that shown in Fig. 1-6a can be replaced by the system in Fig. 1-6b.

As an example of the use of Eq. (1-4), suppose

$$x(n) = \begin{cases} 1, & n \geq 0 \\ 0, & \text{otherwise} \end{cases}$$

and $h(n)$ is a decaying exponential:

$$h(n) = \begin{cases} a^n, & n \geq 0 \\ 0, & \text{otherwise} \end{cases}$$

(where $|a| < 1$), as shown in Fig. 1-7a and b. Then

$$y(n) = \sum_{k=0}^{n} a^{(n-k)}$$

The lower limit is zero because $x(k) = 0$ for $k < 0$, and the upper limit is n because $h(n - k)$ is zero for $k > n$. [This can be seen in Fig. 1-7c, where

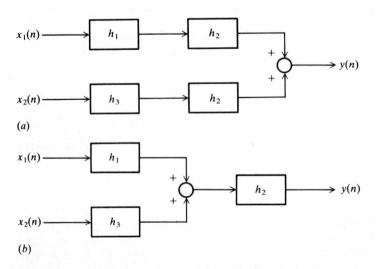

Figure 1-6 A transfer function factored out of a linear system.

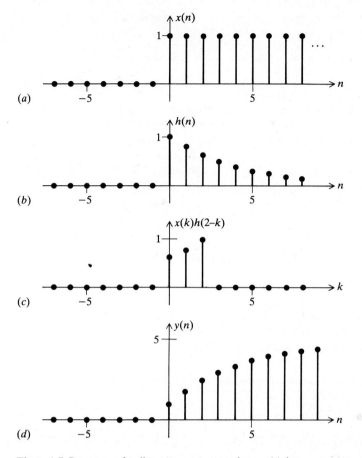

Figure 1-7 Response of a linear system to an input: (*a*) input sequence; (*b*) impulse response; (*c*) evaluation of $y(2)$; (*d*) output sequence.

$x(k)h(n - k)$ is plotted for $n = 2$.] The sum is

$$y(n) = \begin{cases} \dfrac{1 - a^{(n+1)}}{1 - a}, & n \geq 0 \\ 0, & \text{otherwise} \end{cases}$$

as shown in Fig. 1-7*d*.

Duration of the Impulse Response

The detailed connection between the impulse response and the difference equation (1-2) will have to await the introduction of transforms in the next section. We can, however, relate the gross form of Eq. (1-2) to the duration of $h(n)$. We speak of *finite-duration impulse-response* (FIR) systems and *infinite-duration impulse-response* (IIR) systems. The difference is this: if, in the difference equation (1-1) shown above, the coefficients a_i are all zero, then the equation reduces to

$$y(n) = b_0 x(n) + b_1 x(n-1) + \cdots + b_q x(n-q) \qquad (1\text{-}9)$$

In this case the impulse response can be read directly from the right-hand side of (1-9):

$$h(n) = b_n$$

and clearly the impulse response is of finite length—specifically, $q+1$ samples long. If any of the a coefficients are not zero, however, then the impulse response can last forever, because even if the impulse occurred more than q samples ago, it can be "remembered" in the output samples $y(n-1)$, $y(n-2)$, ..., which are being recirculated in the feedback path on the right-hand side of Fig. 1-3. Hence the system will, in general, be an IIR system.

1-3 TRANSFORMS

Transforms are a powerful tool for simplifying the analysis of signals and of linear systems. We have seen that linear systems imply linear differential (or difference) equations and the operation of convolution. Hence it is not surprising that, for the transforms of interest to us:

1. Linearity applies; i.e., if we use $T[x]$ to indicate a transformation operation on x, then for any constants a, b,

$$T[ax + by] = aT[x] + bT[y]$$

2. Convolution is replaced by a simpler operation, namely multiplication; i.e., if convolution of two functions is represented by $*$, then

$$T[x * y] = T[x]T[y]$$

The second property is the reason transforms are important. Since differentiation, integration, differencing, and time delays are all representable by suitable convolutions, it follows that all of these are also representable by simple operations in the transform domain. In fact, our main use of transforms will be as a way of making these operations either computationally or conceptually simpler. In particular, while it is not clear how to express the inverse of a convolution operation, multiplication has a simple and well-understood inverse. We will presently see that a final corollary of these properties is that linear difference and differential equations can be converted to algebraic equations by means of appropriate transforms.

The four transforms most commonly used in communications engineering are:

1. Laplace transforms

2. Continuous Fourier transforms
3. Z transforms
4. Discrete Fourier transforms

The Laplace and continuous Fourier transforms are used with continuous-time systems and signals. The Z and discrete Fourier transforms are used with discrete-time systems and signals. As we have seen, computers are better adapted to discrete-time analysis; hence our primary interest is in the latter two transforms. In all cases of interest to us, the domain of the input function is time. In the Fourier transform, the transform domain is frequency. The domains of the Laplace and Z transforms are sometimes called "complex frequency," but this term cannot be taken too literally.

All of these transforms have corresponding inverse transforms that will undo the original transform, and the defining equations of these transforms come in pairs, one for the direct transform and one for the inverse. The use of transforms is a little like that of logarithms: we may transform one or more functions, do operations in the transform domain, and then take the inverse transform of the result.

1-4 THE Z TRANSFORM

Defining Equations

The direct Z transform of a time sequence $x(n)$ is defined as follows:

$$X(z) = \sum_{n=-\infty}^{\infty} x(n) z^{-n} \tag{1-10}$$

The inverse transform is given by

$$x(n) = \frac{1}{j2\pi} \oint_C X(z) z^{n-1} \, dz \tag{1-11}$$

There is nothing sacred about the use of negative powers of z: some writers use positive powers of z; z^{-n} is consistent with general engineering usage whereby the direct transform is given by the negative exponent.

Notice that although x is discrete time, z is a continuous variable. Furthermore, z is a complex variable, even when x is real. In the inverse transform, the contour C must be in the region of convergence of $X(z)$. The inverse is found by the residue theorem, by partial-fraction expansion, or simply by expansion into a power series in z^{-1}. Since we will be using transforms chiefly as conceptual aids, inversion is not generally important to us. Inversion by the residue theorem can be found in many standard texts (e.g., Jury, 1964; Oppenheim and Schafer, 1975; Rabiner and Gold, 1975).

Inversion by partial-fraction expansion proceeds as follows. If $X(z)$ is a ratio of polynomials, then it can be rewritten as

$$X(z) = \sum_{i=1}^{p} \frac{b_i}{1 - a_i z^{-1}} \qquad (1\text{-}12a)$$

where p is the number of poles in the denominator. Equation (1-12a) applies when there are no repeated roots in the denominator polynomial. If there are repeated roots, then we must write

$$X(z) = \sum_{i=1}^{p} \sum_{j=1}^{n_i} \frac{b_{ij}}{(1 - a_i z^{-1})^j} \qquad (1\text{-}12b)$$

where n_i is the multiplicity of the ith root. Because the Z transform is linear (as will be explained), (1-12) can be inverted term-by-term and the inverses added to obtain the final solution.

Z transforms can frequently be expanded into power series by simple long division. Suppose $X(z) = 1/(1 - az^{-1})$; then

$$\frac{1}{1 - az^{-1}} = 1 + az^{-1} + a^2 z^{-2} + a^3 z^{-3} + \cdots$$

From the defining equation of the direct transform, this must be the transform of an exponential:

$$x(n) = \begin{cases} a^n, & n \geq 0 \\ 0, & n < 0 \end{cases}$$

Elementary Functions and Their Z Transforms

The following transforms are easily derived from the defining equation, mostly by inspection:

1. *Unit impulse:*
$x(n) = \delta(n)$
From the definition of $\delta(n)$,

$$X(z) = \sum_{n=-\infty}^{\infty} \delta(n) z^{-n} = 1 \qquad (1\text{-}13)$$

We will be making considerable use of the unit impulse, and it is well at this point to note two of its properties:
a. Convolution of any function with $\delta(n)$ leaves the function unchanged:

$$a(n) * \delta(n) = \delta(n) * a(n) = a(n)$$

b. Convolution with $\delta(n - p)$ shifts $a(n)$ by p samples:

$$a(n) * \delta(n - p) = a(n - p)$$

2. *Delayed unit impulse.* If $x(n) = \delta(n - k)$,

$$X(z) = \sum_{n=-\infty}^{\infty} \delta(n - k)z^{-n}$$

$$= z^{-k} \qquad (1\text{-}14)$$

3. *Unit step.* The unit step function is defined as follows:

$$u(n) = \begin{cases} 1, & n \geq 0 \\ 0, & \text{otherwise} \end{cases}$$

If $x(n) = u(n)$, then

$$X(z) = \sum_{n=0}^{\infty} z^{-n} = 1 + z^{-1} + z^{-2} + z^{-3} + \cdots$$

$$= \frac{1}{1 - z^{-1}} \qquad (1\text{-}15)$$

4. *Exponential.* If $x(n) = a^n u(n)$,

$$X(z) = \sum_{n=0}^{\infty} a^n z^{-n}$$

$$= \frac{1}{1 - az^{-1}} \qquad (1\text{-}16)$$

(a may be complex).

Elementary Properties of the Z Transform

In all of the following, $Z[x(n)]$ represents the Z transform of $x(n)$:

1. *Linearity.* Let $x(n)$ and $y(n)$ be any two functions and let $X(z)$ and $Y(z)$ be their respective Z transforms. Then for any constants a, b,

$$Z[ax(n) + by(n)] = aX(z) + bY(z) \qquad (1\text{-}17)$$

This can be proved by substituting $ax(n) + by(n)$ in the defining equation.

2. *Convolution.* If $w(n) = x(n) * y(n)$, then

$$W(z) = X(z)Y(z) \qquad (1\text{-}18)$$

Proof:

$$Z[x(n) * y(n)] = \sum_{n=-\infty}^{\infty} \sum_{k=-\infty}^{\infty} x(k)y(n - k)z^{-n}$$

Since $z^{-n} = z^{-k}z^{-(n-k)}$, let $p = n - k$. Then

$$Z[x(n) * y(n)] = \sum_{n=-\infty}^{\infty} x(k)z^{-k} \sum_{p=-\infty}^{\infty} y(p)z^{-p}$$

$$= X(z)Y(z)$$

Example 1-2 We can now recompute our previous convolution example using Z transforms. We had $x(n) = u(n)$ and $h(n) = a^n u(n)$; hence $X(z) = 1/(1 - z^{-1})$ and $H(z) = 1/(1 - az^{-1})$. Therefore, by the convolution property,

$$Y(z) = \frac{1}{1 - z^{-1}} \frac{1}{1 - az^{-1}}$$

$$= \frac{1}{1-a}\left(\frac{1}{1 - z^{-1}} - \frac{a}{1 - az^{-1}}\right)$$

from which

$$y(n) = \frac{1 - a^{(n+1)}}{1 - a} u(n)$$

which agrees with our previous result.

3. *Shifting.* $x(n - k)$ is $x(n) * \delta(n - k)$; hence by the shifting property of $\delta(n)$,

$$Z[x(n - k)] = z^{-k} X(z) \tag{1-19}$$

4. *Differences.* We define the forward and backward differences of a function x as follows:

Forward: $\quad \Delta x(n) = x(n + 1) - x(n)$

Backward: $\quad \nabla x(n) = x(n) - x(n - 1)$

Since $\Delta x(n) = x(n) * [\delta(n + 1) - \delta(n)]$ [and similarly for $\nabla x(n)$], it follows from the shifting theorem that

$$\begin{aligned} Z[\Delta x(n)] &= (z - 1)X(z) \\ Z[\nabla x(n)] &= (1 - z^{-1})X(z) \end{aligned} \tag{1-20}$$

Application to Linear, Discrete-Time Systems

Transfer function We have seen that a linear system's input/output behavior is characterized by its impulse response $h(n)$. In particular, for any input $x(n)$, the output is given by

$$y(n) = \sum_{k=-\infty}^{\infty} x(k)h(n - k)$$

$$= x(n) * h(n)$$

By the convolution property of the Z transform,

$$Y(z) = X(z)H(z)$$

where $H(z) = Z[h(n)]$. In that case,

$$H(z) = \frac{Y(z)}{X(z)}$$

This gives us a way to relate the impulse response of a system to its difference equation. Recall that the difference equation is

$$\sum_{i=0}^{p} a_i y(n-i) = \sum_{j=0}^{q} b_j x(n-j) \qquad (1\text{-}21)$$

Using the shifting and linearity properties of the Z transform, we can write the transform of this equation as follows:

$$\sum_{i=0}^{p} a_i z^{-i} Y(z) = \sum_{j=0}^{q} b_j z^{-j} X(z)$$

or

$$Y(z) \sum_{i=0}^{p} a_i z^{-i} = X(z) \sum_{j=0}^{q} b_j z^{-j} \qquad (1\text{-}22)$$

Note that by using the Z transform, we have been able to convert the difference equation of (1-21) into an algebraic equation. In that case,

$$\frac{Y(z)}{X(z)} = \frac{N(z)}{D(z)}$$

where

$$N(z) = \sum_{j=0}^{q} b_j z^{-j} \qquad (1\text{-}23a)$$

and

$$D(z) = \sum_{i=0}^{p} a_i z^{-i} \qquad (1\text{-}23b)$$

We see that $H(z)$ is a ratio of polynomials in z. The fundamental theorem of algebra tells us that $N(z)$ has q roots; each of these is a value of z for which $H(z) = 0$. The roots of N are called the *zeros* of H. Similarly, $D(z)$ has p roots for which $H(z) = \infty$; roots of D are called the *poles* of H. Since any polynomial is defined (to within a multiplicative constant) by its roots, H is completely characterized (except for a gain factor) by its poles and zeros.

Stability A system is stable if a bounded (i.e., finite-amplitude) input always produces a bounded output; $x(n)$ is a bounded input if

$$|x(n)| < M \qquad \text{for all } n$$

where M is some finite constant. In that case,

$$|y(n)| < M \sum_{k=-\infty}^{\infty} |h(k)|$$

Hence the system is stable if

$$\sum_{k} |h(k)| < \infty \qquad (1\text{-}24)$$

This is a sufficient condition for stability; it can be shown (Prob. 1-9) that it is also a necessary condition.

18 REVIEW MATERIALS

An equivalent requirement is that all poles of $H(z)$ lie within the unit circle. A partial-fraction expansion of $H(z)$ will yield an impulse response that is a sum of exponentials:

$$h(n) = \sum_{i=1}^{N} b_i(a_i)^n$$

If all poles are inside the unit circle, then all of these exponentials will be decaying and $h(n)$ will satisfy Eq. (1-24), while if even one pole lies outside, there will be a growing exponential in $h(n)$ and the system will be unstable.

Example 1-3 We return to the system of Fig. 1-4:

$$y(n) - 1.2y(n-1) + 0.85y(n-2) = x(n) + 0.92x(n-1) + 0.36x(n-2)$$

Taking Z transforms, we have

$$Y(z) - 1.2z^{-1}Y(z) + 0.85z^{-2}Y(z) = X(z) + 0.92z^{-1}X(z) + 0.36z^{-2}X(z)$$

Then

$$H(x) = \frac{Y(z)}{X(z)} = \frac{1 + 0.92z^{-1} + 0.36z^{-2}}{1 - 1.2z^{-1} + 0.85z^{-2}}$$

The zeros of this system are at $z = 0.46 + j0.385$ and the poles are at $z = 0.6 + j0.7$. These poles and zeros are plotted in Fig. 1-8; since the poles are within the unit circle, we see that the system is stable.

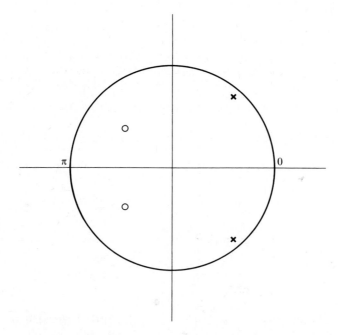

Figure 1-8 Poles and zeros of the system of Fig. 1-4 shown with the unit circle.

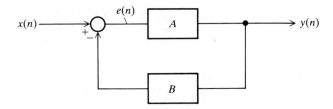

Figure 1-9 A linear system with feedback. The feedback path is through box B.

Feedback; inverse transfer function An important type of system is that in which part of the output is fed back and combined with the input, as shown in Fig. 1-9.

We can determine the transfer function of this system with the aid of Z transforms as follows. Let X, Y, and E be the Z transforms of x, y, and e, respectively. Then by inspection of Fig. 1-9,

$$Y(z) = A(z)E(z)$$

and

$$E(z) = X(z) - E(z)A(z)B(z)$$

Hence the overall transfer function is

$$\frac{Y(z)}{X(z)} = \frac{A(z)}{1 + A(z)B(z)} \tag{1-25}$$

In most applications, $A(z)$ and $B(z)$ are FIR; then the condition for stability is that all the roots of $1 + A(z)B(z)$ lie within the unit circle.

The use of feedback provides a way to realize the inverse of a transfer function $Q(z)$. If we place a $[Q(z) - 1]$ in the feedback path, as shown in Fig. 1-10, then by Eq. (1-25), the overall transfer function is $1/Q(z)$. It is always possible to form the inverse of a transfer function in this way, but the inverse thus formed may not be stable. The requirement for stability is that all zeros of $Q(z)$, and hence all poles of $1/Q(z)$, lie within the unit circle.

Computer simulation If a system is specified by either its difference equation or by its Z transform written as a ratio of polynomials, then its block diagram can be constructed and used as the basis for a computer program for simulating the system. In this case, it is more economical to redraw Fig. 1-3 as shown in Fig. 1-11.

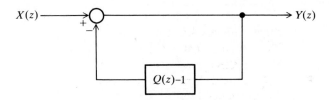

Figure 1-10 Use of feedback to realize the function $1/Q(z)$.

20 REVIEW MATERIALS

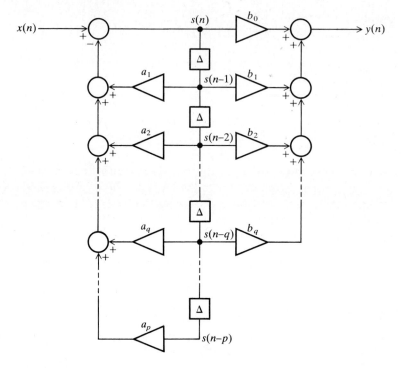

Figure 1-11 Direct-form equivalent of Fig. 1-3.

Here we have placed the denominator part of the system ahead of the numerator part. Clearly, $S(z) = X(z)/D(z)$ and $Y(z) = N(z)S(z)$, so $Y(z)/X(z) = N(z)/D(z)$ as before. Combining the delays into a single chain in this way is more economical than Fig. 1-3, whether the system is to be implemented by hardware or software. This configuration is called the *direct form*.

Figure 1-11 leads immediately to a computer program for simulating its operation. The chain of delays is implemented as an array; the propagation of the *s* values down this chain is represented by shifting the values down this array between output computations. In the Fortran-77 program in Fig. 1-12, the input is the value $x(n)$ and the output is $y(n)$. $S(0)$ holds the value $s(n)$ of Fig. 1-11 and $S(I)$ holds the value $s(n - i)$. The A and B arrays, with upper bounds P and Q, respectively, hold the coefficients of the numerator and denominator polynomials; R, the upper bound of S, is the maximum of P and Q. The main program must set the contents of the S array to zero before the process starts. DFILT is called every time an output sample is to be computed. Upon entry to DFILT, the DO 20 loop updates the contents of the delay chain, after which all the elements of S contain their correct values, except $S(0)$. The DO 40 loop computes the new value of $S(0)$ from the rest of the array and the current input sample. The DO 60 loop then finds the corresponding output sample, which is returned as the value of the function.

```
       function DFILT (x, a, p, b, q, s, r)
*        Returns one output sample of a discrete system
*        Variables
*          x     input sample
*          a     coefficients of numerator polynomial
*          b     coefficients of denominator polynomial
*          s     system state variables
       integer p, q, r
       real a(1:n), b(Ø:m), s(Ø:r),
*        --Update state variables
         do 2Ø i = r, 1, -1
2Ø           s(r) = s(r - 1)
*        --Compute s(Ø)
         s(Ø) = x
         do 4Ø i = 1, p
2Ø           s(Ø) = s(Ø) - a(i)*s(i)
*        --Compute output
         dfilt = Ø
         do 6Ø i = Ø, q
6Ø           dfilt = dfilt + b(i)*s(i)
         return
         end
```

Figure 1-12 Computer program for simulating a linear system.

1-5 THE DISCRETE FOURIER TRANSFORM (DFT)

Defining Equations

The direct DFT of a finite-length sequence of N complex points is

$$X(k) = \sum_{n=0}^{N-1} x(n) \exp \frac{-j2\pi nk}{N} \qquad (1\text{-}26a)$$

It is customary to use the abbreviation

$$W_N = \exp \frac{j2\pi}{N}$$

$$= \cos \frac{2\pi}{N} + j \sin \frac{2\pi}{N}$$

(The N subscript is needed only if it is not apparent from the context.) Then the direct transform is

$$X(k) = \sum_{n=0}^{N-1} x(n) W^{-nk} \qquad (1\text{-}26b)$$

Using the same notation, the inverse transform is

$$x(n) = \frac{1}{N} \sum_{k=0}^{N-1} X(k) W^{nk} \qquad (1\text{-}27)$$

Equation (1-27) represents $x(n)$ as a sum of sinusoids of frequencies 0, 1, 2, ..., $N - 1$. Hence the Fourier transform can be interpreted as a frequency analysis (or "spectrum analysis") of the input signal.

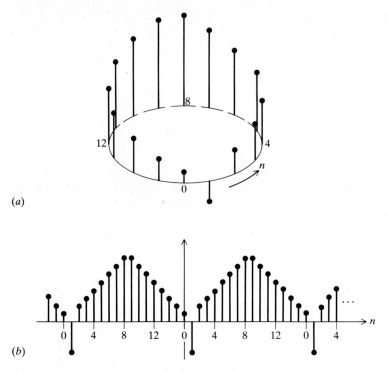

(a)

(b)

Figure 1-13 The time and frequency domains of the DFT can be viewed as (a) circular or (b) periodic.

Note that X and x are in general complex. (Even if x is real, X is usually complex.) The domains of x and X are "circular"—i.e., after $x(N-1)$ comes $X(0)$ again, as shown in Fig. 1-13a. We say that the domains "wrap around" modulo N. This is perhaps the most mystifying characteristic of the DFT for the inexperienced user. Another way to look at this is to consider x and X to be infinitely repeated periodic sequences with period N, as shown in Fig. 1-13b: $x(k + aN) = x(k)$ where a is any integer.

This periodicity, or circularity, leads to unexpected consequences. In particular, if you shift $x(n)$, the samples shifted past $n = N - 1$ reappear at $n = 0$. (The shift is actually a rotation.) Another consequence is that $X(-k) = X(N - k)$. Hence the negative-frequency portion of the transform appears in the samples between $k = N/2$ and $k = N - 1$—i.e., in the top half of the transform. Indeed, it is customary to plot both $x(n)$ and $X(k)$ with the top half displayed to the left of the origin to represent the negative-time and negative-frequency parts.

Example 1-4 $N = 16$ and $x(n)$ is the rectangular pulse shown in Fig. 1-14a:

$$x(n) = \begin{cases} 1, & n = 0, 1, 15 \\ 0, & \text{otherwise} \end{cases}$$

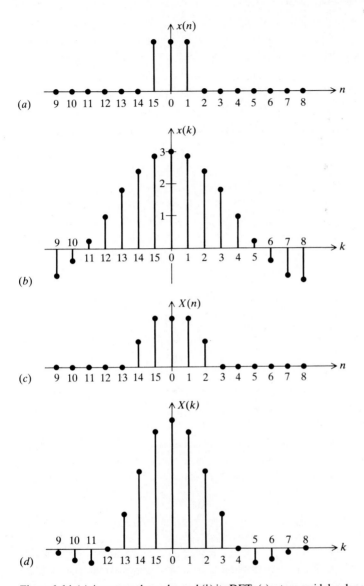

Figure 1-14 (a) A rectangular pulse and (b) its DFT; (c) a trapezoidal pulse and (d) its DFT.

Then

$$X(k) = 1 + W^{-k} + W^k$$

$$= 1 + 2\cos\frac{\pi k}{8}$$

plotted in Fig. 1-14b.

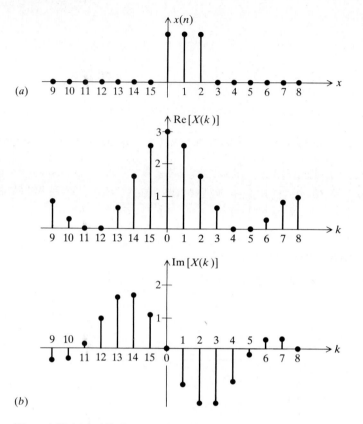

Figure 1-15 (a) A shifted rectangular pulse and (b) the real and imaginary parts of its DFT.

Example 1-5 $N = 16$ and $x(n)$ is as follows:

$$x(n) = \begin{cases} 1, & n = 0, 1, 15 \\ 0.5, & n = 2, 14 \\ 0, & \text{otherwise} \end{cases}$$

plotted in Fig. 1-14c. Then

$$X(k) = 1 + W^{-k} + W^{-k} + \tfrac{1}{2}(W^{-2k} + W^{2k})$$

$$= 1 + 2\cos\frac{\pi k}{8} + \cos\frac{\pi k}{4}$$

plotted in Fig. 1-14d.

Example 1-6 $N = 16$ and $x(n)$ is a shifted rectangular pulse, as in Fig. 1-15a:

$$x(n) = \begin{cases} 1, & 0 \leq n \leq 2 \\ 0, & \text{otherwise} \end{cases}$$

Then

$$\dot{X}(k) = 1 + W^{-k} + W^{-2k}$$
$$= 1 + \cos\frac{\pi k}{8} + \cos\frac{\pi k}{4} - j\left(\sin\frac{\pi k}{8} + \sin\frac{\pi k}{4}\right)$$

The real and imaginary parts of $X(k)$ are plotted in Fig. 1-15b.

There is a family of efficient programs for computing the DFT, collectively known as the "fast Fourier transform" (FFT). The efficiency of the FFT algorithms accounts for much of the popularity of the DFT as a signal-processing technique. FFT programs for transforming complex and real functions are given in Appendix B.

Elementary Functions and Their Transforms

These transforms are easily derived from the defining equation:

1. *Unit impulse*

$$x(n) = \delta(n)$$
$$X(k) = 1 \tag{1-28}$$

2. *Shifted unit impulse*

$$x(n) = \delta(n - p)$$
$$X(k) = W^{-kp} \tag{1-29}$$

3. *Constant*

$$x(n) = 1$$
$$X(k) = N\delta(k) \tag{1-30}$$

It is of particular interest to be able to find the transforms of sinusoids and exponentials. These transforms are messy affairs, and it is probably best to approach them by way of a simple case. We initially consider only the case where the period is an exact fraction of the length of the transform. The term, "cell-centered," is sometimes used for these cases; the term will be explained below.

4. *Complex exponential* (cell-centered)

$$x(n) = e^{j\alpha n}$$
$$X(k) = N\delta\left(k - \frac{N\alpha}{2\pi}\right) \tag{1-31}$$

provided $N\alpha/2\pi$ is an integer (as it will be in the cell-centered case).

5. *Cosine function* (cell-centered)

$$x(n) = \cos 2\pi f_0 n$$

$$X(k) = \frac{N}{2}[\delta(k - Nf_0) + \delta(N - k + Nf_0)] \qquad (1\text{-}32)$$

provided Nf_0 is an integer. This is a pair of impulses located symmetrically about the origin (or about $N/2$).

Elementary Properties

In all of the following, $g(n) \leftrightarrow G(k)$ means that $g(n)$ and $G(k)$ are a transform pair. Most of these properties are presented without proofs, since they arise naturally out of the defining equations. For brevity, we will assume that $-k$ and $-n$ are equivalent to $N - k$ and $N - n$, respectively.

1. *Symmetry.* If $F(k)$ is the DFT of $f(n)$, then

$$f(k) = NF(-n) \qquad (1\text{-}33)$$

2. *Linearity.* If $x(n) \leftrightarrow X(k)$ and $y(n) \leftrightarrow Y(k)$, then for constants a and b,

$$ax(n) + by(n) \leftrightarrow aX(k) + bY(k) \qquad (1\text{-}34)$$

3. *Shifting.* Because of the cyclical nature of the DFT domains, shifting becomes a rotation.

   Example 1-7 If $N = 8$ and x is as shown in Fig. 1-16a, then x shifted by three samples is as shown in Fig. 1-16b.

   Subject to this qualification, we say that if $x(n) \leftrightarrow X(k)$, then

$$x(n - p) \leftrightarrow W^{-kp} X(k) \qquad (1\text{-}35)$$

   where all indices are modulo N.

4. *Time reversal.* If $x(n) \leftrightarrow X(k)$, then

$$x(-n) \leftrightarrow X(-k) \qquad (1\text{-}36)$$

5. *Cyclical convolution.* Recall that convolution is a shift/multiply/add operation. Since all shifts in the DFT are circular, convolution is defined with this circularity included. Thus the convolution is cyclical and is defined as

$$x(n) * y(n) = \sum_{p=0}^{N-1} x(p) y(p - n) \qquad (1\text{-}37)$$

   where all indices are modulo N.

LINEAR SYSTEMS AND TRANSFORMS 27

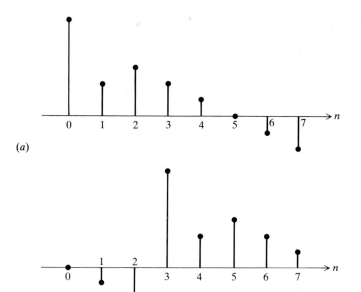

Figure 1-16 Shifting in the DFT domains appears as a rotation. (*a*) Original function, $N = 8$; (*b*) shifted function.

Example 1-8 Let $x(n)$ and $y(n)$ be as shown in Fig. 1-17*a* and *b*, respectively, where $N = 16$. Let $z = x * y$; then the sum for computing $z(2)$ is

$$z(2) = \sum_{p=0}^{15} x(p)y(2 - p)$$

as shown in Fig. 1-17*c*. Notice that $y(2 - p)$ wraps around on the p axis. The result is shown in Fig. 1-17*d*.

The convolution property for the DFT is as follows: if $x(n) \leftrightarrow X(k)$ and $y(n) \leftrightarrow Y(k)$, then

$$x(n) * y(n) \leftrightarrow X(k)Y(k) \qquad (1\text{-}38)$$

The proof of this property parallels that of the Z transform:

$$F[x(n) * y(n)] = \sum_{n=0}^{N-1} \sum_{p=0}^{N-1} x(n)y(n - p)W^{-nk}$$

Since $W^{-nk} = W^{-kp}W^{-k(n-p)}$,

$$F[x(n) * y(n)] = \sum_{n=0}^{N-1} x(n)W^{-nk} \sum_{p=0}^{N-1} y(n - p)W^{-k(n-p)}$$

The first sum is $X(k)$; in the second, the limits $p = 0$ to $N - 1$ comprise the same points as the limits $(n - p) = 0$ to $N - 1$; hence the second sum is $Y(k)$ and the property is proved.

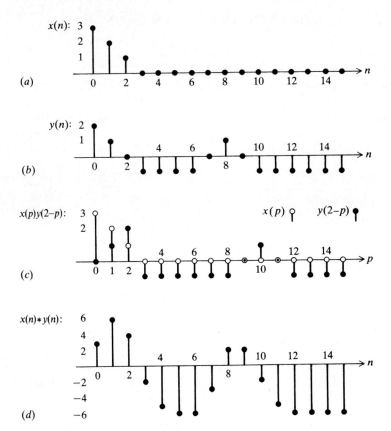

Figure 1-17 Convolution in the DFT domain: (*a*) first function; (*b*) second function; (*c*) shifted functions for computing $z(2)$; (*d*) convolution result.

6. *Real functions.* If $x(n)$ is real and $x(n) \leftrightarrow X(k)$, then

$$X(-k) = X(N - k) = X^*(k) \tag{1-39}$$

where * denotes the complex conjugate.

This property has some practical consequences. If $X(N - k) = X^*(k)$, then
  a. $X(0)$ is a real and $X(N/2)$ is real.
  b. There is no need to compute S for $N/2 < k < N$, since these values can be found from the first half of X.
  c. This symmetry can be exploited to decrease the computation required to transform a real sequence. The program RFFT in Appendix B does this, replacing a real array x with the first half of the complex array X. [Since $X(0)$ is real, the $X(N/2)$ value is tucked into the imaginary part of $X(0)$ and must be removed before use.]
7. *Real, even functions.* If $x(n)$ is real and even, then $X(k)$ is likewise real and even.

1-6 PRACTICAL CONSIDERATIONS IN USING THE DFT

Windowing

In a practical case, one is dealing with a long signal of which the DFT can handle only a finite slice. Cutting out a slice is equivalent to multiplying the signal by a rectangular pulse (Fig. 1-18). We are, in effect, viewing $f(n)$ through a "window" of length N. This means that the transform will be *convolved* with the transform of $P_N(n)$. Hence we must consider the transform of this rectangular window:

$$S(k) = \sum_{n=0}^{N-1} P_N(n) W^{-nk} \tag{1-40}$$

We will assume $P_N(n)$ symmetrical about $n = 0$. Then it can be shown, after a lot of manipulation, that

$$S(k) = \frac{\sin \pi k}{\sin (\pi k/N)} \tag{1-41}$$

[Notice that $S(k)$ is similar to the continuous Fourier transform of a rectangular pulse, $\sin \omega/\omega$. In fact, for $k/N \ll 1$, $S(k) \approx N \sin \pi k/\pi k$.]

Hence if we take transform of (say) $\exp(jan)$, the result will be $S(k)$ convolved with $\delta(k - Na/2\pi)$. That is,

$$X(k) = S(k - Na/2\pi) = \frac{\sin [\pi(k - Na/2\pi)]}{\sin [\pi(k - Na/2\pi)/N]} \tag{1-42}$$

We are interested in this function *only for integer values of k*. (We say that it is *sampled* at those points.) Now if $Na/2\pi$ is an integer, then the samples of $S(k - Na/2\pi)$ will look exactly like those of $\delta(k - Na/2\pi)$ (see Fig. 1-19a), because all samples but one are at zero crossings of S. This is the case we previously

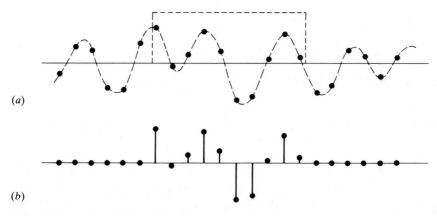

Figure 1-18 Windowing of a sampled time function. (a) Original function, samples, and rectangular window; (b) windowed function.

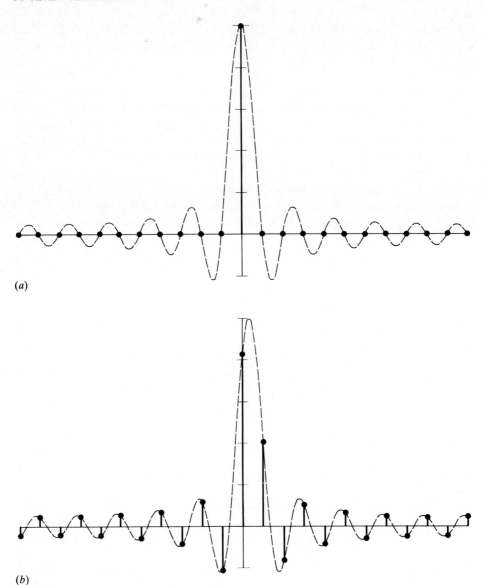

Figure 1-19 Equation (1-42) sampled at integer values of k: (a) cell-centered case; (b) non-cell-centered case.

called "cell-centered"—the window function $S(k)$ is centered with respect to the frequency samples—and it is only because of this coincidence that the transforms previously given for $e^{j\alpha n}$ and for $\cos 2\pi f_0 n$ were correct. However, if $Na/2\pi$ is not an integer, then $S(k)$ will not be sampled at its zero crossings and the appearance of the sampled transform will be radically different, as shown in Fig. 1-19b.

For practical purposes, where we wish to use the transform to estimate the distribution of signal power or amplitude over the frequency domain, this is undesirable for the following reasons:

1. Power for cell-centered frequencies appears to be concentrated at a single point while for other frequencies power is scattered over the entire spectrum.
2. Peak power for cell-centered frequencies is greater than for non-cell-centered frequencies. The difference can be as great as 41 percent. This is a consequence of the sampled nature of the DFT spectrum: if we could see all of $S(k)$ for all frequencies, there would be no nonuniformity; as it is, it is like seeing $S(k)$ through the openings in a picket fence, and this problem is sometimes called the "picket-fence effect."

The simplest solution is to make samples of $S(k)$ closer. This can be done by increasing the size of the transform and filling the new locations with zeros. (This

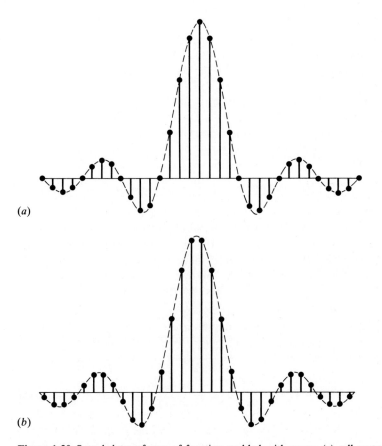

Figure 1-20 Sampled transforms of function padded with zeros: (a) cell-centered case; (b) mid-cell case.

is known as "padding out with zeros.") As a result, the shape of $S(k)$ remains unchanged, but samples are twice as close together and the shape of $S(k)$ is evident regardless of frequency. Note that padding with zeros does not improve the resolution of the transform—it just samples the transform at smaller intervals. Figure 1-20 shows shapes of cell-centered and mid-cell spectra when the time function has been padded to twice its length with zeros. Here the peak power differs by <1 dB between the two cases. Clearly, the difference could be made still smaller by padding out with more zeros.

Leakage

Even when the time function has been padded out with zeros there is another problem associated with the shape of $S(k)$. $S(k)$ does not have just one peak located at $k = 0$, but has in addition numerous smaller peaks, known as *side-lobes*. This has two undesirable consequences: (1) energy which is concentrated at a single point in the spectrum appears to be scattered over a band of frequencies and (2) a small frequency component located near a larger component may be obliterated by one of the larger component's side-lobes.

There is no ideal solution to this problem; when we Fourier-transform a finite-length chunk of signal, there is inevitably a degree of uncertainty in the frequency domain, which shows up as a widening of the central peak of each component. We can, however, mitigate the problem by applying a weighting function to the chunk before transforming it. When we cut a finite slice out of the original time function, we implicitly applied a *rectangular* weighting function to that slice, and we have seen that the side-lobes are a result of convolution with the transform of that rectangle. However, we do not have to use a rectangular function; the only requirement is that the window be finite, and if we can find a finite window whose transform has smaller side-lobes, this will ease the leakage problem. These windows also, without exception, widen the main lobe; this is usually a small price to pay for alleviating the leakage problem. There is a large literature on the choice of suitable weighting (or window) functions (see Harris, 1978). In speech processing the following three functions are used most frequently [these functions are defined in various ways; the forms given here are chosen to yield transforms with $W(0) = N$ and zeros located at integer values of k]:

1. Triangular weighting (Fig. 1-21a; these curves are centered about the origin for greater clarity, and as usual $-n$ and $-k$ are equivalent to $N - n$ and $N - k$, respectively):

$$w_t(n) = \begin{cases} 2 - 4|n|/N, & |n| \leq N/2 \\ 0, & \text{otherwise} \end{cases} \quad (1\text{-}43)$$

The transform of $w_t(n)$ is shown in Fig. 1-21b, c. For triangular weighting, the largest side-lobes are 27 dB down from the main lobe. At the half-power points, the main lobe is wider than that of $S(k)$ by 44 percent.

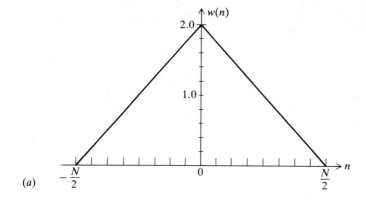

(a)

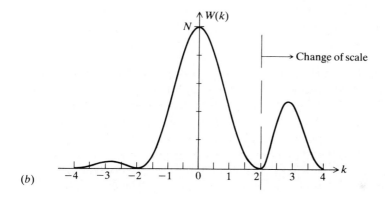

(b)

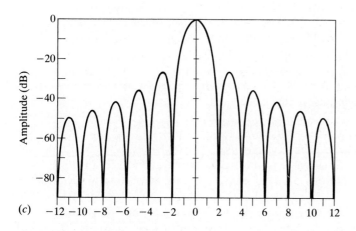

(c)

Figure 1-21 Triangular weighting. (a) Time window; (b) transform (linear); (c) transform (log). The linear transform is scaled up by a factor of 10, starting with $k = 1$.

34 REVIEW MATERIALS

2. Hanning weighting (Fig. 1-22a), also called cosine-squared or raised-cosine weighting:

$$w_c(n) = \begin{cases} 1 + \cos 2\pi n/N, & |n| \leq N/2 \\ 0, & \text{otherwise} \end{cases} \quad (1\text{-}44)$$

The transform of $w_c(n)$ is shown in Fig. 1-22b, c. The largest side-lobes here are approximately 32 dB down from the main lobe. The main lobe is wider by 62 percent.

3. Hamming weighting (Fig. 1-23a):

$$w_h(n) = \begin{cases} 1 + 0.84 \cos 2\pi n/N, & |n| \leq N/2 \\ 0, & \text{otherwise} \end{cases} \quad (1\text{-}45)$$

The transform of $w_h(n)$ is shown in Fig. 1-23b, c. With Hamming weighting, the largest side-lobes are approximately 43 dB down from the main lobe. The main lobe is wider by 46 percent.

Application to Speech

As an analytic tool, the Fourier transform has lost some of its former popularity to linear prediction. Nevertheless, it is still an important technique and is still used in many kinds of processing, so it is worth taking a moment to consider the techniques to be used.

Data preparation System design at this stage must include the usual precautions, especially choosing a suitable sampling rate (usually 8 to 10 kHz) and using a proper antialiasing filter. In digitizing, a word length of at least 12 bits should be used. This should be taken as a minimum; for high-quality processing, 14 to 16 bits should be considered. The performance of all associated hardware should be matched to the resolution used. Particular attention must be paid to the linearity and dynamic range of all analog circuitry, to the sharpness of the antialiasing filter's cutoff and to its transient response, and to the aperture time of the sample-and-hold circuit.

Windowing and weighting Because the DFT is inherently finite, the analysis must be applied to short segments of the speech signal. (These segments are generally referred to as "frames.") We would like the frame to be short enough for the speech to be essentially stationary over its length, but also long enough for consecutive pitch harmonics to be easily resolved. Typical values range from approximately 25 to 75 ms; the final value is almost always chosen to suit a transform of a particular size (for example, 51.2 ms fits 512 points at a sampling rate of 10 kHz).

Time weighting is essential in any application where the spectrum is to be displayed, inspected, or manipulated (we will explain this notion below). Padding with zeros is usually also necessary in order to avoid the picket-fence effect. Any of the three weighting functions given above will do. If the sines and cosines for

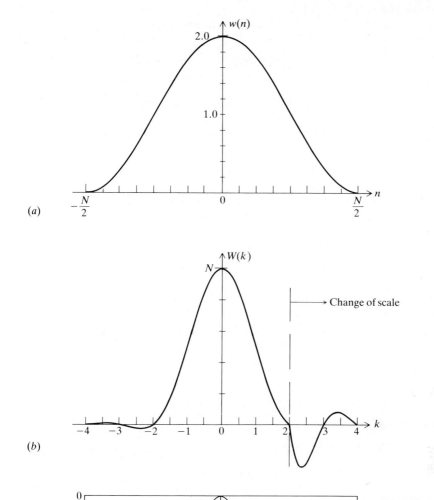
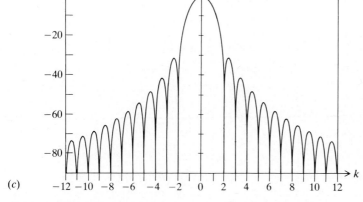

Figure 1-22 Hanning weighting. (*a*) Time window; (*b*) transform (linear); (*c*) transform (log). The linear transform is scaled up by a factor of 10, starting with $k = 1$.

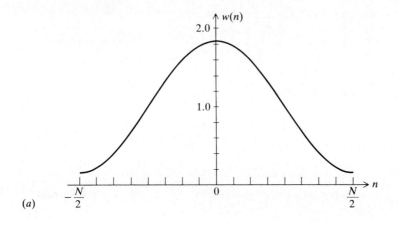

(a)

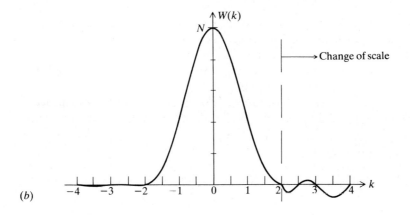

(b)

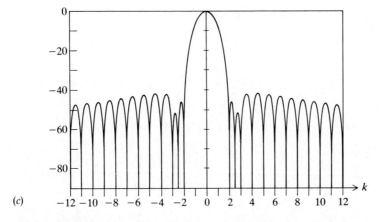

(c)

Figure 1-23 Hamming weighting. (*a*) Time window; (*b*) transform (linear); (*c*) transform (log). The linear transform is scaled up by a factor of 10, starting with $k = 1$.

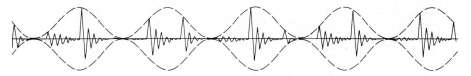

Figure 1-24 Time function modulated by periodic Hanning weighting.

the FFT are precomputed, as they are in the program FFT in Appendix B, then Hanning weighting can be made very economical by stealing the cosine weights from the FFT tables.

Use of overlapping windows There are some speech-enhancement techniques which do processing in the frequency domain, followed by an inverse transformation to reconstruct the speech signal. The processing may take two forms. In *spectrum manipulation*, the process may add or delete peaks, set samples to zero, or otherwise tamper with the transform. In *convolution*, the process simply multiplies two transforms in order to convolve two time functions economically. In either case, we must resort to special devices to compensate for the fact that we are trying to process an essentially endless signal with finite-length transforms. We will find that it is not enough to process contiguous segments; instead, we must include a degree of overlap between frames.

In the case of manipulative processes, if we simply transform and process contiguous segments, the inverse transform will be modulated by the time-weighting function, as shown in Fig. 1-24. It is hopeless to try to remove this weighting. Instead, we process overlapping segments. In reconstructing the time function, the overlapping segments dovetail and can be added to yield unmodulated speech, as shown in Fig. 1-25. This technique unfortunately doubles the

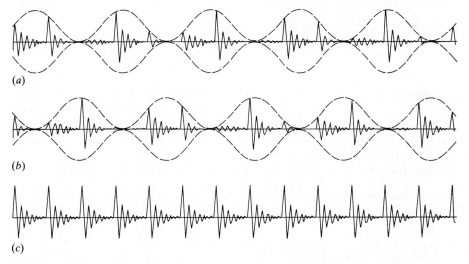

Figure 1-25 Removal of weighting by summing overlapping segments. (*a*) Odd-numbered segments with weighting; (*b*) even-numbered segments with weighting; (*c*) sum of sequences (*a*) and (*b*).

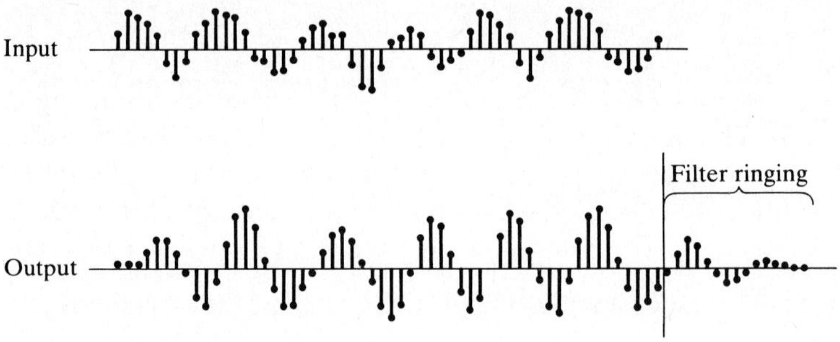

38 REVIEW MATERIALS

Input

Output

Filter ringing

Figure 1-26 Convolution by DFT, showing input sequence and output sequence with filter ringing.

amount of processing that must be done for a given length of speech signal, but it has the compensating advantage that it smoothes out any discontinuities which might result from differences in the processing of consecutive frames, since one frame fades out as its successor fades in.

When DFT processing is used for convolution, the output for any one frame will be longer than the input, because the output will include the response of the filter to the final samples of the input, as shown in Fig. 1-26. To incorporate this extra information, we use nonoverlapping input frames, but overlapping output frames. Assume that we are using a FIR filter and let the length of the filter's impulse response be M. (Alternatively, assume that the filter is an IIR filter whose impulse response can be considered negligible after M samples.) If the order of the transform is N, then we divide the input stream into frames of length $(N - M)$ and pad these frames with M zeros, to leave room for the final transient.

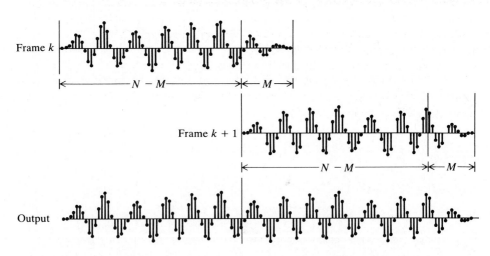

Figure 1-27 Convolution of contiguous segments by the overlap-add technique. Frames are N samples long; $N - M$ samples contain data and the last N points provide room for filter response. Filter ringing from frame k is overlapped with, and added to, the first M samples of frame $k + 1$ to obtain the final output.

In transforming these frames, no time weighting is used. After transformation, filtering, and inverse transformation, the outputs are combined at the original $(N - M)$-sample spacing and the tail of each frame is added to the beginning of the subsequent frame. This is shown in Fig. 1-27 for two frames. The transient response of the filter to the last M samples of frame k, which are missing in the output for frame $k + 1$, is supplied by the overlap from the output for frame k. Not surprisingly, this is known as the *overlap-add* technique. This, and an alternative method called the *overlap-save* technique, are described in greater detail in Oppenheim and Schafer (1975).

PROJECTS

The reader should implement the fast Fourier transform programs given in the Appendix. Readers who can program in assembly language will no doubt want to write assembly language versions of these programs; impressive speedups over the compiled versions are occasionally possible.

A/D and D/A systems are now available for use with personal computer systems, usually as cards which can be plugged into the computer's bus. Readers with access to such hardware should try to set up a complete voice acquisition and playback system. The chief bottleneck is usually transfer of data to disk. The alternatives are (1) use of large amounts of memory as a buffer, writing to disk only after acquisition is complete, or (2) use of a simulated disk in memory (the so-called RAM disk).

An acquisition program should be able to check for overflows (i.e., signals whose amplitude exceeds the range of the A/D converter) and, in the absence of overflows, to compute the peak sample size to indicate how efficiently the converter's dynamic range is being used. If the converter does not provide a two's-complement output, the program should convert the samples to two's-complement form before writing them to a file.

It is a good idea to provide a header record in the file for ancillary data, containing at least the sampling rate and possibly with provision for a brief verbal description of the digitized material.

PROBLEMS

1-1 Show that the system,

$$y(t) = x(t) - C$$

is not a linear system.

1-2 Show that the system,

$$y(t) = x(t - C)$$

is a linear system.

1-3 Show that the operations of differentiation and integration are linear.

1-4 Prove the four properties [Eqs. (1-5) to (1-8)] of convolution.

1-5 Let $h_1(n)$ and $h_2(n)$ be defined as follows:

$$h_1(n) = \begin{cases} 1, & 0 \leq n \leq 5 \\ 0, & \text{otherwise} \end{cases}$$

$$h_2(n) = \begin{cases} 3 - n, & 0 \leq n \leq 3 \\ 0, & \text{otherwise} \end{cases}$$

Compute the impulse response of a system consisting of h_1 cascaded with h_2.

1-6 Use long division to generate a power series expansion for

$$H(z) = \frac{1 + z^{-1}}{1 - az^{-1}}$$

Show that the inverse transform is

$$h(n) = -\frac{1}{a}\delta(n) + \frac{1 + a}{a} a^n u(n)$$

1-7 The numerator of a Z transform must be of lower order than the denominator for the partial-fraction expansion of (1-12) to work. Otherwise, we use division to rewrite the function as a quotient and a remainder:

$$\frac{N(z)}{D(z)} = Q(z) + \frac{R(z)}{D(z)}$$

The new fraction can be expanded as usual. Using this method, find the inverse of

$$H(z) = \frac{1 + 4z^{-1} + 2z^{-2}}{1 + 3z^{-1} + 2z^{-2}}$$

1-8 Decimal numbers are written by concatenating the coefficients of the powers of 10 that make up the number. We could think of the digits as the coefficients of a Z transform which just happens to be evaluated at $z = 0.1$:

$$1984 = z^{-3} + 9z^{-2} + 8z^{-1} + 4 \Big|_{z=1/10}$$

From the convolution theorem, it must follow that to multiply decimal numbers, we must convolve their digits. Show by an example that this is, in fact, what we do.

1-9 Suppose a system's transfer function fails to satisfy Eq. (1-24). Design a bounded input that will result in an unbounded output. Show from this that (1-24) is also a necessary condition for stability.

1-10 Show that if $h(n) = \cos \alpha n u(n)$, then the poles of $H(z)$ lie exactly on the unit circle.

1-11 Show that for $k/N \ll 1$, $\sin \pi k / [\sin (\pi k/N)] \approx N \sin \pi k / \pi k$.

1-12 Show that the transform of the Hanning window is

$$W_c(k) = S(k) * [\delta(k) + \tfrac{1}{2}\delta(k - 1) + \tfrac{1}{2}\delta(k + 1)]$$

1-13 From Fig. 1-22b, it can be seen that the first side-lobe of $W_c(n)$ is at $k = 2.5$. From the previous problem, the value of $W_c(k)$ at this point must be

$$W_c(2.5) = S(2.5) + 0.5S(1.5) + 0.5S(3.5)$$

Using the approximation of Prob. 1-11, find the constant a such that

$$W_h(2.5) = S(2.5) + aS(1.5) + aS(3.5) = 0$$

thus canceling out the side-lobe at that point. Show that this constant yields the Hamming window function (1-45).

REFERENCES

Allen, J. B., and L. R. Rabiner: A unified approach to short-time Fourier analysis and synthesis, *Proc. IEEE*, vol. 65, no. 11, pp. 1558–1564, November, 1977.

Bracewell, R.: *The Fourier Transform and Its Applications*, McGraw-Hill, New York, 1965.

Harris, F. J.: On the use of windows for harmonic analysis with the discrete Fourier transform, *Proc. IEEE*, vol. 66, no. 1, pp. 51–833, January, 1978.

Jury, E. I.: *Theory and Application of the Z-Transform Method*, Wiley, New York, 1964.

Nyquist, H.: Certain topics in telegraph transmission theory, *AIEE Trans.*, p. 617, April, 1928.

Oppenheim, A., and R. Schafer: *Digital Signal Processing*, Prentice-Hall, Englewood Cliffs, 1975.

Oppenheim, A. V., et al. (Eds.): *Selected Papers in Digital Signal Processing*, Vol. II, IEEE Press, New York, 1975.

Papoulis, A.: *The Fourier Integral and Its Applications*, McGraw-Hill, New York, 1962.

Rabiner, L. R., and B. Gold: *Theory and Application of Digital Signal Processing*, Prentice-Hall, Englewood Cliffs, 1975.

Rabiner, L. R., and C. M. Rader (Eds.): *Digital Signal Processing*, IEEE Press, New York, 1972.

Schwartz, M., and L. Shaw: *Signal Processing*, McGraw-Hill, New York, 1975.

Schwarz, R. J., and B. Friedland: *Linear Systems*, McGraw-Hill, New York, 1965.

Shannon, C. E.: Communication in the presence of noise, *Proc. IRE*, vol. 37, pp. 10–21, January, 1949.

CHAPTER
TWO

PROBABILITY THEORY

Many techniques in speech processing require the manipulation of probabilities and statistics. In this section we provide a brief review of those elements of probability theory most frequently encountered in speech work. The two principal application areas we will encounter are (1) statistical pattern recognition and (2) modeling of linear systems. For pattern recognition, we need a knowledge of the elements of probability and a familiarity with Bayes' theorem and with the gaussian probability density for one and for many random variables. For linear systems, we need a grounding in the statistics of random signals and of the response of linear systems to random inputs. The material presented here represents the minimum necessary to cover these topics; for greater depth, the reader is referred to the textbooks listed in the references.

2-1 EVENTS; AXIOMS OF PROBABILITY

It is customary to refer to the probability of an *event*. An event is a certain set of possible outcomes of an experiment or trial. The nature of the experiment and of our interest in it is what determines what we consider an outcome. Outcomes are assumed to be mutually exclusive and, taken together, to cover all possibilities. A classic example is the tossing of a die. The possible outcomes of a single trial (i.e., a single toss) are {1, 2, 3, 4, 5, 6}. From these possible outcomes we can select events, or sets of outcomes, such as {even}, {greater than 3}, {2}, {2 *or* 5}, {prime *and* greater than 2}. ("And" and "or" are used in the conventional set theory sense; in writing, "and" can be represented by concatenation and "or" by the + symbol if there is no likelihood of confusion with multiplication or addition.) There are two special events: S, the certain event, and 0, the impossible event. In the case of the die, $S = \{1 + 2 + 3 + 4 + 5 + 6\}$ (since one of these is bound to come up) and $0 = \{$no face at all$\}$.

To any event A we can assign a number, $P(A)$, which satisfies the following axioms:

1. $P(A) \geq 0$.
2. $P(S) = 1$.
3. If A and B are mutually exclusive, then $P(A + B) = P(A) + P(B)$.

The number $P(A)$ is called the *probability* of A; it reflects our belief in how likely A is to occur. In practice, we arrive at an estimate of $P(A)$ on the basis of experience or observation. Probability theory does not tell us how to form this estimate, but it does tell us how to manipulate these estimates and draw inferences from them once we have them.

The axioms of probability have some immediate consequences. First, if $\bar{A}$ is the complement of A, then since A and $\bar{A}$ are mutually exclusive and $(A + \bar{A}) = S$, $P(\bar{A}) = 1 - P(A)$. Second, $P(0)$, the probability of the impossible event, is 0. Finally, $P(A) \leq 1$.

If two events A and B are not mutually exclusive, then to express the probability of the event $(A + B)$, we must break it down into the mutually exclusive components AB, $A\bar{B}$, and $\bar{A}B$. From this analysis and the axioms of probability, we can show that $P(A + B) = P(A) + P(B) - P(AB)$.

2-2 CONDITIONAL PROBABILITY; INDEPENDENCE

The conditional probability of an event A, given that event B has occurred, is written $P(A|B)$. We define

$$P(A|B) = \frac{P(AB)}{P(B)} \quad (2\text{-}1)$$

If we know $P(A|B)$, we may be able to infer $P(B|A)$ by means of Bayes' theorem:

$$P(B|A) = P(A|B) \frac{P(A)}{P(B)} \quad (2\text{-}2)$$

Of course, events A and B may have nothing to do with each other. In that case, they are said to be *independent*. Formerly, two events are independent if $P(AB) = P(A)P(B)$. In that case, from the definition of conditional probability, $P(A|B)$ reduces to $P(A)$ and $P(B|A)$ to $P(B)$. Furthermore, $P(A + B) = P(A) + P(B) - P(A)P(B)$.

When more than two events are involved, all of their joint probabilities must be similarly factorable for them to be independent. For example, three events A, B, and C, are independent only if

$$P(AB) = P(A)P(B)$$
$$P(AC) = P(A)P(C)$$
$$P(BC) = P(B)P(C)$$

and
$$P(ABC) = P(A)P(B)P(C)$$

2-3 RANDOM VARIABLES; PROBABILITY DENSITY; MOMENTS

A random variable is a number chosen at random, i.e., as the outcome of an experiment. Random variables may be real or complex and may be discrete or continuous. In speech processing, the random variables encountered are most often real and discrete; hence we will consider chiefly real, discrete random variables in what follows.

We can characterize a random variable by its *probability distribution* or by its *probability density function*. The distribution function for a random variable y is the probability that y does not exceed some value u. Thus

$$F_y(u) = P(y \leq u)$$

(The subscript y identifies the random variable in question; it is frequently omitted if the random variable is clear from the context.) From this definition, it follows that

$$P(u < y \leq v) = F_y(v) - F_y(u) \tag{2-3}$$

The probability density function is the derivative of the distribution:

$$f_y(u) = \frac{d}{du} F_y(u)$$

As the term implies, the probability density function describes how densely the probability of the variable is spread over its range. For a continuous random variable, $f_y(u)\, du$ is the probability that the variable will take on a value lying between u and $u + du$. Then the probability that x lies between u and v is

$$P(u < y \leq v) = \int_u^v f_y(y)\, dy$$

which is consistent with (2-3).

Since probabilities are always nonnegative, it follows that $f_y(u)$ is also nonnegative. For a discrete random variable, $p(x)$ is simply the probability that the random variable resulting from an experiment will be equal to x.

We can also characterize a random variable by its statistics. The statistics of a random variable will be defined as weighted averages of certain functions of the variable. Given any function $g(x)$, the weighted average, or *expected value*, of $g(x)$ is written $E\{g(x)\}$ or $\langle g(x) \rangle$ and defined as

$$\langle g(x) \rangle = \int_{-\infty}^{\infty} g(x) f(x) \, dx \tag{2-4a}$$

for a continuous random variable and

$$\langle g(x) \rangle = \sum_{x} g(x) p(x) \tag{2-4b}$$

where the sum is taken over all possible values of x.

The statistics of greatest interest are the *moments* of $p(x)$. The kth moment of $p(x)$ is the expected value of x^k. For a discrete random variable, this is

$$m_k = \langle x^k \rangle = \sum_{x} x^k p(x) \tag{2-5}$$

Of these moments, the most important are the first two. The first moment, m_1, is the *mean* of x, also written $\langle x \rangle$, $\bar{x}$, or μ_x. If $p(x)$ were a physical object, $\bar{x}$ would be its center of gravity. Similarly, the second moment, m_2, would correspond to its moment of inertia. We are usually more interested in the second *central* moment of x, which describes the degree to which x is spread about its mean. The second central moment, also known as the *variance* of $p(x)$, is given by

$$\sigma^2 = \sum_{x} (x - \bar{x})^2 p(x)$$
$$= m_2 - \bar{x}^2 \tag{2-6}$$

σ itself is known as the *standard deviation* of $p(x)$. It is left to the reader to prove that, if x is multiplied by a constant c, the variance of cx is c^2 times the variance of x.

In order to estimate the statistics of a random variable, we repeat the experiment which generates the variable a large number of times and note the values which result. If the experiment is run N times, then each value x will occur roughly $Np(x)$ times. Thus

$$\hat{m}_k = \frac{1}{N} \sum_{i=1}^{N} x_i^k \tag{2-7}$$

where x_i is the value found in the ith experiment. For example,

$$\hat{\mu}_x = \frac{1}{N} \sum_{i=1}^{N} x_i$$

[The circumflexes ("hats") indicate estimates.] It can be shown that $\hat{m}_k$ converges to m_k as N goes to infinity. In practice, N is not only finite but is in fact frequently determined by the number of available measurements.

Uniform and Gaussian Densities

A number of specific probability densities have been widely studied; the two of greatest interest to us are the uniform and gaussian densities.

A random variable has a uniform density on the interval (a, b) if

$$F_x(x) = \begin{cases} 0, & x < a \\ (x - a)/(b - a), & a \le x \le b \\ 1, & x > b \end{cases}$$

and

$$f_x(x) = \begin{cases} 1/(b - a), & a \le x \le b \\ 0, & \text{otherwise} \end{cases}$$

The mean is obviously $\tfrac{1}{2}(a + b)$; the variance is then

$$\sigma^2 = \frac{1}{b - a} \int_a^b [x - \tfrac{1}{2}(a + b)]^2 \, dx$$
$$= \tfrac{1}{12}(b - a)^2$$

The gaussian, or normal, density function is given by

$$n(x; \mu, \sigma) = \frac{1}{\sigma\sqrt{2\pi}} e^{-(x-\mu)^2/2\sigma^2} \tag{2-8}$$

where μ and σ are the mean and standard deviation of x; $n(x; 0, 1)$ is plotted in Fig. 2-1. Gaussian or nearly gaussian random variables are found frequently in nature, and random data are often assumed to have a gaussian density even in the absence of firm evidence. This is done because (1) the gaussian density is well understood and relatively tractable mathematically and (2) when the number of data is small, the gaussian assumption tends to be less risky than any alternative density function.

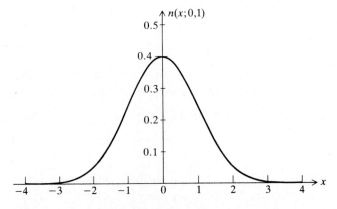

Figure 2-1 The normal density function.

The probability distribution of a normal random variable is

$$N(x; \mu, \sigma) = \int_{-\infty}^{x} n(u; \mu, \sigma) \, du$$

This integral cannot be expressed in closed form. It is usually expressed in terms of the *error function*,

$$\text{erf } x = \frac{1}{\sqrt{2\pi}} \int_{-\infty}^{x} e^{-u^2/2} \, du$$

which is tabulated in many books (e.g., Papoulis, 1984) and is built into some scientific calculators. Clearly,

$$N(x; \mu, \sigma) = \frac{1}{2\sigma} + \frac{\text{erf } (x - \mu)}{\sigma} \qquad (2\text{-}9)$$

2-4 TWO OR MORE RANDOM VARIABLES

If two random variables x and y are to be considered together, they can be described in terms of their joint probability density $f(x, y)$ or, for discrete variables, $p(x, y)$. For the latter, $p(x, y)$ is the probability that the first variable will take on the value x and the second will take on the value y. Two random variables are *independent* if

$$p(x, y) = p(x)p(y)$$

Given a function $g(x, y)$, its expected value is defined analogously to the case for a single random variable. $\langle g(x, y) \rangle$ is given by

$$\langle g(x, y) \rangle = \int_{-\infty}^{\infty} \int_{-\infty}^{\infty} g(x, y) f(x, y) \, dx \, dy \qquad (2\text{-}10a)$$

for the continuous case and by

$$\langle g(x, y) \rangle = \sum_{x, y} g(x, y) p(x, y) \qquad (2\text{-}10b)$$

if x and y are discrete. (The sum is taken over all possible values of x and y.) We can now define joint moments for two discrete random variables:

$$m_{ij} = \sum_{x, y} x^i y^j p(x, y) \qquad (2\text{-}11)$$

As in the case of a single random variable, moments are estimated in practice by averaging repeated measurements:

$$\hat{m}_{ij} = \frac{1}{N} \sum_{i=1}^{N} x^i y^j \qquad (2\text{-}12)$$

A measure of the dependence of two random variables is their *correlation*. The correlation of two random variables is their joint second moment:

$$m_{11} = \langle xy \rangle = \sum_{x,y} xy p(x, y) \qquad (2\text{-}13)$$

The joint second *central* moment of x and y is their *covariance*:

$$\sigma_{xy} = \langle (x - \bar{x})(y - \bar{y}) \rangle = m_{11} - \bar{x}\bar{y} \qquad (2\text{-}14)$$

If x and y are independent, then $m_{11} = \bar{x}\bar{y}$ and their covariance is zero. The *correlation coefficient* of x and y is their covariance normalized to their standard deviations:

$$r_{xy} = \frac{\sigma_{xy}}{\sigma_x \sigma_y} \qquad (2\text{-}15)$$

Gaussian Random Variables

The gaussian density function which we discussed above can be extended to more than one random variable. Two random variables x and y are jointly gaussian if their density function is

$$N(x, y) = \frac{1}{2\pi \sigma_x \sigma_y \sqrt{1 - r^2}} \exp\left[-\frac{1}{2(1-r^2)}\left(\frac{x^2}{\sigma_x^2} - \frac{2rxy}{\sigma_x \sigma_y} + \frac{y^2}{\sigma_y^2}\right)\right] \qquad (2\text{-}16)$$

[The variables in this example have means of zero, in order to avoid further complexity. For nonzero mean variables, we would substitute $(x - \bar{x})$ for x and $(y - \bar{y})$ for y.] Here σ_x and σ_y are the standard deviations of x and y, respectively, and r is their correlation coefficient. The terms in brackets will be recognized as a quadratic form in x and y; this form is positive-definite, i.e., it is positive for all nonzero x, y and zero only for $x = y = 0$. Hence $N(x, y)$ has a maximum of $1/(2\pi \sigma_x \sigma_y \sqrt{1 - r^2})$ located at the means of x and y.

Sums of Random Variables; The Central Limit Theorem

The expected value of a sum of two random variables is equal to the sum of their individual expected values:

$$\langle x + y \rangle = \langle x \rangle + \langle y \rangle \qquad (2\text{-}17)$$

This is true whether x and y are independent or not. Clearly this can be extended to the sum of any number of random variables. A corollary of (2-17) is that multiplication by a constant can be taken outside the expected-value operation:

$$\langle cx \rangle = c \langle x \rangle$$

Another corollary is that we can interchange the order of the operations of summation and, taking the expected value,

$$\left\langle \sum_i x_i \right\rangle = \sum_i \langle x_i \rangle$$

A somewhat more restrictive rule applies to variances. The variance of the sum of two *independent* random variables is the sum of their individual variances:

$$\sigma_{x+y}^2 = \sigma_x^2 + \sigma_y^2$$

If two random variables are independent, the probability density of their sum is the convolution of the densities of the individual variables. For continuous random variables,

$$f_{x+y}(z) = \int_{-\infty}^{\infty} f_x(u) f_y(z-u)\, du$$

and for discrete random variables,

$$p_{x+y}(z) = \sum_{u=-\infty}^{\infty} p_x(u) p_y(z-u)$$

Since we have seen that the operation of convolution is associative, this can clearly be extended to any number of independent random variables:

$$f_{x_1+x_2+\cdots+x_n}(x) = f_{x_1}(x) * f_{x_2}(x) * \cdots * f_{x_n}(x)$$

If many independent random variables are summed, the probability density function of the sum tends toward the gaussian density, no matter (within reasonable limits) what their individual densities are. This is an informal paraphrase of the *central limit theorem* (CLT), which states: subject to certain conditions, the probability density function of the sum of independent random variables tends, in the limit as the number of random variables becomes infinite, to the normal density. The conditions are difficult to state; probably the most important requirement is that the variances of the individual variables be on roughly the same scale, so that the sum is not dominated by a small number of the constituents. (In addition, the sum must be scaled in some way to keep the variance finite in the limit.) For more details, see Papoulis (1984).

The CLT provides an important justification for assuming that an unknown phenomenon is gaussian. As likely as not, the reasoning goes, the phenomenon will turn out to be the result of a large number of independent causes working together, in which case the CLT can be expected to apply.

The Multivariate Normal Density

The normal density function can be generalized to any number of random variables. The argument of the exponential again involves a quadratic in the random variables. In this *multivariate* case, it is more concise to use vector-matrix notation. Let $\mathbf{x}$ be the random vector, col $[x_1, x_2, \ldots, x_n]$, where the x_i are random variables. Let $\bar{\mathbf{x}}$ be $\langle \mathbf{x} \rangle = \text{col}\,[\langle x_1 \rangle, \langle x_2 \rangle, \ldots, \langle x_n \rangle]$. Then

$$N(\mathbf{x}) = (2\pi)^{-n/2} |\mathbf{R}|^{-1} \exp\left[-\tfrac{1}{2} Q(\mathbf{x} - \bar{\mathbf{x}})\right] \quad (2\text{-}18a)$$

where $Q(\mathbf{x} - \bar{\mathbf{x}})$ is the quadratic form,

$$Q(\mathbf{x} - \bar{\mathbf{x}}) = (\mathbf{x} - \bar{\mathbf{x}})^T \mathbf{R}^{-1} (\mathbf{x} - \bar{\mathbf{x}}) \quad (2\text{-}18b)$$

This form is also occasionally written as

$$Q(\mathbf{x} - \bar{\mathbf{x}}) = \operatorname{tr}\left[\mathbf{R}^{-1}(\mathbf{x} - \bar{\mathbf{x}})(\mathbf{x} - \bar{\mathbf{x}})^T\right] \qquad (2\text{-}18c)$$

(tr being the trace of a matrix: the sum of the elements on the main diagonal). The reader should verify that (2-18b) and (2-18c) are the same, and that, for $n = 2$, the (2-18) form is equivalent to (2-16). The matrix $\mathbf{R}$ is the *covariance matrix* of $\mathbf{x}$; its (i, j) element is the covariance of x_i and x_j. $\mathbf{R}$ can be written compactly as

$$\mathbf{R} = \langle (\mathbf{x} - \bar{\mathbf{x}})(\mathbf{x} - \bar{\mathbf{x}})^T \rangle$$

The matrix $\mathbf{R}$ is positive-definite.

2-5 RANDOM FUNCTIONS; AUTOCORRELATION AND POWER SPECTRUM

Just as a random variable was defined as one associated with the outcome of an experiment, a random function is one arising as the outcome of an experiment. More specifically, a random function is considered as arising from an underlying random process, called a *stochastic process*. For example, the annual rainfall in a given locality is a random function arising from the weather system, which is taken to be the underlying stochastic process. Random functions need not necessarily be functions of time, but in all cases of interest to us they will be.

A given stochastic process is capable of giving rise to many different random functions (usually infinitely many). Each one of these functions is said to be a *realization* of the process, and all of these realizations taken together constitute the *ensemble* of functions defined by the process. In practice, we usually have only one realization available to us for study. (We cannot rerun the weather system for, say, the past 50 years to see what other patterns of rainfall might have occurred.) The extent to which we are entitled to take the realization before us as representative of all the others is discussed below.

Random functions may be real or complex, may be defined for either continuous or discrete time, and may be continuous or discrete in range. Signals sampled and digitized for computer processing are usually real and discrete in both domain (time) and range. We will restrict our discussion to such signals, which we will call simply discrete random functions.

In general, a discrete stochastic process is characterized by many probability densities of the form,

$$p(x_1, x_2, x_3, \ldots, x_n, t_1, t_2, t_3, \ldots, t_n)$$

This is the probability that the signal will have values x_1 at t_1, x_2 at t_2, etc. In practice, most signals in which we are interested are describable by their second-order statistics, which require only $p(x, t)$ and $p(x_1, x_2, t_1, t_2)$.

If the individual values of the random signal are independent, then this joint probability density can be factored into densities of the individual variables:

$$p(x_1, x_2, x_3, \ldots, x_n, t_1, t_2, t_3, \ldots, t_n) = p(x_1, t_1)p(x_2, t_2)p(x_3, t_3) \cdots p(x_n, t_n)$$

If these individual probability densities are all the same, then one speaks of a sequence of independent, identically distributed samples, frequently abbreviated in the literature to "i.i.d. samples."

The statistics of a random function are defined in terms of weighted averages, as they were for random variables. The statistics of greatest interest to us will be the mean and the autocorrelation.

The mean is the expected value of $x(t)$:

$$\bar{x}(t) = \langle x(t) \rangle = \sum_x x p(x, t) \tag{2-19}$$

where the sum is, as usual, taken over all possible values of x.

The autocorrelation function is the expected value of the product $x(t_1)x(t_2)$:

$$r(t_1, t_2) = \langle x(t_1)x(t_2) \rangle = \sum_{x_1, x_2} x_1 x_2 \, p(x_1, x_2, t_1, t_2) \tag{2-20}$$

In principle, these averages can be determined in two ways. First, the experiment can be repeated many times, yielding many different functions, and the average can be taken over all these functions. Such an average is called an *ensemble average*. For example, the emissions of a radioactive substance have been used as a source of random numbers (random tapes used for encryption purposes have been made in this way). If we take the sequences of random numbers generated by many separate specimens of the radioactive substance, we will have an ensemble of realizations of the underlying stochastic process by which the decay is modeled. We could then use these realizations to estimate the mean and autocorrelation from (2-19) and (2-20).

Second, we may take any one of these functions as being representative of the ensemble and find the average from a number of samples of this one function. This is called a *time average*. There is, in general, no assurance that these two approaches will give the same answers. If the time averages and ensemble averages of a random function are the same, it is said to be *ergodic*.

A random function is said to be *stationary* if its statistics do not change as a function of time. Any ergodic function is also stationary. In speech signals, some parts can be treated as short segments of a stationary signal while other parts must be treated as nonstationary.

In a stationary signal, the mean $\bar{x}(t)$ becomes simply $\bar{x}$. The joint density $p(x_1, x_2, t_1, t_2)$ reduces to $p(x_1, x_2, \tau)$, where $\tau = t_2 - t_1$. Then the autocorrelation is a function simply of τ:

$$r(\tau) = \sum_{x_1, x_2} x_1 x_2 \, p(x_1, x_2, \tau)$$

When $x(t)$ is ergodic, its mean and autocorrelation can be expressed much more simply:

$$\bar{x} = \lim_{N \to \infty} \frac{1}{N} \sum_{t=-N}^{N} x(t) \tag{2-21}$$

$$r(\tau) = \langle x(t)x(t - \tau) \rangle = \lim_{N \to \infty} \frac{1}{N} \sum_{t=-N}^{N} x(t)x(t - \tau) \tag{2-22}$$

The time shift τ is frequently referred to as a *lag*, since it makes one copy of x lag in time behind the other and $r(\tau)$ is sometimes referred to in the literature as a sum of lagged products. Note that since x is a discrete-time function, so is $r(\tau)$; it is defined only for values of τ which are multiples of the sampling period. The autocorrelation function is an even function of τ: $r(-\tau) = r(\tau)$. It has its maximum value at $\tau = 0$ and $r(0)$ is equal to the *variance* of x. If $x(t)$ were an electrical signal, then $r(0)$ would be the power of x, and $r(0)$ is frequently referred to as the signal power.

The concept of the sum of lagged products is very powerful and finds wide application in signal processing. It is therefore very common in the technical literature to refer to any sum of the form of (2-22) as an autocorrelation, even for finite N and even if x is known not to be ergodic or even stochastic.

The *cross-correlation* of two ergodic random functions is similarly defined:

$$r_{xy}(\tau) = \langle x(t)y(t-\tau)\rangle = \lim_{N\to\infty} \frac{1}{N} \sum_{t=-N}^{N} x(t)y(t-\tau) \qquad (2\text{-}23)$$

The subscript xy indicates a cross-correlation; when it is necessary to distinguish among cross- and autocorrelations, we write r_{xx}, r_{xy}, r_{yx}, and r_{yy}.

The Fourier transform of $r(\tau)$ is called the *power spectral density* (or simply the *power spectrum*) of $x(t)$:

$$S(\omega) = \sum_{\tau=-\infty}^{\infty} r(\tau) e^{-j\omega\tau} \qquad (2\text{-}24)$$

The *cross-spectral density* of two ergodic random functions is, similarly,

$$S_{xy}(\omega) = \sum_{\tau=-\infty}^{\infty} r_{xy}(\tau) e^{-j\omega\tau} \qquad (2\text{-}25)$$

As with correlations, we use subscripts, if necessary, to distinguish among S_{xx}, S_{xy}, S_{yx}, and S_{yy}.

The name, power spectrum, implies that $S(\omega)$ provides some sort of spectral analysis of $x(t)$. That this is indeed so may be seen from the fact that if the Fourier transform of $x(t)$ is $X(\omega)$, then for $x(t)$ ergodic,

$$S(\omega) = |X(\omega)|^2$$

First, note that for ergodic signals $r(\tau)$ can be written as a convolution of x and its time reversal:

$$r(\tau) = x(\tau) * x(-\tau) \qquad (2\text{-}26)$$

Then from elementary Fourier transform properties,

$$S(\omega) = X(\omega)X(-\omega)$$
$$= X(\omega)X^*(\omega)$$
$$= |X(\omega)|^2$$

where X^* indicates the complex conjugate of X.

White Noise

If all values of a random signal are uncorrelated, then

$$r(\tau) = \sigma^2 \delta(\tau)$$

and the noise is called "white." The reason for this description can be seen from the fact that its power spectrum is a constant:

$$S(\omega) = \sigma^2$$

Thus just as white light is a mixture of all colors in equal amounts, white noise is likewise an equal mixture of all frequencies.

2-6 RANDOM SIGNALS IN LINEAR SYSTEMS

If a random function is applied to a linear system, we will call it and the output of the system random signals. We usually assume ergodicity. The most important results are the following.

Linear operations are interchangeable with the expected-value operation. Let $T[\ ]$ represent the linear operation; then

$$\langle T[x(t)] \rangle = T[\langle x(t) \rangle] \qquad (2\text{-}27)$$

(This is a corollary of the interchangeability of addition and averaging.) In particular, given a system with impulse response $h(n)$, we know that for input $x(n)$, the output is given by $y(n) = x(n) * h(n)$. Equation (2-27) tells us that

$$\langle y(n) \rangle = \langle x(n) * h(n) \rangle = \langle x(n) \rangle * h(n) \qquad (2\text{-}28)$$

This result should be compared with Eq. (1-7b).

A stationary signal applied to a linear system yields a stationary output. The autocorrelations of the output and input are related as follows. Let $h(t)$ be the impulse response of the system. Then

$$r_{yy}(\tau) = r_{xx}(\tau) * h(\tau) * h(-\tau) \qquad (2\text{-}29)$$

where $*$ indicates convolution. This result is most easily shown by writing the correlation functions as convolutions, as we did in (2-26). Then we proceed in two steps. Step 1 gives us

$$\begin{aligned} r_{xy}(\tau) &= x(\tau) * y(-\tau) \\ &= x(\tau) * x(-\tau) * h(-\tau) \\ &= r_{xx}(\tau) * h(-\tau) \end{aligned}$$

The second line follows from the time-reversal property of convolution: see Eq. (1-8). For step 2,

$$\begin{aligned} r_{yy}(\tau) &= y(\tau) * y(-\tau) \\ &= h(\tau) * x(\tau) * y(-\tau) \\ &= h(\tau) * r_{xy}(\tau) \\ &= r_{xx}(\tau) * h(\tau) * h(-\tau) \end{aligned}$$

This assumes that $h(n)$ is real; for complex $h(n)$, the second convolution must be with the complex conjugate $h^*(-\tau)$.

It is frequently convenient to consider $h(\tau) * h(-\tau)$ as the autocorrelation of $h(t)$, $r_{hh}(\tau)$. In that case, we can write,

$$r_{yy}(\tau) = r_{xx}(\tau) * r_{hh}(\tau) \tag{2-30a}$$

or

$$r_{yy}(\tau) = \sum_{n=-\infty}^{\infty} r_{xx}(n) r_{hh}(n - \tau) \tag{2-30b}$$

In particular, the signal power of y, $\langle y^2(n) \rangle = r_{yy}(0)$, is given by

$$r_{yy}(0) = \sum_{n=-\infty}^{\infty} r_{xx}(n) r_{hh}(n)$$

A similar relation can be given for power spectral densities of the input and output. Let the Fourier transform of $h(t)$ be $H(\omega)$. Then

$$S_{yy}(\omega) = S_{xx}(\omega) |H(\omega)|^2 \tag{2-31}$$

This follows directly from (2-28) and the convolution property of the Fourier transform. Notice that $|H(\omega)|^2$ is the squared magnitude of the frequency response of h.

To illustrate the foregoing principles, let us consider the case of white noise applied to a leaky integrator. An integrator is a device whose output is

$$y(t) = \int_{-\infty}^{t} x(u) \, du$$

or, for discrete signals,

$$y(n) = \sum_{k=-\infty}^{n} x(k) \tag{2-32}$$

Integration is clearly equivalent to convolution with a unit step. For discrete signals,

$$y(n) = \sum_{k=-\infty}^{\infty} x(k) u(n - k)$$

For $k > n$, $u(n - k)$ is zero, so the upper limit is n and the sum of (2-32) results. Hence we can do integration with a linear system whose impulse response is $u(n)$.

A leaky integrator is one which gradually forgets the past or lets it leak away. The impulse response of a leaky integrator is a slowly decaying exponential:

$$h(n) = (1 - a) a^n u(n)$$

where a is very nearly 1. The factor is included to make the integral of $h(n)$ unity. Leaky integrators are useful where the signal being integrated may have a nonzero constant component which would make a conventional integrator overflow or where we wish to smooth the signal by means of a weighted average in which the most recent values contribute the most.

If we apply white noise to $h(n)$, then the output has a mean

$$\langle y(n)\rangle = \langle x(n)\rangle * h(n)$$
$$= \frac{\langle x(n)\rangle}{1-a} \sum_{k=-\infty}^{n} a^{n-k}$$
$$= \langle x(n)\rangle$$

The autocorrelation of white noise is $\sigma^2\delta(n)$; hence by (2-30b) the autocorrelation of the output is

$$r_{yy}(\tau) = \sigma^2\delta(n) * r_{hh}(\tau)$$

The autocorrelation of the integrator is

$$r_{hh}(\tau) = (1-a)^2 \sum_{n=-\infty}^{\infty} a^n u(n) a^{n-\tau} u(n-\tau)$$

which can be shown to be $(1-a)^2/(1-a^2)a^{|\tau|}$. Hence the autocorrelation of the output is

$$r_{yy}(\tau) = \frac{\sigma^2(1-a)^2}{1-a^2} a^{|\tau|}$$

since convolution with the delta function leaves the result unchanged. The variance of the output is $r_{yy}(0) = \sigma^2(1-a)^2/(1-a^2)$; notice that the leaky integrator reduces the variance of the signal which is passed through it, as we would expect.

PROBLEMS

2-1 Prove that $P(A+B) = P(A) + P(B) - P(AB)$.

2-2 Prove that $P(A|BC) = P(AB|C)/P(B|C)$.

2-3 A researcher has examined 450 cats and has yet to find one that will not purr. Presumably such cats are very rare, and the researcher may simply have looked at the wrong cats. Let N be the event {there exists a cat that does not purr} and let $P(N)$ be the probability of the event N.

(a) For what value of $P(N)$ could the researcher have missed such a cat on 450 tries with probability 0.5?

(b) For what value of $P(N)$ would the researcher have missed such a cat with probability 0.05?

2-4 Prove that $\sigma_{xy} = m_{11} - \bar{x}\bar{y}$.

2-5 A random variable has the probability density function

$$f_y(y) = \begin{cases} ae^{-ay}, & y \geq 0 \\ 0, & \text{otherwise} \end{cases}$$

(a) Compute the mean and standard deviation of y.

(b) What is the probability that $y > 3.5a$?

2-6 The random variables x and y have probability density functions

$$f_x(x) = -[\delta(-3) + \delta(3)]$$
$$f_y(y) = n(y; 0, 0.75)$$

and the density of the random variable z is uniform on the interval $(-0.5, 0.5)$. Sketch the probability density functions of $x + y$, $x + z$, and $y + z$.

2-7 Prove Eq. (2-9).

2-8 Prove that the quadratic forms $\mathbf{x}^T\mathbf{A}\mathbf{x}$ and tr $(\mathbf{A}\mathbf{x}\mathbf{x}^T)$ are the same.

2-9 Samples from a stochastic process have the following values:

0.81	0.19	0.63	0.23	0.34	−0.04	0.42	0.51
0.06	1.12	0.40	−0.13	0.27	0.51	0.16	−0.10
0.44	0.27	0.53	0.75	0.91	0.47	0.45	0.22

(a) Estimate the mean and variance from these data.

(b) Estimate the autocorrelation function for the first nine lags (that is, 0 to 8) from these data.

2-10 Prove Eq. (2-27).

2-11 Prove Eq. (2-30).

2-12 A random signal with zero mean and the autocorrelation function

$$r(n) = 0.6^{-|n|}$$

is applied to a digital filter with the impulse response

$$h(n) = 0.8^n u(n)$$

What are the mean, variance, and autocorrelation function of the output?

REFERENCES

Anderson, T. W.: *An Introduction to Multivariate Statistical Analysis*, Wiley, New York, 1958.

Feller, W.: *An Introduction to Probability Theory and Its Applications*, Wiley, New York, 1959.

Papoulis, A.: *Probability, Random Variables, and Stochastic Processes*, McGraw-Hill, New York, 1984.

Van Trees, H. L.: *Detection, Estimation, and Modulation Theory*, Part I, Wiley, New York, 1968.

PART TWO

LINGUISTIC AND TECHNICAL FUNDAMENTALS

In this part, we will turn to the specific background of modern speech processing. We will start with the physiology and psychology of speech communication: how speech sounds are generated and perceived. We will then take up phonetics. This subject has two main subdivisions, articulatory and acoustic phonetics. In articulatory phonetics, we apply our anatomical knowledge of the speech organs to the task of describing and classifying speech sounds. This will summarize the taxonomic and behavioral background on which researchers draw in addressing specific applications. Acoustic phonetics applies the laws of physics and the theory of linear systems to the acoustics of the vocal tract and attempts to relate the articulatory gestures studied previously to measurable characteristics of the corresponding speech signals.

A large portion of this section is devoted to the topic of linear prediction of speech. It has been said that the importance of linear prediction arises from the fact that, of all the various analytical techniques which have been brought to bear on speech, it was the first one which really worked. That statement exaggerates, but not by much. The information provided by this technique is intimately related to the model of the vocal tract developed in Chapter 5, and few indeed are the application areas in which linear prediction is not embedded somewhere. Many other breakthroughs have occurred since, but linear prediction remains the single most important analytic technique currently used in speech processing.

We end this part of the book with a brief survey of the elements of pattern recognition. The speech community has had to develop its own techniques, some of which lie outside the domain of what is conventionally considered pattern recognition. The chief common ground comprises the topics of distance measurement, feature evaluation, and clustering, and these are the topics covered in this chapter.

CHAPTER
THREE

SPEECH GENERATION AND PERCEPTION

The study of the anatomy of the organs of speech is required as a background for articulatory and acoustic phonetics. In this chapter, we will provide a description of the speech organs and discuss their operation. An understanding of hearing and perception is needed in the fields of both speech synthesis and speech enhancement and is useful in the field of automatic recognition of speech. We will describe the structure of the ear and what little is currently known, or believed, about the nature of speech perception.

3-1 ORGANS OF SPEECH

We can divide the vocal organs into three main subsystems: (1) lungs and trachea, (2) larynx, (3) vocal tract. The lungs and trachea are the power supply of the system; the larynx contains the principal sound-generating mechanism; and the vocal tract modulates the resulting sound.

Lungs and Trachea

The vocal organs work by using compressed air; this is supplied by the lungs and delivered to the system by way of the trachea. These organs also control the loudness of the resulting speech, but they seldom make an audible contribution to speech, except possibly for gasps.

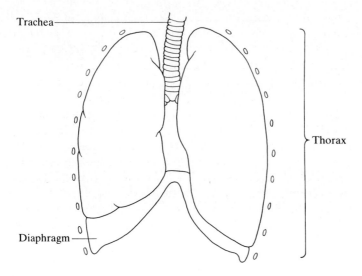

Figure 3-1 The lungs, diaphragm, rib cage, and trachea.

The lungs and trachea are shown schematically in Fig. 3-1. The primary function of the lungs is to exchange gases between the bloodstream and the air; oxygen is absorbed into the blood and carbon dioxide is removed from the blood and exhaled into the atmosphere. The lungs are a mass of spongy tissue designed to offer a large area over which this exchange can take place. Their capacity is 4 to 5 litres in an adult. They are passive structures, in the sense that they are not able in themselves to inhale or exhale. Instead, they are contained in an airtight chamber called the *pleura*. The pleura is enclosed on the sides by the ribs and on the bottom by the diaphragm; the lungs are expanded and compressed, and thus made to draw in and expel gases, by changing the size of the pleura.

The diaphragm is a dome-shaped muscle attached to the bottom of the rib cage; when this muscle contracts, the dome flattens out, the volume of the pleura increases, and air rushes into the lungs. When the diaphragm relaxes, it resumes its dome shape and the process reverses. When air is forcibly expelled from the lungs, as when blowing, shouting, sneezing, or coughing, additional force may be brought to bear by contraction of the abdominal musculature, which by compressing the abdomen applies added pressure to the bottom of the diaphragm. Inhalation may also be assisted by expanding the rib cage. When this is done, breathing is said to be *thoracic*; breathing due to the diaphragm is called *abdominal* breathing. Most breathing is a mixture of both kinds, the proportions depending on circumstances.

We speak while breathing and must manage to reconcile linguistic and physiological requirements; we learn to do this as children. The physiological requirement is the oxygenation of the blood and the removal of carbon dioxide; this process is regulated by a feedback loop controlled by the concentration of carbon dioxide in the blood. Nonspeech breathing consists normally of regular, even inhalation and exhalation of roughly equal length.

The chief linguistic requirement is to provide a degree of continuity in speech. Hence we speak in breath groups, and speech breathing consists of short inhalations and long, controlled exhalations. Some aspects of sentence structure may be related to breath groups, but there seems to be no fixed rule.

The trachea or windpipe is approximately 12 cm long by 2 cm across, joining the lungs and the larynx. It is made of rings of cartilage joined by connective tissue. This construction provides a tube which is rigid in cross section but which can bend and twist readily in response to motions of the head. At the bottom, the trachea branches into the right and left *bronchus*; the bronchi lead into the lungs and complete the connection between the spongy interior of the lungs and the air. At the top, the trachea joins the *larynx*. The trachea and lungs together constitute the *pulmonary tract*.

The Larynx

This is a complicated system of cartilages and muscles containing and controlling the vocal cords. Its principal parts are:

1. Cricoid cartilage
2. Thyroid cartilage
3. Arytenoid cartilages
4. Vocal cords

The cricoid and thyroid cartilages are mostly framework. The cricoid cartilage is essentially another of the rings making up the trachea, but much higher at the rear in order to support the back ends of the vocal cords. The thyroid cartilage is located in front, approximately opposite the raised part of the cricoid cartilage. The shape of the thyroid is designed to give it strength to resist the pull of the vocal cords; the domed shape of the thyroid cartilage, visible as a projection at the front of the throat, is the "Adam's apple."

The vocal cords are folds of flesh stretched between the front and the back of the larynx, as shown in Fig. 3-2. The front ends are supported by the thyroid car-

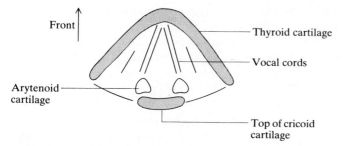

Figure 3-2 The vocal cords and their supporting cartilages. The vocal cords are shown open, in the normal position for breathing.

tilage and the back ends by the arytenoid cartilages, which in turn are connected to the raised portion of the cricoid cartilage. These cartilages are controlled by sets of muscles attached to the cricoid cartilage and can move the ends of the vocal cords together or apart. When the ends of the cords are apart, they are open; this is the normal position for breathing. (The space between the vocal cords is called the *glottis*.) When the ends are together, the cords are closed and provide an airtight seal at the top of the pulmonary tract.

The functions of the vocal cords are biological and acoustical. The biological function is to close off the trachea, either to protect the pulmonary tract or to permit building up pressure inside the thorax and abdomen. The pulmonary tract is protected (1) by sealing off the trachea during swallowing, to keep food particles out of the pulmonary tract, and (2) by coughing, in which the sudden opening of the vocal cords causes a gust of rapidly moving air, helping to dislodge particles in the trachea. Building up thoracic pressure increases its rigidity, aiding in heavy exertions like lifting and pushing; building up abdominal pressure is an aid in defecation and childbirth. The acoustical function of the vocal cords is to provide the principal excitation source for speech. We will detail their operation below.

The Vocal Tract

This term usually means everything past the vocal cords. The general structure can be seen from the sagittal cross section shown in Fig. 3-3. The vocal tract is conventionally divided into the following regions:

1. Laryngeal pharynx (beneath epiglottis)
2. Oral pharynx (behind tongue, between epiglottis and velum)
3. Nasal pharynx (above velum, rear end of nasal cavity)
4. Oral cavity (forward of the velum and bounded by lips, tongue, and palate)
5. Nasal cavity (above the palate and extending from the pharynx to the nostrils)

In addition, the vocal tract is bounded by the following structures:

1. Epiglottis
2. Lower jaw
3. Tongue
4. Velum
5. Palate
6. Teeth
7. Lips

The epiglottis is a plate of cartilage lying above the vocal cords and behind the tongue. It is commonly believed that it aids in swallowing, but Heffner (1964) points out that this is not so, and indeed that the epiglottis can be removed without impairment of the ability to swallow. The lower jaw, or mandible, is used in mastication and also supports the front end of the tongue.

SPEECH GENERATION AND PERCEPTION 63

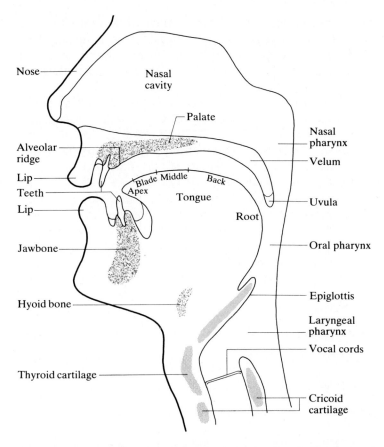

Figure 3-3 Sagittal section of the human head, showing the principal organs of speech.

The roof of the mouth can be divided into two principal regions. In front, the roof is formed by a bone called the palate which separates the mouth from the nasal cavities and supports the upper teeth. At the back of the palate, the roof is formed of muscle and connective tissue; this structure is called the velum, or soft palate. (Writers who call the velum the soft palate refer to the palate as the hard palate to distinguish the two.) The uvula is a small fleshy appendage at the rear of the velum. The velum can be lifted by a muscle and pressed against the back wall of the pharynx to seal the nasal passages off from the rest of the vocal tract. At the front of the palate there is a ridge, formed by the thickening of the bone where the front teeth are inserted; this is called the alveolar ridge.

The tongue is a large system of muscles connected in front to the lower jaw and in back to bones in the throat and head. Its biological functions include tasting and manipulation of food during mastication. For articulatory purposes it is convenient to divide the tongue into regions. In the absence of distinct landmarks, it is difficult to define these regions precisely, but they are approximately as follows. The *blade* of the tongue is its front end, roughly that part which can be stuck out of the mouth, and especially its upper surface; the very front of the blade is the *tip*. Behind the blade and opposite the back of the (hard) palate is the *middle* of the tongue; the *back* of the tongue is beneath the velum. Finally, the *root* of the tongue is that portion which faces the pharynx.

The functions of the vocal tract, like those of the larynx, are biological and vocal. The biological functions include respiration, olfaction, tasting, mastication, and swallowing. The vocal function is the coloring and articulation of the voice; the vocal tract also contains the principal points from which the speech sounds are radiated. With the exception of the epiglottis, all of these parts are involved in speech; the principal participants in coloring and articulation are the tongue, lips, and lower jaw.

The vocal tract in the adult male is approximately 17 cm long. As the acoustical wave passes through the vocal tract, its frequency content is affected by cavity resonances in the tract. These resonances depend on the shapes of the various regions of the vocal tract. By moving the tongue, we can alter the shapes of the oral cavity and oral pharynx. We can also decouple the nasal cavity from the system by raising the velum so that it seals the nasal cavity off at the pharynx.

3-2 SPEECH PRODUCTION

The operation of the system as a whole is most readily divided into two functions, *excitation* and *modulation*, as shown schematically in Fig. 3-4. Excitation takes place mostly at the glottis but also at some other points; modulation is done by the various organs of the vocal tract.

Excitation

Excitation is done in several ways, comprising phonation, whispering, frication, compression, and vibration.

Phonation This, the most important excitation source, is the oscillation of the vocal cords. The arytenoid cartilages close and stretch the vocal cords, as shown in Fig. 3-5a. When air is forced through the vocal cords, they vibrate, like the lips of a trumpeter. The oscillations are governed by the mass and tension of the cords and also by the Bernoulli effect of the air passing through. A detailed analysis of this action is to be found in Flanagan (1972). The opening and closing of the cords breaks the airstream up into pulses, as shown in Fig. 3-6. The shape and duty cycle of these pulses depend on circumstances (loudness, pitch,

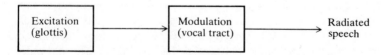

Figure 3-4 The excitation-modulation model of speech production.

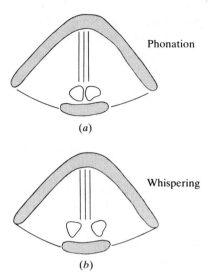

Figure 3-5 Position of the vocal cords and cartilages (a) for phonation and (b) for whispering.

Figure 3-6 A typical glottal pulse train.

"breathy" speech, etc.); the shape and duty cycle shown are typical of normal speech. The repetition rate of the pulses is termed *pitch*. Pitch is controlled mainly by tension on vocal cords and regulated by feedback through the ears and brain. Different modes of vibration are possible. Singers call these modes "registers" ("chest tone," "head tone," "falsetto"). At low levels of air pressure (e.g., in unaccented parts of speech or at the ends of sentences), oscillations may become irregular, occasionally dropping pitch an octave as the repetition rate halves, or with pulses coming in pairs, as shown in Fig. 3-7. These irregularities are known as "vocal fry." Speech sounds accompanied by phonation are called *voiced*; others, *unvoiced* or *mute*.

Whispering Here the vocal cords are drawn together, but with a small triangular opening between arytenoid cartilages, as shown in Fig. 3-5b. Air rushing through this opening generates turbulence, causing wideband noise which serves as the excitation signal.

The remaining sound sources serve as modulation as well as excitation, since they are generally perceived as interruptions of the voice, forming consonants,

Figure 3-7 Glottal pulses in pairs, one form of *vocal fry*.

syllable boundaries, and the like. These functions will be discussed in greater detail in the following chapter.

Frication If the vocal tract is constricted at any other point, the air flow past the constriction is turbulent and generates broadband noise whose frequency spectrum reflects (to a limited degree) the location of the constriction. Sounds so produced are called *fricatives* or *sibilants*. Frication can occur with or without phonation.

Compression If the vocal tract is completely shut off at any point while the talker continues to try to exhale, pressure builds up, and upon release (i.e., when the vocal tract is reopened) a small explosion will occur. The combination of a short silence followed by a short noise burst has a characteristic sound. If the release is abrupt and clean, the sound is a *stop* or *plosive* (e.g., [p], [t]); if gradual and turbulent, the sound can pass into the related fricative (e.g., tch or German pf) and is termed an *affricate*.

Vibration If air is forced through a closure other than the vocal cords, vibrations may be set up, especially at the tongue (trilled r) or uvula (French or Prussian r), and occasionally between the lips.

Modulation

This is what we do to impose information on the glottal output. Linguists think of this as articulation and the division of speech stream into vowels and consonants. If we think of it as modulation, we must consider (1) from a physiological point of view, how the articulatory information is imposed on the sound; (2) from an acoustical point of view, what the vocal organs do to the signal emanating from the glottis. Answering (1) leads us into the domain of *articulatory phonetics*: how the organs of speech are positioned to produce any given speech sound. Answering (2) takes us into the field of *acoustic phonetics*: what the measurable acoustical correlates of any given speech sound are and how acoustical features in general correspond to phonetic and articulatory ones.

We will go into both articulatory and acoustical phonetics in detail later, but a brief summary will be in order here. Physiologically, the sound is modulated by moving the speech organs (mainly the tongue) in order to change the quality of the voice and to interpose additional sounds or interruptions on the voice.

Acoustically, the principal means of modulation is the operation of *filtering*. The glottal waveform is very rich in harmonics, and the vocal tract, like any acoustical tube, has natural frequencies which are a function of its shape. These natural resonances are called *formants*, and they are the single most important way of modulating the voice—they account for all of the vowels and some of the consonants, and we will see that they also provide crucially important information about the rest of the consonants as well. Additional types of modulation are the various interruptions and the interposed and added wideband noise bursts (described above) which form the consonants.

3-3 HEARING AND PERCEPTION

By hearing we mean the process by which sound is received and converted into nerve impulses; by perception we mean, approximately, the postprocessing within the brain by which the sounds heard are interpreted and given meaning.

Hearing

We will start with the anatomy of the ear. The ear is divided into three parts: the outer ear, the middle ear, and the inner ear (Fig. 3-8).

The outer ear consists of the *pinna* (the visible, convoluted cartilage), the external canal (*external auditory meatus*), and the eardrum (*tympanic membrane*). The pinna protects the opening; its convoluted shape is thought to provide some directional cues (Schroeder, 1975). The external auditory meatus is a nearly uniform tube approximately 2.7 cm long by 0.7 cm across through which the sound passes to reach the eardrum. Like all tubes, it has a number of resonant frequencies, of which only one, at approximately 3 kHz, falls in the frequency range of speech. The tympanic membrane is a stiff, conical structure at the end of the meatus. It vibrates in response to the sound and is the first link in a chain of structures which transmit the sound to the neural transducers in the inner ear.

The middle ear is an air-filled cavity separated from the outer ear by the tympanic membrane and connected to the inner ear by two apertures called the *oval* and *round windows*. The middle ear is also connected to the outside world by way of the *eustachian tube*, which permits equalization of air pressure between the middle ear and the surrounding atmosphere.

The middle ear contains three tiny bones or *ossicles* which provide the acoustical coupling between the tympanic membrane and the oval window. These bones are called the *malleus* (hammer), *incus* (anvil), and *stapes* (stirrup). The malleus is attached to the tympanic membrane, the stapes to the oval window, and the incus connects the two. The function of the ossicles is twofold: (1) impedance transformation and (2) amplitude limiting.

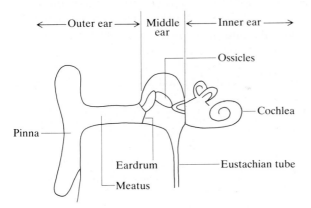

Figure 3-8 Sectional view of the human ear.

Impedance transformation provides more efficient transfer of acoustical energy from the air to the fluid-filled inner ear. The transformation has two components, the mechanical advantage of the ossicular linkage and the ratio of the area of the tympanic membrane to that of the oval window. The overall impedance stepup is about 15 to 1 (Békésy, 1960).

Limiting protects the ear at high sound levels. Limiting is done by the inner ear muscles, which can attenuate the transmission through the ossicles by contracting (this contraction is known as the *acoustic reflex*). Specifically, at high sound intensities the *stapedius muscle* contracts in such a way as to change the mode of vibration of the stapes to a direction which provides reduced excitation of the oval window (Békésy, 1960; Flanagan, 1972).

The inner ear consists of the *vestibular apparatus*, the round and oval windows, and the *cochlea*. The vestibular apparatus comprises the semicircular canals and associated organs, used for balance and sensing orientation and not of interest to us here.

The cochlea is a snail-shaped passage communicating with the middle ear via the round and oval windows. It contains the transducers which convert acoustical vibrations to nerve impulses. If the cochlea were uncoiled, it would look like Fig. 3-9; in cross section, a single turn looks like Fig. 3-10. The cochlea is divided down its middle by a partition bounded by a flexible sheet called the *basilar membrane* and by a thinner membrane called *Reissner's membrane*. The partition divides the cochlea into two passages, the *scala vestibuli* and the *scala tympani*. The two passages are connected by an opening at the far end of the cochlea called the *helicotrema*. The acoustical energy enters by way of the oval window, which is driven by the stapes. The sound travels down one side of the cochlea (the scala vestibuli), passes to the other side via the helicotrema, travels back along the other side (the scala tympani), and exits by way of the round window. The basilar membrane vibrates in response to this sound.

The *organ of Corti* and the *tectorial membrane* run the length of the basilar membrane. The organ of Corti is on the basilar membrane; the tectorial membrane is mounted on a projection of the wall of the cochlea and lies just over the organ of Corti. The latter contains *hair cells* which span the gap between the organ of Corti and the tectorial membrane. These hair cells sense the vibration of the membrane. Next to the base of each hair cell is a nerve synapse by which the frequency information is passed to the brain.

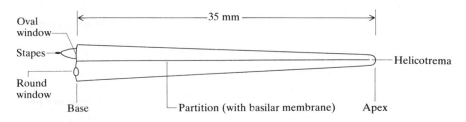

Figure 3-9 The cochlea as it would appear if unwound.

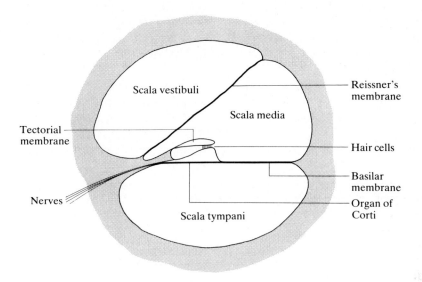

Figure 3-10 Cross section of one turn of the cochlea.

The function of this structure is to produce a spatial dispersion of frequency components along the length of the basilar membrane. Békésy (1928, 1960) analyzed the vibration of the basilar membrane in response to the passage of sound through the two scalae and was able to show that its vibration in response to an applied sound reaches a maximum at one point along its length and that the location of this maximum is a function of the frequency of the sound. The location of the maximum-amplitude point is plotted against frequency in Fig. 3-11. The cochlea thus acts as a mechanical-neural spectrum analyzer. The typical frequency response of one point on the basilar membrane is shown in Fig. 3-12. The basilar membrane thus appears to be the primary mechanism for frequency analysis of the incoming sound. (Figure 3-12 is based on Rhode, 1971; Békésy's curves showed a less sharp response, leading many investigators to assume that postprocessing was responsible for the pitch discrimination actually observed in psychological experiments. The possibility of postprocessing has by no means been ruled out, but Rhode's measurements make it appear less necessary than had previously been thought.)

This is known as the *place theory* of frequency resolution (see, for example, Nordmark, 1970). It is also known, however, that firings of the auditory nerves occur with a frequency equal to that of the incoming sound; this correspondence has been observed for frequencies up to 5 kHz; hence some researchers believe that the brain determines frequency by, in effect, measuring the rate at which firings take place. This is the *temporal*, or *frequency*, theory. There is no decisive evidence to rule out either possibility. There are some phenomena which are hard to explain by means of the place theory. For example, if the fundamental frequency component is missing from a complex tone, the ear will supply it and the

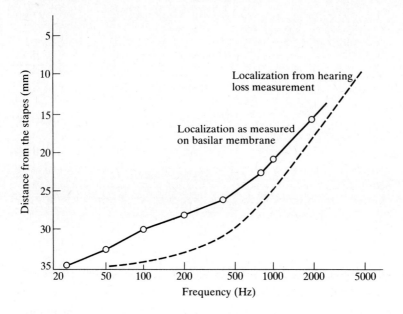

Figure 3-11 Position of maximum amplitude along basilar membrane as a function of applied frequency. (*After Békésy, 1960.*)

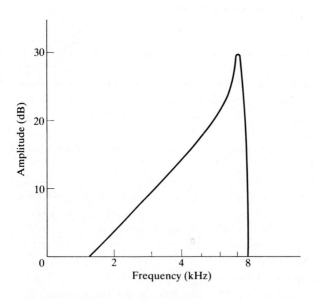

Figure 3-12 Frequency response of a point on the basilar membrane. (*After Rhode, 1971.*)

listener will perceive the fundamental. (This is especially remarkable in the case of the perception of the sound of bells, where partials which are only approximately harmonic can give rise to an apparent fundamental.) On the other hand, if the temporal theory is correct, it is not easy to see why the elaborate structure of the cochlea exists. One school of thought is that both mechanisms contribute to the perception of frequency.

The nerves from the cochlea converge in a cluster called the cochlear nucleus. From there the path to the brain passes through the superior olivary complex, the lateral lemnisci, the inferior colliculus, the medial geniculate body, and the auditory cortex. It is believed that additional processing of the sound data takes place in one or more of these intermediate stages on the path. There are crossovers at several points along this path, with the result that the most important path from each ear leads to the opposite hemisphere of the brain.

Perception

We will consider first the performance of the auditory organs and then take up what is known about speech perception.

Performance Determining the capabilities of the human auditory system is one of the classical functions of experimental psychology. We summarize the results briefly here, starting with the limits of the domain. The frequency range is from approximately 16 Hz to 16 kHz. The upper limit falls off with increasing age; among the young, it occasionally reaches 20 kHz; in old age it may be as low as 10 kHz. At the low end of the frequency range, the perceived sound becomes a pulse train; at the high end, it fades off into silence. The intensity range is from 0 to 130 dB spl. (The reference level is 10^{-16} W/cm^2 or 0.0002 dyn/cm^2.) At the high end, sound turns to pain; at the low end, it becomes silence.

Loudness Perceived loudness is a function of both frequency and level. By comparing tones at different frequencies and amplitudes, contours of equal subjective loudness can be found; these contours take the general form shown in Fig. 3-13. These are sometimes called the Fletcher-Munson (1933) curves, although similar estimates have been made by Churcher and King (1937) and by Robinson and Dadson (1956) and Robinson (1958). The slight dip in the neighborhood of 3 to 4 kHz, indicating an increased sensitivity in this region, is probably due to the resonance of the external auditory meatus. The unit of loudness level when compensated for frequency dependence is the *phon*.

Psychologists distinguish between loudness and loudness level. The perceived loudness scale is derived by asking subjects to set the loudness of a sound to $\frac{1}{2}$, 2, $\frac{1}{10}$, or 10 times the loudness of a reference. The scale is set up after many repetitions; the unit is the *sone*. Figure 3-14 shows the relation between loudness in sones and loudness level in phons. This curve is sometimes approximated by the equation,

$$N = 0.063 \times 10^{0.03L},$$

where N is loudness in sones and L is loudness level in phons.

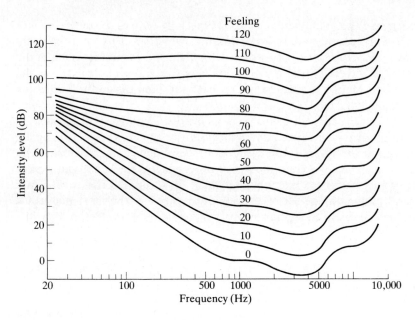

Figure 3-13 Contours of equal loudness level. The numbers on the curves indicate the loudness in phons. (*After Fletcher and Munson, 1933.*)

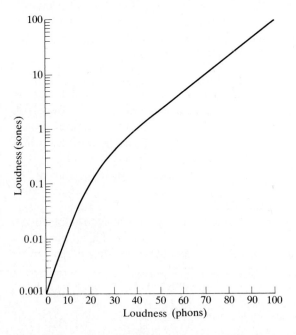

Figure 3-14 Conversion from phons to sones. (*After Fletcher and Munson, 1937.*)

Pitch Among musicians and physicists, pitch is defined relative to some reference frequency. The difference in pitch between two notes is equal to 1200 times the logarithm to the base 2 of their frequency ratio. The unit of musical pitch is the *cent*. (One cent is $\frac{1}{100}$ of an equally tempered semitone.) Psychologists, on the other hand, have started with the assumption that humans perceive a pitch in absolute terms, and their measurements yield results generally at variance with the physical model. By applying the same experimental method as was used for loudness (setting pitch $\frac{1}{2}$, 2 times a reference, etc.), a pitch scale can also be derived (Stevens and Volkmann, 1940). The unit of pitch is the *mel*; pitch in mels is plotted against frequency in Fig. 3-15. In the figure, frequency is plotted on a logarithmic scale and is therefore linear in musical pitch. Notice that the mel scale does not correspond either to frequency or to musical pitch. Koenig (1949) approximates this scale by a function which is linear below 1 kHz and logarithmic above; Fant (1959) gives the approximation,

$$y = k \log \left(1 + \frac{f}{1000}\right)$$

where $k = 1000/\log 2$.

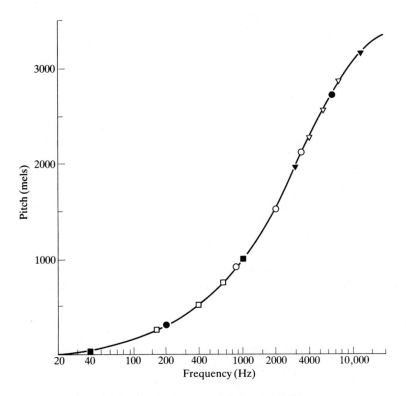

Figure 3-15 The mel scale. (*After Stevens and Volkmann, 1940.*)

Complex periodic sounds We saw in an earlier chapter that periodic, non-sinusoidal sounds can be analyzed by Fourier transform methods into a set of harmonically related pure tones. Harmonics are not ordinarily heard as separate tones; instead, the ensemble seems to be a single tone whose pitch is at the fundamental; the presence of the higher harmonics is perceived as giving the sound a "tone quality" or "timbre." (This is a difficult thing to explain if the "place" theory of frequency resolution is correct.) The perceptual phenomenon of timbre is important to us because vowel sounds are distinguished by their differing harmonic content.

In complex tones, pitch (i.e., fundamental frequency) is perceived even if the fundamental is actually absent. For example, the pitch of a male voice, which typically lies below 120 Hz, is clearly perceived over a telephone system in which the frequency response cuts off below 300 Hz. It is not clear how the fundamental is reconstructed in the brain. The following theories have been proposed to explain this effect:

1. A fundamental is generated by nonlinearities in the ear. (This theory has been challenged on the basis that the effects of nonlinearities are dependent on amplitude, while perception of the fundamental is not.)
2. The fundamental is derived in the brain by postprocessing.
3. The fundamental results from phase coherence among neuron firings in response to the harmonics.

Masking This is the name for the phenomenon in which one sound interferes with our perception of another ("drowning out"). The degree to which masking occurs is a function of relative levels and frequencies. Tones nearby are more effectively masked than tones of widely differing frequency. Fletcher and Munson (1937) found that when a pure tone (i.e., a sinusoid) was masked by wideband noise, only a small band centered about the tone contributed to the masking effect; they named this the critical band. The critical band has since been shown to be related to a large number of frequency-dependent perceptual effects, including masking by a second tone, sensitivity to phase modulation, perception of musical dissonance, among others (Scharf, 1970). Critical bands are of almost constant width on the mel scale; the width of a critical band ranges from 100 mels at 50 mels to approximately 250 mels at 3600 mels (13,500 Hz).

Speech perception The primary question addressed by theories of speech perception is how the acoustical input to the ear is translated by the brain into speech sounds. A large body of experimental evidence has been accumulated which answers parts of this question, although a complete answer does not appear to be likely soon. We will summarize the consensus as it currently exists. (Some issues in speech perception deal with the significance of formants and formant transitions. Formants are an essentially acoustical phenomenon, and we will defer these topics to Chapter 5, where the acoustical characteristics of vowels and consonants will be discussed in detail.)

It appears that the brain makes a fundamental distinction between speech sounds and nonspeech sounds. Experiments (House et al., 1962) suggest that this distinction is either/or: when listeners hear nonspeech synthetic sounds which are gradually made more speechlike, an abrupt boundary is found, on one side of which the sounds are perceived as speech and on the other side of which they are not.

The brain appears to process speech sounds in a fundamentally different way from nonspeech sounds. It is believed that the speech-processing center is located in the left hemisphere of the brain. The evidence for this is, first, that the right ear shows generally better performance in listening to speech than does the left ear (e.g., Kimura, 1961b) and, second, that damage to the left hemisphere of the brain results in impaired speech perception (Kimura, 1961a).

It is believed that there is an innate predisposition in the human nervous system to decode speech inputs. It is noteworthy that acousticians using white noise for test purposes report hearing "voices" in the noise after long exposure. Although this may simply be an expression of a natural tendency to impose patterns on random events, it also suggests that the brain may continually attempt to detect speech in any auditory input.

The brain tends to impose a categorization on speech sounds. (This is termed *categorical perception*.) Just as sounds are classified as speech or nonspeech, so speech sounds themselves are sorted by the brain into different types. A particularly striking example of the latter property is provided by an experiment by Liberman *et al.* (1957) using synthetic sounds which varied gradually in acoustical characteristics from /bæ/ (as in "bad") to /gæ/ (as in "gad"). The results are shown in Fig. 3-16. Listeners did not hear this gradual variation, but instead made sharp distinctions among initial consonants.

It is thought that this categorization is done by a preprocessor which separates speech from nonspeech, separates the fundamental frequency from the spectral coloration due to harmonic components, and outputs a set of features. A central processor then performs recognition using these features as its input. The processor almost certainly draws on other things in addition to the data from the peripheral processor: the listener's knowledge of the language, of the talker's characteristics, and of the topic under discussion are drawn upon to combine the

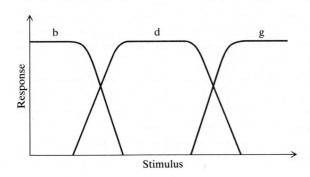

Figure 3-16 Consonant identifications as a function of stimulus value. As the stimulus is varied smoothly from the low end of the scale to the high end, the perceived consonant changes abruptly from b to d, then from d to g. (*Adapted from Liberman et al., 1957.*)

features into a coherent whole and also to correct possible errors resulting from ambiguities in the input data.

Other research indicates that perception of specific speech sounds depends on the same features as those identified by articulatory and acoustical analysis of speech. Details on these topics will have to await the chapters on articulatory and acoustical phonetics.

Perception is influenced by context. A number of researchers have attempted to measure the ease with which speech is perceived by measuring subjects' ability to understand speech obscured by noise, on the assumption that easily understood speech is more resistant to such degradation. Nonsense syllables and words have been found to be more easily obscured than is sense; incoherent sentences made up of real words are likewise more easily obscured than coherent sentences; short utterances are more easily obscured than long ones; and ungrammatical utterances than grammatical ones. This has led to the belief that lexical, grammatical, and semantic cues are all used as aids in verifying the correctness of the brain's analysis of the incoming speech.

The importance of context on ease and accuracy of perception has led some researchers (Halle and Stevens, 1962; and Miller and Chomsky, 1963) to believe that we perceive speech by modeling the talker internally. That is, as we listen to a talker, we duplicate the speech mentally, tracking and if possible anticipating it. This process is known as analysis by synthesis. Such a model requires coherence and continuity in the speech, and under this hypothesis nonsense is less intelligible because it makes it impossible to maintain the internal model. This theory of internally modelling perceived speech has had a powerful influence on the development of "speech-understanding" systems.

The motor theory, set forth in Liberman *et al.* (1967), among other places, suggests that speech is perceived in terms of articulation. That is, the mind analyzes speech by maintaining a mental simulation of the articulatory processes of speech generation. Using this simulation, the mind constructs one or more hypothetical articulatory models of the incoming speech and matches it against a library of possibilities. Categorical perception has been linked with the motor theory by the suggestion that distinct categories of perceived speech sounds correspond to distinct articulations.

Both of these theories appeal to a knowledge of the language and of the articulatory process on the part of the listener. Other theorists, e.g., Fant (1967), suggest that perception depends primarily on the ability to recognize distinguishing traits in the received sound without any extensive reliance on a local duplication of the process. This belief appears to have been influenced by our experience in attempting to do speech recognition by computer, and it is closely related to the distinctive feature theory of Jakobson *et al.* (1952), to be discussed in the following chapter. One area of current research is whether such features are indeed the raw material of speech recognition by humans, or whether we in fact process speech at several levels more or less concurrently.

High-level approaches like the motor theory are probably trying to explain too much too soon, and this is perhaps why they do not command a significant following today. Modern theories of perception tend to be at once less ambitious and more specific. For example, Cole and Jakimik (1980), on the basis of many experiments in perception, have developed the following theory:

1. Knowledge of the language and of the environment generally plays a significant part in perception of speech. Speech is not recognized by pure analysis of the acoustic signal alone; such analysis is not adequate to remove ambiguities from the message or to clarify obscure speech sounds. As the utterance proceeds, it is analyzed and the analysis checked against knowledge of the phonological constraints of the language, the grammatical rules of the language, and the listener's knowledge of the subject of the utterance. On the other hand, the primary input to the analysis is still the incoming signal: "word recognition is conceptually guided but data *driven.*"
2. The input speech is processed one word at a time, in the order in which the words are received. Information extracted from each word is used to guide the analysis of subsequent words. In particular, recognition of a word immediately identifies the approximate location of the start of the next word, and the meaning and sound of the word provide constraints which limit the number of possibilities which must be considered in recognizing subsequent words.
3. In the recognition of an individual word, the sounds of which it is composed are likewise processed in order of their appearance, and each new sound is used to narrow the number of possibilities. The initial sound is of particular importance in this analysis, since it usually does more to limit the number of possibilities than the subsequent syllables. (There are probably computational advantages in using the first syllable immediately as well.) The early part of the word, and particularly the first syllable, thus receive the closest attention from the listener. As soon as enough information has been received to exclude all but one possible word, recognition is complete and the listener pays only slight attention to the remainder of the word.

This model is based on experiments on listeners' ability to detect mispronunciations of words; the experiments typically measure the number of mispronunciations detected, the reaction time in detecting them, or the listeners' ability to correct them. The assumption is that performance will depend on (1) how closely the listener is paying attention to the word (so that mispronunciations occurring after recognition is essentially complete will be detected less often) and (2) how essential the mispronounced sound is to recognition (so that mispronunciations in important sounds—particularly those at the beginning of the word—are detected more slowly than those of less important sounds).

Recognition in this model is essentially a bottom-up process, starting from the data and working toward the structure, as opposed to a top-down process which starts with a hypothetical sentence and tries to fit the data to it. Readers who are familiar with the design of compilers for programming languages will recognize this distinction, since compilers can be made to parse the program input either top-down or bottom-up. At this writing, bottom-up parsers, which also analyze the input elements in the order in which they appear, offer generally superior performance in speed and in error detection. While the use of the computer as a model of human thought processes is risky, the coincidence is undeniably appealing.

The experience of researchers in writing programs for recognition of continuous speech has also influenced thought about models of perception, and there are affinities between existing recognizers and the Cole-Jakimik model. In particular, most recognizers use some sort of left-to-right, bottom-up process, starting from an analysis of the incoming signal, and the level-building process, which we discuss in Chapter 12, also uses the recognition of the current word to estimate the location of the beginning of the next word.

Effects of severe distortion on intelligibility A number of investigators have observed the effects of various types of signal degradation on speech intelligibility. These experiments have been made partly as explorations of the perceptual apparatus and partly in order to improve existing speech-transmission facilities. The findings of greatest interest are summarized here.

Filtering French and Steinberg (1947) investigated the effects of low-pass and high-pass filtering on the intelligibility of speech. They estimated intelligibility by scoring the number of nonsense syllables correctly recognized by listeners to the filtered speech. When high-pass filtering was used, the intelligibility decreased as the cutoff frequency was increased. Intelligibility was essentially unimpaired for cutoff frequencies below approximately 400 Hz; at approximately 1.7 kHz, the number of syllables correctly recognized was reduced by half, and a cutoff frequency above 6 kHz rendered speech unintelligible. Low-pass filtering had the opposite effect; intelligibility decreased as the cutoff frequency was lowered. Intel-

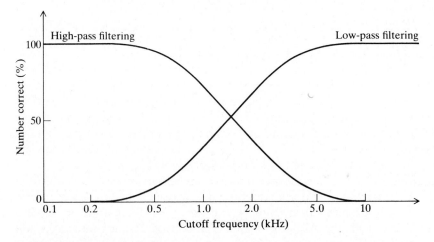

Figure 3-17 Effect of low-pass and high-pass filtering on accuracy of speech recognition. (*After French and Steinberg, 1947.*)

ligibility was unaffected for cutoff frequencies above 6 kHz; the number of correct syllables was reduced by half at approximately 1.5 kHz; and a cutoff below 400 Hz rendered speech unintelligible. These results were affected somewhat by variations in amplitude, but the overall pattern was unchanged. These results are summarized in Fig. 3-17.

Clipping Licklider (1946) investigated the effects of clipping on the intelligibility of speech. He considered several types of clipping; of these the most important to us are infinite clipping and center clipping. The action of infinite clipping is shown in Fig. 3-18; it removes all information from speech except the zero cross-

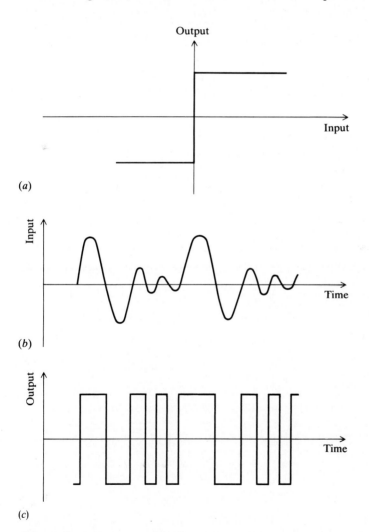

Figure 3-18 (*a*) Input/output function of infinite clipper; (*b*) input speech waveform; (*c*) infinitely clipped waveform.

ings. Somewhat surprisingly, Licklider found that infinitely clipped speech retains its intelligibility.

Center clipping is in a sense the complement of infinite clipping: high-amplitude information is preserved and low-amplitude information (i.e., below some minimum value) is destroyed, as shown in Fig. 3-19. Center clipping above

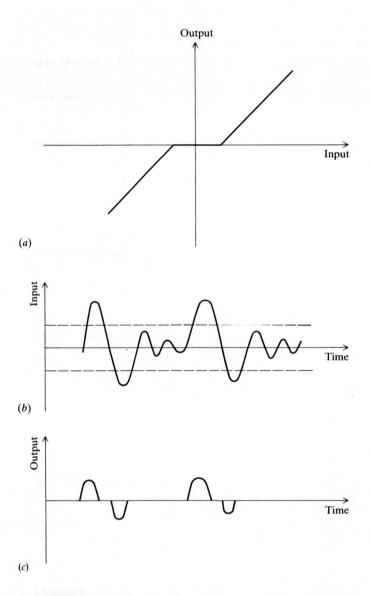

Figure 3-19 (a) Input/output function of center clipper; (b) input speech waveform; (c) center-clipped waveform.

some relatively small threshold destroys intelligibility. These two observations suggest that most of the information in speech is carried in the low-amplitude portions; this belief is reenforced by the fact that if speech is infinitely clipped with reference to some off-axis point, intelligibility decreases.

Disruptions Huggins (1964) investigated the effect of switching the speech signal between the right and left ears. He found that listeners understood the speech well when the switching rate was low and when it was high. At an intermediate rate, approximately 3 to 4 times per second, intelligibility was degraded. Huggins observed that this critical rate was approximately equal to the syllable rate. It appeared that a full syllable had to be presented to one ear or the other for it to be understood; the syllable could either be presented whole, as when the switching rate was low, or it could be sampled so rapidly that the rest of the syllable could be reconstructed, possibly by some sort of interpolation. He concluded from this that preprocessing of speech at approximately the syllabic level occurs separately in portions of the signal path before they are finally merged in a central processor.

The effects of interrupting the speech signal were studied by Miller and Licklider (1950). Interruptions degrade intelligibility, as we would expect, but in peculiar ways. If the speech signal is pulsed on and off with a 50 percent duty cycle (i.e., equal on and off times), then the worst degradation occurs at pulse frequencies in the neighborhoods of 1 and 500 Hz. Interruptions at rates from 10 to 100 Hz have only a minor effect on intelligibility.

Cherry and Wiley (1967) investigated amplitude-dependent interruptions, passing high-amplitude segments of speech and rejecting the rest. This was found to have "extremely low" intelligibility (typically 20 percent); however, if the gaps in the signal were filled in with white noise, intelligibility increased typically to 70 percent. This same effect was observed by Weiss (1970) in a similar experiment in which voiced speech was passed and unvoiced speech rejected.

REFERENCES

Ainsworth, W. A.: The perception of speech signals, *Sci. Prog., Oxf.*, vol. 62, pp. 33–57, 1975.
———: *Mechanisms of Speech Recognition*, Pergamon Press, Oxford, 1976.
Békésy, G. von.: Zur Theorie des Horens; die Schwingungen der Basilarmembran, *Phys. Z.*, vol. 29, pp. 793–810, 1928.
———: *Experiments in Hearing*, McGraw-Hill, New York, 1960.
Beranek, L.: *Acoustics*, McGraw-Hill, New York, 1954.
Cherry, C., and R. Wiley: Speech communication in very noisy environments, *Nature*, vol. 214, p. 1164, June 10, 1967.
Churcher, B. G., and A. J. King: The performance of noise meters in terms of the primary standard, *J. Inst. Elec. Engrs.*, vol. 81, pp. 57–90, July, 1937.
Cole, R. A., and J. Jakimik: A model of speech perception, in R. A. Cole (Ed.), *Perception and Production of Fluent Speech*, Erlbaum, Hillsdale, Chap. 6, 1980.
Delattre, P.: Acoustic cues in speech, First Report, Haskins Labs, New York, 1958.

Denes, P. B., and E. N. Pinson: *The Speech Chain*, Doubleday, Garden City, 1973.
Fant, C. G. M.: Acoustic description and classification of phonetic units, *Ericsson Technics*, no. 1, 1959; reprinted in Fant, *Speech Sounds and Features*, MIT Press, Cambridge, 1973.
——: Sound, features, and perception, *Proc. Sixth Int. Cong. Phonetic Sci.*, Prague, 1967; reprinted in Fant, *Speech Sounds and Features*, MIT Press, Cambridge, 1973.
Flanagan, J. L.: *Speech Analysis Synthesis and Perception*, Springer-Verlag, Berlin, 1972.
Fletcher, H., and W. A. Munson: Loudness, its definition, measurement, and calculation, *JASA*, vol. 5, pp. 82–108, 1933.
—— and ——: Relation between loudness and masking, *JASA*, vol. 9, pp. 1–10, 1937.
French, N. R., and J. C. Steinberg: Factors governing the intelligibility of speech sounds, *JASA*, vol. 19, no. 1, pp. 90–119, 1947.
Halle, M., and K. N. Stevens: Speech recognition: a model and a program for research, *IRE Trans.*, vol. IT-8, pp. 155–159, 1962.
Heffner, R-M. S.: *General Phonetics*, University of Wisconsin Press, Madison, 1964.
House, A. S., et al.: On the learning of speechlike vocabularies, *J. Verb. Learn. Verb. Behav.*, vol. 1, pp. 133–143, 1962.
Huggins, A. W. F.: Distortion of the temporal pattern of speech: interruption and alternation, *JASA*, vol. 36, pp. 1055–1064, 1964.
Jakobson, R., et al.: *Preliminaries to Speech Analysis*, MIT Press, Cambridge, 1952.
Kimura, D.: Some effects of temporal-lobe damage on auditory perception, *Can. J. Psychol.*, vol. 15, no. 3, pp. 156–165, 1961(*a*).
——: Cerebral dominance and the perception of verbal stimuli, *Can. J. Psychol.*, vol. 15, no. 3, pp. 166–171, 1961(*b*).
Koenig, W.: A new frequency scale for acoustic measurements, *Bell Telephone Lab. Record*, vol. 27, pp. 299–301, 1949.
Liberman, A. M., et al.: The discrimination of speech sounds within and across phoneme boundaries, *J. Exp. Psych.*, vol. 54, pp. 358–368, 1957.
—— et al.: Perception of the speech code, *Psych. Rev.*, vol. 74, pp. 431–461, 1967.
Licklider, J. C. R.: Effects of amplitude distortion upon the intelligibility of speech, *JASA*, vol. 16, no. 2, pp. 429–434, October, 1946.
—— and I. Pollack: Effects of differentiation, integration, and infinite peak clipping upon the intelligibility of speech, *JASA*, vol. 20, pp. 42–51, 1948.
Miller, G. A., and N. Chomsky: Finitary models of language users, in R. D. Luce et al. (Eds.), *Handbook of Mathematical Psychology*, vol. 2, Wiley, New York, 1963.
—— and J. C. R. Licklider: The intelligibility of interrupted speech, *JASA*, vol. 22, no. 2, pp. 167–173, March, 1950.
Nordmark, J. O.: Time and frequency analysis, in J. V. Tobias (Ed.), *Foundations of Modern Auditory Theory*, Academic Press, New York, pp. 57–83, 1970.
Pickles, J. O.: *Introduction to the Physiology of Hearing*, Academic Press, New York, 1982.
Pisoni, D. B.: Speech perception: some new directions in research and theory, *JASA*, vol. 78, no. 1, part 2, pp. 381–388, July, 1985.
Pollack, I., and J. M. Pickett: Intelligibility of peak-clipped speech at high noise levels, *JASA*, vol. 31, no. 1, pp. 14–16, January, 1959.
Rhode, W. S.: Observations of the vibration of the basilar membrane in squirrel monkeys using the Mössbauer technique, *JASA*, vol. 49, no. 4, pp. 1218–1231, April, 1971.
Robinson, D. W.: A new determination of the equal-loudness contours, *IRE Trans. Audio*, vol. AU-6, no. 1, pp. 6–13, January–February, 1958.
—— and R. S. Dadson: A redetermination of the equal-loudness relation for pure tones, *Brit. J. Appl. Phys.*, vol. 7, pp. 166–181, May, 1956.
Scharf, B.: Critical bands, in J. V. Tobias (Ed.), *Foundations of Modern Auditory Theory*, Academic Press, New York, pp. 159–202, 1970.
Schroeder, M. R.: Models of hearing, *Proc. IEEE*, vol. 63, no. 9, pp. 1332–1350, September, 1975.
Stevens, S. S., and J. Volkmann: The relation of pitch to frequency, *Am. J. Psychol.*, vol. 53, p. 329, 1940.

――― et al.: The masking of speech by sine waves, square waves, and regular and modulated pulses, *JASA*, vol. 18, no. 2, pp. 418–424, 1946.
Tobias, J. V. (Ed.): *Foundations of Modern Auditory Theory*, Academic Press, New York, 1970.
Weiss, M. R.: Personal communication, 1970.
Zwislocki, J. J., et al.: Symposium on cochlear mechanics: where do we stand after 50 years of research?, *JASA*, vol. 18, no. 2, pp. 1679–1745, May, 1980. (A collection of seven papers.)

CHAPTER
FOUR

ARTICULATORY PHONETICS AND PHONEMICS

The principal goal of phonetics is to provide an exact and unambiguous description of every known speech sound. We shall see that the domains of phonetics are anatomy and physics; thus phonetics is independent of any particular language. The term *phonemics* is used for the study of speech sounds as they are perceived and thought of by speakers of a particular language.

Articulatory phonetics considers how any given speech sound is produced, with particular emphasis on anatomical detail. A large part of articulatory phonetics is intensive ear training, preferably in small groups with a trained phonetician and native speakers of a wide variety of languages—clearly impractical here. A written text usually concentrates on familiarizing the reader with terminology and notation, and this is what we will do.

In *acoustic phonetics*, the emphasis is on observable, measurable characteristics in the waveforms of speech sounds, especially those which enable them to be distinguished from one another. An important related goal is relating these acoustical characteristics to corresponding positions of speech organs. Acoustic phonetics thus provides theoretical and experimental background for speech recognition and synthesis by electronic hardware.

In this chapter we will consider articulatory phonetics and phonemics; these will lay the necessary anatomical and linguistic groundwork for acoustic phonetics, which will be taken up in the following chapter.

4-1 ARTICULATORY PHONETICS

The first task of articulatory phonetics is to describe speech sounds in terms of the positions of the vocal organs when producing any given sound. An important goal is to provide a common notation and frame of reference so one linguist can understand another and reproduce accurately any unknown utterance which has been written down in "close phonetic transcription."

Phonetic Alphabets

We shall see shortly that there is a wealth of different speech sounds, more than can be encompassed in any traditional alphabet. Hence phoneticians have had to devise their own system of notation. The oldest and most widely accepted notation is the international phonetic alphabet (IPA). It dates from a time when type was hand-set and derives many of its symbols by printing Roman characters upside down or by borrowing from the alphabets of other languages. These symbols clearly cannot readily be produced on most computer printers; hence in recent years a substitute has been developed, called the "Arpabet" [after the

Table 4-1 Phonetic alphabets

IPA symbol	Arpabet		Examples	IPA symbol	Arpabet		Examples
i	i	IY	heed	v	v	V	verve
ɪ	I	IH	hid	θ	T	TH	thick
e	e	EY	hayed	ð	D	DH	those
ɛ	E	EH	head	s	s	S	cease
æ	@	AE	had	z	z	Z	pizzaz
ɑ	a	AA	hod	ʃ	S	SH	mesh
ɔ	c	AO	hawed	ʒ	Z	ZH	measure
o	o	OW	hoed	h	h	HH	heat
ʊ	U	UH	hood	m	m	M	mom
u	u	UW	who'd	n	n	N	noon
ɝ	R	ER	heard	ŋ	G	NX	ringing
ə	x	AX	*a*head	l	l	L	lulu
ʌ	A	AH	bud	l̩	L	EL	batt*l*e†
aɪ	Y	AY	hide	m̩	M	EM	botto*m*†
aʊ	W	AW	how'd	n̩	N	EN	butto*n*†
ɔɪ	O	OY	boy	ɾ	F	DX	bat*t*er‡
ɨ	X	IX	ros*e*s	ʔ	Q	Q	§
p	p	P	pop	w	w	W	wow
b	b	B	bob	j	y	Y	yoyo
t	t	T	tug	r	r	R	roar
d	d	D	dug	tʃ	C	CH	church
k	k	K	kick	dʒ	J	JH	judge
g	g	G	gig	ʍ	H	WH	where
f	f	F	fife				

† Vocalic l, m, n ‡ Flapped t § Glottal stop

Some sounds from other European languages (IPA notation):

y	F rue, G Bühne		x	G ich, S México
Y	G Hütte		ɛ̃	F vin
ø	F peu, G Söhne		ã	F vent
œ	F boeuf, G Götter		ɔ̃	F vont
ɯ	R ы		œ̃	F un

Other marks (IPA):

   : indicates preceding vowel is long
   ' precedes an accented syllable

Advanced Research Projects Agency (ARPA) of the Department of Defense, which has funded much recent speech research]. The Arpabet comes in two different versions: a single-character form which uses lower-case characters for some sounds and a two-character version to accommodate printers which have no lower-case characters.

Corresponding IPA and Arpabet symbols are listed in Table 4-1. This table is not an exhaustive list of the IPA; complete tables of the IPA symbols are to be found in Brosnahan and Malmberg (1970) and also in the Random House unabridged dictionary *sv* "phonetic alphabet." The English words provided as examples in Table 4-1 should be used only as a rough guide, especially in the case of vowels, since English vowel sounds, as we shall see, are generally not pure.

We will use the IPA notation in this chapter for both phonetics and phonemics. The convention is to enclose the character in square brackets, [b], in phonetic notation; phonemes are written between solidi, /b/.

Categories

The conventional division of speech sounds is into vowels and consonants. Although these terms are also used in phonetics, it is difficult to define them precisely. Attempts at definition usually involve questions of their function within specific languages and thus encroach on the territory of phonemics. Some writers (e.g., Pike, Hockett, Brosnahan) use the terms *vocoid* and *contoid*. Vocoids are characterized by phonation and a relatively unobstructed vocal tract, and their most important feature is the tone color imparted to the sound by resonances in the vocal tract. Contoids are characterized by obstruction of the vocal tract; phonation is of secondary interest and the most important feature is audible turbulence or other interruption of the speech stream.

The reason for the vocoid/contoid dichotomy is the fact that in many cases the same sound can function as either a vowel or a consonant. For example, "you" and "eat" both begin with very nearly the same speech sound, but in "eat" it is a vowel, followed by the consonant /t/, while in "you" the sound is a consonant followed by the vowel /u/. Similarly, "early" and "rate" begin with essentially the same sound, but in "early" it serves as a vowel (the so-called *vocalic* r) and in "rate" it is a consonant. The sounds in both examples, however, are unmistakably vocoids, and their vocalic or consonantal roles are simply a question of application in a particular context.

Contoids and Consonants

Consonants are relatively easy to define in anatomical terms. Most consonants are describable by a few well-recognized features, principally:

1. Point of articulation
2. Manner of articulation
3. Voicing (phonation)

Point of articulation This is the location of the principal constriction in the vocal tract, defined (usually) in terms of participating organs. Table 4-2 is a list of the principal points of articulation and the names given to the corresponding consonants:

Table 4-2 Principal points of articulation

Name	Description	
Bilabial	Between lips	
Labiodental	Between lower lip and upper teeth	
Apicodental	Tip of tongue on teeth	All frequently
Apicogingival	Tip of tongue on gums	lumped together
Apicoalveolar	Tip of tongue on alveolar ridge	as "dentals"
Apicodomal	Tip of tongue on hard palate (also called "retroflex")	
Laminoalveolar	Blade of tongue on alveolar ridge ("palatalized")	
Laminodomal	Blade of tongue on hard palate	
Centrodomal	Middle of tongue on back of hard palate ("palatal")	
Dorsovelar	Back of tongue on velum ("velar")	
Pharyngeal	Root of tongue constricting oral pharynx	
Glottal	Between vocal cords	

Manner of articulation This is principally the degree of constriction at the point of articulation and the manner of release into the following sound. Table 4-3 gives the principal categories and their names. Most of these terms should prove self-explanatory. Aspiration is an attribute of stops; in most European languages aspiration, if it occurs at all, is associated with unvoiced stops (defined below); in other languages voiced stops may be aspirated. The trill corresponds to the modulation by vibration mentioned in Chapter 3. Heffner (1950) identifies four types of trill: the laryngeal, uvular, dental, and labial trills. The uvular trill is the

Table 4-3 Principal categories of articulation

Name	Description
Plosive	Vocal tract shut off at point of articulation; nasal passages shut off at velum. Plosives have clean, sharp release. Also called *stops*
Aspirated	Vocal tract initially shut, as with plosives; release marked by a puff of air before next speech sound
Affricate	Initial closure of vocal tract followed by gradual release producing turbulence
Fricative	Vocal tract partially open at point of articulation, velum shut. Turbulent noise created at point of articulation. Also called *spirants* or *sibilants*
Lateral	Vocal tract closed at point of articulation but open at sides (may or may not be fricative)
Semivowel	Vocal tract partly open at point of articulation without turbulence. (These are consonantal vocoids; glides [w] and [j] are in this category.)
Nasal	Vocal tract closed at point of articulation; velum open
Trill	Oscillatory opening and closure at point of articulation

French or Prussian "r;" the dental trill is the Spanish rolled "rr." A dental trill of only one beat is called a tap; in English it occurs in the "dd" of some pronunciations of the word "ladder."

Voicing This indicates the presence or absence of phonation. Even during a stop, it is possible to force air through the vocal cords for a short time. Consonants accompanied by voicing are called (not surprisingly) voiced—the others, unvoiced. There are fine points here which allow for semivoiced sounds as well; we will not go into these details. We will also see that perception of voicing is influenced by other factors in addition to phonation.

These three features—voicing, point of articulation, and manner of articulation—provide a terminology by which we can define any contoid. For example:

[b]   Voiced bilabial stop
[d]   Voiced dental plosive
[tʃ] Unvoiced apicoalveolar affricate
[θ]   Unvoiced apicodental spirant
[ʔ]   Glottal stop

Notice that the description of a consonant is virtually a formula for producing the sound; it is very specific and related immediately to the anatomy of the vocal tract.

Vocoids and Vowels

The first thing to be said about vowels is that they are much less well defined than consonants. This is because the tongue typically never touches another organ when making a vowel; hence there are no specific landmarks corresponding to the point of articulation, and vowels are somewhat vaguely defined in terms of "position"—i.e., distances from other parts of the mouth. Vowels are described by these variables:

1. Tongue high or low
2. Tongue front or back
3. Lips rounded or unrounded
4. Nasalized or unnasalized

These parameters are mostly self-explanatory. High or low and front or back refer roughly to the position of the highest part of the tongue. (Some authors prefer the terms close and open instead of high and low.) Front is toward the lips and back is toward the pharynx. In nasalized vowels, the velum is open, so that sound passes through the nasal cavity as well as through the mouth; in unnasalized vowels, the velum is shut and the sound passes through the mouth only.

Vowel diagrams If we consider only tongue position, we can map the high/low and front/back positions by means of a diagram like that in Fig. 4-1. The space spanned by these two dimensions is sometimes called the *vowel space*. As we move the tongue from (front, high) to (front, low) there is a sensation of the tongue sliding slightly backward; furthermore, in the (front, high) position, the highest part of the tongue is apt to be the blade, while in the (front, low) position it is more apt to be the middle. These considerations explain the sloping line in the vowel diagram. In order to make this diagram useful, we must show the position of some known vowels in order to provide points of reference. This is done in the diagram; the symbols are the IPA signs for the vowels. This diagram should be studied in connection with the IPA alphabet given in Table 4-1.

In an attempt to provide more reliable landmarks on this diagram, the English phonetician Daniel Jones identified the vowels corresponding to its extreme points as "cardinal vowels." In pronouncing the cardinal vowels, the positions of tongue and lips are to be exaggerated to the point of physical discomfort; they represent extremes which are intended to be reproducible by trained phoneticians and beyond which it is assumed no naturally occurring vowels will go. (As an aid to standardizing the pronunciation of the cardinal vowels, Jones recorded them; the recording is available from the Linguaphone Institute.)

The vowels shown in the diagram of Fig. 4-1 are those most common in English and other European languages, but the diagram as shown contains an element of inconsistency: the front vowels shown are pronounced with the lips unrounded and the back vowels with lips rounded. This is customary in English, but not in all languages, and we must discriminate. In fact, we need two vowel diagrams to accommodate the differences. This leads us to the representation shown in Fig. 4-2. The front rounded vowels include ö and ü in German and Hungarian and the French u; the unrounded back vowel [ɯ] is found in Russian and Turkish. Figure 4-2 also includes some symbols not listed in Table 4-1; these sounds do not occur in the better-known European languages and it is thus not practical to give examples. It will be instructive to the reader to try to pronounce these unlisted vowels, using their positions relative to known vowels in the vowel diagram.

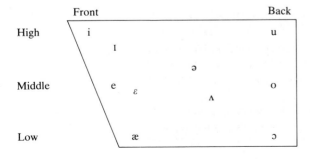

Figure 4-1 Basic vowel diagram.

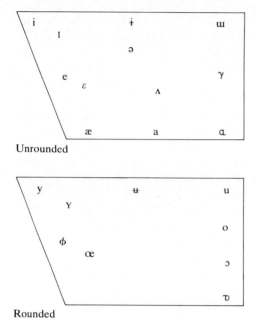

Figure 4-2 Vowel diagrams for unrounded and rounded vowels.

One vowel deserves particular comment. The *neutral vowel*, [ə], is one of the most commonly used vowels in the English language. This vowel, "for which," as George Bernard Shaw (1964) wrote, "our wretched alphabet has no letter," is given the name *schwa*, from the Hebrew name for their neutral vowel. It is the first vowel in "above," the final vowel in "soda," and the vowel in the most common pronunciation of "the." Pronounced lower and further back, it becomes [ʌ]. The absence of letters for [ə] and [ʔ] make the common English informal negative, [ʔə'ʔə] (or [ʔə̃'ʔə̃]—the tildes indicate nasalization), impossible to spell in English; it is frequently written "Unh-unh."

Phoneticians sometimes distinguish between *tense* and *lax* vowels. The vowels [i, e, o, u] are termed tense, and the corresponding vowels [ɪ, ɛ, ɔ, ʊ] are termed lax. The tense vowels are associated with the more extreme positions on the vowel diagram, which require somewhat greater muscular tension to produce. Higher breath pressures and greater muscular tension in the vocal tract generally are also associated with tense vowels. The tense/lax dichotomy is a source of some confusion, since these terms are also used to describe one of the *distinctive features*, described in a later section. In the present context the distinction is primarily articulatory, while in distinctive-feature theory it is primarily acoustical.

These vowel diagrams are the nearest thing to an equivalent to the detailed articulatory instructions given for the consonants. They must be used in conjunction with examples such as those given in Table 4-1, and in any case should be taken only as a rough guide and the most superficial introduction. Vowel sounds can be learned accurately only by long and intensive ear-training.

Nasalization In the pronunciation of any vowel, the velum can be open or closed. If the velum is closed, the nasal cavity is for all practical purposes disconnected from the system and the vowel sound is determined only by the position of the tongue and lips. If the velum is open, the sound passes through the nasal cavity as well. This cavity has its own acoustics and gives the vowel a characteristic color. Such vowels are said to be nasalized. In many languages, including English, no distinction is made between nasalized and unnasalized vowels, and the talker is free to nasalize vowels or not as idiosyncracy or dialect dictate. In others, e.g., Portuguese and French, the nasalized vowels form a separate category. (Nasalization may also be combined with subtle differences in tongue position.) The pronunciation of these vowels is a stumbling block for many students; part of the trick appears to be to take care that unnasalized vowels are consistently pronounced as such, in order to maintain the contrast between them and the nasals. In the IPA, nasalization is indicated by a tilde (˜) placed over the corresponding vowel symbol.

Diphthongs It is possible to combine two vowel sounds in a single syllable by moving the tongue from one position to another. Such a combination is called a diphthong; examples in English are the vowels in b*oy* ([ɔɪ]), *few* ([ju]), n*ow* ([aʊ]). On the vowel diagram, these sounds do not appear as points but as trajectories from an initial position to a final position.

Native speakers of English are usually quite aware of these composite vowels; what is less well known is that in English the high and middle tense ("long") vowels are also diphthongs. Thus *hay* is not [he:] but [heɪ], *he* is not [hi:] but [hij]; *hoe* is not [ho:] but [hoʊ], and *who* is not [hu:] but [huw]. (These diphthongs can be heard most easily by taping a sequence like "he, he, he, he" and playing the tape backwards; the downward glide in the vowel will be clearly audible.) To anticipate the following section for a moment, these diphthongizations are not *phonemic* in English—i.e., they do not serve to distinguish the meaning of the words in which they occur from that of contrasting, non-diphthongized forms—and so we are not conscious of them.

In most other European languages (with the notable exception of Dutch), vowels are pronounced more or less uniformly throughout their duration, and one of the peculiarities of English as heard by foreign ears is the unsteadiness of our long vowels. [The Spanish writer Salvador de Madariaga (1928) speaks of the English language as having no distinct vowels at all, but only a "vowel cloud."] The existence of this vowel cloud makes it extremely difficult for the aspiring English-speaking phonetician to get a true picture of the principal long vowel sounds, since they are actually single vowels, not diphthongs, and therefore he has probably never heard them. In Table 4-1, where long vowels are illustrated by means of English words, these examples must thus be taken as only suggestive. It helps to hear them pronounced by a nonnative speaker of English who will not diphthongize them.

Coarticulation

Everything that we have said about phonetics so far is misleading in one respect. It suggests that every phone is executed perfectly and uniformly and in a manner independent of context. Language learning, and the synthesis and recognition of speech, would be simple tasks if this were so. In fact, no speech sound is produced accurately in the context of other sounds. Instead, each phone can be considered as a *target* at which the vocal organs aim but which they never reach. As soon as the target has been approached nearly enough to be intelligible to the listener, the organs change their destinations and start to head for a new target. This is done to minimize the effort expended in speaking and makes for greater fluency.

In most cases, the production of a phone will thus include some articulatory features left over from the previous phone and some anticipation of features in a subsequent phone. For example, most English speakers do not pronounce the word "man" as [mæn], but as [mæ̃n]. English does not distinguish between nasalized and unnasalized vowels, and it is too much trouble to raise the velum for the [æ] when it is going to be lowered again for the [n]. This overlapping of phonetic features from phone to phone is termed *coarticulation*. The phenomenon of coarticulation adds to the problems of speech synthesis and recognition. Since coarticulation occurs naturally, speech in which it does not occur does not sound natural to our ears; hence for high-quality synthesis from an input description in phonemic terms, we must include an appropriate degree of coarticulation as we go from phonemes to the final utterance. In recognition, coarticulation means that the features of isolated phones are never found in connected syllables; hence any recognition system based on identifying phonemes is going to have to correct for contextual influences.

4-2 PHONEMICS

Whereas phonetics is a view of speech sounds considered in isolation from any language, phonemics is the view *from within some specific language*. It would be only a slight overstatement to say that phonetics is not really a division of linguistics but rather a resource which linguistics draws upon. Phonemics, on the other hand, is decidedly a branch of descriptive linguistics.

Phonemes

In phonetics, an individual sound is a *phone*; in phonemics, the smallest unit is the *phoneme*. We have seen that phones are written inside square brackets: [b]; a large number of symbols are used, often with modifying diacritics. Phonemes are written between solidi: /b/; a small number of symbols is used, and their meanings, while close to the equivalent phonetic symbols, do not always match exactly.

We will take the following as a working definition of the phoneme, to be expanded presently: a phoneme is the smallest sound unit in a given language that is sufficient to differentiate one word from another. If changing a particular phone in an utterance changes the utterance's meaning, then the changed phone is also a phoneme. If the change goes unnoticed, or if it merely "sounds funny," then the inserted phone is not a phoneme—at least, not in that particular context. Similarly, if changing a phonetic variable changes the meaning of a word, then that variable marks a distinction between two phonemes; if it fails to change the meaning of the word, then we say that that feature is not phonemic in that language.

Some examples should make this clear. If we change the initial sound of English "got" from voiced to unvoiced, we get "cot." The two words clearly have different meanings; hence voicing is a feature which distinguishes between two phonemes, /g/ and /k/. Furthermore, this distinction works at the ends of words as well: "bug" contrasts with "buck." The fact that German *Tag* can be pronounced either [ta:g] or [ta:k] indicates that in some contexts voicing is not phonemic in German.

A pair of words which, like "got" and "cot," differ in only one phone is known as a *minimal pair*. In linguistic field work, the analysis of an unknown language into phonemes is based in part on finding minimal pairs which separate all phones from one another in the way that "got" and "cot" separate /g/ and /k/ in English. In many cases the process must be aided by inference from other evidence: e.g. (Gleason, 1961), there appear to be no minimal pairs in English to distinguish between /ŋ/ (as in "ring") and /ʒ/ (as in "rouge").

The number of phones is vast, limited only by our ability to distinguish them. The number of phonemes in any language is small. The largest number known for sure is 45 phonemes (in Chipewyan); the smallest number is 13 (in Hawaiian) (Hockett, 1958). English has 31 to 38, depending on how they are analyzed (Gleason, 1961, by including prosodic elements as well as phonemes, finds a total of 46).

In discussing the perception of speech, we remarked on the tendency to quantize in perceiving speech. Phonemes represent an extreme case of this tendency. For example, English vowel space is divided into regions, as shown in Fig. 4-3, and any intermediate sounds are forced into one or another of these categories. For example, some dialects do not have /ɨ/; to native speakers of these dialects, this sound is perceived as /ɪ/. Since the English alphabet has no symbol

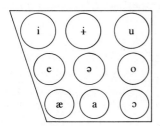

Figure 4-3 Schematic diagram of English vowel phonemes.

for /ɨ/, writers using dialects must improvise; e.g., "just" is spelled "jist." It is easy to see that the distinction between /ɨ/ and /ɪ/ is phonemic in dialects where both occur by comparing the sentences, "I jist got here," and "The Supreme Court's ruling was very jist."

Allophones

We can relate phonemes to phonetics by observing that a phoneme is actually a *set* of phonetically similar sounds which are accepted by the speakers of the language as being the *same* sound. Members of the set are called *allophones*. For example, if, having decided that /k/ is a phoneme in English, we look at some examples more closely, we will observe subtle differences among them. For example, the /k/ in "kin" is, in most dialects, articulated closer to the front of the mouth than the /k/ in "cup." In fact, the former is a centrodomal, [c], while the latter is a dorsovelar, [k]. Furthermore, the /k/ in "cope" is aspirated—i.e., pronounced with a little puff of air after it: [k^{h}oʊp], while the /k/ in "scope" is not: [skoʊp]. However, these are all regarded as /k/ by native speakers of English; furthermore, if one manages to pronounce "cope" without the aspiration, it will "sound funny," but it will not change the meaning of the word. Finally, careful analysis will show that [k] occurs in one set of contexts, while [k^h] occurs in a different set of contexts, and these two sets do not overlap. Such context dependence is known as *complementary distribution*; clearly if such a distribution is found, minimal pairs distinguishing between [k] and [k^h] are impossible. These different pronunciations, [c], [k], [c^h], and [k^h], are allophones of /k/.

Which allophone is used in any given case depends on a number of variables, the two most important of which are context and social custom. We saw the influence of context in "scope" and "cope;" in standard English unvoiced stops beginning accented syllables are aspirated unless they are preceded by /s/. The existence of allophones creates problems in speech synthesis. We would like to go from a stored phonemic representation of a word to a natural-sounding pronunciation of the word. To do so, we must be able to select the correct allophone for each phoneme; otherwise the synthesized speech "sounds funny." It is only recently that algorithms have been found that can do this reliably.

Nonphonemic differences are usually ignored and frequently unheard by native speakers. (We mentioned previously the nonphonemic diphthongization of English vowels, of which most English speakers are unaware.) This leads to difficulty in learning and understanding foreign languages. One of the reasons we speak foreign languages with an accent is the fact that we unconsciously impose the phonemic organization of our native language, complete with its allophones, on the other language.

4-3 DISTINCTIVE FEATURES

The theory of distinctive features, advanced by Jakobson, Fant, and Halle (1952, 1956) has its origins in acoustics, the psychology of speech perception, and boolean algebra.

The distinctive features are a set of 12 attributes which a phoneme may have. Each attribute is an acoustical characteristic and is considered as having only two possible values. Ideally, each feature is independent of all the others. Thus each phoneme can be regarded as a bundle of distinctive features and could in principle be completely defined by a boolean vector or, equivalently, by a 12-bit binary number, although the usual notation is $(+ - - + - \cdots)$.

The features are as follows:

1. Vocalic/nonvocalic. Refers to presence or absence of a well-defined formant structure. (Formants will be discussed in detail in the next chapter.)
2. Consonantal/nonconsonantal. Consonantal implies a relatively small amount of total energy.
3. Compact/diffuse. Refers to distribution of spectral energy.
4. Tense/lax. Tense implies larger total energy with wider bandwidth and longer duration.
5. Voiced/voiceless. Voicing indicates the presence of low-frequency components due to vibration of the vocal cords.
6. Nasal/oral. Nasal shows a wider distribution of spectral energy resulting from additional nasal resonances.
7. Discontinuous/continuous. Discontinuous phonemes show abrupt changes in spectral energy spread.
8. Strident/mellow. Strident phonemes have stronger and more random noise components.
9. Checked/unchecked. Energy in checked phonemes appears as a burst, as in plosives.
10. Grave/acute. Grave sounds are dominated by low-frequency resonances, acute ones by high-frequency resonances.
11. Flat/plain. Difference is one of relative energy of high-frequency resonances: flat weaker, plain stronger.
12. Sharp/plain. Sharp phonemes show a raising in the relative frequency of higher-frequency resonances.

Note that these features are capable of defining 4096 phonemes; hence there is no expectation that every combination will be represented in any given language.

The theory of distinctive features was published in 1952. At that time, spectrographic displays (to be described in the next chapter) were the principal analytic tool for speech research, and it is significant that all but two of the features are defined in terms of frequency content. The distinctive features were revised by Chomsky and Halle (1968); the new set is somewhat larger, and in it the features are defined in articulatory terms rather than acoustically.

The distinctive features have been proposed as a possible model for human speech perception and also as a tool in automatic speech recognition. Fant (1973) gives a decision tree showing how 18 Swedish vowels can be distinguished on the basis of four distinctive features. In his diagram, features are not always binary (he uses ± to mean "partly true") and some features may be irrelevant (/o:/ is grave, semicompact, and long, but flatness does not appear). In discussing the Chomsky-Halle revision, Fant (1971) raises additional points: features are not independent and may even be contradictory; not only is the binary principle not necessary, but a single feature may take three or more different levels. He notes that contrasts in phonemes do not correlate well with the number of feature contrasts and doubts whether anyone will ever come up with a universally acceptable distinctive-feature set.

Other questions have also been raised. It is not clear whether the features characterizing a phoneme are independent of allophones or whether, conversely, we are able to distinguish among allophones by their distinctive features. The effect of coarticulation on the features is also not well understood; we do not know whether the appropriate features appear all at once in the utterance of a phoneme or indeed whether there is always a moment at which they are all present. This latter point is especially problematical in the case of *checked* and *continuous*, which are essentially time-domain features, unlike the others.

Nevertheless, distinctive-feature theory represents an inspired first attempt to relate acoustical observables to the perception of speech sounds in a systematic manner. If a generally applicable and measurable distinctive-feature set could be found, it would provide a new universal description of language and might be the basis for a phonetic taxonomy of the world's languages. In any case, it has had a lasting effect on the study of phonetics. In addition, the theory has been found to be of value as a diagnostic tool. Since the features have well-defined acoustical correlates, it has been found possible to diagnose flaws in speech-processing systems by working backwards from failures on specific speech sounds and identifying faults which may have given rise to them. This is the basis of the diagnostic rhyme test (Voiers, 1977), about which we will have more to say in Chapter 13.

4-4 SYLLABLES, JUNCTURE, AND PROSODICS

Up to this point we have discussed only the individual speech sound. Speech is made by concatenating these sounds, however, and we conclude this chapter with some of the terminology that is associated with larger units of speech.

Phonemes go together to form syllables; this is an elementary fact in all languages (although Brosnahan and Malmberg, 1970, p. 140f, cite a possible exception). Phoneticians have had a great deal of difficulty defining a syllable, because syllables take different forms in different languages. (For a detailed survey, see Hockett, 1955.)

In English, every syllable contains a vowel, known as the nucleus or peak. Since vowels are generally characterized by greater energy than consonants, the syllable peak is usually also an amplitude peak. Indeed, at the acoustic level, the simplest and safest definition of a syllable is as a local power maximum in the speech stream. There are many exceptions to this, but it is significant that segmentation algorithms for speech recognition typically take amplitude as a starting point. Figure 4-4, which shows an utterance, part of a weather report, plotted as a function of time, illustrates some of the problems associated with this definition.

It should be clear from a comparison with the text that virtually every syllable is associated with an amplitude maximum. The problem is that not every amplitude maximum is associated with a syllable. The /ɪr/ in "clear" shows two maxima, and the second syllable of "tonight" shows three or four. These fluctuations are very small, to be sure, but they should be compared with the transitions between "low" and "in" or between "clear" and "and." The latter boundary is marked by the rapidity of the glide between /r/ and /æ/ and in part by timing. Such features frequently serve to divide syllables where amplitude provides no cue. Syllables tend to be separated by nonvowel sounds; we could say that syllables are an alternation of vowels and consonants, except that languages vary so widely in their handling of even so elementary a thing as the syllable that it is risky to generalize.

In English, words are frequently separated by a *juncture*, commonly written /+/. (Gleason, 1961, calls this the *open transition*.) Acoustically the juncture may be a pause, a lengthening of the previous syllable, a momentary glottal closure, or a momentary dip in amplitude. The classic minimal pair which shows that juncture is phonemic is the pair, *nitrate/night rate*, which are written /naɪtreɪt/ and

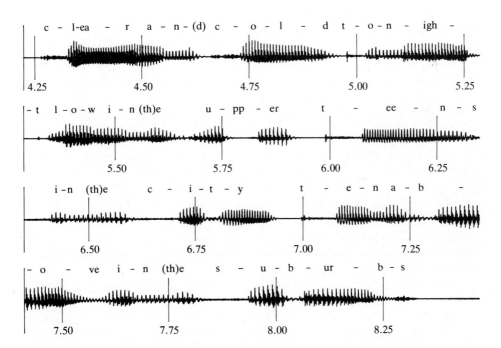

Figure 4-4 Sample speech waveform of the weather report utterance. The time scale is in seconds; the text is: "Clear and cold tonight, low in the upper teens in the city, ten above in the suburbs."

/naɪt + reɪt/, respectively. Whether a juncture is required between words depends on the words involved; Hockett (1958) provides many examples, but we can say briefly that if two adjacent words do not provide enough contrast where they abut to make the boundary between them plain, then a juncture is supplied to mark the boundary.

Prosodics is a general term for those aspects of speech which span groups of syllables or words. The principal prosodic variables of interest are pitch and stress. Pitch variation over a sentence, also called *intonation*, is used in most languages to give shape to a sentence and indicate its structure, although the way in which this is done varies widely between languages. In some languages pitch is also used to help indicate the meanings of words. Pitch ranges between 80 and 160 Hz for male talkers and between 160 and 400 Hz for females. Just as phones are quantized in any individual language into phonemes, pitch is similarly quantized; English has four pitch levels and three terminal contours. The levels are sometimes marked by numbers and sometimes termed low, mid, high, and extra high; the terminals are fading (decreasing pitch and amplitude), rising (increasing pitch, amplitude nearly constant until the end), and sustained (pitch and amplitude approximately constant).

Stress reflects the degree of emphasis with which a word or syllable is spoken; stressed sounds are usually louder, but they are also usually longer and more tense. That is, stress tends to move vowels out toward the extremes of the vowel diagram, while in English and some other languages unstressed vowels tend to be pronounced closer to the neutral position. Stress tends to raise pitch as well; stress-produced pitch irregularities are superimposed on the pitch contour. Stress, like pitch, is quantized; English has four stress levels.

Stress is applied to words and to larger units of speech. Individual words normally have one syllable which is stressed, or accented. In English this is primarily a stress accent, although in some languages the accented syllable is marked by pitch. Over phrases and sentences, the combination of stress and pitch patterns is used in English to provide shades of meaning beyond what is conveyed by the words themselves.

PROJECTS

It is extremely valuable to acquire a reading knowledge of the IPA character set. One way to do this is to practise reading aloud from phonetic transcriptions. The Appendixes in Kantner and West (1960) provide a rich collection of training material for this purpose. Papers published in *Le Maître Phonétique* are all printed in IPA notation; although this is a difficult periodical to obtain, it is a first-rate training tool, particularly since its contents are in a number of different languages. It is also helpful to transcribe into IPA notation, but the student must be on guard against errors, and it is best if the transcriptions can be checked by a phonetician, or at least by a fellow student.

REFERENCES

Bloomfield, L.: *Language*, Holt, Rinehart, & Winston, New York, 1933.
Brosnahan, L. F., and B. Malmberg: *Introduction to Phonetics*, Cambridge University Press, Cambridge, 1970.
Chomsky, N., and M. Halle: *The Sound Pattern of English*, Harper & Row, New York, 1968.
Denes, P., and E. Pinson: *The Speech Chain*, Doubleday, New York, 1973.
Fant, C. G. M.: Structural classification of Swedish phonemes, Speech Transmission Laboratory Quarterly Progress and Status Report 2/1960; reprinted in Fant, *Speech Sounds and Features*, MIT Press, Cambridge, 1973.
———: Distinctive features and phonetic dimensions, in G. E. Perren and J. L. M. Trim (Eds.), *Applications of Linguistics. Selected Papers of the Second International Congress of Applied Linguistics, Cambridge, 1969*, Cambridge University Press, London, 1971; reprinted in Fant, *Speech Sounds and Features*, MIT Press, Cambridge, 1973.
Flanagan, J. L.: *Speech Analysis, Synthesis, and Perception*, Springer-Verlag, New York, 1972.
Gleason, H.: *An Introduction to Descriptive Linguistics*, Holt, Rinehart, & Winston, New York, 1961.
Heffner, R-M. S.: *General Phonetics*, University of Wisconsin Press, Madison, 1950.
Hockett, C.: *A Manual of Phonology*, Mem. 11, Indiana University Publications in Anthropology and Linguistics, 1955.
———: *A Course in Modern Linguistics*, Macmillan, New York, 1958.
Jakobson, R., C. G. M. Fant, and M. Halle: *Preliminaries to Speech Analysis*, MIT Press, Cambridge, 1952.
——— and M. Halle: *Fundamentals of Language*, Janua Linguarum, no. 1, Mouton, 's-Gravenhage, 1956 (paperback).
Kantner, C., and R. West: *Phonetics*, Harper & Bros., New York, 1960.
Ladefoged, P.: *Elements of Acoustic Phonetics*, University of Chicago Press, 1962 (paperback).
Lehiste, I.: *Readings in Acoustic Phonetics*, MIT Press, Cambridge, 1967.
Madariaga, S. de: *Englishmen, Frenchmen, and Spaniards*, Oxford University Press, London, 1928.
Pike, K.: *Phonetics*, University of Michigan Press, Ann Arbor, 1966.
Potter, R., et al.: *Visible Speech*, Dover, New York, 1966.
The Random House Dictionary of the English Language, Unabridged edition, Random House, New York, 1967.
Shaw, G. B.: *Pygmalion*, Penguin Books, Baltimore, 1964.
Voiers, W. D.: Diagnostic evaluation of speech intelligibility, in M. E. Hawley (Ed.), *Speech Intelligibility and Speaker Recognition*, Dowden, Hutchinson, & Ross, Stroudsburg, pp. 374–387, 1977.

CHAPTER
FIVE

ACOUSTIC PHONETICS

The study of acoustic phonetics dates back to the eighteenth century, when von Kempelen devised the first known speech synthesizer (Dudley and Tarnoczy, 1950), a bellows-driven device in which the vocal tract was modeled by a flexible leather tube whose shape was controlled by the operator's hand. The rapid growth of modern acoustic phonetics, however, dates roughly from the invention of the sound spectrograph at Bell Telephone Laboratories in 1941. The importance of this invention is hard to overestimate. Newer techniques have supplemented the sound spectrograph, but not supplanted it; spectrograms appear as regularly in the speech literature of today as they did in the 1950s. We will therefore introduce this chapter with a brief description of this device.

In its simplest form, the sound spectrograph consists of (1) a loop of magnetic tape, attached to the rim of a large disk; (2) a tunable analyzing filter, (3) a drum around which a sheet of recording paper is wrapped (see Fig. 5-1). In the "record" mode, speech is recorded onto the tape loop, which can accommodate approximately 2 s of speech (i.e., up to a short sentence). In the "analyze" mode, the speech is played back repetitively at high speed and analyzed by the filter. On each repetition, the filter tuning is changed slightly so a different band of frequencies is analyzed. The output of the filter is sent to a stylus which darkens the paper proportionately to the amplitude of the filter output. The filter tuning and the stylus position are linked together so that each new analysis appears in a new position on the paper.

The result of the analysis is a graphic representation of the frequency content of the speech versus time, with frequency on the vertical axis and time on the horizontal axis, as with musical notation. The intensity of any given frequency component at any time is indicated by the darkness of the corresponding spot on

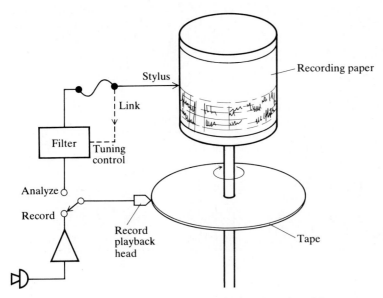

Figure 5-1 Schematic diagram of the sound spectrograph. (*Adapted from Koenig et al., 1946.*)

the paper. Figure 5-2 shows a spectrogram of a part of the weather report utterance from Fig. 4-4.

The spectrograph offers the user a choice of two bandwidths: narrowband (45 Hz) and wideband (300 Hz). Since essentially all voices have fundamental frequencies greater than 45 Hz, narrowband spectrograms show the pitch and its harmonics as horizontal lines. Since most speakers' pitches are lower than 300 Hz, however, the pitch harmonics are not resolved in the wideband mode; on the other hand, individual glottal pulses are visible and the formants (the resonances in the vocal tract) show up as dark bars. The spectrogram in Fig. 5-2 is a wideband spectrogram.

In this figure, time and frequency scales have been added below and at the left, and the text ("Ten above in the suburbs") is written in phonetic transcription along the bottom of the figure. Notice that all vocoids have a characteristic appearance consisting of regular vertical striations of varying density. Each striation corresponds to a single pitch period; the onset of the striation corresponds approximately to the beginning of a glottal pulse. The spacing of the striations provides an indication of pitch. The pitch is highest where the striations are close together, as in the [ɛ] of "ten;" the pitch reaches its minimum in the [ə] of "the." Resonances in the vocal tract emphasize certain frequency components in the pulse, and these show up in the display as wider or darker regions in the striations. In the figure, four such resonances are visible in most places. Fricatives show up as irregular striations predominantly above 2.5 kHz; these striations indicate the presence of wideband noise. The initial [s] of "suburbs" clearly has the most energy and the highest frequency components, with the final [zs], a close second.

102 LINGUISTIC AND TECHNICAL FUNDAMENTALS

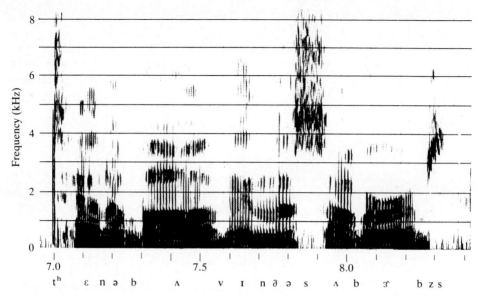

Figure 5-2 Spectrogram of a phrase from the weather report utterance. (Provided by courtesy of Kay Elemetrics, Pine Brook, New Jersey.)

To appreciate the importance of this invention, we must consider it in the light of technology previously available. High-speed spectrum analysis was not available until the 1950s and was not available cheaply until the introduction of the fast Fourier transform in 1965. Previously only hand computation or filter-bank analysis was available. Hand computation was prohibitively laborious, and filter banks did not give satisfactory resolution. The analysis of 2 s of speech took approximately 5 min on the original sound spectrograph and showed results that would otherwise have taken weeks to obtain.

Resonances had already been observed in speech sounds before this time and the acoustical characteristics of most speech sounds were understood after a fashion, but the sound spectrograph provided a wealth of detail such as had never been available before. It was also expected to provide an aid to the deaf, enabling them to understand speech by viewing spectrograms. Results in this area have been inconsistent, but generally disappointing. These disappointments led to the conclusion that it was impossible to recognize speech from spectrographic displays alone (see, for example, Liberman *et al.*, 1968). This belief was upset when a researcher demonstrated the ability to read spectrograms of unknown utterances with high accuracy (Cole *et al.*, 1980) and to teach others to do so. A renewed interest in the study of speech spectrograms has resulted from this discovery. Spectrograms have also been used to identify unknown talkers, especially in forensic applications. These methods have come under heavy attack; we will address the issue in Chapter 12. The sound spectrograph has found its principal use in the field of acoustic phonetics; the ultimate origin of much of what follows lies in the lights and shadows of the speech spectrogram.

5-1 ACOUSTICS OF THE VOCAL TRACT

We have seen the complex and articulated structure of the vocal tract as it is seen by the phonetician. In analyzing the acoustics of these organs, we use a far simpler model. Acoustically, the vocal tract is a tube of nonuniform cross section, approximately 17 cm long in adult males, usually open at one end and nearly closed at the other. Branching off this main tube, approximately at its midpoint, is the nasal cavity, a tube approximately 13 cm long, with a valve at the branch (the velum), as shown in Fig. 5-3. We will initially assume the velum closed; this excludes nasal cavities from consideration and greatly simplifies analysis.

Such a tube is a distributed-parameter structure and thus has many natural frequencies (i.e., frequencies at which the transfer function of the tube is at a maximum). If the vocal tract were of uniform cross section, these frequencies would occur at

$$f_n = \frac{(2n-1)c}{4l}, \qquad n = 1, 2, 3, \ldots$$

In air, $c = 350$ m/s; for a tube of length $l = 17$ cm, the natural frequencies occur at odd multiples of ~ 500 Hz. Actually, the area is not uniform; as a result, resonances are not equally spaced, but the average density of vocal tract resonances is still approximately 1 per kilohertz of bandwidth, as the above relation suggests.

These resonances are known as *formants*; they were the dark bands observed in the speech spectrogram of Fig. 5-2 and are the most important acoustical characteristics of the vocal tract. The glottal pulse train is rich in harmonics, and these harmonics interact strongly with the vocal tract resonances to affect the tone quality of the voice. Formants thus provide the listener's primary source of information about the position of the speaker's vocal organs.

Note that these resonant frequencies correspond to *poles* of the transfer function. As long as the nasal tract is blocked off and the glottis is the sole source of excitation, the vocal tract transfer function has no finite-frequency zeros. This will prove to be an important simplification.

Formants are identified by number in order of increasing frequency: F_1, F_2, etc. (For uniformity, pitch is sometimes designated F_0.) In classical acoustic phonetics, usually only F_1 and F_2 are considered, but, for recognition, at least three

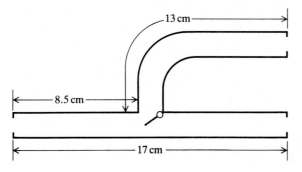

Figure 5-3 Simplified diagram of the vocal tract. The straight section runs from the glottis (left end) to the lips (right end); the curved section runs from the velum (hinged valve) to the nostrils.

Table 5-1 Frequency ranges for the first three formants

	Frequency ranges, Hz		Bandwidths, Hz
	Adult males	Adult females	
F_1	200–800	250–1000	40–70
F_2	600–2800	700–3300	50–90
F_3	1300–3400	1500–4000	60–180

are meaningful and, for synthesis, five are recommended for greatest realism. Table 5-1 gives the approximate ranges for the first three formants (in hertz). These numbers are only a guide; humans are capable of infinite variability. Values of $F_1 < 100$ Hz have been observed in males; this means that F_1 can lie at or below the pitch frequency in both sexes.

Relation to Speech Sounds

We produce different vowel sounds by changing the shape of the vocal tract; hence we would expect a correspondence between vowel sounds and formant frequencies. This expectation is borne out by the evidence: (1) consistent formant frequencies can be recovered from speech and mapped onto vowel sounds; (2) artificial speech with selected formant frequencies is perceived as having the intended vowel quality. If we set up a coordinate system using F_1 and F_2 as a basis, vowels lie in specific regions. This is shown in Fig. 5-4, in which measured formant frequencies are plotted on a Koenig scale. The exact partitioning of the F_1-F_2 space varies with age, sex, language, and from one talker to another, but the overall pattern does not vary. A table of typical values for specific vowels is given in Table 5-2.

Table 5-2 Typical formant frequencies for selected vowels. (*Adapted from Peterson, 1961.*)

Values are means and are given in hertz. F_1 and F_2 blend in females for some vowels; figures for these vowels are tabulated midway between F_1 and F_2 columns

Vowel	Adult males			Adult females		
	F_1	F_2	F_3	F_1	F_2	F_3
[i]	255	2330	3000	340	2610	3210
[ɪ]	350	1975	2560	425	2170	2900
[ɛ]	560	1875	2550	690	2015	2815
[æ]	735	1625	2465	950	1955	2900
[ɑ]	760	1065	2550	1085		2810
[ʌ]	640	1250	2610	750	1300	2610
[ɔ]	610	865	2540	785		2565
[ʊ]	475	1070	2410	515	1070	2280
[u]	290	940	2180	390	995	2585

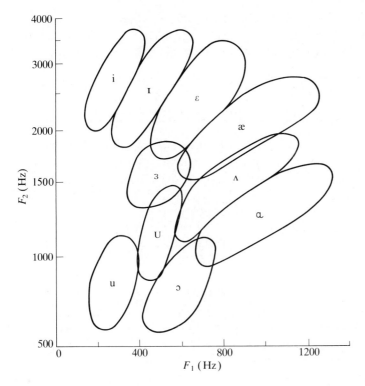

Figure 5-4 Typical F_1-F_2 loci for various English vowels. (*After Peterson and Barney*, 1952.)

There is an additional piece of persuasive evidence. If we reverse the directions of the F_1 and F_2 axes, as in Fig. 5-5, we see that the vowel loci correspond roughly with the positions assigned to these vowels in the articulatory vowel diagram.

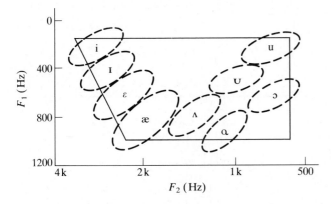

Figure 5-5 Vowel diagram with F_1-F_2 loci superimposed. Note the inversion of the frequency scales.

Formant frequencies are also associated with the sonorants /w/, /j/, /r/, and /l/ (Lehiste, 1964). We will see that the formants also have a bearing on consonants (contoids), but the relationship is a more subtle one and will be taken up in a later section.

5-2 ANALYSIS OF THE ACOUSTICS OF VOCOIDS

Because of the importance of formants, much effort has been devoted to analyzing vocal tract acoustics, particularly with a view to relating specific vocal tract shapes to the corresponding formant frequencies. The problem is complicated by the fact that the area of the vocal tract varies irregularly along its length. Exact analysis of nonuniform acoustic tubes is possible only in a few special cases; hence it is necessary to resort to some simplification. The most popular approximation is the piecewise-cylindrical model shown in Fig. 5-6. Use of this model dates as far back as the 1950s (see, for example, Fant, 1961). Its advantage is that cylindrical sections are well understood and easy to model and analyze; furthermore, the results agree well with actual measurements made (for example) by x-ray photographs. We will analyze this model as follows. We will start by reviewing the acoustics of a single cylindrical tube; then we will consider how cylindrical sections interact in a model such as the one shown above and derive an expression for the overall transfer function.

Acoustics of a Cylindrical Tube

A tube of uniform cross section is the acoustical analogue of an electrical transmission line, and we will take advantage of this analogy in analyzing the vocal tract. As with the line, waves can travel in either direction in the tube, and these waves are governed by the *wave equation*. The difference is that the waves in an acoustic tube are waves of pressure and velocity, instead of voltage and current.

The wave equation is derived in detail in many physics and acoustics texts; we will be brief here. We assume plane waves and lossless, nondispersive transmission.

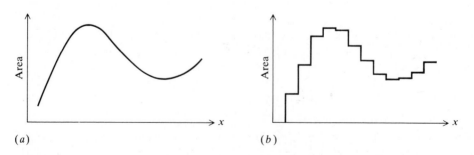

Figure 5-6 Smooth and piecewise-cylindrical approximations of vocal tract area function.

First, from Newton's equation, we have a relation between the pressure gradient in the direction of the wave and the acceleration of the gas:

$$\frac{\partial p}{\partial x} = -\rho_0 \frac{\partial u}{\partial t} \qquad (5\text{-}1)$$

where p = fluctuation in pressure
 u = particle velocity
 ρ_0 = density of air

Second, from consideration of the compression and rarefaction of the medium, we can relate the velocity gradient to the rate of change in pressure:

$$\frac{\partial u}{\partial x} = -\frac{1}{\eta P_0} \frac{\partial p}{\partial t} \qquad (5\text{-}2)$$

where η = ratio of constant-volume to constant-pressure specific heats of air
 P_0 = normal atmospheric pressure

Combining (5-1) and (5-2) gives us the wave equation:

$$\frac{\partial^2 p}{\partial x^2} = \frac{\rho_0}{\eta P_0} \frac{\partial^2 p}{\partial t^2} \qquad (5\text{-}3)$$

The solution to (5-3) is the sum of any arbitrary combination of rightward- and leftward-traveling pressure waves moving with velocity $\pm c$:

$$p = f_1\left(t - \frac{x}{c}\right) + f_2\left(t + \frac{x}{c}\right) \qquad (5\text{-}4a)$$

The only restriction on f_1 and f_2 is that they be differentiable at least twice. That this is indeed a solution can be verified by substituting it into (5-3); doing so also shows that the velocity of propagation must be

$$c = \sqrt{\frac{\eta P_0}{\rho_0}}$$

We can also solve (5-3) for the particle velocity $u(x, t)$. When dealing with waves in a tube, however, we are more interested in the *volume velocity*, the rate of flow through the cross-sectional area S in cubic units per second. If particle velocity is u and volume velocity is U, then $U = Su$. We can find a solution for U from (5-3) and (5-1); it is

$$U = \frac{S}{\rho_0 c}\left[f_1\left(t - \frac{x}{c}\right) - f_2\left(t + \frac{x}{c}\right)\right] \qquad (5\text{-}4b)$$

Note that $\rho_0 c/S$ is a ratio of pressure to volume velocity. It is therefore analogous to electrical impedance and we term it the *characteristic impedance* of the tube Z_c.

(Acoustics has borrowed the following terms and symbols from electrical circuit theory: *impedance*, the ratio of pressure to volume velocity, Z, and *admittance*, the ratio of volume velocity to pressure, Y. These ratios refer strictly to transforms of pressure and velocity, but are also used for time-domain ratios when no ambiguity will result.)

Sample values of c and Z_c are readily computed. For air, $\eta = 1.4$, $\rho_0 = 1.14 \times 10^{-3}$ gm/cm^3, and $P_0 = 1$ bar $= 10^6$ dyn/cm. Hence $c = 3.5 \times 10^4$ cm/s and $Z_c = 1.11S$ acoustic Ω. For $S = 6$ cm^2 (a typical figure for parts of the vocal tract), then $Z_c = 6.66$ acoustic Ω.

Sine Wave Solution; Input Impedance

It is also of interest to know the form of the solution to the wave equation for sinusoidal waves, since this permits frequency-domain analysis and the consideration of input impedance of a tube. For sinusoidal waves, the solutions are

$$p(x, t) = (P_1 e^{-j\beta x} + P_2 e^{j\beta x}) e^{j\omega t} \tag{5-5}$$

$$U(x, t) = \frac{1}{Z_c} (P_1 e^{-j\beta x} - P_2 e^{j\beta x}) e^{j\omega t} \tag{5-6}$$

where ω = frequency of the sine wave (in radians per second)
$\beta = \omega/c$, the propagation constant

If the tube is of length l and terminated at the end with an impedance Z_L (Fig. 5-7), then $p(l, t) = Z_L U(l, t)$. Combining this with (5-5) and (5-6) leads (after some manipulation) to this expression for the input acoustic impedance Z_{in}:

$$Z_{in} = Z_c \frac{Z_L \cos \omega T + jZ_c \sin \omega T}{Z_c \cos \omega T + jZ_L \sin \omega T} \tag{5-7}$$

where T is the time required for the wave to propagate over the length l: $T = l/c$. There are two special cases. First, if the end of the tube is open, $Z_L = 0$ and

$$Z_{in} = jZ_c \tan \omega T \tag{5-8a}$$

Second, if the tube is closed at the end, $Z_L = \infty$ and

$$Z_{in} = -jZ_c \cot \omega T \tag{5-8b}$$

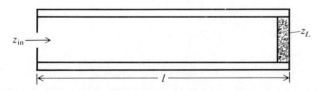

Figure 5-7 Acoustic tube terminated in a load impedance Z_L.

The corresponding input admittances are the reciprocals of these. Let $Y_c = 1/Z_c$; then for $Z_L = 0$,

$$Y_{in} = -jY_c \cot \omega T \tag{5-8c}$$

and for $Z_L = \infty$,

$$Y_{in} = jY_c \tan \omega T \tag{5-8d}$$

Note that the input impedance always has finite-frequency poles and zeros; in these special cases, these poles and zeros are real.

Analysis of the Cylindrical Model of the Vocal Tract

If the vocal tract is divided into a large number of cylindrical segments, a fairly close approximation to its actual shape, and hence to its transfer function, is possible. If the segments are short enough, each one can be approximated as a lumped-parameter system; hence this model also permits us to start with a distributed-parameter system and end up with a lumped-parameter approximation. This approximation is more tractable computationally and has a form which we will encounter again in our study of linear prediction. As an additional simplification, we will assume that transmission throughout the vocal tract is lossless.

Figure 5-8 shows the general appearance of the model and the numbering conventions we will use. All sections are of length Δ. They are numbered from right to left for two reasons: first, this is the numbering used by Wakita (1973), whose development we will (roughly) follow; second, this order makes it simpler to establish certain similarities which will appear in the chapter on linear prediction. In the literature, the transfer function is given in terms of volume velocity rather than pressure, and we will follow suit.

We must start by finding the relation between the traveling waves in adjacent cylindrical sections. In any section n, f_n is the forward volume-velocity wave departing from the left end of the section and b_n is the backward wave arriving at the same point. Since we assume lossless and nondispersive transmission, the corresponding pressure waves are just $R_n f_n$ and $R_n b_n$, where R_n is the acoustic

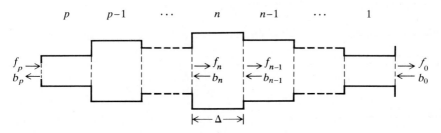

Figure 5-8 Notation and section numbering used for analysis of piecewise-cylindrical vocal tract model.

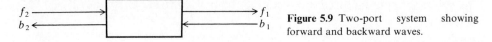

Figure 5.9 Two-port system showing forward and backward waves.

impedance of the section. If the section has a cross-sectional area S_n, then $R_n = \rho_0 c / S_n$.

We will initially analyze each cylindrical section as a distributed-parameter system. It is appropriate to do this analysis in terms of the forward and backward waves of (5-4); this will permit us to draw on the body of theory developed for transmission lines and waveguides. In particular, we will analyze the section in terms of the *wave transformation matrix*. In any two-port linear passive system (Fig. 5-9), let f_1 and b_1 be the forward and backward waves at port 1 and f_2 and b_2 be the forward and backward waves at port 2. (The numbering is reversed to agree with the conventions above.) Then the transformation matrix T is defined as follows:

$$\begin{bmatrix} f_1 \\ b_1 \end{bmatrix} = T \begin{bmatrix} f_2 \\ b_2 \end{bmatrix}$$

This matrix has the important property that the T matrix for two or more cascaded sections is equal to the product of the T matrices of the corresponding sections. This will permit us to go from a typical single section to the entire cylindrical model simply by multiplying matrices. The T matrix also has structural features which will be of interest to us later.

A related matrix, occasionally also seen, is the *scattering matrix S*. This matrix relates the waves leaving (or "scattered from") the two-port system to the waves entering it. In our case, the incident waves are f_2 and b_1 and the scattered waves b_2 and f_1; hence we write

$$\begin{bmatrix} b_2 \\ f_1 \end{bmatrix} = S \begin{bmatrix} f_2 \\ b_1 \end{bmatrix}$$

Analysis of a single section We will divide the section into a uniform tube of length Δ followed by a discontinuity where it abuts the following section. To find the T matrix for such a section, we will take advantage of the multiplication property of these matrices; i.e., we will find the T matrices of the discontinuity and the tube separately and then multiply them.

1. At the discontinuity, we have the following relations (Fig. 5-10): on the left, we have

$$p_2 = R_2(f_2 + b_2) \quad \text{(pressure)}$$
$$U_2 = f_2 - b_2 \quad \text{(volume velocity)} \tag{5-9}$$

and on the right, we have

$$p_1 = R_1(f_1 + b_1) \quad \text{(pressure)}$$
$$U_1 = f_1 - b_1 \quad \text{(volume velocity)} \tag{5-10}$$

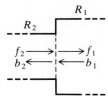

Figure 5-10 Forward and backward volume-velocity waves at discontinuity between cylindrical sections.

Since pressure and volume velocity must be continuous across the junction, we have

$$f_2 - b_2 = f_1 - b_1$$
$$R_2(f_2 + b_2) = R_1(f_1 + b_1)$$

Solving for f_1 and b_1 gives

$$\begin{bmatrix} f_1 \\ b_1 \end{bmatrix} = \frac{1}{2R_1} \begin{bmatrix} R_2 + R_1 & R_2 - R_1 \\ R_2 - R_1 & R_2 + R_1 \end{bmatrix} \begin{bmatrix} f_2 \\ b_2 \end{bmatrix} \quad (5\text{-}11)$$

We define the *reflection coefficient k* as follows:

$$k = \frac{R_1 - R_2}{R_1 + R_2}$$
$$= \frac{S_2 - S_1}{S_2 + S_1} \quad (5\text{-}12)$$

Then the T matrix for the junction is

$$T_j = \frac{1}{1+k} \begin{bmatrix} 1 & -k \\ -k & 1 \end{bmatrix} \quad (5\text{-}13)$$

2. The rest of the cylindrical section which precedes the junction is shown in Fig. 5-11. Here there is a delay as the waves travel from end to end. Hence, by inspection,

$$f_1(t) = f_2\left(t - \frac{\Delta}{c}\right)$$
$$b_1(t) = b_2\left(t + \frac{\Delta}{c}\right) \quad (5\text{-}14)$$

since f_1 lags f_2 by Δ/c seconds and b_1 leads b_2 by the same amount.

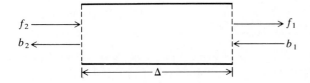

Figure 5-11 Forward and backward waves at ends of cylindrical section.

Z transforms In order to combine (5-14) with (5-13), we will carry our results into the Z-transform domain. If we sample this system at a rate $F_s = c/2\Delta$, then a delay of Δ/c corresponds to a factor of $z^{-1/2}$ in the Z-transform domain. Then we may write the T matrix for the cylindrical section as

$$T_c = \begin{bmatrix} z^{-1/2} & 0 \\ 0 & z^{1/2} \end{bmatrix} \tag{5-15}$$

We can now multiply the matrices of (5-13) and (5-15) to obtain the T matrix for the entire nth section:

$$\begin{aligned} T_n &= \frac{1}{1+k_n} \begin{bmatrix} 1 & -k_n \\ -k_n & 1 \end{bmatrix} \begin{bmatrix} z^{-1/2} & 0 \\ 0 & z^{1/2} \end{bmatrix} \\ &= \frac{1}{1+k_n} \begin{bmatrix} z^{-1/2} & -k_n z^{1/2} \\ -k_n z^{-1/2} & z^{1/2} \end{bmatrix} \\ &= \frac{z^{-1/2}}{1+k_n} \begin{bmatrix} 1 & -k_n z \\ -k_n & z \end{bmatrix} \end{aligned} \tag{5-16}$$

where the subscripts refer to the beginning and end of the section, as shown in Fig. 5-12. The inverse of this matrix will be of interest to us later; it is

$$T_n^{-1} = \frac{z^{1/2}}{1-k_n} \begin{bmatrix} 1 & k_n \\ k_n z^{-1} & z^{-1} \end{bmatrix} \tag{5-17}$$

Notice what we have done here. By choosing a sampling interval $(2\Delta/c)$ equal to the round-trip travel time over the segment, we have ignored all the details of what goes on inside the segment and have essentially reduced it to a lumped-parameter system. Equation (5-16) also displays the transformation matrix as the product of a delay ($z^{-1/2}$, half of the round-trip travel time) and a matrix made up of polynomials in z.

Scattering matrix Equation (5-16) may be recast in a form that uses the scattering matrix S. Note that the incident waves are f_n and b_{n-1}, because they are headed into the section, and that the scattered waves are b_n and f_{n-1}. After some

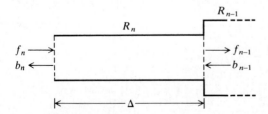

Figure 5-12 Forward and backward waves for entire cylindrical section.

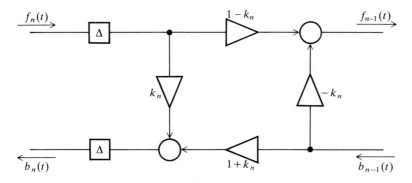

Figure 5-13 Block diagram of system modeled by the Kelly-Lochbaum equations.

manipulation, we have

$$b_n(t) = (1 + k_n)b_{n-1}\left(t - \frac{\Delta}{c}\right) + k_n f_n\left(t - \frac{2\Delta}{c}\right)$$

$$f_{n-1}(t) = -k_n b_{n-1}(t) + (1 - k_n)f_n\left(t - \frac{\Delta}{c}\right)$$

(5-18)

or, using Z transforms,

$$\begin{bmatrix} B_n(z) \\ F_{n-1}(z) \end{bmatrix} = \begin{bmatrix} (1 - k_n)z^{-1/2} & k_n z^{-1} \\ -k_n & (1 + k_n)z^{-1/2} \end{bmatrix} \begin{bmatrix} B_{n-1}(z) \\ F_n(z) \end{bmatrix}$$

(5-19)

These are the *Kelly-Lochbaum* equations; they may be represented by the structure shown in Fig. 5-13. Kelly and Lochbaum (1962) used this structure in a vocal tract model for computer generation of synthetic speech.

Overall T matrix We can now write the wave transformation matrix for the entire model; since the T matrices for cascaded sections multiply, it is simply

$$\begin{bmatrix} F_0(z) \\ B_0(z) \end{bmatrix} = T \begin{bmatrix} F_p(z) \\ B_p(z) \end{bmatrix}$$

(5-20a)

where

$$T = \prod_{i=1}^{p} T_i$$

(5-20b)

We will discuss economical ways of evaluating this transfer function later. At the moment, however, we can use (5-20) to establish a basic property of the vocal tract.

The velocity transfer function of any system can be computed from its T matrix as follows:

$$A_U = \frac{f_0 - b_0}{f_p - b_p} = \frac{|T|(1 - k_L)}{t_{21} + t_{22} - k_L(t_{11} + t_{12})}$$

(5-21)

where k_L is the reflection coefficient of the load: $k_L = b_0/f_0$. The t_{ij} are elements of the T matrix, which in our case is the overall T matrix we just derived. Now if we try evaluating T by multiplying component matrices of the form of (5-16), we will find that the t_{ij} are all polynomials in z. Hence the denominator of A_U is likewise a polynomial in z. The numerator, $|T|(1 - k_L)$, can be shown to be a constant. This leads to the important conclusion that the vocal tract transfer function is an *all-pole function*. We had stated this previously without proof; here we have the justification. This condition holds as long as the vocal tract can be represented as a single tube with no side branches—in particular, provided the velum is closed so that the nasal passages are not coupled to the rest of the vocal tract.

Losses Our derivations have assumed lossless transmission throughout. We conclude this section with a brief discussion of the losses. Clearly these losses are small and their effect on the vocal tract transfer function is minimal; otherwise our model would not be a useful one. There are three principal sources of energy loss within the vocal tract:

1. Implicit in our model is the assumption that the walls of the vocal tract are rigid. In fact, they vibrate perceptibly in response to the voice; hence energy is being lost to them from the vocal tract.
2. The compression and rarefaction result in motion of the air relative to the walls of the vocal tract; some energy is lost through friction associated with this motion.
3. Equation (5-1) assumed adiabatic expression of the air; i.e., that heat transfer in and out of the gas during compression and rarefaction was zero. In fact, there is a small amount of heat exchanged between the air and the walls of the vocal tract.

In addition to these effects within the tract, there are further losses due to the resistive parts of the radiation impedance at the lips and to the effective source impedance at the glottis.

The effect of these losses on our model is mainly to move the transmission poles in from the unit circle. This means that each formant has an associated nonzero bandwidth. Strictly speaking, these bandwidths vary from formant to formant and as a function of formant frequency. In practice (e.g., in speech encoding and synthesis), a bandwidth in the neighborhood of 60 to 100 Hz is an acceptable approximation.

5-3 PROPERTIES OF VOWEL WAVEFORMS

We will ultimately examine the time function of a sample of live speech in detail, but at this point it is convenient to summarize the properties of the vowel waveforms resulting from the system we have just been analyzing. These properties are of interest in nearly all types of speech processing and will be referred to repeatedly in the chapters to follow.

Figure 5-14 Glottal pulse train.

Time-Domain Properties

We have seen in Chapter 4 that the glottal waveform takes the form of a pulse train, as shown in Fig. 5-14. Let this function be called $g(t)$. It is applied to the vocal tract, and the resulting speech signal is the convolution of $g(t)$ with the impulse response of the vocal tract $h(t)$. Most experimental evidence suggests that the interaction between the vocal cords and the input impedance of the vocal tract is slight; hence we can assume that $g(t)$ is unaffected by the shape of the vocal tract. If the vocal tract transfer function is all-pole, then its impulse response will be a sum of decaying sinusoids, one for each pole-pair in $H(z)$. The resulting time function typically looks like Fig. 5-15. Each of the large peaks represents the onset of a new glottal pulse, and they are therefore spaced at an interval equal to the glottal pulse period.

Frequency-Domain Characteristics

The pulse train $g(t)$ is naturally rich in harmonics. If we consider $g(t)$ as an impulse train convolved with the glottal pulse shape, then the spectrum will be an impulse train spaced at a frequency equal to the pitch frequency and multiplied by the transform of the glottal pulse shape. This transform generally has complex zeros falling within the frequency range of interest to us, and those zeros can cause minima in the excitation spectrum envelope which can interact with formants. Observed glottal pulse shapes, however, vary widely with pitch, speaking conditions, talker, and other variables (including, possibly, experimental method), and hence the exact zero locations are hard to specify exactly. It is customary to approximate these effects by a 12-dB/octave rolloff above approximately 0.8 to 1.0 kHz, which is common to most experimental results.

There is an additional factor to be considered. The radiation of speech from the lips has the property that the sound pressure is proportional to the derivative of the volume velocity in the mouth. This fact introduces a 6-dB/octave boost in the sound spectrum. We would like to reflect this boost back to the glottis in order to keep the vocal tract filter uncluttered by radiation effects. This leaves us

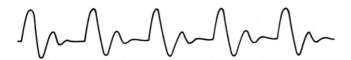

Figure 5-15 Output of vocal tract in response to glottal pulse train.

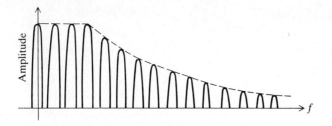

Figure 5-16 Idealized spectrum of glottal pulse train.

with a "virtual" excitation spectrum consisting of an impulse train with a net 6-dB/octave rolloff. After windowing, which is a part of any practical spectral analysis, the excitation spectrum looks like Fig. 5-16.

This excitation is then applied to the vocal tract. Then if the effective spectrum shown above is called $G(f)$ and the vocal tract transfer function is $H(f)$, the spectrum of the output will be $G(f)H(f)$. $H(f)$ is characterized by maxima corresponding to the formant poles, as shown in Fig. 5-17.

The output spectrum is then the product of these two spectra (Fig. 5-18). The dotted curve is called the *spectrum envelope*; its shape is the product of $H(f)$ and the envelope of $G(f)$. Recovering this spectrum envelope is a major part of many speech-processing applications, since it is our main source of articulatory information. Much of the importance of linear prediction, the subject of Chapter 6, arises from the fact that it provides a fast, accurate, and theoretically justifiable means of recovering this envelope.

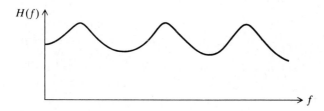

Figure 5-17 Frequency response of vocal tract. The peaks correspond to formants.

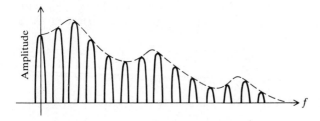

Figure 5-18 Output speech spectrum.

5-4 ACOUSTIC CHARACTERISTICS OF NASALS

Among nasals we include not only nasal consonants [m n ŋ] but also nasalized vowels—i.e., vowels in which the velar flap is open and the nasal passages are coupled to the vocal tract. This includes not only the French and Portuguese nasalized vowels but also the numerous nasalized allophones of English vowels.

The common element is the presence of an additional acoustical element. Using the transmission-line analog, we can draw the equivalent circuit shown in Fig. 5-19. Here we have represented the indicated sections of the vocal tract by transmission lines. Since these sections are not uniform tubes, they have been drawn as nonuniform transmission lines. In nasal consonants, the mouth is sealed off and $Z_{rm} = \infty$. In nasalized vowels, the two paths appear in parallel.

In either case, the presence of a parallel path means that the transfer function is no longer all-pole. The easiest way to see this is probably to note that the input impedance of the extra tube shunts the main tube. This impedance will always have finite-frequency zeros, as we saw in Sec. 5-2. If there is a zero in Z_n at some frequency f_z, then at that frequency Z_n looks like a short-circuit, as shown in Fig. 5-20. Hence there will also be a zero in transfer function at f_z. The dimensions of the cavities involved are such that there is typically only one zero in the F_1 to F_4 range.

To show the effects of the input impedance of the side-branch, Fujimura (1962) took advantage of another theorem from electrical circuit analysis: at any pole of the transfer function, the sum of the input admittances at any point in the vocal tract, looking in all possible directions, is zero. Our model assumes that the vocal tract is lossless; if we further assume that all passages are terminated with either zero or infinite impedances, then the input admittances will all be of the form of (5-8c) or (5-8d). (This assumption is, in fact, very shaky, because the radiation impedances at lips and nostrils are finite and the source impedance at the glottis is nonzero, but it is good enough to provide a reasonable conceptual model for understanding the effects of nasals, and it yields plausible results.)

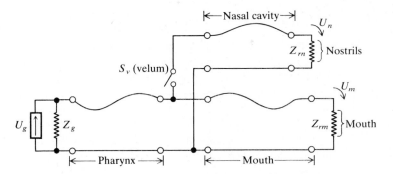

Figure 5-19 Electrical model of speech production, showing sections of the vocal tract modeled by nonuniform transmission lines.

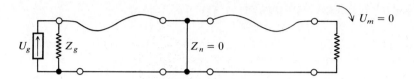

Figure 5-20 Vocal tract short-circuited at velum by zero nasal input impedance.

To apply this theorem, we sit at point A in Fig. 5-21, where the vocal tract branches into the oral and nasal paths, and observe the three admittances Y_g, Y_m, and Y_n. At any transmission pole, $Y_g + Y_m + Y_n = 0$.

In nasal consonants, the main branch is the nasal cavity and the oral cavity is the side-branch. To get an estimate of $Y_g + Y_n$, Fujimura used the consonant [ŋ], since the occlusion is far enough back that the oral cavity can be assumed to be of zero length and hence out of the picture. Representative formant frequencies for [ŋ] were 350, 1050, 1900, and 2750 Hz. Since these frequencies represent zeros of $Y_g + Y_n$, and since Y_g and Y_n are assumed pure imaginary [from (5-8c) and (5-8d)], we arrive at the solid curve in Fig. 5-22, where the formants are marked by the circles on the f axis.

For the consonant [m], we can plot $-Y_m$ on the same scale, and its intersections with $Y_g + Y_n$ will give us the formants of [m]. The first pole of Y_m is at $f = c/4l_m$; with l_m approximately 8.5 cm, this places the pole at approximately 1 kHz and gives us the dotted curve in the figure. The formants are marked by crosses on the plot; there is also a transmission zero, marked by a dot on the f axis and corresponding to the admittance pole of the side-branch.

The predicted formant values can be read off the curve and compared with measurements. The agreement is good:

	F_1	F_2	F_3	F_4	Zero
Predicted	270	900	1300	1750	1000
Observed	250	900	1150	1950	950

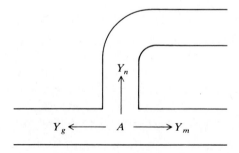

Figure 5-21 Transmission paths at junction of pharynx, nasal cavity, and mouth.

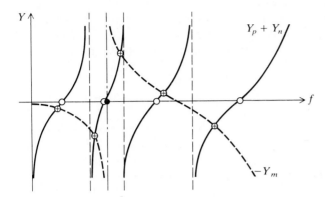

Figure 5-22 Admittances at junction of pharynx, nasal cavity, and mouth.

It will be seen from this that the presence of the added admittance function makes itself felt in the following ways:

1. The transmission zero is added (typically somewhere between 1 and 2 kHz, depending on the point of articulation).
2. Formants falling below the zero are lowered in frequency.
3. Formants falling above the zero are raised in frequency.
4. An additional formant appears in the neighborhood of the zero.
5. The density of formants is somewhat greater than that typical of vowels.

A further effect, which this analysis does not give us, is a somewhat increased damping of all formants, due to the greater transmission losses in the nasal cavity.

In the case of nasal consonants, the nasal and pharyngeal passages constitute the main path. The shape of this path is approximately constant; hence the formant frequencies are also constant. The location of the zero depends on the effective length of the oral cavity, and that in turn depends on the point of articulation. Thus we have constant formants being perturbed by a movable zero.

In the case of nasalized vowels, the mouth provides the main path and the nasal passage is the shunt. Because the shape of the nasal passage is constant, the location of this zero is constant (typically at about 1500 Hz). Hence instead of a movable zero being added to (and perturbing) a stationary set of poles, we now have a fixed zero added to (and perturbing) the variable poles of the vocal tract.

5-5 ACOUSTIC CHARACTERISTICS OF STOPS AND FRICATIVES

Acoustically, a fricative appears as a stretch of more-or-less wideband noise. A stop appears as a short period of silence followed by an abrupt release. The release is often not "clean" (even in nonaffricates) and usually shows up as a very short burst of noise with an abrupt onset.

If voicing is present during a stop or fricative, then a formantlike structure may also be visible in the spectrum of the sound. (In some languages, however, phonation may not be present, even in "voiced" consonants. In Danish, for example, the difference between /b/ and /p/ is the amount of aspiration at the end.)

Acoustical traits of stops and fricatives may be divided into two groups:

1. Spectral makeup of noise
2. Transitions of formants in adjacent vocoids

We shall see that the second group is by far the more important.

Noise

Various researchers (e.g., Hughes and Halle, 1956; Strevens, 1960; Heinz and Stevens, 1961) have investigated the acoustical characteristics of fricative noise. Their findings are not entirely unanimous, probably because of differences in language, experimental methods, and contexts. The following points represent a consensus:

1. Alveolar/dental noise (i.e., in [t, d, s]) is generally high frequency (the bulk of the energy above 4 kHz) and of high energy.
2. Labial noise [p, b] is generally low frequency (most of the energy below 2 kHz) and of low energy.
3. Velar noise [k, x] is of medium frequency with "formantlike" character and medium energy. The formant results from cavity resonance beyond the point of articulation but is also heavily dependent on the adjacent vowel.

Heinz and Stevens (1961) presented a model for the generation of fricative noise; they included the effects of the portions of the vocal tract lying behind the source as well as those in front of it. The combined system can be expected to have a formant structure, as vowels have, but the formants are more heavily damped because of frictional losses at the constriction and because of losses at the glottis, which is usually open. In addition, the cavities behind the source introduce zeros into the transfer function. Using a very simple two-tube cylindrical model, they were able to adjust its parameters to get very good matches to the fricative spectra observed by Hughes and Halle (1956).

The most striking feature of these results, however, is their relative imprecision, as compared with the detailed formant maps found for vowels. Fricative noise is not strongly dependent upon the point of articulation, and attempts to distinguish among fricatives by examination of their noise spectra alone have not been conspicuously successful. We might add that talkers do not generally take care to maintain as high a standard of uniformity in producing fricatives as they do in producing vowels. This lack of uniformity goes a long way toward explaining the absence of a well-defined consensus. In speech synthesis, also, it has been found that convincing stops and fricatives do not generally require a detailed match to the observed spectral characteristics of the intended sounds. On the other hand, this imprecision runs directly counter to the nearly universal observation that consonants, with their well-defined points and manner of articulation, carry most of the information in speech, while vowels, vaguely defined in terms of relative tongue position, carry mostly prosodic information. This leads us to suspect that there must be more to the acoustics of stops and fricatives than noise spectra; we shall see that there is.

Formant Transitions

In early experiments with sound spectrograms, it was noticed that formant tracks were curved in the neighborhood of consonants. That is, the tracks did not hold steady over a word, as in Fig. 5-23a, but were continuously changing, especially in regions adjacent to consonants, as in Fig. 5-23b. These curves are called *formant transitions*; they were extensively investigated in a series of classic studies at Haskins Laboratories in the 1950s. Their experimental method was to synthesize speech from drawings of speech spectrograms using a device called the *pattern playback*.

The pattern playback (Cooper *et al.*, 1951) functions as an inverse sound spectrograph. A diagram is shown in Fig. 5-24. A lamp and optical system produce a narrow, fan-shaped light beam; this beam passes through a "tone wheel," a rotating disk with a system of concentric annular patterns on it. The patterns represent a fundamental frequency and fifty harmonics, and as the light passes through the disk it is modulated along its width by the patterns. The modulated beam is projected onto a transparent film on which the spectrogram is drawn. A collector beneath the film applies the transmitted light to a photocell. Alternately, a collector above the film can be used to receive the reflected light. In either case, the resulting signal is amplified and played back through a loudspeaker.

The pattern playback permitted researchers to make speech to order with any desired spectral-temporal content. They could test hypotheses by creating

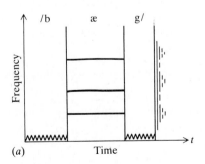
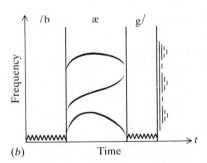

Figure 5-23 (a) Idealized and (b) realistic formant values over utterance of the word "bag."

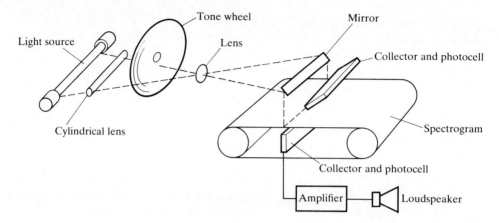

Figure 5-24 Schematic diagram of the pattern playback. (*After Cooper et al., 1951.*)

speech as desired and having it evaluated by listeners. The patterns drawn for the playback were abstract representations of spectrograms. In the consonant research, plosive noise bursts were represented by blips and formant tracks by heavy lines, as shown in Fig. 5-25. Using these techniques, they reached the following conclusions:

1. The stop perceived by listeners depended on the frequency at which the blip was placed. These perceptions were not uniformly consistent but were in general agreement with the noise-spectrum results summarized above.
2. The perceived stop was strongly affected by transitions in formants, especially F_2 (Fig. 5-26).
3. The formant transition for each point of articulation was characterized by a target frequency or *locus* largely independent of the following vowel. For example, for apicoalveolars, the locus is as shown in Fig. 5-27. They found that the best formant 2 locus for [b] was at 720 Hz; for [d], at 1800 Hz; and for [g], at 3000 Hz.

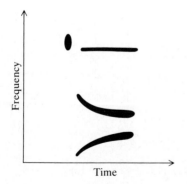

Figure 5-25 Typical pattern applied to pattern playback.

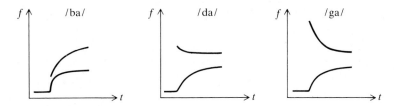

Figure 5-26 Pattern-playback diagrams showing effect of F_2 transitions on perceived consonant type. (*After Liberman et al., 1959.*)

Formant transitions generally present a more orderly and detailed pattern than do the noise bursts. It is clear that they are caused by (and provide clues to) the movement of speech organs from the preceding vowel position to the consonant position and from the consonant position to the following vowel. In fact, because of formant transitions, more detailed articulatory information is to be found in the adjacent vowels than in the consonants themselves. It would appear, then, that this is the place to look for the precision which we missed in the fricative noise spectra. There is additional experimental evidence to support this view. Parsons (1976) synthesized speech from pitch and harmonic-content data alone in a form that was inherently limited to producing vowel-like sounds only. When the process was tried on speech containing consonants, however, the proper consonants seemed to be present in the output speech. These results suggest that the ear will accept almost any random sound as a consonant, provided it is flanked by the appropriate formant transitions. The intelligibility experiments of Cherry and Wiley (1967) and Weiss (1970), cited in Chapter 3, can also be explained in part by this observation.

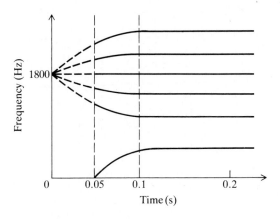

Figure 5-27 Formant 2 locus for transitions from [d]. The solid lines are the actual patterns; the dotted lines show the projection back to the frequency locus. The F_1 curve (bottom) is constant; the family of F_2 curves show the shapes for different vowels. (*After Delattre et al., 1955.*)

5-6 MODEL OF SPEECH PRODUCTION

We started our discussion of phonetics with the mention of an excitation-modulation model. It is time now to develop this model in greater detail. If we try to include everything, we will get the equivalent circuit shown in Fig. 5-28, where

U_g is glottal excitation current (corresponding to volume velocity)
V_p is pharyngeal fricative-noise voltage
V_m is oral fricative-noise voltage
S_v is the velar flap

Here the transmission characteristics of the various segments of the vocal tract are represented by tunable filters. The combined transfer functions of the pharynx and mouth filters realize the transmission matrix of Eqs. (5-20); the nasal filter provides the interactions described in Sec. 5.4. Fricative noise sources are located in the pharynx and the mouth, as approximations to the wide variety of possible sites.

This complete model may be found in, for example, Fant (1961). For most synthesis and analysis purposes, however, it is needlessly complicated. Hence it is customary to make the following simplifications:

1. Replace the fricative-noise sources by an equivalent source in parallel with U_g. (We can modify the filters to compensate for the move.) Filters F_{p1}, F_{p2} and F_{m1}, F_{m2} can now be consolidated.
2. Ignore the nasal tract. Since nasals are just another transfer function, we can implement it using the oral filter.

These simplifications lead to the model shown in Fig. 5-29. Here U_g is the glottal source for voicing and U_n is the noise source; F_g and F_n are shaping filters as

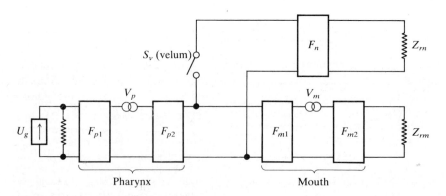

Figure 5-28 General model of the vocal tract.

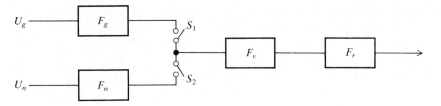

Figure 5-29 Simplified model of the vocal tract.

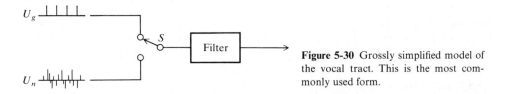

Figure 5-30 Grossly simplified model of the vocal tract. This is the most commonly used form.

required. Switches S_1 and S_2 permit selection of vocoids and either voiced or unvoiced contoids. F_v is the vocal tract and F_r takes care of radiation impedance. We now make further simplifications:

3. Replace U_g by an impulse train and modify F_g to compensate.
4. Ignore the possibility of voiced stops and fricatives and replace S_1 and S_2 by a single-pole, double-throw switch. (This is justified by the persuasive force of formant transitions.)
5. Consolidate F_g, F_n, F_v, and F_r into one filter (Fig. 5-30).
6. Ignore zeros (since humans do not notice missing zeros as much as they do missing poles); then the filter is an all-pole filter.

This final form is found in numerous places in the literature. It is the conceptual model on which most analysis is based; it is also the basis for the "terminal-analogue" type of speech synthesizer.

5-7 STATISTICS OF SPEECH SIGNALS

We conclude with a brief summary of gross statistical characteristics of speech.

The probability density of speech has been studied by McDonald (1966). He found two approximations; the better of the two is a variant of the gamma density

$$f_g(x) = \frac{\sqrt{k}}{2\sqrt{\pi}} \frac{e^{-k|x|}}{\sqrt{|x|}} \tag{5-22}$$

The less accurate is the laplacian density

$$f_\lambda(x) = 0.5\alpha e^{-\alpha|x|} \tag{5-23}$$

Finding the standard deviations of these density functions is left as an exercise for the reader. These densities are plotted in Fig. 5-31. A histogram of the absolute values from the weather report data of Fig. 4-4 is shown on the same axes, and a gaussian density function has been added for purposes of comparison. The reader should compare these curves with those in Paez and Glisson (1972). Notice that speech tends to be very heavily concentrated in the low-amplitude region. If the speech has been passed through a compressor, as is frequently done in commercial radio, the probability density may not agree with the shape shown here, since the density reflects the general variation of speech loudness as well as the distribution of moment-to-moment sample values, and the former is what is modified by the compressor.

The autocorrelation function of speech is heavily dependent on what is being said at the moment. Figure 5-32 shows autocorrelations taken from three points in the weather report data of Fig. 4-4. The sampling rate is 8 kHz; hence each point along the horizontal axis represents a lag of 125 μs. In this figure, curve (a) is for the [ʌ] of "above," at approximately 7.45 s; (b) is for the [n] of "in" at approximately 7.70 s; and (c) is for the [s] of "suburbs" at approximately 7.85 s.

It is also occasionally useful to have long-term averaged autocorrelation estimates. The curves in Fig. 5-33 show long-term averages for 20-s samples of speech from six male talkers recorded from commercial radio and sampled at 8 kHz.

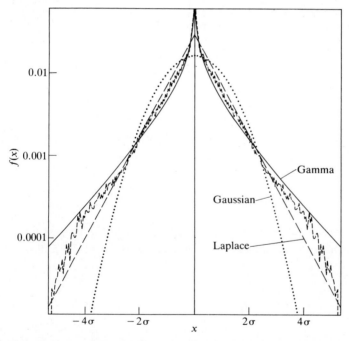

Figure 5-31 Long-term amplitude distribution of weather report utterance (irregular dashed curve), shown with modified gamma density (solid curve), Laplace density (dashed curve), and gaussian density (dotted curve).

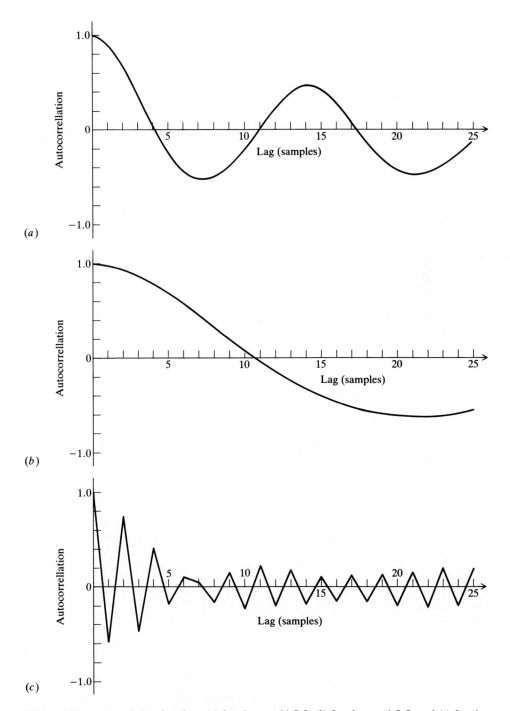

Figure 5-32 Autocorrelation functions (*a*) for the vocoid [ʌ], (*b*) for the nasal [n], and (*c*) for the contoid [s], all from the weather report data. The lags are in steps of 125 μs.

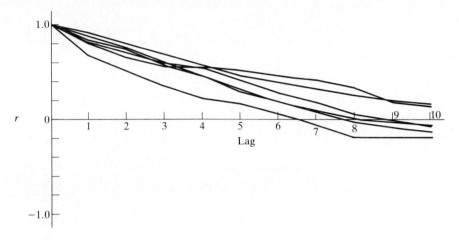

Figure 5-33 Long-term average autocorrelation functions for six male talkers.

5-8 EXAMINATION OF A SAMPLE UTTERANCE

Before concluding, let us study a specific sample of voice in the light of what we have covered so far. Figure 5-34 shows a portion of the weather report voice sample of Fig. 4-4 in greater detail. The words being spoken are, "ten above in the suburbs." This speech was sampled at 8000 points/s; the elapsed time is marked on the figure at intervals. The reader should compare the time function plotted in Fig. 5-34 with the spectrogram of the same words shown in Fig. 5-2.

Probably the first thing to observe in this figure is the fact that there are virtually no abrupt boundaries between phones; nearly every sound fades gradually into the next sound. In the following discussion, we will describe phones as starting at certain points, which are identified by letters in the figure, but it must be remembered that these are approximate locations. In speech sounds, gradual transitions from one phone to the next are the rule rather than the exception, and even experienced phoneticians, when asked to locate boundaries between phones and words precisely from plotouts like this, or from spectrograms, do not always agree.

The release of the initial [t] occurs almost exactly at the 7-s point, marked A on the figure. Notice that it is not a clean click; there is a volley of three bursts at this point, reflecting the fact that the motion away from the alveolar ridge is gradual. The low-level noise which follows is aspiration after release of the /t/; we are looking at the [tʰ] allophone of /t/. These aspirations are made with a relatively unobstructed vocal tract; the amplitude of the noise suggests that the air is moving fairly fast during the aspiration. Phonation does not begin until point B. This is the [ɛ] of "ten;" here we see the characteristic shape of a speech waveform: each cycle begins with a marked peak and is followed by a set of gradually decaying oscillations. The initial peak results from the onset of the glottal pulse,

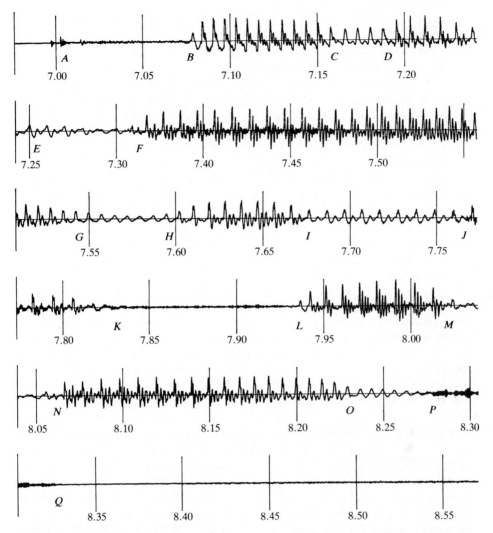

Figure 5-34 Time waveform of the words, "ten above in the suburbs," taken from the weather report data.

and the oscillations which follow are the ringing of the cavity resonances in the mouth in response to the pulse. (In fact, some low-level, predominantly high-frequency ringing can be seen at the release of the initial [t] as well.) Between the time marks at 7.10 and 7.15 s, there are approximately $7\frac{1}{2}$ cycles; hence the speaker's pitch in this region is about 150 Hz, a reasonable figure for a male voice.

If the [ɛ] were constant, then all the cycles would have the same shape. However, three things are happening during this vocoid: the vocal cords take three or four cycles to reach a steady state; the tongue is continually in motion, moving from the [ɛ] position gradually toward the apicoalveolar closure of the [n]; and the velum is moving from the closed position of the [t] to the open position needed for the [n] (unless, in fact, it was lowered during the aspiration). These changes, which are examples of coarticulation and formant transitions, are reflected in the continually changing shapes of the 10 or 11 cycles of the [ɛ], and also in the slope of the formant bars in the corresponding portion of Fig. 5-2.

The [n] begins at point C and lasts about four cycles, to point D. The [ə] of "above" follows immediately; the words are not separated by a juncture here. The [ə] is five or possibly six cycles long; during this time the lips are moving together for the [b] closure, which begins at about point E. Oscillations can still be seen through the [b]; air is moving into the oral cavity and building up pressure behind the lips. In speech spectrograms, phonation during a voiced stop usually shows up as a dark band at the low-frequency end, called a "voice bar." The voice bar for the [b] is clearly visible in Fig. 5-2.

The following [ʌ] starts at point F without any noticeable plosive noise burst, in spite of the pressure buildup; it lasts until point G. Again, the formant transitions away from the [b] and toward the [v] can be seen in the changing waveforms of Fig. 5-34 and the sloping formants in Fig. 5-2. Supposedly, the following [v], which ends at point H, should be marked by noise arising from turbulence between the lip and teeth; in fact, this noise level is so low as to be a barely discernible roughening of the waveform.

The phrase, "in the suburbs," begins at point H on the figure. Another instance of coarticulation may be seen at the transition between the [n] of "in" and the [ð] of "the;" the waveform of the [n] continues virtually unchanged until the mouth opens for the [ə] of "the;" the initial [ð] of "the" shows up only as low-level noise riding on the last two or three cycles of the [n] and a slight roughening of the first cycle or two of the [ə]. This "the," in fact, is reduced to hardly more than a simple [ə]; such is the fate of most English "the"s unless they are preceded by vowels. The [s] of "suburbs" lasts from point K to point L, where it releases relatively cleanly into the [ʌ]. The release of the initial [b], at point N, is marked; in contrast, there is no sharp plosive release to the second [b] at the end of this word; instead it merges gradually into the following [z]. The latter no sooner starts than phonation dies out: the phoneme is /z/, but the phones are [zs]. This is another allophone, and [zs] for final /z/ is very common in English.

The sentence of which "ten above in the suburbs" is a part ends here; almost complete silence prevails after point Q, marking the end unambiguously. We are not always so lucky; speakers frequently control their breath carefully until the end of the utterance and then relax with a puff of air which, among other things, makes it difficult for speech-recognition programs to identify the word boundary. Here, on the other hand, we see a gradual buildup of noise after 8.35 s as the speaker inhales for the next sentence.

Figure 5-35 shows a Fourier transform of the [ʌ] of "above," at approximately 7.45 s. The time waveform was 256 samples long, embracing approximately four pitch periods. The samples were differenced in order to remove any

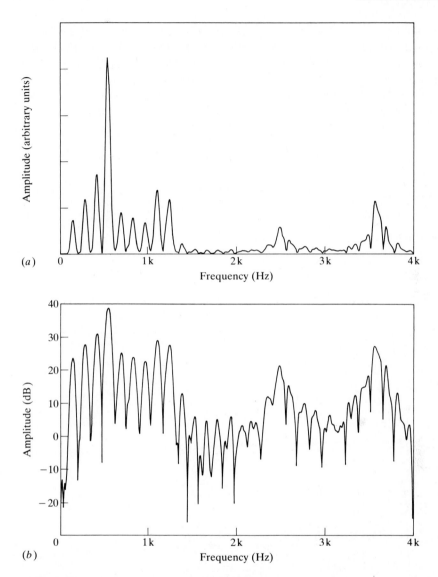

Figure 5-35 Amplitude spectrum of the vocoid [ʌ] from the weather report data: (a) linear amplitude scale, (b) decibel scale.

dc component and to provide high-frequency preemphasis; they were also Hamming-weighted and padded to twice their length with zeros before transformation, as described in Chapter 1. In Fig. 5-35a, the amplitudes are plotted on a linear scale; in Fig. 5-35b, they are plotted on a decibel scale. The linear plot is more appealing to the inexperienced observer, but the logarithmic plot shows more low-level detail, and this is the form which is most generally used.

The pitch harmonics show up very clearly in the spectrum. There are almost 11 peaks between 0 and 1500 Hz; hence the pitch must be approximately 136 Hz. We can verify this by observing the spacing of the cycles in Fig. 5-34; there are approximately $6\frac{1}{2}$ periods between 7.45 and 7.50 s, leading to an estimate of 130 Hz, which is satisfactory agreement for such crude measurements. The spectrum shows four strong concentrations of energy, at approximately 550, 1150,

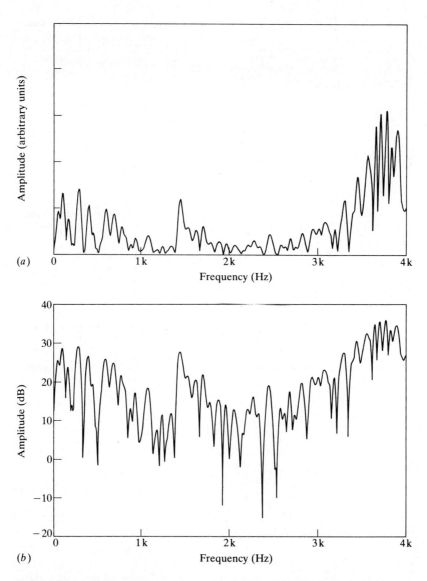

Figure 5-36 Amplitude spectrum of the contoid [s] from the weather report data: (*a*) linear amplitude scale, (*b*) decibel scale.

2450, and 3600 Hz; these are the formants, and their frequencies agree well with the bands in Fig. 5-2. The frequencies of the first three formants also show good agreement with the values for [ʌ] given in Table 5-1.

A Fourier transform of the initial [s] of "suburbs" is shown in Fig. 5-36. Here no high-frequency preemphasis is used, because our primary interest is in the overall spectrum shape, and because there is, as can be seen, no shortage of high-frequency energy. Careful examination of this spectrum will show that the peaks are randomly spaced; there is no periodic component in this sound, which is as we would expect for an unvoiced sound. Notice the abrupt rise in energy starting at approximately 4 kHz. This is in good agreement with the spectrum shapes observed for [s] by Hughes and Halle (1956).

PROJECTS

5-1 Write a program for computing speech spectra. This program should accept 12-bit speech samples as its input. Use Hamming (or Hanning) weighting and pad each segment of input speech to twice its length with zeros. Have the program compute the absolute value of each frequency component. The output may be (1) a tabulation of the amplitude spectrum or (2) a plot. Plots can be printed as histograms if an xy plotter is not available.

5-2 If an xy plotter is available, experiment with various representations of the spectrum. It is desirable to provide a choice of linear or log spectra. This program can be developed into a valuable research tool; in such a case it is desirable to have the program calculate its own time and frequency scaling from the sampling rate and the length of the input segments.

5-3 Using this program and the data-acquisition program of Chapter 1, determine your own formant frequencies for the vowels in Table 5-1. (Estimate them from the maxima in the log spectra.) Repeat this experiment after a week or two and note how much variation there is. Compare the spectrum of a vowel pronounced with the velum closed with that of the same vowel pronounced with the velum open.

5-4 A rough equivalent to a spectrogram can be made with an xy plotter by plotting spectra of consecutive speech segments immediately underneath one another. Motion pictures of speech spectra can be made with the aid of a microfilm plotter.

5-5 Some laboratories have real-time spectrum analyzers which can show an amplitude spectrum on a video display while the word is spoken. If you have access to such a system, try having one person mimic the vowels of another speaker by matching the formants to those of the unknown vowel.

PROBLEMS

5-1 Verify Eq. (5-6) (for volume velocity in the sinusoidal case) from Eqs. (5-5) and (5-1).

5-2 At 20°C and normal atmospheric pressure ($= 10^6$ dyn/cm^2), helium gas has the following properties:

$$\rho_0 = 0.1664 \text{ g/litre}$$

$$\eta = 1.659$$

(a) Compute the velocity of sound in helium.
(b) For a tube with a cross-sectional area of 6 cm^2 in a helium atmosphere, compute Z_c.
(c) Discuss the implications of result (a) for speakers communicating in a helium atmosphere (e.g., while working in a diving bell).

5-3 Derive the expression for input impedance of a uniform cylindrical tube:

$$Z_{in} = Z_c \frac{Z_L \cos \omega T + jZ_c \sin \omega T}{Z_c \cos \omega T + jZ_L \sin \omega T}$$

5-4 Derive the Kelly-Lochbaum equations, Eqs. (5-18) and (5-19).

5-5 Verify Eq. (5-21), using (5-9), (5-10), and the fact that $k_L = b_0/f_0$.

5-6 Show that $|T|$ in Eq. (5-21) is a constant depending on the cross-sectional areas of the lips and of the glottis.

5-7 Assume that the vocal tract consists of three uniform tubes as in Fig. 5-3, with dimensions as shown. Let $Z_g = \infty$, $Z_m = 0$, and $Z_c = 6$ acoustic Ω.

(a) Find the first three formant frequencies when the velum is closed by computing the sum of Y_g and Y_m.

(b) With the velum open, find the first three formant frequencies by computing the sum, $Y_g + Y_m + Y_n$. (Rough numerical calculations of the roots are sufficient.) Determine the frequency of the transmission zero introduced by Y_n.

5-8 Show that the standard deviation of the modified gamma density is

$$\sigma = \frac{\sqrt{3}}{2k}$$

5-9 Show that the standard deviation of the laplacian density function is

$$\sigma = \frac{\sqrt{2}}{\alpha}$$

5-10 Using the time scale provided in Fig. 5-34, estimate the pitch of each oscillatory portion.

5-11 Account for the continually changing shapes of the oscillations in the [ʌ] of "above" in Fig. 5-34 from 7.30 to 7.55 s.

5-12 The pitch was changing slowly over the waveform from which Fig. 5-35 was obtained. Use this fact to explain the gradually increasing irregularity of the harmonic peaks above approximately 1500 Hz.

REFERENCES

Atal, B. S., and S. L. Hanauer: Speech analysis and synthesis by linear prediction of the speech wave, *JASA*, vol. 50, no. 2, pp. 637–655, August, 1971.

Cherry, C., and R. Wiley: Speech communication in very noisy environments, *Nature*, vol. 214, p. 1164, June 10, 1967.

Cole, R. A., et al.: Speech as patterns on paper, in R. A. Cole (Ed.), *Perception and Production of Fluent Speech*, Erlbaum, Hillsdale, 1980.

Cooper, F. S., et al.: The inter-conversion of audible and visible patterns as a basis for research in the perception of speech, *Proc. Nat. Acad. Sci.*, vol. 37, pp. 318–325, 1951.

——— et al.: Some experiments on the perception of synthetic speech sounds, *JASA*, vol. 24, no. 6, pp. 597–606, November, 1952.

Davenport, W. B., Jr.: An experimental study of speech-wave probability distributions, *JASA*, vol. 24, no. 4, pp. 390–399, July, 1952.

Delattre, P. C., et al.: Acoustic loci and transitional cues for consonants, *JASA*, vol. 27, no. 4, pp. 769–773, July, 1955.

Dudley, H., and T. H. Tarnoczy: The speaking machine of Wolfgang von Kempelen, *JASA*, vol. 27, no. 2, pp. 151–166, March, 1950.

Dunn, H. K.: The calculation of vowel resonances, and an electrical vocal tract, *JASA*, vol. 22, no. 5, pp. 740–753, November, 1950.

Fant, C. G. M.: The acoustics of speech, in L. Cremer (Ed.), *Proc. Third Int. Congr. Acous., Stuttgart,* 1961; reprinted in Fant, *Speech Sounds and Features,* MIT Press, Cambridge, 1973.

Fischer-Jørgensen, E.: Acoustic analysis of stop consonants, *Miscellanea Phonetica,* vol. 2, pp. 42–59, 1954.

Fujimura, O.: Analysis of nasal consonants, *JASA,* vol. 34, no. 12, pp. 1865–1875, December, 1962.

Halle, M., et al.: Acoustic properties of stop consonants, *JASA,* vol. 29, no. 1, pp. 107–116, January, 1957.

Heinz, J. M., and K. N. Stevens: On the properties of voiceless fricative consonants, *JASA,* vol. 33, no. 5, pp. 589–596, May, 1961.

Hughes, G. W., and M. Halle: Spectral properties of fricative consonants, *JASA,* vol. 28, no. 2, pp. 303–310, March, 1956.

Kelly, Jr., J. L., and C. C. Lochbaum: Speech synthesis, in *Proc. Fourth Int. Congr. Acoust.,* vol. G42, pp. 1-4, 1962.

Koenig, W., et al.: The sound spectrograph, *JASA,* vol. 17, pp. 19–49, 1946.

Lehiste, I.: Acoustical characteristics of selected English consonants, *Int. J. Am. Ling.,* vol. 30, pp. 1–97, 1964.

Liberman, A. M., et al.: Minimal rules for synthesizing speech, *JASA,* vol. 31, no. 11, pp. 1490–1499, November, 1959.

—— et al.: Why are speech spectrograms hard to read?, *Am. Annals for the Deaf,* vol. 113, pp. 127–133, 1968.

McDonald, R. A.: Signal-to-noise and idle channel performance of differential pulse code modulation systems—Particular applications to voice signals, *BSTJ,* vol. 45, pp. 1123–1151, September, 1966.

Paez, M. D., and T. H. Glisson: Minimum mean-squared-error quantization in speech PCM and DPCM systems, *IEEE Trans.,* vol. COM-20, pp. 225–230, April, 1972.

Parsons, T. W.: Separation of speech from interfering speech by means of harmonic selection, *JASA,* vol. 60, no. 4, pp. 911–918, October, 1976.

Peterson, G. E.: Parameters of vowel quality, *J. Speech & Hearing Res.,* vol. 4, no. 1, pp. 10–29, March, 1961.

—— and H. L. Barney: Control methods used in a study of the vowels, *JASA,* vol. 24, no. 2, pp. 175–184, March, 1952.

Potter, R. K., et al.: *Visible Speech,* Dover, New York, 1966.

Strevens, P.: Spectra of fricative noise in human speech, *Language & Speech,* vol. 3, pp. 32–49, 1960.

Wakita, H.: Direct estimation of the vocal tract shape by inverse filtering of acoustic speech waveforms, *IEEE Trans.,* vol. AU-21, no. 5, pp. 417–427, October, 1973.

Weiss M. R.: Personal communication, 1970.

CHAPTER
SIX

LINEAR PREDICTION

The concept of predicting the future of a signal from its past is nothing new—it dates back at least to the late 1940s and is mentioned in many probability texts. The appeal of linear prediction as applied to speech, however, is not only its predictive function but also the fact that it gives us a very good model of the vocal tract which is useful for both theoretical and practical purposes. In addition, the goodness of the model means that linear prediction is a particularly appropriate way to encode speech and that the predictor parameters are a valuable source of information for recognition purposes.

In this chapter, after introducing the concept of linear prediction itself, we will derive the equations for the linear predictor and will then show how these equations are solved. For one case, we will derive an iterative solution which is of particular interest, both theoretically and practically. We will then introduce the concept of the *reverse* linear predictor and, with its aid, establish a number of widely used recurrence relations among predictors and prediction errors.

At that point we will be ready to relate linear prediction to speech. We will do this by exhibiting the predictor as a filter and relating it to the piecewise-cylindrical model of the vocal tract which we analyzed previously. Next, we will take up some special algorithms for linear prediction and explain their motivation. Finally, we will discuss some of the details that come up in applying linear prediction to practical speech problems.

Figure 6-1 A system viewed as a black box with its input and output.

6-1 INTRODUCTION

Given a linear, discrete-time system, the object of linear prediction is to estimate the output sequence—or, specifically, the forthcoming output sample—from a linear combination of input samples, past output samples, or both (see Fig. 6-1):

$$\hat{y}(n) = \sum_{j=0}^{q} b(j)x(n-j) - \sum_{i=1}^{p} a(i)y(n-i) \qquad (6\text{-}1)$$

(The hat indicates an estimate.) The factors $a(i)$ and $b(j)$ are called *predictor coefficients*. Intuitively, we would feel that a process which predicted a system's output in this way must be a pretty good model of the system. However, there is more to it than that. Very many systems of interest to us are describable, at least approximately, by a linear, constant-coefficient difference equation:

$$\sum_{i=0}^{p} a(i)y(n-i) = \sum_{j=0}^{q} b(j)x(n-j) \qquad (6\text{-}2)$$

Notice that the form of (6-2) is essentially the same as that of (6-1); if we solve (6-2) for $y(n)$, we get the right-hand side of (6-1). Hence the predictor is an inherently reasonable way of modeling such a system. Indeed, if the predictor is a good one, we can derive an approximate system function right from the predictor coefficients. From elementary Z transforms, if $Y(z)/X(z) = H(z)$, where $H(z)$ is a ratio of polynomials $N(z)/D(z)$, then

$$N(z) = \sum_{j=0}^{q} b(j)z^{-j} \quad \text{and} \quad D(z) = \sum_{i=0}^{p} a(i)z^{-i}$$

Thus the predictor coefficients give us immediate access to the poles and zeros of $H(z)$, provided we have chosen p and q properly.

6-2 TYPES OF SYSTEM MODEL

The model resulting from (6-1) is termed the *mixed pole–zero* model and is the most general. There are two important variants, however:

1. In an *all-pole* model (in statistics, the *autoregressive* (AR) model), the numerator $N(z)$ is a constant. Then $b(j) = 0$ for $j > 0$ and the predictor essentially works only from output samples.
2. In an *all-zero* model (in statistics, the *moving-average* (MA) model), the denominator $D(z)$ is equal to unity and the predictor works only from input samples.

To round out the terminology, we note that the mixed pole–zero model is also called the autoregressive moving-average (ARMA) model.

In practice, the most frequently used model is the *all-pole* model, for two important reasons:

1. It is the easiest to compute. Deriving a predictor with finite zeros involves us in simultaneous nonlinear equations, which are expensive to solve.
2. We may not know the input sequence x—as in some seismic or EEG applications, or in "blind deconvolution."

In speech, we have an additional reason for using an all-pole model:

3. If we ignore the case of nasals and some fricatives, the transfer function of the vocal tract is, as we have seen, an all-pole function.

Contemporary literature in linear prediction of speech uses the all-pole model in the overwhelming majority of cases, and this is the model which we will discuss from here on.

We might reasonably ask why one bothers with these special models. Is it not somehow unreasonable to pretend there are no finite poles (or zeros) in the system? The answer is that it may in some cases prove impractical, or inexact, but it is not unreasonable. We may instance two examples. First, the basic convolution equation

$$y(n) = \sum_{k=-\infty}^{\infty} x(k)h(n-k)$$

depends only on the input and hence is all-zero. In practice, the duration of h may be infinite, and hence a finite all-zero model may not be exact; however, it may be sufficient to our purpose. Second, a zero may be approximated by many poles:

$$1 - az^{-1} = \frac{1}{1 + az^{-1} + a^2z^{-2} + a^3z^{-3} + \cdots}$$

and if the denominator converges fast enough, we may be able to get by with only a few terms. Therefore the all-pole and all-zero models frequently provide adequate and reasonable approximations for practical applications.

6-3 DERIVATION OF THE LINEAR PREDICTION EQUATIONS

Given a zero-mean signal $y(n)$, in the all-pole predictor, we wish to estimate the value at point n as a linear combination of past values (Fig. 6-2):

$$\hat{y}(n) = - \sum_{i=1}^{p} a(i)y(n-i) \qquad (6\text{-}3)$$

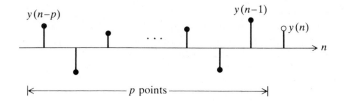

Figure 6-2 The prediction problem. The sample at time n (open circle) is to be estimated as a linear combination of the preceding p samples (dots).

(The minus sign is used here to simplify notation later.) Then the error is

$$e(n) = y(n) - \hat{y}(n)$$
$$= \sum_{i=0}^{p} a(i)y(n-i) \quad (6\text{-}4)$$

where $a(0) = 1$. [We will use $a(0) = 1$ throughout because it simplifies notation.]

To derive the predictor, we compute the coefficients a which will minimize this error in the mean-squared sense, i.e., that will minimize $E = \langle e^2 \rangle$. The coefficients can be found by expanding $\langle e^2 \rangle$ with (6-4) and taking partial derivatives with respect to $a(i)$, but it is quicker and easier to use the *orthogonality principle*. This principle states that the desired coefficients are those which make the error orthogonal to the samples $y(n-1), y(n-2), \ldots, y(n-p)$. (Two functions u and v are orthogonal if $\langle uv \rangle = 0$. For a proof of the orthogonality principle, see Appendix A or Papoulis, 1984, p. 407ff.) Thus we require that

$$\langle y(n-j)e(n) \rangle = 0 \quad \text{for } j = 1, 2, \ldots, p$$

i.e., that

$$\left\langle y(n-j) \sum_{i=0}^{p} a(i)y(n-i) \right\rangle = 0$$

Interchanging the operations of averaging and summing, and representing $\langle \ \rangle$ by summing over n, we have

$$\sum_{i=0}^{p} a(i) \sum_{n} y(n-i)y(n-j) = 0, \quad j = 1, \ldots, p \quad (6\text{-}5)$$

The required predictors are found by solving these equations.

The orthogonality principle also states that the resulting minimum error is given by

$$E = \langle e^2(n) \rangle = \langle y(n)e(n) \rangle$$

In the same way in which we found (6-5), this leads to

$$\sum_{i=0}^{p} a(i) \sum_{n} y(n-i)y(n) = E \quad (6\text{-}6)$$

The limits on n in these sums depend on details of the way in which we will minimize the error. There are two ways of proceeding:

1. We can minimize the error over N points of the signal. In that case, the limits on n are 0 and $N - 1$, and our equations become

$$\sum_{i=0}^{p} a(i)c_{ij} = 0, \qquad j = 1, 2, \ldots, p \qquad (6\text{-}7a)$$

and

$$E = \sum_{i=0}^{p} a(i)c_{i0} \qquad (6\text{-}7b)$$

where

$$c_{ij} = \sum_{n=0}^{N-1} y(n-i)y(n-j) \qquad (6\text{-}7c)$$

(Note that to compute c_{00} through c_{pp}, we need to have $N + p$ samples of the signal.)

2. We can minimize the error over all time. In that case, limits of n are $-\infty$ and ∞. Then (with a little juggling)

$$\sum_{i=0}^{p} a(i)r_{i-j} = 0, \qquad j = 1, 2, \ldots, p \qquad (6\text{-}8a)$$

and

$$E = \sum_{i=0}^{p} a(i)r_i \qquad (6\text{-}8b)$$

where

$$r_i = \sum_{n=-\infty}^{\infty} y(n)y(n-i) \qquad (6\text{-}8c)$$

Since we know only a finite number, N, of points, we assume that y has been "windowed" (as with a DFT), i.e., that $y = 0$ outside the range $(0, N - 1)$; then

$$r_i = \sum_{n=i}^{N-1} y(n)y(n-i) \qquad (6\text{-}9)$$

The form in (6-8) is commonly called the *autocorrelation* method. [Note that (6-8c) is the autocorrelation function of $y(n)$.] The form in (6-6) has come to be known as the "covariance" method—a slightly misleading term since c_{ij} is not a covariance in the usual probability sense. The autocorrelation of a time series x is

$$R(n_1, n_2) = \langle x(n_1)x(n_2) \rangle$$

The autocovariance is

$$C(n_1, n_2) = \langle [x(n_1) - \bar{x}(n_1)][x(n_2) - \bar{x}(n_2)] \rangle$$

(i.e., with the means removed). If the time series is stationary, then

$$R(k) = \langle x(n+k)x(n) \rangle$$

and

$$C(k) = \langle [x(n+k) - \bar{x}][x(n) - \bar{x}] \rangle$$

It would probably be better to say *stationary* and *nonstationary* rather than autocorrelation and covariance, but there appears to be no trend toward this terminology.

The choice of method depends on experience and on the assumptions made about y. The autocorrelation method is indicated for stationary signals and the covariance method for non-stationary signals. In speech processing, we know from experience that the autocorrelation method gives better results with fricatives and the covariance method is better with periodic speech sounds. (In speech encoding, of course, we cannot switch back and forth between methods, and have to settle for one or the other.) The autocorrelation method is slightly cheaper to compute, and it leads to a number of interesting theoretical insights. For that reason, we will discuss the autocorrelation equations first.

6-4 SOLVING THE AUTOCORRELATION EQUATIONS

The equations of (6-8) can be represented as follows:

$$
\begin{aligned}
r_{-1}a(0) + r_0 a(1) + r_1 a(2) + \cdots + r_{p-1} a(p) &= 0 \\
r_{-2}a(0) + r_{-1}a(1) + r_0 a(2) + \cdots + r_{p-2} a(p) &= 0 \\
r_{-3}a(0) + r_{-2}a(1) + r_{-1}a(2) + \cdots + r_{p-3} a(p) &= 0 \\
&\cdots \\
r_{-p}a(0) + r_{1-p}a(1) + r_{2-p}a(2) + \cdots + r_0 a(p) &= 0
\end{aligned}
\qquad (6\text{-}10)
$$

Note, however, that for a real sequence y, $r_{-i} = r_i$, and recall also that $a(0) = 1$. Then, rewriting (6-10) in matrix form, we have

$$
\begin{bmatrix}
r_1 & r_0 & r_1 & r_2 & \cdots & r_{p-1} \\
r_2 & r_1 & r_0 & r_1 & \cdots & r_{p-2} \\
r_3 & r_2 & r_1 & r_0 & \cdots & r_{p-3} \\
\cdots \\
r_p & r_{p-1} & r_{p-2} & r_{p-3} & \cdots & r_0
\end{bmatrix}
\begin{bmatrix} 1 \\ a(1) \\ a(2) \\ \cdots \\ a(p) \end{bmatrix}
=
\begin{bmatrix} 0 \\ 0 \\ 0 \\ \cdots \\ 0 \end{bmatrix}
\qquad (6\text{-}11)
$$

If we move the constant terms to the right-hand side, this will be recognized as a set of p equations in p unknowns:

$$
\begin{bmatrix}
r_0 & r_1 & r_2 & \cdots & r_{p-1} \\
r_1 & r_0 & r_1 & \cdots & r_{p-2} \\
r_2 & r_1 & r_0 & \cdots & r_{p-3} \\
\cdots \\
r_{p-1} & r_{p-2} & r_{p-3} & \cdots & r_0
\end{bmatrix}
\begin{bmatrix} a(1) \\ a(2) \\ a(3) \\ \cdots \\ a(p) \end{bmatrix}
= -
\begin{bmatrix} r_1 \\ r_2 \\ r_3 \\ \cdots \\ r_p \end{bmatrix}
\qquad (6\text{-}12)
$$

We will not, in fact, be using this form, for reasons that will appear shortly, and we include it only for reference. Notice the structure of the **R** matrix in these equations, however: all the elements along any diagonal are equal. Such a matrix is called a Toeplitz matrix. **R** is in fact not only Toeplitz but also symmetric.

Although these equations can be solved by any standard method, the fact that **R** is Toeplitz and symmetric permits a recursive solution that is not only computationally efficient but also of considerable theoretical interest. This recursion is variously attributed to Levinson and to Durbin; the derivation presented here is based on Burg (1975).

The recursive solution proceeds in steps. In each step, we already have a solution a_{n-1} for a predictor of order $(n-1)$, and we use this solution to compute the coefficients a_n for an nth-order predictor. (We will use subscripts to keep track of the order of the predictor.)

We can find the recursive solution most easily if we set ourselves a slightly more ambitious task. Let us go back to the form of (6-11) and include the prediction-error formula (6-8b) as an auxiliary equation:

$$\sum_{i=0}^{p} a(i) r_i = E \qquad (6\text{-}8b)$$

Appending this to (6-11), we have

$$\begin{bmatrix} r_0 & r_1 & r_2 & r_3 & \cdots & r_p \\ \hline r_1 & r_0 & r_1 & r_2 & \cdots & r_{p-1} \\ r_2 & r_1 & r_0 & r_1 & \cdots & r_{p-2} \\ r_3 & r_2 & r_1 & r_0 & \cdots & r_{p-3} \\ \cdots & \cdots & \cdots & \cdots & \cdots & \cdots \\ r_p & r_{p-1} & r_{p-2} & r_{p-3} & \cdots & r_0 \end{bmatrix} \begin{bmatrix} 1 \\ \hline a(1) \\ a(2) \\ a(3) \\ \cdots \\ a(p) \end{bmatrix} = \begin{bmatrix} E \\ \hline 0 \\ 0 \\ 0 \\ \cdots \\ 0 \end{bmatrix} \qquad (6\text{-}13)$$

The equations below the partition are the ones to be solved for a_p; the auxiliary equation above the partition gives the resulting prediction error. Note that again we have a matrix that is symmetric and Toeplitz.

Suppose we have solved (6-13) for $p = 2$. This means that we know $a_2(1)$ and $a_2(2)$ for which

$$\begin{bmatrix} r_0 & r_1 & r_2 \\ \hline r_1 & r_0 & r_1 \\ r_2 & r_1 & r_0 \end{bmatrix} \begin{bmatrix} 1 \\ \hline a_2(1) \\ a_2(2) \end{bmatrix} = \begin{bmatrix} E_2 \\ \hline 0 \\ 0 \end{bmatrix} \qquad (6\text{-}14)$$

and we wish to use this to solve

$$\begin{bmatrix} r_0 & r_1 & r_2 & r_3 \\ \hline r_1 & r_0 & r_1 & r_2 \\ r_2 & r_1 & r_0 & r_1 \\ r_3 & r_2 & r_1 & r_0 \end{bmatrix} \begin{bmatrix} 1 \\ \hline a_3(1) \\ a_3(2) \\ a_3(3) \end{bmatrix} = \begin{bmatrix} E_3 \\ \hline 0 \\ 0 \\ 0 \end{bmatrix} \qquad (6\text{-}15)$$

The key to the solution is to note that, because **R** is symmetric and Toeplitz, the solution to (6-14) also works if the vectors are reversed:

$$\begin{bmatrix} r_0 & r_1 & r_2 \\ r_1 & r_0 & r_1 \\ r_2 & r_1 & r_0 \end{bmatrix} \begin{bmatrix} a_2(2) \\ a_2(1) \\ 1 \end{bmatrix} = \begin{bmatrix} 0 \\ 0 \\ E_2 \end{bmatrix}$$

This is the trick. Using this, we try writing the solution to (6-15) as

$$\begin{bmatrix} 1 \\ a_3(1) \\ a_3(2) \\ a_3(3) \end{bmatrix} = \begin{bmatrix} 1 \\ a_2(1) \\ a_2(2) \\ 0 \end{bmatrix} + k_3 \begin{bmatrix} 0 \\ a_2(2) \\ a_2(1) \\ 1 \end{bmatrix} \qquad (6\text{-}16)$$

where k_3 is some constant. Substituting in (6-15), we get

$$\begin{bmatrix} r_0 & r_1 & r_2 & r_3 \\ \hline r_1 & r_0 & r_1 & r_2 \\ r_2 & r_1 & r_0 & r_1 \\ r_3 & r_2 & r_1 & r_0 \end{bmatrix} \left\{ \begin{bmatrix} 1 \\ a_2(1) \\ a_2(2) \\ 0 \end{bmatrix} + k_3 \begin{bmatrix} 0 \\ a_2(2) \\ a_2(1) \\ 1 \end{bmatrix} \right\} = \begin{bmatrix} E_2 \\ \hline 0 \\ 0 \\ q \end{bmatrix} + k_3 \begin{bmatrix} q \\ \hline 0 \\ 0 \\ E_2 \end{bmatrix} \qquad (6\text{-}17)$$

where q is some other term we do not need to worry about yet. Now, for (6-17) to be a solution, we require only that the right-hand side have all zeros below the partition. However, we already have zeros everywhere except in the bottom element, and we can force that element to be zero by forcing k_3 to satisfy

$$q + k_3 E_2 = 0$$

Hence the solution to (6-15) is indeed (6-16), where

$$k_3 = -\frac{q}{E_2}$$

$$= -\frac{1}{E_2} \sum_{i=0}^{2} a(i) r_{3-i}$$

Notice that the new prediction error, E_3, is equal to $E_2 + k_3 q$, or

$$E_3 = E_2(1 - k_3^2) \qquad (6\text{-}18)$$

It can be shown that the absolute value of k can never exceed 1; in practice it is strictly less than unity. Thus each new prediction error tends to be less than the preceding one but greater than zero. This agrees with intuition: we would expect the accuracy of the predictor to increase with its order but never to become perfect.

We can now generalize to the nth recursive step:

$$\begin{bmatrix} a_n(0) \\ a_n(1) \\ a_n(2) \\ \vdots \\ a_n(n-1) \\ a_n(n) \end{bmatrix} = \begin{bmatrix} a_{n-1}(0) \\ a_{n-1}(1) \\ a_{n-1}(2) \\ \vdots \\ a_{n-1}(n-1) \\ 0 \end{bmatrix} + k_n \begin{bmatrix} 0 \\ a_{n-1}(n-1) \\ a_{n-1}(n-2) \\ \vdots \\ a_{n-1}(1) \\ a_{n-1}(0) \end{bmatrix} \quad (6\text{-}19a)$$

or, briefly,

$$a_n(i) = a_{n-1}(i) + k_n a_{n-1}(n-i) \quad (6\text{-}19b)$$

[recall that $a_n(0) = 1$ for any n]; and

$$k_n = \frac{-1}{E_{n-1}} \sum_{i=0}^{n-1} a_{n-1}(i) r_{n-i} \quad (6\text{-}19c)$$

Finally,

$$E_n = E_{n-1}(1 - k_n^2) \quad (6\text{-}19d)$$

These three equations are the recursion relation we were after.

The key to each recursion step is clearly the coefficient k_n. These coefficients are of particular interest in themselves. For reasons that will appear later, they are known variously as *partial-correlation* (PARCOR) coefficients or *reflection coefficients*. It remains to show how the recursion is started up and to present the whole process in an orderly form. We can start the recursion at $n = 0$, for which the equations are

$$[r_0][1] = [E_0]$$

Hence $E_0 = r_0$.

The algorithm can then be stated as follows:

1. For $n = 0$, $E_0 = r_0$.
2. For step n,

    a.
    $$k_n = \frac{-1}{E_{n-1}} \sum_{i=0}^{n-1} a_{n-1}(i) r_{n-i}$$

    b.
    $$a_n(n) = k_n$$

    c. For $i = 1$ to $n - 1$,
    $$a_n(i) = a_{n-1}(i) + k_n a_{n-1}(n-i)$$

    d.
    $$E_n = E_{n-1}(1 - k_n^2)$$

This algorithm is implemented in the program LPCA in Appendix B.

There is one other piece of information to be obtained from the autocorrelation equations. Recall that for any predictor $\{a\}$, the prediction error was given in (6-4) as

$$e(n) = \sum_{i=0}^{n} a(i)y(n-i)$$

Then

$$e^2(n) = \sum_{i=0}^{n} a(i)y(n-i) \sum_{j=0}^{n} a(j)y(n-j)$$

Taking the expected value and interchanging the expected-value and summing operations gives us

$$\langle e^2(n) \rangle = \sum_{i=0}^{n} a(i) \sum_{j=0}^{n} a(j) \langle y(n-i)y(n-j) \rangle \qquad (6\text{-}20)$$

The quantity $\langle y(n-i)y(n-j) \rangle$ is, of course, r_{ij}. If we represent the predictor coefficients by the vector $\mathbf{a}$, then the right-hand side of (6-20) can be written as the quadratic form, $\mathbf{a}^T \mathbf{R} \mathbf{a}$. Then the prediction error can be written as

$$E = \langle e^2(n) \rangle = \mathbf{a}^T \mathbf{R} \mathbf{a} \qquad (6\text{-}21)$$

This expression for the prediction error is frequently used in speech recognition, and we will have occasion to refer to it in a later section. Note that this does not apply only to the optimum predictor. (Indeed, the autocorrelation equations can be derived by differentiating $\mathbf{a}^T \mathbf{R} \mathbf{a}$ with respect to $\mathbf{a}$.)

6-5 THE REVERSE PREDICTOR; RECURRENCE RELATIONS

In (6-19a, b) we saw the predictor-coefficient vector reversed. It happens that this reverse vector is useful enough to merit its own symbol. We will therefore introduce a new set of coefficients $\{b(i)\}$, defined as follows:

$$b_p(i) = a_p(p+1-i), \qquad i = 1, 2, \ldots, p+1 \qquad (6\text{-}22a)$$

where p is the order of the predictor, as usual. For all p,

and

$$\left. \begin{array}{l} a_p(0) = b_p(p+1) = 1 \\ a_p(q) = 0 \quad \text{for } q < 0 \text{ and } q > p \\ b_p(q) = 0 \quad \text{for } q < 1 \text{ and } q > p+1 \end{array} \right\} \qquad (6\text{-}22b)$$

Given a set of p data samples, $y(n-1)$ through $y(n-p)$, we can show that the b vector forms a "postdictor" which will estimate the value of the *preceding* sample, $y(n-p-1)$. The derivation for this follows the lines of Secs. 6-3 and 6-4; we will not repeat it here. If the reverse-prediction error is E^- and we rename the forward-prediction error E^+, then this derivation will also show that $E^+ = E^-$.

These results are in accord with intuition: since $r_{-i} = r_i$, the statistics do not seem to take the direction of time into account, in which case the same predictor *should* work both ways.

The combination of the concept of reverse prediction and the symmetry implied by (6-22) allows us to represent compactly a number of useful recurrence relations among autocorrelation-based predictors and their prediction errors.

Recurrence for Forward Predictor

This is an alternate formulation of (6-19a):

$$a_p(i) = a_{p-1}(i) + k_p b_{p-1}(i) \tag{6-23}$$

Recurrence for Backward Predictor

$$b_p(i) = b_{p-1}(i-1) + k_p a_{p-1}(i-1) \tag{6-24}$$

Z Transforms

Let the Z transform of the forward predictor be

$$A_p(z) = \sum_{i=-\infty}^{\infty} a_p(i) z^{-i} \tag{6-25a}$$

Because of (6-22b), these limits in practice are 0 to p. Let the Z transform of the postdictor be

$$B_p(z) = \sum_{i=-\infty}^{\infty} b_p(i) z^{-i} \tag{6-25b}$$

Again, because of (6-22b), these limits in practice are 1 to $p+1$. Note that

$$B_p(z) = z^{-(p+1)} A_p\left(\frac{1}{z}\right) \tag{6-25c}$$

Then the prediction and postdiction equations can be written as

$$A_p(z) = A_{p-1}(z) + k_p B_{p-1}(z) \tag{6-26}$$

$$B_p(z) = z^{-1}[B_{p-1}(z) + k_p A_{p-1}(z)] \tag{6-27}$$

These equations are frequently written in matrix form as follows:

$$\begin{bmatrix} A_p(z) \\ B_p(z) \end{bmatrix} = \begin{bmatrix} 1 & k_p \\ k_p z^{-1} & z^{-1} \end{bmatrix} \begin{bmatrix} A_{p-1}(z) \\ B_{p-1}(z) \end{bmatrix} \tag{6-28}$$

Recurrence Relations among Errors

Let the forward prediction error at point n be $e_p^+(n)$ for an order-p predictor:

$$e_p^+(n) = \sum_{i=0}^{p} a_p(i) y(n-i)$$

[for $p = 0$, $e_p^+(n) = y(n)$]. Let the reverse error *for the same set of p points* be $e_p^-(n)$:

$$e_p^-(n) = \sum_{i=1}^{p+1} b_p(i) y(n-i)$$

$$= \sum_{i=1}^{p+1} a_p(p+1-i) y(n-i)$$

[for $p = 0$, $e_p^-(n) = y(n-1)$]. Then the forward- and reverse-prediction errors of consecutive filter orders can be represented as follows:

$$e_p^+(n) = e_{p-1}^+(n) + k_p e_{p-1}^-(n) \tag{6-29}$$

$$e_p^-(n) = e_{p-1}^-(n-1) + k_p e_{p-1}^+(n-1) \tag{6-30}$$

Z Transforms of Errors

Defining Z transforms in the usual way,

$$E_p^+(z) = E_{p-1}^+(z) + k_p E_{p-1}^-(z) \tag{6-31}$$

$$E_p^-(z) = z^{-1}[E_{p-1}^-(z) + k_p E_{p-1}^+(z)] \tag{6-32}$$

Again, these last two equations are frequently combined in matrix form:

$$\begin{bmatrix} E_p^+(z) \\ E_p^-(z) \end{bmatrix} = \begin{bmatrix} 1 & k_p \\ k_p z^{-1} & z^{-1} \end{bmatrix} \begin{bmatrix} E_{p-1}^+(z) \\ E_{p-1}^-(z) \end{bmatrix} \tag{6-33a}$$

and when $p = 0$,

$$\begin{bmatrix} E_0^+(z) \\ E_0^-(z) \end{bmatrix} = \begin{bmatrix} Y(z) \\ z^{-1} Y(z) \end{bmatrix} \tag{6-33b}$$

6-6 APPLICATIONS: FILTERING AND MODELING

Before continuing, let us review briefly what we have done and consider how this applies to speech analysis. We start by giving an alternative interpretation of the prediction process based on spectrum and autocorrelation matching.

Autocorrelation Matching

We return now to the concept of system modeling. Suppose we have a signal $y(n)$ with known autocorrelation $r_{yy}(n)$. [We will have occasion to discuss several different autocorrelations in this section, so we will temporarily use the notation

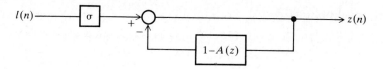

Figure 6-3 An autoregressive system used to match a specified autocorrelation function.

$r_{qq}(n) = r_n$ for signal $q(n)$.] We wish to model this with the autoregressive system shown in Fig. 6-3, where $e(n)$ is an excitation with autocorrelation $r_{ee}(n) = \delta(n)$ and A is of order p. We will consider a satisfactory model one which produces a signal $z(n)$ whose second-order statistics match those of $y(n)$, and in particular whose autocorrelations are the same as those of $y(n)$ for lags out to p. We will now show that $A(z)$ is our linear predictor.

The transfer function of this system is

$$H(z) = \frac{\sigma}{A(z)} \qquad (6\text{-}34)$$

and the autocorrelation of $z(n)$ is therefore

$$r_{zz}(n) = r_{ee}(n) * h(n) * h(-n)$$
$$= r_{hh}(n)$$

where $r_{hh}(n)$ is the autocorrelation of the impulse response of H:

$$r_{hh}(n) = \sum_{i=-\infty}^{\infty} h(i)h(i-n) \qquad (6\text{-}35)$$

Hence we wish to find $A(z)$ such that

$$r_{hh}(n) = r_{yy}(n), \qquad n = 0, \ldots, p \qquad (6\text{-}36)$$

(Since the autocorrelations are even functions, they must also match for negative lags out to $-p$, but we will not use this in what follows.)

From Eq. (6-34),

$$A(z)H(z) = \sigma$$

Taking inverse Z transforms, we have

$$\sum_{i=0}^{p} a(i)h(n-i) = \sigma\delta(n) \qquad (6\text{-}37)$$

Multiply this by $h(n-j)$ and sum over n:

$$\sum_{n=-\infty}^{\infty} h(n-j) \sum_{i=0}^{p} a(i)h(n-i) = \sum_{n=-\infty}^{\infty} h(n-j)(n)$$

From (6-35), this is

$$\sum_{i=0}^{p} a(i)r_{hh}(i-j) = \sigma h(-j)$$

Since $h(n)$ is assumed causal, $h(-j) = 0$ for $j > 0$; furthermore, if we require $a(0) = 0$ as usual, then $h(0)$ is clearly σ [from Eq. 6-37)]. Hence we end up with a set of normal equations

$$\sum_{i=0}^{p} a(i) r_{hh}(i-j) = \begin{cases} \sigma^2, & j = 0 \\ 0, & j > 0 \end{cases} \quad (6\text{-}38)$$

These equations depend on the first $p + 1$ values of $r_{hh}(n)$. If we now enforce our modeling requirement that $r_{hh}(n)$ match $r_{yy}(n)$ for these values, we have once again arrived at the autocorrelation equations (6-8). We conclude, therefore, that the predictor we have been talking about all along can also be used to model the signal it predicts. Notice also that σ, the gain constant of the model, can be found from the prediction error:

$$\sigma^2 = E_p \quad (6\text{-}39)$$

Nothing has been said in all this about the origin of the signal $y(n)$. If $y(n)$ happens indeed to be the product of an order-p autoregressive (i.e., all-pole) process, then the model is particularly apt. This is frequently the case in speech, as we have seen.

Spectrum Matching

Because of the intimate connection between autocorrelations and power spectra, we should be able to do the entire linear prediction derivation in the frequency domain. Let $Y(z)$ and $E(z)$ be the transforms of $y(n)$ and $e(n)$; then

$$E(z) = A(z) Y(z)$$

By Parseval's theorem, the prediction error power is given by

$$E = \frac{1}{2\pi} \int_{-\pi}^{\pi} |E(e^{j\omega})|^2 \, d\omega$$

$$= \frac{1}{2\pi} \int_{-\pi}^{\pi} A(e^{j\omega}) A(e^{-j\omega}) Y(e^{j\omega}) Y(e^{-j\omega}) \, d\omega$$

The last two factors in this equation are the power spectrum of $y(n)$:

$$S_y(\omega) = |Y(z)|^2_{z=e^{j\omega}}$$

Hence the prediction problem is now to find $A(z)$ to minimize

$$E = \frac{1}{2\pi} \int_{-\pi}^{\pi} S_y(\omega) A(\omega) A(-\omega) \, d\omega \quad (6\text{-}40)$$

where we use $A(\omega)$ as an abbreviation for $A(e^{j\omega})$. Makhoul and Wolf (1972) have shown that E can be minimized by expanding $A(\omega)$ and $A(-\omega)$ and differentiating with respect to the coefficients a. Doing so leads back to our system (6-8), with the autocorrelation obtained by inverse Fourier transformation of $S_y(\omega)$.

In discussing the autocorrelation-matching problem, we found our solution in the filter $H(z) = \sigma/A(z)$. In view of the foregoing, we would expect the power spectrum of $H(z)$ to match $S_y(\omega)$. Let

$$H_p(\omega) = \frac{\sigma^2}{|A_p(z)|^2}\bigg|_{z=e^{j\omega}} \tag{6-41}$$

where the subscript p indicates the order of A. Then from (6-40),

$$E = \frac{\sigma^2}{2\pi} \int_{-\pi}^{\pi} \frac{S(\omega)}{H_p(\omega)} d\omega \tag{6-42}$$

Notice that because this error criterion depends on a ratio, cases where $S(\omega) > H_p(\omega)$ make a larger contribution to the error than cases where $S(\omega) < H_p(\omega)$. Hence this criterion will make $H_p(\omega)$ tend to follow the peaks in $S(\omega)$ rather than the valleys. In particular, if $S(\omega)$ is a speech spectrum, as in Sec. 5-3, $H_p(\omega)$ will try to approximate the *spectrum envelope* as it was defined in that section. It will, in fact, tend to approximate $S(\omega)$ most closely in the neighborhoods of the formant peaks.

This fact accounts for much of the importance of linear prediction in speech analysis. $H(z)$ gives us immediate access to the formant frequencies, and the filter $\sigma/A(z)$ is a plausible model of the vocal tract, provided its order is chosen properly. (The question of the order of A will be taken up below.) In fact, we will term this filter the *vocal tract* filter, and we will call the prediction error filter $A(z)$ the *inverse filter*. If the input to the inverse filter is the signal from which it was

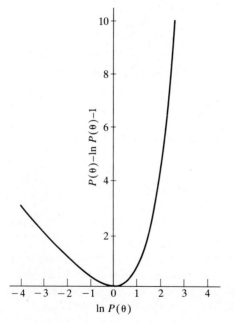

Figure 6-4 The integrand of (6-43) plotted against ln $P(\theta)$.

derived, it will tend to remove the frequency-dependent components in the spectrum envelope of the signal. Hence we say that $A(z)$ *flattens* the spectrum of the signal to which it is matched.

Another explanation of the peak-matching properties of this model is occasionally found in the literature. In a derivation of linear prediction based on the concept of maximum likelihood, Itakura and Saito (1970) showed that finding the optimum predictor was equivalent to minimizing the quantity

$$D = \frac{1}{2\pi} \int_{-\pi}^{\pi} [P(\theta) - \ln P(\theta) - 1] \, d\theta \qquad (6\text{-}43)$$

where $P(\theta)$ is the integrand of (6-42). If $P(\theta) - \ln P(\theta) - 1$ is plotted against $\ln P(\theta)$, as in Fig. 6-4, it will be seen that positive values of $\ln P(\theta)$ make a much greater contribution to the integral than do negative values.

Frequency-Domain Properties

Stability of the all-pole model In practical applications, such as speech synthesis, where the model of (6-34) is used, it is clearly essential that the vocal-tract filter be stable. The requirement for stability is that the roots of $A(z)$ lie inside the unit circle.

We will show that where the recursion of (6-19a) applies, stability is guaranteed. This can be proved by induction on the order of filter, in which we show that each step in the Levinson recursion adds a new zero to $A(z)$ inside the unit circle. Since the zero-order predictor $A_0(z) = a_0$ has no zeros outside the unit circle, neither do any of the others. The proof is based on Rouché's theorem:

Theorem Given a polynomial $F(z)$, let n_p and n_z be the number of its poles and zeros, respectively, lying inside the unit circle. Form a new polynomial, $F(z) + G(z)$, and let the number of its poles and zeros inside the unit circle be n'_p and n'_z. If $|G(e^{j\omega})| \le |F(e^{j\omega})|$, then $n'_p - n'_z = n_p - n_z$.

In the case of the Levinson recursion, we have, from Eq. (6-26),

$$A_p(z) = A_{p-1}(z) + k_p B_{p-1}(z)$$

On the unit circle, $|B_{p-1}(z)| = |A_{p-1}(z)|$, from (6-25c). We also know that $|k_p| < 1$; therefore the Rouché condition is met and $n'_p - n'_z$ for $A_p(z)$ is the same as $n_p - n_z$ for $A_{p-1}(z)$. However, $A_p(z)$ is one degree higher than $A_{p-1}(z)$, and so has one extra pole at the origin; hence the new zero must also be inside the unit circle.

When we take up the covariance method of linear prediction, we will find that the recursion of (6-19a) is not applicable. In fact, filters computed from the covariance equations cannot be guaranteed to be stable. In addition, numerical errors in solving the autocorrelation equations may occasionally produce an apparently unstable filter.

When a filter used for synthesis purposes is found to be unstable, one possible fix is to find the roots of $A(z)$ and for each root outside the unit circle substitute its reciprocal. The new filter will have the same Fourier transform and will be stable. Since the computational cost of finding complex roots of polynomials is usually prohibitive, however, this is not a practical way out. In practice, we frequently simply use the coefficients of the previous timeframe and hope for better luck on the next frame. We can get away with this because we find these filters are stable almost all of the time.

Minimum prediction error The recursion relation of (6-19d), $E_n = E_{n-1}(1 - k_n^2)$, tells us that the error tends to decrease with increasing p. It is of interest to know whether a predictor of infinite order would give an error of zero. That it will not can be seen from an examination of the log power spectra of the model and the signal. For an order-p predictor, we have (Markel and Gray, 1976)

$$\frac{1}{2\pi} \int_{-\pi}^{\pi} \ln \left| \frac{\sigma}{A(\omega)} \right|^2 d\omega = \ln \sigma^2 - \frac{1}{2\pi} \int_{-\pi}^{\pi} \ln |A(\omega)|^2 \, d\omega \qquad (6\text{-}44)$$

Papoulis (1984) provides a proof that the second integral is equal to $\ln a(0)$, which in our case is zero. Hence

$$\frac{1}{2\pi} \int_{-\pi}^{\pi} \ln \left| \frac{\sigma}{A(\omega)} \right|^2 d\omega = \ln \sigma^2 \qquad (6\text{-}45)$$

From considering the autocorrelation-matching problem, we know that σ^2 is equal to the prediction error E_p. From autocorrelation matching, we also know that in the limit as $p \to \infty$, the autocorrelation function of the model matches that of the signal. Then their power spectra match as well; hence we have

$$\ln(E_\infty) = \frac{1}{2\pi} \int_{-\pi}^{\pi} \left| \frac{\sigma_\infty}{A_\infty(\omega)} \right|^2 d\omega = \frac{1}{2\pi} \int_{-\pi}^{\pi} \ln |S_y(\omega)|^2 \, d\omega \qquad (6\text{-}46)$$

Hence the infinite-order predictor has an error equal to the geometric mean of the power spectrum of the input signal.

Filter Structures

Clearly, the inverse filter can be realized in a regular FIR filter structure (Fig. 6-5). We will call such a configuration a predictor-coefficient-controlled (PCC) filter. In many cases, however, the user may find it useful to control the filter with reflection coefficients rather than predictor coefficients. A reflection-coefficient-controlled (RCC) filter can be built using a *lattice structure* based on the recurrence relations among prediction errors. Repeating (6-31) and (6-32),

$$E_n^+(z) = E_{n-1}^+(z) + k_n E_{n-1}^-(z)$$

and

$$E_n^-(z) = z^{-1}[E_{n-1}^-(z) + k_n E_{n-1}^+(z)]$$

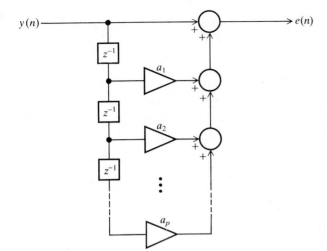

Figure 6-5 Direct-form digital filter structure for the inverse filter.

The *n*th stage of the corresponding filter therefore has the structure shown in Fig. 6-6. If we recall that $E_0^+(z) = Y(z)$ and $E_0^-(z) = z^{-1}Y(z)$, the entire filter structure looks like Fig. 6-7.

The vocal tract model,

$$\frac{Y(z)}{E(Z)} = \frac{1}{A(z)}$$

can similarly be implemented in either PCC or RCC versions. The PCC version takes the form of a standard all-pole IIR filter configuration (Fig. 6-8). The RCC

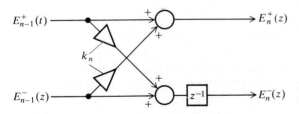

Figure 6-6 Lattice filter structure corresponding to (6-31) and (6-32).

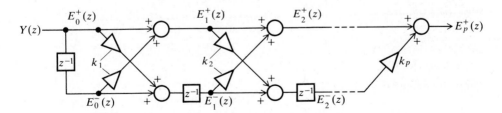

Figure 6-7 Lattice filter structure for the inverse filter.

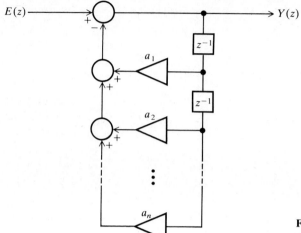

Figure 6-8 Direct-form digital filter structure for the vocal tract model.

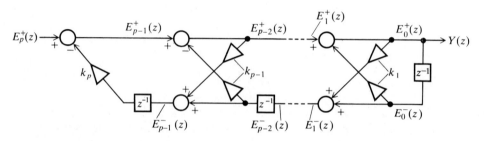

Figure 6-9 Lattice filter structure for the vocal tract model.

version again takes the form of a lattice structure derived from repeated application of (6-31) and (6-32), as shown in Fig. 6-9.

The advantage of reflection-coefficient control, in spite of its greater complexity, is more apparent in the vocal tract filter, where stability is important. All that is necessary to guarantee stability in an RCC filter is to ensure that $|k_n| < 1$ for all reflection coefficients. In many synthesizers, it is important to minimize data storage, and one way to do this is to store only key values of the filter coefficients and generate the rest by interpolation. There is no guarantee that interpolated predictor coefficients will result in a stable filter; on the other hand, interpolated reflection coefficients will always give a stable filter if the reference values do.

Significance of the Constants k_n

The pivotal coefficients are known variously as reflection coefficients and partial-correlation (PARCOR) coefficients. The justification for these names is as follows.

Reflection coefficients Recall that the inverse transfer function for any one section of the cylindrical model of the vocal tract is

$$\begin{bmatrix} F_i(z) \\ R_i(z) \end{bmatrix} = \frac{z^{1/2}}{1 + k_i} \begin{bmatrix} 1 & k_i \\ k_i z^{-1} & z^{-1} \end{bmatrix} \begin{bmatrix} F_{i-1}(z) \\ R_{i-1}(z) \end{bmatrix} \qquad (6\text{-}47)$$

Notice that the matrix of (6-47) is identical in form to that of (6-33) and that the k's play the same rôle in (6-33) that the reflection coefficients do in (6-47). The relations from which (6-33) was derived are also those from which the lattice filter forms were obtained. We thus have a close correspondence [except for the scalar factors $z^{1/2}/(1 + k_i)$] among the prediction errors, the lattice filter model, and the cylindrical model. The lattice filter is, in fact, the analog of the cylindrical model.

PARCOR coefficients Itakura and Saito (1972) define k_{p+1} as the correlation of the previous forward and backward prediction errors:

$$k_{p+1} = -\frac{\langle e_p^+(n) e_p^-(n) \rangle}{\langle [e_p^+(n)]^2 [e_p^-(n)]^2 \rangle^{1/2}} \qquad (6\text{-}48)$$

We will show that this is exactly the same as our recursion formula,

$$k_{p+1} = \frac{-1}{E_p} \sum_{i=0}^{p} a_p(i) r_{p+1-i} \qquad (6\text{-}49)$$

Recall that $E_p^+ = \langle [e_p^+(n)]^2 \rangle$. We have already established that $E_p^+ = E_p^-$, so clearly $1/E_p$ can be written as $1/\sqrt{E_p^+ E_p^-}$, which leads to the denominator of (6-49).

The numerator is

$$\langle e_p^+(n) e_p^-(n) \rangle = \left\langle \sum_i a_p(i) y(n-i) \sum_j b_p(j) y(n-j) \right\rangle$$

$$= \sum_{j=1}^{p+1} b_p(j) \sum_{i=0}^{p} a_p(i) r_{j-i} \qquad (6\text{-}50)$$

For $j = 1, 2, \ldots, p$, the second sum is equal to zero. [For these values, the second sum is simply the autocorrelation equations (6-8a).] Hence the only term left in the first sum is the one for which $j = p + 1$. However, for $j = p + 1$, $b_p(p + 1) = 1$; hence (6-50) reduces to

$$\langle e_p^+(n) e_p^-(n) \rangle = \sum_{i=0}^{p} a_p(i) r_{p+1-i} \qquad (6\text{-}51)$$

which is the sum in (6-49).

In introducing their lattice structure, in fact, Itakura and Saito built computation of the PARCOR coefficients into the model. Their typical filter stage looks like Fig. 6-10, where the symbol ⊠ denotes a correlator.

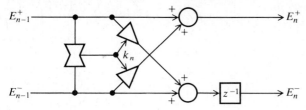

Figure 6-10 The Itakura-Saito lattice structure, showing computation of the PARCOR coefficients by cross-correlation of the error signals.

6-7 SOLUTION OF THE COVARIANCE EQUATIONS

We now return to the mathematics of linear prediction. The equations for the covariance method (6-7) can be expanded and rewritten as follows:

$$\begin{bmatrix} c_{11} & c_{12} & c_{13} & \cdots & c_{1p} \\ c_{21} & c_{22} & c_{23} & \cdots & c_{2p} \\ c_{31} & c_{32} & c_{33} & \cdots & c_{3p} \\ \vdots & & & & \vdots \\ c_{p1} & c_{p2} & c_{p3} & \cdots & c_{pp} \end{bmatrix} \begin{bmatrix} a_1 \\ a_2 \\ a_3 \\ \vdots \\ a_p \end{bmatrix} = - \begin{bmatrix} c_{10} \\ c_{20} \\ c_{30} \\ \vdots \\ c_{p0} \end{bmatrix} \qquad (6\text{-}52)$$

Computationally, the difference between solving the system (6-52) and the system (6-11) lies in the fact that the $\mathbf{C}$ matrix, although symmetric, is not Toeplitz ($c_{ij} = c_{ji}$, but $c_{i+k, j+k} \neq c_{ij}$). This means that the interesting shortcuts of the autocorrelation method are no longer usable.

Choleski Decomposition

The most commonly used solutions to (6-52) are variants of a general method known as LU decomposition (also known as Crout reduction or Choleski decomposition). The matrix $\mathbf{C}$ is factored into a lower triangular matrix $\mathbf{L}$ and an upper triangular matrix $\mathbf{U}$. If the system to be solved is written as

$$\mathbf{Ca} = \mathbf{c} \qquad (6\text{-}53)$$

and if $\mathbf{C} = \mathbf{LU}$, then we can break the solution of (6-23) into two simpler problems. Solve

$$\mathbf{L\kappa} = \mathbf{c} \qquad (6\text{-}54a)$$

and then solve

$$\mathbf{Ua} = \mathbf{\kappa} \qquad (6\text{-}54b)$$

There are actually three general ways to do the factorization of $\mathbf{C}$, all of which can be found in the literature. Any positive-definite symmetric matrix can be factored as follows:

$$\mathbf{C} = \mathbf{BDB}^T$$

or

$$\mathbf{C} = \mathbf{QQ}^T$$

or

$$\mathbf{C} = \mathbf{LU}$$

In the first case, **B** is lower-triangular with ones on the main diagonal and **D** is a diagonal matrix. The second factorization is neat and elegant, but has two disadvantages. First, it is unnecessarily expensive to compute. The expense comes about because $\mathbf{Q} = \mathbf{B}\sqrt{\mathbf{D}}$, where $\sqrt{\mathbf{D}}$ is a diagonal matrix whose elements are the square roots of the elements of **D**. Since computation time is usually limited, we would like to avoid taking square roots. The second problem is that **C** is occasionally not positive-definite, in which case the elements of **D** will not all be positive and some of the square roots will be imaginary. In the third factorization, $\mathbf{L} = \mathbf{BD}$ and $\mathbf{U} = \mathbf{B}^T$. Note that in this case the diagonal elements of **L** are identical to the corresponding elements of **D**.

Of these decompositions, the third is probably the easiest to program. The details can be found in any elementary book on numerical methods; we will only summarize briefly here.

The procedure is to evaluate **L** one column at a time and to find the rows of **U** from these results. (We will use $\mathbf{L} = [s_{ij}]$ to avoid confusion between l's and ones.) The elements of **L** are found as follows:

First column: $\quad s_{i1} = c_{i1}, \qquad\qquad i = 1, p \qquad\qquad$ (6-55a)

jth column: $\quad s_{ij} = c_{ij} - \sum_{k=1}^{j-1} \dfrac{s_{ik} s_{jk}}{s_{kk}}, \qquad i = j, p \qquad\qquad$ (6-55b)

As each column of **L** is found, we can compute each row of **U**, because

$$u_{ij} = \frac{s_{ji}}{s_{ii}}$$

This follows from the fact that $\mathbf{U} = \mathbf{D}^{-1}\mathbf{L}^T$. It is common practice to save storage by replacing the lower half of the **C** matrix by **L** and the upper half by **U**. (The diagonal elements of **U**, being ones, do not need to be saved.) These replacements can be so sequenced that nothing in **C** is wiped out until after it has been used. (This algorithm is implemented in program LPCC in Appendix B.)

Solution by LU decomposition can also be made recursive, but the process is (1) of less theoretical interest than the Durbin/Levinson recursion and (2) not as tidy. The solution is arrived at by bordering the **C**, **L**, and **U** matrices in (6-53) and (6-54) and deriving expressions for the border elements from the remaining partitions.

Prediction Error

From Eq. (6-7b), the sum-squared prediction error is

$$\begin{aligned} E &= \sum_{i=0}^{p} a(i) c_{i0} \\ &= c_{00} - \sum_{i=1}^{p} a(i) c_{i0} \\ &= c_{00} - \mathbf{a}^T \mathbf{c} \end{aligned} \qquad (6\text{-}56)$$

From (6-54),
$$\mathbf{a}^T\mathbf{c} = \boldsymbol{\kappa}^T(\mathbf{U}^{-1})^T\mathbf{L}\boldsymbol{\kappa} \tag{6-57}$$

This can be simplified by recalling that $\mathbf{L} = \mathbf{BD}$ and $\mathbf{U} = \mathbf{B}^T$. Substituting in (6-56) and (6-57) gives us
$$E = c_{00} - \boldsymbol{\kappa}^T\mathbf{D}\boldsymbol{\kappa}$$

The elements of $\mathbf{D}$ are clearly the diagonal elements of $\mathbf{L}$; hence
$$E = c_{00} - \sum_{i=1}^{p} s_{ii}\kappa_i^2 \tag{6-58}$$

As was mentioned above, covariance method predictors may generate unstable inverse filters. If this happens, the prediction error computed by (6-58) will provide an early warning of the condition by going negative at some point in the solution of (6-52).

Reflection Coefficients

The intermediate vector in (6-49), labeled $\boldsymbol{\kappa}$, corresponds very roughly to the reflection coefficients of the autocorrelation method. In particular, $\boldsymbol{\kappa}$ has the following traits in common with $\mathbf{k}$:

1. The pth element of $\boldsymbol{\kappa}$ is the last order-p predictor coefficient: that is,
$$\kappa_p = a_p(p)$$
2. For any predictor order $m < n$, $\boldsymbol{\kappa}_m$ is a prefix of $\boldsymbol{\kappa}_n$. That is, if the normal equations for an order-m predictor are solved, the $\boldsymbol{\kappa}$ vector computed in the course of the solution will consist of the first m elements of $\boldsymbol{\kappa}_n$.
3. If $\mathbf{C}$ is Toeplitz, $\boldsymbol{\kappa} = \mathbf{k}$. That is, if the LU method is used to solve the autocorrelation equations (6-12) the κ_i values will be equal to the reflection coefficients.

On the other hand, the two vectors are not the same, as the following differences indicate:

1. The covariance prediction error is given by
$$E_p = E_{p-1} - s_{pp}\kappa_p^2$$
while the autocorrelation prediction error is given by
$$E_p = E_{p-1}(1 - k_p^2)$$
2. The recursion relation
$$a_p(i) = a_{p-1}(i) + k_p a_{p-1}(p-i)$$
does not apply to the elements of $\boldsymbol{\kappa}$.

In spite of these differences, the κ's obtained in solving (6-49a, b) are also often called "reflection coefficients," or sometimes (more correctly) "generalized" reflection coefficients (GRCs). The fact that these correspondences are not exact does not deter engineers from deriving lattice filters from GRCs or even computing predictor coefficients from GRCs using the Levenson recursion. We can get away with this if the time window from which $\mathbf{C}$ is computed is long, because in such cases the difference between $\mathbf{C}$ and $\mathbf{R}$ is slight. For a detailed discussion of this question, see Gibson (1977).

Atal (Atal, 1977; Atal and Schroeder, 1979) has shown a way to obtain Levinson reflection coefficients from the LU decomposition. From (6-19d), we have

$$k_n = \sqrt{\frac{E_{n-1} - E_n}{E_{n-1}}}$$

From (6-52), we have

$$E_{n-1} - E_n = s_{nn} \kappa_n^2$$

Hence

$$k_n = \kappa_n \sqrt{\frac{s_{nn}}{E_{n-1}}} \qquad (6\text{-}59a)$$

where

$$E_{n-1} = c_{00} - \sum_{i=1}^{n-1} s_{ii} \kappa_i^2 \qquad (6\text{-}59b)$$

In Eq. (6-59a), the positive square root is assumed and k_n takes its sign from κ_n. If the sum in Eq. (6-59b) is accumulated term by term, as it is in the routine LPCC, the added cost of computing k_n from Eq. (6-59) is negligible. Note, however, that this procedure requires that $\mathbf{C}$ be positive-definite so that the elements s_{nn} in (6-59a) will always be positive.

In some applications, e.g., speech compression, the reflection coefficients are encoded for economy in transmission. In such cases, computing Atal's equivalent reflection coefficients may be a superfluous step, since the improvement resulting from the computation will usually be wiped out by the quantization errors resulting from the encoding.

6-8 SPECIAL TECHNIQUES: THE METHODS OF SCHUR AND BURG

Schur's Recursion for Reflection Coefficients

In the normal equations for the order-p linear predictor, we had

$$\sum_{i=0}^{p} a_p(i) r_{i-j} = 0, \qquad j = 1, 2, \ldots, p \qquad (6\text{-}8a)$$

Let us consider the sequence

$$q_p(j) = \sum_{i=0}^{p} a_p(i) r_{i-j} \tag{6-60}$$

for general values of j and p. This sequence has the following properties:

1. If $p = 0$, $q_p(j)$ is the same as r_{-j}.
2. If $p > 0$, $q_p(j)$ is zero for $j = 1, 2, \ldots, p$.
3. $q_p(0)$ is the order-p prediction error E_p.
4. $q_p(p + 1)$ is the quantity labeled q in (6-17).
5. For successive values of p, q obeys the recurrence relation

$$q_p(j) = q_{p-1}(j) + k_p q_{p-1}(p - j) \tag{6-61}$$

   where k_p is the pth reflection coefficient.
6. $|q_p(j)| \le r_0$, with equality only if $p = j = 0$.

These properties all follow from the recursive solution of Sec. 6-4. The proof of property 6 is as follows. From the derivation of (6-8a),

$$q_p(j) = \sum_n e(n) y(n - j)$$

Then

$$|q_p(j)|^2 = \left| \sum_n e(n) y(n - j) \right|^2$$

$$\le \sum_n |e(n)|^2 \sum_n |y(n - j)|^2$$

(This follows from the Schwartz inequality.) The first sum is the order-p prediction error E_p; the second sum is just r_0. Since $E_p \le r_0$, we have

$$|q_p(j)|^2 \le r_0^2$$

and property 6 follows.

These properties lead to yet another recursive solution to the autocorrelation equations:

1. For $-p < i < p$, $q_0(i) = r_{|i|}$.
2. For step n:
   a. $k_n = -q_{n-1}(n)/q_n(0)$.
   b. For $i = n - p$ to p, $q_n(i) = q_{n-1}(i) + k_n q_{n-1}(n - i)$.

This algorithm is implemented in the program LPCS in Appendix B.

This recursion was devised by Schur (1917) and subsequently rediscovered by Le Roux and Guegen in 1977. Its usefulness is this: if we normalize the r's by dividing through by r_0, then all the quantities in the recursion are of magnitude <1 (except r_0) and can be represented by fractions. For computation by hardware, fixed-point arithmetic is simpler and faster than floating-point arithmetic.

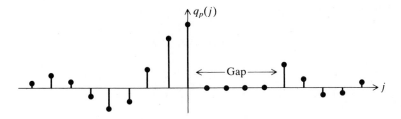

Figure 6-11 The function $q_p(j)$ for $p = 4$.

In fixed-point arithmetic, we would prefer to work with either all-integer or all-fraction data. Hence the Schur recursion is particularly handy for hardware computation of PARCOR coefficients.

If we plot $q_p(j)$, as shown in Fig. 6-11, it shows a p-point gap just past the origin, as a result of property 2. For this reason, $q_p(j)$ has been named the *gapped function* by Robinson and Treitel (1980). The Schur recursion can be regarded as a process for widening this gap by one additional point in each step.

Burg's Method for Computing Reflection Coefficients

Both the autocorrelation and covariance methods leave something to be desired. In computing r_i for the autocorrelation method, we run into a problem when $i \neq 0$, since in any time frame we do not know the values of $y(n)$ outside the current window $(0, N - 1)$. This is the reason for using (6-9), but this has two other problems associated with it. First, as i increases, fewer and fewer samples of y contribute to the estimate of r_i. Second, it means that this method implicitly assumes that $y(n)$ is zero outside the window.

In the covariance method there are also difficulties. First, as has been mentioned, there is no guarantee that the resulting vocal tract filter will be stable. Second, none of the recursive relations of Sec. 6-5 are applicable.

Burg (1975) seems to have been the first to realize that the estimation of the autocorrelations could be sidestepped altogether. This is done by assuming that y is stationary, that therefore the autocorrelation method is applicable, and that therefore the recursions of Sec. 6-5 apply. By using (6-31) and (6-32), we can derive a recursive procedure which finds each new reflection coefficient from the previous prediction error. [The prediction error can be found by running the predictor over the data, although in practice this step is also avoided by means of (6-31) and (6-32).]

For brevity, let $f_p(n) = e_p^+(n)$ and let $r_p(n) = e_p^-(n)$. We will find the value of k_p which minimizes the sum of the squares of the forward and backward prediction errors over the window. This is

$$E = \frac{1}{2(N - p)} \sum_{j=p}^{N-1} f_p^2(j) + r_p^2(j + 1) \qquad (6\text{-}62)$$

Using (6-31) and (6-32), these become

$$E = \frac{1}{2(N+p)} \sum_{j=p}^{N-1} [f_{p-1}(j) + k_p r_{p-1}(j)]^2 + [r_{p-1}(j) + k_p f_{p-1}(j)]^2 \quad (6\text{-}63)$$

where k_p is the desired PARCOR coefficient and f_{p-1} and r_{p-1} are known from the previous pass. To minimize the error, we differentiate with respect to k_p, getting (after some juggling)

$$\frac{\partial E}{\partial k_p} = \frac{1}{N-p} \sum_{j=p}^{N-1} k_p[f_{p-1}^2(j) + r_{p-1}^2(j)] + 2f_{p-1}(j)r_{p-1}(j)$$

Setting this derivative to zero gives the following recursive formula for k_p:

$$k_p = -\frac{2P}{Q} \quad (6\text{-}64a)$$

where

$$P = \sum_{j=p}^{N-1} f_{p-1}(j) r_{p-1}(j) \quad (6\text{-}64b)$$

and

$$Q = \sum_{j=p}^{N-1} f_{p-1}^2(j) r_{p-1}^2(j) \quad (6\text{-}64c)$$

Once the reflection coefficient is known, the predictor coefficients can be computed using (6-19a) as usual. If the autocorrelations themselves are required, Burg shows that R_p can be estimated by applying the new order-p predictor to the previous estimates $R_0, R_1, \ldots, R_{p-1}$:

$$R_p = -\sum_{i=1}^{p} a_p(i) R_{p-1} \quad (6\text{-}65)$$

(We use R here to avoid confusion with the reverse prediction error r.) Burg has also shown that these estimates of R have the property that they make minimal assumptions about the nature of y outside the window $(0, N-1)$. For this reason, Burg's method is also known as the *maximum-entropy method* (MEM). Entropy is a measure of uncertainty; in this case the uncertainty refers to that portion of y lying outside the window.

Burg's recursion can be summarized as follows:

1. For $n = 0$:
   a. $R_0 = \sum y^2$.
   b. $f_0(j) = y(j); r_0(j) = y(j-1)$.
2. For step n:
   a. $k_n = -2P/Q$, where P and Q are computed as in (6-64).
   b. $a_n(n) = k_n$.
   c. For $i = 1$ to $n-1$,

   $$a_n(i) = a_{n-1}(i) + k_n a_{n-1}(n-i)$$

d. $R_n = -\sum_{i=1}^{n} a_n(i) r_{p-i}$.

e. For $j = n$ to $N - 1$,

$$f_n(j) = f_{n-1}(j) + k_n r_{n-1}(j)$$
$$r_n(j) = r_{n-1}(j - 1) + k_n f_{n-1}(j - 1)$$

This algorithm is implemented in the program LPCB given in Appendix B.

If the Burg algorithm can be faulted, it is for being almost too perfect. It relies heavily on the stationarity of the input signal, and could be thought of as being ideally matched to stationary signals. Much of speech, however, is nonstationary, and the performance of Burg's algorithm tends to be erratic when applied to vocoids. In particular, formant-frequency measurements based on Burg predictors show more scatter than those based on either the autocorrelation or covariance methods. Nevertheless, the Burg algorithm appears frequently in the speech literature, and it is well to be familiar with it. (For a unified development of Burg's algorithm and its relation to the autocorrelation method, see also the tutorial by Papoulis, 1981.)

6-9 PRACTICAL CONSIDERATIONS

Spectrum Envelope

In the all-pole model of the vocal tract,

$$H(z) = \frac{\sigma}{A(z)}$$

The power spectrum is given by

$$|H(\omega)|^2 = \left| \frac{\sigma}{A(z)} \right|^2_{z=e^{j\omega}}$$

It is clearly more practical to start by finding $A(e^{j\omega})$. This can be done using the DFT. If we wish to evaluate H for N points about the unit circle, then we may write

$$H(k)^{-1} = \frac{1}{\sigma} A(e^{-2\pi jk/N}), \quad k = 0, 1, \ldots, N - 1$$

$$= \frac{1}{\sigma} A(W^{-k}) \tag{6-66}$$

where W is defined as in the DFT. Then since

$$A(z) = \sum_{i=0}^{p} A(i) z^{-i}$$

we have

$$H(k)^{-1} = \frac{1}{\sigma} \sum_{i=0}^{p} a(i) W^{-ik}$$

$$= \frac{1}{\sigma} \sum_{i=0}^{N-1} a(i) W^{-ik} \qquad (6\text{-}67)$$

We can change the upper limit because, by (6-22b), $a(i) = 0$ for $i > p$. Then the sum in (6-67) is simply the DFT of the sequence $[a(0), a(1), a(2), \ldots, a(p), 0, 0, \ldots, 0]$.

In such a sequence, p is typically 10 to 15 and N is typically 512 or 1024. When there are so few nonzero elements, the FFT algorithm can profitably be "pruned" by omitting groups of unnecessary operations. This is described in Markel (1971, 1972).

Order of Predictor

The choice of predictor order depends on the analysis bandwidth, which in turn depends on the sampling frequency f_s. The rule of thumb is

$$p = \frac{f_s}{1000} + \gamma \qquad (6\text{-}68)$$

We justify this as follows. For a normal (17-cm) vocal tract, there is an average of about one formant per kilohertz of bandwidth. (Actually it is one formant per $c/2l$ hertz.) One formant requires two conjugate complex poles. Hence, for every formant, we require two predictor coefficients, or two coefficients per kilohertz of bandwidth. The total bandwidth is equal to $f_s/2$ (Nyquist's rate); hence $p = f_s/1000$. Note also that this makes the sampling rate the same as that used in finding the Z transform of the transformation matrix in Sec. 5-2:

$$p = \frac{2lf_s}{c}$$

Thus

$$f_s = \frac{pc}{2l}$$

$$= \frac{c}{2\Delta}$$

The γ in (6-68) is a fudge constant, empirically determined, and typically 2 or 3. These extra poles take care of such things as the rolloff in the glottal excitation function, and also give the predictor a little extra flexibility.

Linear Prediction of Noisy Speech

When the speech signal is corrupted by noise, the assumptions of the all-pole model are violated and the quality of the estimate suffers. Low signal-to-noise ratios (e.g., below 5 to 10 dB) can cause serious distortion of the model spectral density.

We have seen that the spectrum-matching action of linear prediction tends to favor spectrum peaks over spectrum valleys. If the noise consists of periodic functions (e.g., from rotating machinery), the predictor will try to fit the spectral peaks corresponding to these components. White noise has the effect of flattening the formant peaks and smoothing out the model spectrum. The poles are moved inward, away from the unit circle and toward the origin (Jackson et al., 1978; Kay, 1979).

There are no sure-fire solutions to these problems. The most common recourses involve preprocessing the speech to attenuate the noise or applying corrections to the autocorrelation estimates: these will be discussed in greater detail in Chapter 13. Kay (1980) describes a method for correcting the reflection coefficients; this offers the advantages that stability is easy to guarantee and that the corrections can, in principle, be tailored to the individual reflection coefficients.

Autocorrelation Method Details

We said initially that the autocorrelation method assumes a stationary, infinite sequence that has been "windowed." Experiments with autocorrelation-based predictors show that the window shape affects the values of the predictor coefficients obtained and the appearance of the spectrum envelope. In particular, if we use the rectangular window implied by our basic autocorrelation definition (6-9), the side-lobes of its transform will frequently mask the higher formants. This is true of the spectrum taken from the DFT of the time series itself and of the spectrum envelope as well. Hence the autocorrelation method requires a window that will suppress the side-lobes; the Hamming window is probably the one most commonly used. (This problem does not arise with the Burg and covariance methods.)

Covariance Method Details

We mentioned that an extra p samples had to be prefixed to the N-sample window in order to evaluate (6-7b) for c_{00} through c_{pp}. Presumably one could avoid this necessity by defining c_{ij} as

$$\sum_{n=p}^{N-1} y(n-i)y(n-j)$$

but in practice, the extra p samples are taken from the end of the previous time window. This has the virtue that every point in the time series makes an equal contribution to the predictors: points at the end of one frame which are omitted from some values of c_{ij} are included in those values when they are prepended to the subsequent frame.

General

When digitizing data for linear prediction, the usual precautions concerning aliasing must be observed. Digitized data are frequently differenced before being passed to the prediction programs, in order (1) to ensure that there is no dc component present and (2) to preemphasize the high-frequency regions of the signal. As an alternative, many processing programs will compute and remove the dc value in one step and in a subsequent step will apply high-frequency preemphasis, typically at 6 dB per octave with a corner frequency between 800 Hz and 1 kHz.

PROJECTS

6-1 Get the LPC programs up and running on a system available to you.

6-2 Investigate the possibility of further subdividing LPCA into subprograms which (a) compute the autocorrelation function, (b) find the reflection coefficients, and (c) do Levinson recursion.

6-3 Write a computer program which implements the lattice filters of Figs. 6-7 and 6-9.

6-4 Write a version of the Choleski decomposition which factors **C** into $\mathbf{QQ}^T$. Notice that it is not necessary to store the entire matrix in this case, and the upper or lower triangular part can be stored in condensed form. Implement this in your program and compare its complexity with that of LPCC.

6-5 Implement Atal's procedure for obtaining reflection coefficients from the LU decomposition. Compare the results obtained in this way with those from LPCA.

6-6 Speech data are generally acquired and stored as two's-complement binary integers; LPC programs usually employ floating-point arithmetic. Explore and evaluate the possible points at which the conversion from fixed- to floating-point data can be made and compare the speed, storage requirements, and accuracy of the alternatives.

6-7 Investigate the techniques for representing binary fractions using fixed-point numbers. Write a version of the Schur algorithm which uses fixed-point arithmetic throughout.

PROBLEMS

6-1 Show that for an autocorrelation predictor of order $p = 1$, $a_1(1) = -r_1/r_0$.

6-2 Derive the recursion relations corresponding to (6-19) for the reverse predictor of Sec. 6-5.

6-3 Prove (a) that $|k_i| \leq 1$; (b) that if $|k_p| = 1$, then the order-p predictor is perfect and all higher-order predictors will be the same; that is,

$$a_{p+n}(i) = \begin{cases} a_p(i), & i \leq p \\ 0, & i > p \end{cases}$$

6-4 Derive the autocorrelation normal equations by differentiating

$$E = \mathbf{a}^T \mathbf{R} \mathbf{a}$$

with respect to the vector **a**.

6-5 We are now in a position to relate the piecewise-cylindrical model of the vocal tract to the equivalent filter, $1/A(z)$. The following cross-sectional areas (in arbitrary units) are given for the model:

$$S_0 = 5.70 \quad S_4 = 1.85 \quad S_8 = 12.36$$
$$S_1 = 3.03 \quad S_5 = 4.12 \quad S_9 = 7.27$$
$$S_2 = 1.56 \quad S_6 = 8.77 \quad S_{10} = 3.52$$
$$S_3 = 1.35 \quad S_7 = 13.42 \quad S_{11} = 1.85$$
$$S_{12} = 1.50$$

(a) Find the reflection coefficients.
(b) Use the Levinson recursion to find the predictor coefficients.
(c) Find the roots of the polynomial, if you have access to a program for doing so.
(d) Find and plot the spectrum envelope.

6-6 If $A(z)$ has a quadratic factor $(1 + bz^{-1} + cz^{-2})$ with complex roots, show that $1/A(z)$ has a pole with frequency and bandwidth given by

$$f = \frac{f_s}{2\pi} \cos^{-1}\left(\frac{-b}{2\sqrt{c}}\right)$$

$$\text{BW} = \frac{-f_s}{\pi} \ln c$$

6-7 (a) Show that in the LU decomposition, the pth element of κ is the last order-p predictor coefficient: i.e., that $\kappa_p = a_p(p)$.
(b) Show that if LU decomposition is used to solve the autocorrelation equations, the κ_i values will be the reflection coefficients.

6-8 Show that if LU decomposition is used to solve the autocorrelation equations, the diagonal elements of **L** will contain the prediction errors: specifically,

$$s_{ii} = E_{i-1}$$

6-9 The following autocorrelation data are given:

i	r_i	i	r_i
0	1.0000	4	-0.2222
1	0.8404	5	-0.2174
2	0.4492	6	0.0083
3	0.0300	7	0.3322

Verify the results of the preceding problems by solving the autocorrelation equations (a) by the recursion of Sec. 6-4 and (b) using LU decomposition. Compare the values of the reflection coefficients obtained in (a) with the **k** vector obtained in (b).

Note: If this problem is done on the computer, use extended-precision arithmetic; otherwise roundoff errors may interfere with the comparison of (a) and (b).

6-10 Derive an inverse Levinson recursion which will accept a vector of predictor coefficients as input and will compute the reflection coefficients which gave rise to them.

REFERENCES

Atal, B. S.: Linear prediction of speech—recent advances with applications to speech analysis, in D. R. Reddy (Ed.), *Speech Recognition: Invited Papers Delivered at the 1974 IEEE Symposium*, Academic Press, New York, pp. 221–230, 1975.
———: On determining partial correlation coefficients by the covariance method of linear prediction, *JASA*, vol. 62, suppl. 1, p.s64, Fall, 1977.
——— and S. L. Hanauer: Speech analysis and synthesis by linear prediction of the speech wave, *JASA*, vol. 50, no. 2, pp. 637–655, August, 1971.
——— and M. R. Schroeder: Predictive coding of speech signals and subjective error criteria, *IEEE Trans.*, vol. ASSP-27, no. 3, pp. 247–254, June, 1979.
Barnwell III, T. P.: Windowless techniques for LPC analysis, *IEEE Trans.*, vol. ASSP-28, no. 4, pp. 421–427, August, 1980.
Burg, J. P.: Maximum entropy spectral analysis, PhD Thesis, Stanford University, May, 1975.
Chandra, S., and W. C. Lin.: Experimental comparison between stationary and nonstationary formulations of linear prediction applied to voiced speech analysis, *IEEE Trans.*, vol. ASSP-22, no. 6, pp. 403–416, December, 1974.
Gibson, J. D.: On reflection coefficients and the Cholesky decomposition, *IEEE Trans.*, vol. ASSP-25, no. 1, pp. 93–96, February, 1977.
Gray, Jr., A. H., and J. D. Markel: A spectral-flatness measure for studying the autocorrelation method of linear prediction speech analysis, *IEEE Trans.*, vol. ASSP-22, no. 3, pp. 207–217, June, 1974.
——— and D. Y. Wong: The Burg algorithm for LPC speech analysis, *IEEE Trans.*, vol. ASSP-28, no. 6, pp. 609–615, December, 1980.
Itakura, F.: Minimum prediction residual principle applied to speech recognition, *IEEE Trans.*, vol. ASSP-23, no. 1, pp. 67–72, February, 1975.
——— and S. Saito: A statistical method for estimation of speech spectral density and formant frequencies, *Electron. Commun. Japan*, vol. 53-A, pp. 36–43, 1970.
——— and ———: On the optimum quantization of feature parameters in the PARCOR speech synthesizer, *Proc. 1972 Conf. Speech Commun. Process.*, pp. 434–437, 1972.
———, et al.: An audio response unit based on partial autocorrelation, *IEEE Trans.*, vol. COM-20, no. 4, pp. 792–797, August, 1972.
Jackson, L. B., et al.: Frequency estimation by linear prediction, *Proc. ICASSP-78*, IEEE Press, New York, 1978.
Kay, S. M.: The effects of noise on the autoregressive spectral estimator, *IEEE Trans.*, vol. ASSP-27, no. 5, pp. 478–485, October, 1979.
———: Noise compensation for autoregressive spectral estimates, *IEEE Trans.*, vol. ASSP-28, no. 3, pp. 292–303, June, 1980.
——— and S. L. Marple, Jr.: Spectrum analysis—a modern perspective, *Proc. IEEE*, vol. 69, no. 11, pp. 1380–1419, November, 1981.
Le Roux, J., and C. Guegen: A fixed point computation of partial correlation coefficients in linear prediction, *Proc. ICASSP-77*, IEEE Press, New York, pp. 742–743, 1977.
Makhoul, J. I.: Spectral analysis of speech by linear prediction, *IEEE Trans.*, vol. AU-21, no. 3, pp. 140–149, June, 1973.
———: Linear prediction: a tutorial review, *Proc. IEEE*, vol. 63, no. 4, pp. 561–580, April, 1975(*a*).
———: Spectral linear prediction: properties and applications, *IEEE Trans.*, vol. ASSP-23, no. 3, pp. 283–296, June, 1975(*b*).
———: Linear prediction in automatic speech recognition, in D. R. Reddy (Ed.), *Speech Recognition*, Academic Press, New York, pp. 183–220, 1975(*c*).
———: Stable and efficient lattice methods for linear prediction, *IEEE Trans.*, vol. ASSP-25, no. 5, pp. 423–428, October, 1977.
——— and J. J. Wolf: Linear prediction and the spectral analysis of speech, Bolt, Beranek, &

Newman, Inc., Report No. 2304, August, 1972 (available from NTIS: no. AD 749 066).

Markel, J. D.: FFT pruning, *IEEE Trans.*, vol. AU-19, no. 4, pp. 305–312, December, 1971.

————: Digital inverse filtering—a new tool for formant trajectory estimation, *IEEE Trans.*, vol. AU-20, no. 2, pp. 129–138, June, 1972.

———— and A. H. Gray, Jr.: On autocorrelation equations as applied to speech analysis, *IEEE Trans.*, vol. AU-21, no. 2, pp. 69–80, April, 1973.

———— and ————: Fixed-point truncation arithmetic implementation of a linear prediction autocorrelation vocoder, *IEEE Trans.*, vol. ASSP-22, no. 4, pp. 273–282, August, 1974.

———— and ————: *Linear Prediction of Speech*, Springer-Verlag, New York, 1976.

Marple, L.: A new autoregressive spectrum analysis algorithm, *IEEE Trans.*, vol. ASSP-28, no. 4, pp. 441–454, August, 1980.

Morf, M., *et al.*: General speech models and linear estimation theory, in D. R. Reddy (Ed.), *Speech Recognition*, Academic Press, New York, pp. 157, 182, 1975.

————, *et al.*: A classification of algorithms for ARMA models and ladder realizations, *Proc. ICASSP-77*, IEEE Press, New York, pp. 13–19, 1977(a).

————, *et al.*: Efficient solution of covariance equations for linear prediction, *IEEE Trans.*, vol. ASSP-25, no. 5, pp. 429–433, October, 1977(b).

Papoulis, A.: Maximum entropy and spectral estimation: a review, *IEEE Trans.*, vol. ASSP-29, no. 6, pp. 1176–1186, December, 1981.

————: *Probability, Random Variables, and Stochastic Processes*, McGraw-Hill, New York, 1984.

Rabiner, L. R., and R. W. Schafer: *Digital Processing of Speech Signals*, Prentice-Hall, Englewood Cliffs, 1978.

Robinson, E. A., and S. Treitel: Maximum entropy and the relationship of the partial autocorrelation to the reflection coefficients of a layered system, *IEEE Trans.*, vol. ASSP-28, no. 2, pp. 224–235, April, 1980.

Sambur, M. R., and N. S. Jayant: LPC analysis/synthesis from speech inputs containing quantizing noise or additive white noise, *IEEE Trans.*, vol. ASSP-24, no. 6, pp. 488–494, December, 1976.

Schafer, R. W., and L. R. Rabiner: Parametric representations of speech, in D. R. Reddy (Ed.), *Speech Recognition*, Academic Press, New York, pp. 99–150, 1975.

Schur, J.: *J. fur die Reine und Angew. Math.*, vol. 147, pp. 205–232, 1917.

Tierney, J.: A study of LPC analysis of speech in additive noise, *IEEE Trans.*, vol. ASSP-28, no. 4, pp. 389–397, August, 1980.

Wakita, H.: Direct estimation of the vocal-tract shape by inverse filtering of acoustic speech waveforms, *IEEE Trans.*, vol. AU-21, no. 5, pp. 417–427, October, 1973.

————: Estimation of vocal-tract shapes from acoustical analysis of the speech wave: the state of the art, *IEEE Trans.*, vol. ASSP-27, no. 3, pp. 281–285, June, 1979.

———— and A. H. Gray, Jr.: Numerical determination of the lip impedance and vocal-tract area functions, *IEEE Trans.*, vol. ASSP-23, no. 6, pp. 574–580, December, 1975.

CHAPTER
SEVEN

RECOGNITION: FEATURES AND DISTANCES

Two important application areas in speech processing are speech recognition and speaker recognition. Both of these are problems in *pattern recognition*. Pattern recognition is a large and varied field in its own right; in this chapter, we will take up only those aspects of pattern recognition which bear on speech processing and which have appeared to a significant extent in the literature. These aspects are *feature evaluation* and *distance measurement*. (We will also touch briefly on the topic of clustering.) For a thorough grounding in pattern recognition, the reader should consult the References at the end of this chapter, especially the books by Fukunaga (1972) and by Tou and Gonzalez (1974).

7-1 INTRODUCTION TO PATTERN RECOGNITION

In pattern recognition, comparison is made between a *test pattern*, representing the unknown to be recognized or identified, and one or more *reference patterns* which characterize known items.

Each pattern takes the form of a vector; each element in the vector is the measured value of some *feature*. (A feature is some measurable characteristic of the input which has been found to be useful for recognition.) In many isolated-word recognition systems, the pattern takes the form of a set of time functions—i.e., values for each feature are recorded over the length of the word rather than at particular points; such patterns are often called *templates*.

A recognition system operates like this: suppose we have a talker-recognition system for 50 talkers. When a word or test phrase is spoken, the system processes the sound, extracts features (i.e., isolates and measures them), and forms a test pattern. The system has a *library* of 50 reference patterns, one for each talker. Comparison is made to all patterns in the library and the talker whose reference pattern is the best match to the test pattern is taken to be the identity of the unknown talker.

Since automatic recognition systems may in general be applied to many kinds of unknown besides words and talkers, we will follow the custom of referring to *classes* of unknown (instead of words or talkers). For example, in a digit-recognition system, the classes are the words, {"zero," "one," "two," "three," ..., "nine"}. The system maintains a library of patterns, one for each class, and in the recognition process it assigns the unknown to a particular class on the basis of its similarity to the corresponding pattern.

Recognition system operation typically consists of two phases:

1. *Learning* (also called *training*): compilation of the library of reference patterns
2. *Recognition:* use of the completed library with unknown inputs

In learning, data for known classes are fed to the system; the system forms a reference pattern or template for each class by averaging many patterns and files the reference in the library under the given class. In recognition, the system computes the pattern of features for the unknown input and identifies the input with the class whose reference pattern matches these features most closely.

The design of a recognition system generally centers around two problems:

1. Feature selection and evaluation
2. Choice of decision rule

The first problem is the more important and the more difficult. We will start by considering the second problem, however, because it will introduce a number of concepts on which we will draw when discussing feature selection.

This summary is greatly simplified and intended only as an introduction. Speech recognition, in particular, requires solving many more problems than just the two listed above. To cite just one example, the unknown and reference must be properly aligned in time before a comparison can be made. Until recently, no satisfactory solution to this problem was known and performance of recognition systems suffered in consequence. Solutions to this problem, however, will be taken up in Chapter 11 rather than here.

7-2 DECISION RULES AND DISTANCE MEASURES

Patterns are vectors of features and thus span a multidimensional vector space which we will call feature space. The pattern vectors are usually assumed to have multivariate gaussian densities. Features are not often gaussian, but this assumption leads to the most tractable and well-understood mathematics, and in many cases the data are too scanty to justify any other assumption. In practical applications the densities associated with different classes overlap. This overlap is a source of recognition errors and it explains why both decision rules and feature evaluation must be based on statistical considerations

Given an unknown feature vector **f**, we will write the probability that it represents word i as $P[i|\mathbf{f}]$ (the probability of word i given the feature vector **f**). Given any two words i and k, we decide we have received word i rather than word k if $P[i|\mathbf{f}] > P[k|\mathbf{f}]$, or if $P[i|\mathbf{f}]/P[k|\mathbf{f}] > 1$. Now the learning process gives us only the statistics of each word's features, and from these we can only determine $P[\mathbf{f}|i]$, the probability that word i has given rise to the features **f**.

At first glance, these two probabilities may seem to be saying the same thing, but careful thought will show that they are not. One works from the observed features to the presumed word and the other works from the presumed word to the observed features; we must take some trouble to show that we can use $P[\mathbf{f}|i]$ as well as $P[i|\mathbf{f}]$.

Conditional probabilities are related by Bayes' theorem, which we stated in Chapter 2:

$$P[i|\mathbf{f}] = P[\mathbf{f}|i] \frac{P[i]}{P[\mathbf{f}]}$$

It is customary to assume that all words are equally likely (so $P[i] = P[k]$). Then

$$\frac{P[i|\mathbf{f}]}{P[k|\mathbf{f}]} = \frac{P[\mathbf{f}|i]}{P[\mathbf{f}|k]}$$

because the $P[\mathbf{f}]$'s cancel. Therefore, our rule is, for any unknown feature vector **f**, choose the word that maximizes $P[\mathbf{f}|i]$.

Pattern vectors for each word are assumed to be multivariate-gaussian, unless we have definite evidence to the contrary. Let $\mathbf{f}_i$ be a vector of m features associated with word i, and let $\bar{\mathbf{f}}_i$ be the mean of all $\mathbf{f}_i$. Then we will write the probability density for word i as

$$f_i(\mathbf{f}) = (2\pi)^{-m/2} |\mathbf{R}_i|^{-1/2} \exp[-\tfrac{1}{2}(\mathbf{f} - \bar{\mathbf{f}}_i)^T \mathbf{R}_i^{-1}(\mathbf{f} - \bar{\mathbf{f}}_i)] \qquad (7\text{-}1)$$

where $\mathbf{R}_i$ is the covariance matrix for feature i. We can now say that $P[\mathbf{f}|i] > P[\mathbf{f}|k]$ if $f_i(\mathbf{f}) > f_k(\mathbf{f})$. Hence we choose that i which maximizes $f_i(\mathbf{f})$ over all i. For computational simplicity, we can as well maximize $\ln[f_i(\mathbf{f})]$. Furthermore, we can ignore the constant factor of $(2\pi)^{-m/2}$. Hence we seek to maximize

$$\ln\{|\mathbf{R}_i|^{-1/2} \exp[-\tfrac{1}{2}(\mathbf{f} - \bar{\mathbf{f}}_i)^T \mathbf{R}_i^{-1}(\mathbf{f} - \bar{\mathbf{f}}_i)]\}$$

or, dropping the minus signs and the factor of $\tfrac{1}{2}$, to *minimize* the "distance,"

$$D_i(\mathbf{f}) = (\mathbf{f} - \bar{\mathbf{f}}_i)^T \mathbf{R}_i^{-1}(\mathbf{f} - \bar{\mathbf{f}}_i) + \ln|\mathbf{R}_i| \qquad (7\text{-}2)$$

This is the basic *maximum-likelihood* criterion.

We will see shortly that this measure gives rise to a number of related likelihood estimates. However, since we have brought up the word distance, this is the appropriate point to observe that a distance measure $d(x, y)$ is strictly required to have the following characteristics (Duda and Hart, 1973):

1. Nonnegativity: $d(x, y) \geq 0$ with equality only for $x = y$.
2. Symmetry: $d(x, y) = d(y, x)$.
3. The triangle inequality: $d(x, z) \leq d(x, y) + d(y, z)$.

We wrote distance in quotation marks above since $D_i(\mathbf{f}_i) = \ln |\mathbf{R}_i|$, which may not be zero, and therefore (7-2) is not a distance by this definition. The point here is that it is desirable, for both intuitive and analytic reasons, for a distance to bear a general similarity to the intuitive concept of distance in euclidean space.

Given a suitable distance measure, there are two ways of using it. We can partition the feature space into regions, one for each class, and define the boundaries by hyperplanes or other surfaces. A great deal of the pattern-recognition literature is devoted to ways of finding these boundary surfaces. The alternative is simply to compute the distance from the unknown input to the centroid of each class and select the class for which the distance is a minimum. In speech and talker recognition, the latter procedure is almost universally used. The computational load is no greater than for finding boundary surfaces.

Simplified Distance Measures

The maximum-likelihood criterion is rarely used in the form given in (7-2), for two reasons. First, many recognition systems are developed on a data base of limited size, and from a limited-size data base we cannot generally get reliable estimates of the **R** matrices. Second, using the maximum-likelihood measure in its exact form is not nearly as important to good recognition performance as making an intelligent choice of features in the first place. Since computational resources are generally limited, it is preferable to deploy them where they will bring the greatest return. Hence in practice we back down to one of the following simplifications:

1. Assume that the features are uncorrelated. Then $\mathbf{R} = \text{diag}(\sigma_{i1}^2, \sigma_{i2}^2, \ldots)$ and $\mathbf{R}_i^{-1} = \text{diag}(1/\sigma_{i1}^2, 1/\sigma_{i2}^2, \ldots)$. In that case,

$$D_i(\mathbf{f}) = \sum_{j=1}^{m} \left(\frac{f_j - \bar{f}_{ij}}{\sigma_{ij}} \right)^2 + 2 \ln \sigma_{ij} \qquad (7\text{-}3)$$

where f_j is the jth element of $\mathbf{f}$, $\bar{f}_{ij}$ is the jth element of $\bar{\mathbf{f}}_i$, and σ_{ij} is the (j, j) element of $\mathbf{R}_i$.

2. Assume that $\mathbf{R}_i$ is the same for all words. Then $\ln |\mathbf{R}|$ is constant and can be ignored:

$$D_i(\mathbf{f}) = (\mathbf{f} - \bar{\mathbf{f}}_i)^T \mathbf{R}^{-1} (\mathbf{f} - \bar{\mathbf{f}}_i) \qquad (7\text{-}4)$$

This is one of the most frequently used distance measures. It is often referred to as the Mahalanobis (1936) distance.

3. Combine assumptions 1 and 2. Then $\mathbf{R} = \mathrm{diag}\,(\sigma_1^2, \sigma_2^2, \ldots)$ and

$$D_i(\mathbf{f}) = \sum_{j=1}^{m} \left(\frac{f_j - f_{ij}}{\sigma_j}\right)^2 \tag{7-5}$$

This is known as the weighted (or normalized) euclidean distance.

4. Assume all of the above, and assume that all features have equal variances. Then we get the euclidean distance

$$D_i(\mathbf{f}) = \sum_{j=1}^{m} (f_j - f_{ij})^2 \tag{7-6}$$

(The euclidean distance as we normally use the term is, of course, the square root of this quantity.)

5. Some authors use only the middle term of the weighted euclidean distance. The expression for this distance can be expanded as

$$D_i(\mathbf{f}) = \sum_j \left(\frac{f_j}{\sigma_{ij}}\right)^2 - 2\sum_j \frac{f_j f_{ij}}{\sigma_{ij}} + \sum_j \left(\frac{f_{ij}}{\sigma_{ij}}\right)^2$$

and the middle term is the correlation between unknown and reference as

$$D_i(\mathbf{f}) = -\sum_j \frac{f_j f_{ij}}{\sigma_{ij}} \tag{7-7}$$

LPC-Based Distance Measures

In speech and talker recognition, the predictor coefficients are frequently among the features used. In this case, the prediction error can be used to test similarity, since the error is a minimum when the predictor matches the applied speech. Two formulations are of particular interest.

The Itakura-Saito measure A derivation of linear prediction by Itakura and Saito (1970) is based on an approximate maximum-likelihood formulation. Given a vector $\mathbf{x}$, their derivation seeks that predictor vector $\mathbf{a}$ which maximizes the likelihood of $\mathbf{x}$ given $\mathbf{a}$. As we mentioned in Chapter 6, they show that maximizing the likelihood of $\mathbf{x}$ given $\mathbf{a}$ is equivalent to minimizing the integral

$$D(\mathbf{x}, \mathbf{a}) = \frac{1}{2\pi} \int_{-\pi}^{\pi} [\ln P(\theta) + P(\theta) - 1]\, d\theta$$

where $P(\theta)$ is the ratio between the spectrum of the input and the spectrum of the predictor. It can be shown (Markel and Gray, 1976) that this integral is given by

$$D(\mathbf{x}, \mathbf{a}) = \frac{E}{\sigma^2} + \ln \frac{\sigma^2}{E_\infty} - 1$$

where σ is the predictor gain factor, E is the error output power when $\mathbf{x}$ is applied to $\mathbf{a}$, and E_∞ is the infinite-order prediction error given by Eq. (6-46). This measure has been used in speech recognition and in the vector quantization technique pioneered by Buzo et al. (1980) and described in Chapter 10.

Itakura's minimum-prediction residual The prediction error itself has also been used as a measure of difference. Recall that for a given autocorrelation matrix **R** and a predictor-coefficient vector **a**, the prediction error is given by

$$E = \mathbf{a}^T \mathbf{R} \mathbf{a}$$

(This was shown in Sec. 6-4.) Then if **a** is the optimum predictor and **b** is any predictor at all,

$$\frac{\mathbf{b}^T \mathbf{R} \mathbf{b}}{\mathbf{a}^T \mathbf{R} \mathbf{a}} \geq 1 \tag{7-8}$$

with equality only for **b** = **a**. Therefore we might expect this ratio to serve as a test for the difference between **a** and **b**.

Itakura (1975) has carried this reasoning further by showing that in fact the likelihood that an unknown word is word *i* is given by the log of (7-8), or

$$\ln(\mathbf{b}^T \mathbf{R} \mathbf{b}) - \ln(\mathbf{a}^T \mathbf{R} \mathbf{a})$$

where **b** is the prediction vector for the unknown word and **R** and **a** belong to word *i*. The rule of choosing that word which minimizes (7-8) is known as the *minimum-prediction residual principle*.

7-3 FEATURE SELECTION

Input data to any recognizer consist of a mix of relevant and irrelevant information. Feature selection is the process of jettisoning as much irrelevant information as possible and representing relevant data in compact and meaningful form. For example, any utterance contains information about the words being spoken and also about the identity of the speaker. In a speech-recognition system we wish to select the first type of feature and ignore the second; in a speaker-recognition system we wish to do just the opposite.

It is obviously of the utmost importance to select features with great care; this is the chief design function in most pattern recognizers. Ideally, features selected should meet the following criteria:

1. Varying widely from class to class
2. Insensitive to extraneous variables (i.e., text, context, health and emotional state of talker, system transmission characteristics, etc.)
3. Stable over long periods of time
4. Frequently occurring
5. Easy to measure
6. Not correlated with other features

It is generally impossible to find features which meet all of these requirements at once, and compromises are inevitable.

Features are usually selected intuitively. One reason for studying anatomy, phonetics, etc., is to lay the groundwork for that intuition. Much published material deals with features which some researcher thought *ought* to be good. One group tried to mechanize the entire feature-selection process—pick out features at random and cull them statistically (Andrews *et al.*, 1968). This was a failure; the problem is that the number of *possible* features is vast and the number of *good* ones is limited, so the probability of finding good ones by chance is virtually nil.

7-4 FEATURE EVALUATION

After features are selected, we must try them out and see how well they separate the different classes. This is usually done by statistical evaluation on a body of test data. A feature is judged by how well it separates recognition classes from one another. There are many measures of separability; we will consider only a small number here. We start by considering measures for evaluating a single feature and then proceed to ways of evaluating a set of features.

Fisher's Discriminant; The *F* Ratio

The ability of a feature to separate two classes depends on the distance between classes and the scatter within classes. Suppose we have a two-word word-recognition system and are evaluating two possible features, V_1 and V_2. We make a large number of measurements and find the distributions sketched in Fig. 7-1. The features are not ideal characterizations of the words, so there is some extraneous variation resulting in a certain degree of scatter in the measurements.

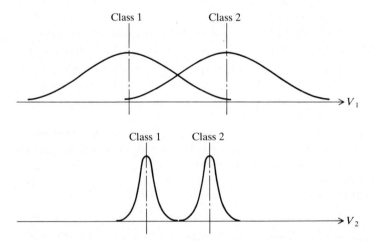

Figure 7-1 Performance of a recognition feature depends on the class-to-class difference relative to the scatter within classes; feature V_2 is superior to V_1 in spite of the fact that the means of the two classes are farther apart for V_1.

Clearly, although the means of V_1 are more widely separated, V_2 is better at separating the two classes, because there is no overlap between the distributions. Overlap depends on two things: (1) the distance between distributions for the two classes and (2) the width of (i.e., scatter within) the distributions. A reasonable way to characterize this numerically would be to take the ratio of the difference of the means to the standard deviation of the measurements—or, since there are two sets of measurements, to find the average of the two standard deviations. Fisher's discriminant is based on this principle: if the results for the two classes have means μ_1 and μ_2 and variances σ_1^2 and σ_2^2, then

$$f = \frac{(\mu_1 - \mu_2)^2}{\sigma_1^2 + \sigma_2^2} \qquad (7\text{-}9)$$

Generally there will be many more than two classes. In that case, we consider the class-to-class separation of the feature over all classes. We estimate this separation by representing each class by its mean and taking the variance of the means. This variance is then compared to the average width of the distribution for each class—i.e., the mean of the individual variances. This measure is commonly called the F ratio:

$$F = \frac{\text{variance of the means (over all classes)}}{\text{mean of the variances (within classes)}}$$

If we have n measurements for each of m different classes, then

$$F = \frac{1/(m-1) \sum_{j=1}^{m} (\mu_j - \bar{\mu})^2}{1/m(n-1) \sum_{j=1}^{m} \sum_{i=1}^{n} (x_{ij} - \mu_j)^2} \qquad (7\text{-}10)$$

where x_{ij} = ith measurement for class j
μ_j = mean of all measurements for class j
$\bar{\mu}$ = mean of all measurements over all classes

Note that when $m = 2$, Eq. (7-10) reduces to Fisher's discriminant; for this reason the F ratio is also referred to as the generalized Fisher's discriminant. Notice also that a high F ratio says only that the scatter among classes tends, on the average, to be greater than the spread for each class. It does not guarantee that none of the distributions will overlap.

The F ratio is used for evaluating a single feature. In practice, we need many features. When many potential features are to be evaluated, it is not safe just to rank features by the F ratio and pick the best ones for use unless all the features are uncorrelated (which, we may assume, they never are). There are two possible responses to this problem, both of which are found in the speech-processing literature:

1. Use various techniques for evaluating combinations of features.
2. Transform features into independent ones and then pick the best ones in the transformed space.

Measures of Separability

The solutions we will consider are all generalizations of one kind or another of the *F*-ratio concept. Recall that the covariance matrix of a random vector **x** is

$$C = \langle (\mathbf{x} - \bar{\mathbf{x}})(\mathbf{x} - \bar{\mathbf{x}})^T \rangle$$

In the case of pattern recognition, we have vectors of features, **f**, and we accumulate observed values of **f** for all the classes we are interested in recognizing. Then we can form two covariance matrices, depending on how we group our data.

First, we can find the covariance for a single recognition class, selecting only feature measurements for class *i*. Let any vector from this class be $\mathbf{f}_i$. Then the *intraclass* covariance matrix for class *i* is

$$\mathbf{W}_i = \langle (\mathbf{f}_i - \bar{\mathbf{f}}_i)(\mathbf{f}_i - \bar{\mathbf{f}}_i)^T \rangle \qquad (7\text{-}11)$$

where $\bar{\mathbf{f}}_i$ represents the mean vector for the *i*th class: $\bar{\mathbf{f}}_i = \langle \mathbf{f}_i \rangle$. (*W* stands for "within.") Notice that each of these covariance matrices describes the scatter within a class; hence it corresponds to one term of the average in the denominator of (7-10). If we make the common assumption that the vector $\mathbf{f}_i$ is normally distributed, then **W** is the covariance matrix of the corresponding density function:

$$f_i(\mathbf{f}) = (2\pi)^{-m/2} |\mathbf{W}_i|^{-1/2} \exp\left[-\tfrac{1}{2}(\mathbf{f} - \bar{\mathbf{f}}_i)^T \mathbf{W}_i^{-1}(\mathbf{f} - \bar{\mathbf{f}}_i)\right]$$

Then we can associate the denominator of the *F* ratio with the average of $\mathbf{W}_i$ over all *i*; we call this the pooled intraclass covariance matrix:

$$\mathbf{W} = \langle \mathbf{W}_i \rangle \qquad (7\text{-}12)$$

Second, we can ignore variation within classes and find the covariance between classes, representing each class by its centroid. The feature centroid for class *i* is $\bar{\mathbf{f}}_i$; hence the *interclass* covariance matrix is

$$\mathbf{B} = \langle (\bar{\mathbf{f}}_i - \bar{\mathbf{f}})(\bar{\mathbf{f}}_i - \bar{\mathbf{f}})^T \rangle \qquad (7\text{-}13)$$

where $\bar{\mathbf{f}}$ is the mean of $\mathbf{f}_i$ over all classes. Here we are ignoring the detailed distribution within each class and representing all the data for that class by its mean. Hence **B** describes the scatter from class to class regardless of the scatter within a class and in that sense corresponds to the numerator of (7-10). (*B* stands for "between.")

Then the generalization we seek should involve a ratio in which the numerator is based on **B** and the denominator on **W**, since we are looking for features with small covariances within classes and large covariances between classes. Fukunaga (1972) lists four such measures:

$$J_1 = \operatorname{tr}(\mathbf{W}^{-1}\mathbf{B})$$

$$J_2 = |\mathbf{W}^{-1}\mathbf{B}| = \frac{|\mathbf{B}|}{|\mathbf{W}|}$$

$$J_3 = \operatorname{tr}\mathbf{B} - \mu(\operatorname{tr}\mathbf{W} - c)$$

$$J_4 = \frac{\operatorname{tr}\mathbf{B}}{\operatorname{tr}\mathbf{W}}$$

Some authors use $\ln(|\mathbf{B}|/|\mathbf{W}|)$ for J_2.

The motivation for these measures is probably clearest in the case of J_3 and J_4. We will see, when we take up transformations, that the trace of a covariance matrix provides a measure of the total variance of its associated variables. If tr $\mathbf{B}$ > tr $\mathbf{W}$, then there is apparently more scatter between classes than within classes, and the feature set is a good one. J_4 tests this ratio directly; the same logic lies behind J_3, except that here we seek to maximize tr $\mathbf{B}$ while holding tr $\mathbf{W}$ constant; μ is a Lagrange multiplier.

The motivation for J_1 and J_2 is less obvious and will have to await the presentation of new material below. Note that for a single feature, J_1 reduces to the F ratio. Note also that J_1 and J_2 are invariant under any reasonable (i.e., nonsingular) rotation or scaling of the coordinate system, while J_3 and J_4 are invariant under rotations only. This point is of interest because the transformations we will presently consider involve rotation and, in one case, scaling of the coordinates.

Figure 7-2 shows the scatter diagram of four classes as measured by two features. For these data, the J_1, J_2, and J_4 measures are:

$$J_1 = 3.529$$
$$J_2 = \ln(1.863) = 0.622$$
$$J_4 = 1.134$$

(Note that for J_2, the breakeven point is zero, while for J_1 and J_4 it is unity.)

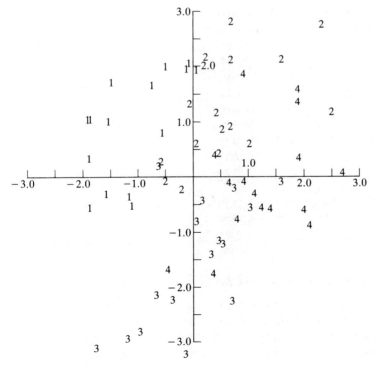

Figure 7-2 Scatter diagram for four classes as measured by two features, f_1 and f_2.

The divergence The divergence (Kullback, 1959) between two classes is defined as the difference in the expected values of their log-likelihood ratios:

$$D_{ik} = \int_{\mathbf{f}} p(\mathbf{f}|i) \ln \frac{p(\mathbf{f}|i)}{p(\mathbf{f}|k)} d\mathbf{f} - \int_{\mathbf{f}} p(\mathbf{f}|k) \ln \frac{p(\mathbf{f}|i)}{p(\mathbf{f}|k)} d\mathbf{f}$$

where the integrals are taken over the entire feature space. This measure has its roots in information theory (see Kullback, 1959) and is a measure of the average amount of information available for discriminating between class i and class k. Kullback shows that for features with multivariate normal densities, the divergence is given by

$$D_{ik} = \tfrac{1}{2} \operatorname{tr}(\mathbf{W}_i - \mathbf{W}_k)(\mathbf{W}_i^{-1} - \mathbf{W}_k^{-1}) + \tfrac{1}{2} \operatorname{tr}[(\mathbf{W}_i^{-1} + \mathbf{W}_k^{-1})(\bar{\mathbf{f}}_i - \bar{\mathbf{f}}_k)(\bar{\mathbf{f}}_i - \bar{\mathbf{f}}_k)^T]$$

(7-14)

We can relate this to more familiar material as follows. If the covariance matrices of the two classes are equal, or if we can replace $\mathbf{W}_i$ and $\mathbf{W}_k$ by an average covariance matrix $\mathbf{W}$, then the first term vanishes and the divergence reduces to

$$D_{ik} = \operatorname{tr}[\mathbf{W}^{-1}(\bar{\mathbf{f}}_i - \bar{\mathbf{f}}_k)(\bar{\mathbf{f}}_i - \bar{\mathbf{f}}_k)^T]$$
$$= (\bar{\mathbf{f}}_i - \bar{\mathbf{f}}_k)^T \mathbf{W}^{-1} (\bar{\mathbf{f}}_i - \bar{\mathbf{f}}_k)$$

In the case of more than two classes, we can average the divergence over all pairs of classes. If $D = \langle D_{ik} \rangle$, then

$$D = \operatorname{tr}[\mathbf{W}^{-1} \langle (\bar{\mathbf{f}}_i - \bar{\mathbf{f}}_k)(\bar{\mathbf{f}}_i - \bar{\mathbf{f}}_k)^T \rangle]$$

This average, $\langle (\bar{\mathbf{f}}_i - \bar{\mathbf{f}}_k)(\bar{\mathbf{f}}_i - \bar{\mathbf{f}}_k)^T \rangle$, is the interclass covariance matrix $\mathbf{B}$; hence in this case D reduces to our separability measure $J_1 = \operatorname{tr}(\mathbf{W}^{-1}\mathbf{B})$. [Some authors in fact call J_1 the divergence; we prefer to reserve that term for (7-14).]

Subset Selection

The purpose of feature evaluation is ultimately to decide which of a large number of possible features to include and which to ignore. That is, if we have an initial set of N possible features under consideration, we wish to select the subset of k features which will yield the best recognition performance. The only sure way to find the best subset is to consider all such subsets and evaluate every one. This means examining a total of $\binom{N}{k}$ subsets; for large N and intermediate k, the numbers involved usually make this approach prohibitive. For example, if we wish to select 10 features from an initial set of 24, we must evaluate 1,961,256 subsets. Since we cannot be sure in advance that 10 features will do the job, the total task may be even bigger. We will discuss three shorter approaches here.

Knock-out and add-on algorithms One way to evaluate a feature in combination with other features is to try leaving it out. If omitting the feature causes no degradation in recognition accuracy, then it can be dropped; otherwise we had better leave it in. This notion gives rise to a simple way to rank features, due to Sambur (1975). Suppose there is an initial set of N features under consideration. Measure the performance of the entire set, using some realistic criterion such as recognition accuracy. Then measure the performance of every subset of $N - 1$ features obtained by omitting each of the features in turn. Eliminate ("knock out") the feature whose omission degrades the performance the least. Then continue recursively; i.e., using the surviving features, test all subsets of $N - 2$ features and again knock out the feature whose omission makes the least difference. Repeat until all features have been knocked out. The order of knocking-out gives the ranking of the features: the most important was knocked out last and the least important was knocked out first. As a byproduct of this procedure, we have subsets of all possible sizes together with measures of their performance. If we are looking for a subset of k features, we must make a total of $[N(N + 1) - k(k - 1)]/2$ evaluations.

The reverse of the knock-out procedure is the add-on procedure (Goldstein, 1976). Each of the N features under consideration is evaluated in isolation and the best feature is selected as the nucleus of the final set. Then all pairs of features comprising the nucleus and one other feature are evaluated; the feature whose addition results in the greatest enhancement of performance is incorporated into the nucleus. This process is repeated, each time adding the one feature which gives the greatest improvement, until all N features have been considered, or until the desired level of performance has been obtained. Selecting a subset of k features by this method requires $k(2N + 1 - k)/2$ evaluations. For $N = 24$ and $k = 10$, the knock-out method requires 255 evaluations and the add-on method, 195. If the size of the subset is to be less than $N/2$, adding-on is clearly more efficient than knocking-out. In either case, each feature being considered for addition or deletion is always tested in combination with the other features. This means that correlation effects among features are always taken into account.

Dynamic programming The knock-out and add-on procedures are used as quick ways of finding a good subset of features. Neither technique guarantees that the resulting subset will be the best possible combination of k features, however. If we have selected a set of, say, three features and have then expanded it to a set of four features by the add-on method, we are committed to including the initial set in the larger one. However, the best possible set of four features does not have to embrace the best possible set of three; thus there could conceivably be some other set of four features which is better than the one the add-on method gave us. A similar line of argument applies to the knock-out procedure. In certain circumstances, however, the optimum subset can be found by means of dynamic programming.

The principles of dynamic programming are beyond the scope of this book. Its motivation, however, in our case, is to select the optimum subset of k features in a series of k steps. It resembles the add-on technique, except that where the latter grows a single subset, dynamic programming grows many subsets in parallel and ultimately selects the best. Suppose we have an initial set of N features from which to choose. Then we proceed as follows:

1. Form N initial subsets of one feature each and evaluate the performance of each subset.
2. For each feature x_i, append the feature to each of the existing subsets and evaluate the performance of the combination. Attach the feature to the subset which gave the best-performing combination. (After this step is complete, the subset size has been increased by one.)
3. Repeat step 2 until the subsets contain k features.
4. Select the subset with the best performance.

If the performance measure is a monotonically increasing function of the subset size, and if the performance at any stage is a function of components from the current feature and from the previous subset, then this process will yield the optimum subset of k features. (The second requirement is termed the *separability requirement*; see Nemhauser, 1966). In step 2, the existing subsets to be considered are only those which do not already include the feature under consideration.

The dynamic programming procedure requires consideration of $N(k-1)(N-k/2)$ subsets; if $N = 24$ and $k = 10$, as in our previous examples, this is 4104 subsets. The cost of the dynamic programming technique is thus intermediate between the exhaustive search and the knock-out and add-on methods. With many performance criteria, however, including $J_1 = \text{tr}(\mathbf{W}^{-1}\mathbf{B})$ (Cheung and Eisenstein, 1978), the separability requirement is not met, and in that case the resulting subset is not optimum. The dynamic programming technique thus has not superseded the knock-out and add-on methods; in fact, Cheung and Eisenstein found only relatively small differences in performance between feature sets chosen by the two methods.

Transformations

Transformation here refers to rotations or other modifications of the coordinates of the feature space. The general object of these transformations is to identify those features, or combinations of features, which contribute most to separating the classes we wish to recognize.

There are two types of coordinate transformation of interest to us: transformation to uncorrelate the features and transformation to maximize separability.

Removal of correlations Suppose we have many features, all with gaussian density and a covariance matrix $\mathbf{W}$. The diagonal elements of $\mathbf{W}$ are measures of the variances of the various features and the off-diagonal elements indicate the degree of correlation between features. If we could transform **W** into a form in which the off-diagonal elements were all zero, the transformed components would be uncorrelated.

We can effect such a transformation by rotating the cluster of features by some matrix **A**:

$$\mathbf{y} = \mathbf{A}\mathbf{x}$$

where **x** is the original set of features and **y** is the transformed set.

In doing this transformation, we assume that there is an underlying set of "real" features, all independent, and that each of the measures we are working with is an "impure" feature in the sense that it is a linear combination of these "real" features. The object of finding the transformation **A** is to recover the "real" features by unscrambling the linear combinations with which we started out.

The technique of rotating the features is well known. If we can find a matrix **A** such that

$$\mathbf{A}^T\mathbf{W}\mathbf{A} = \text{diag}\,(\lambda_1, \lambda_2, \ldots, \lambda_n) = \boldsymbol{\Lambda}$$

then the transformation **A** accomplishes the desired rotation. The elements of **y** are uncorrelated and $\lambda_i = \sigma_{yi}$—i.e., the λ's give the variances of the y's. (In matrix algebra, finding the transformation **A** is called *diagonalization*. In communication theory, it is called the discrete form of the Karhunen-Loève (KL) expansion; pattern recognition has adopted this term, although the term *orthogonalization* is also used.) Once we have these transformed features, we can rank them by their variances by examining the λ's. It is usually assumed that the components with the largest variances are the "true" features and that those with the smallest variances are noise. There is some risk associated with this assumption, as we will describe below, and the researcher must proceed with caution.

The procedure for finding **A** is as follows:

1. Solve the equation, $|\mathbf{W} - \lambda\mathbf{I}| = 0$.
2. For each root λ_i, find a vector $\mathbf{a}_i$ that satisfies $(\mathbf{W} - \lambda_i\mathbf{I})\mathbf{a}_i = 0$. (The vectors $\mathbf{a}_i$ are known as the *characteristic vectors*, or *eigenvectors*, of **W**.) Scale $\mathbf{a}_i$ so that its length is 1.
3. The desired matrix **A** is formed from the vectors $\mathbf{a}_i$:

$$\mathbf{A} = [\mathbf{a}_1, \mathbf{a}_2, \ldots, \mathbf{a}_n].$$

A derivation of this method will be found in any good book on matrix algebra.

It is worth fixing this rotation in the mind by means of a two-dimensional example. Suppose the covariance matrix is

$$\mathbf{W} = \begin{bmatrix} 0.7 & 0.5 \\ 0.5 & 0.5 \end{bmatrix}$$

The quadratic form $\mathbf{x}^T\mathbf{W}^{-1}\mathbf{x}$ is then

$$5x_1^2 - 10x_1x_2 + 7x_2^2$$

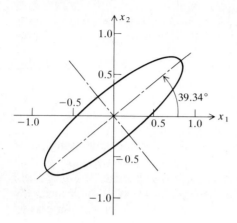

Figure 7-3 Contour of equal probability density for the covariance matrix in the accompanying example.

This is exactly the quadratic form found in the multivariate gaussian probability density and the family of ellipses $\mathbf{x}^T\mathbf{W}^{-1}\mathbf{x} = k$ are contours of equal probability density. The curve $\mathbf{x}^T\mathbf{W}^{-1}\mathbf{x} = 1$ is plotted as an ellipse in Fig. 7-3. The reader should verify that $|\mathbf{W} - \lambda\mathbf{I}| = \lambda^2 - 1.2\lambda + 0.1$ and that the roots are $\lambda = 1.1099$ and 0.0901. For $\lambda_1 = 1.1099$, $\mathbf{a}_1^T = (0.7733, 0.6340)$ after normalization, and for $\lambda_2 = 0.0901$, $\mathbf{a}_2^T = (-0.6340, 0.7733)$. The resultant transformation $\mathbf{A}$ is given by

$$\mathbf{A} = \begin{bmatrix} 0.7733 & -0.6340 \\ 0.6340 & 0.7733 \end{bmatrix} = \begin{bmatrix} \cos \alpha & \sin \alpha \\ -\sin \alpha & \cos \alpha \end{bmatrix}$$

where $\alpha = -39.34°$, the angle through which the features have been rotated. The axes shown as dotted lines in Fig. 7-3 are thus lined up with the x_1 and x_2 axes. The transformed covariance matrix is

$$\mathbf{\Lambda} = \mathbf{A}^T\mathbf{W}\mathbf{A} = \begin{bmatrix} 1.1099 & 0 \\ 0 & 0.0901 \end{bmatrix}$$

The variances of the two components are thus 1.1099 and 0.0901.

We said above that $\mathbf{x}^T\mathbf{W}^{-1}\mathbf{x} = k$ defined a set of contours of constant probability density for gaussian variables. Because we usually have many features, we usually deal with a multidimensional feature space; these contours can be thought of as hyperellipsoids in that space, and the features can be thought of as forming hyperellipsoidal clouds. The KL transformation performs a coordinate rotation that aligns the directions of maximum variance (corresponding with the axes of the hyperellipsoids) with the new coordinate axes.

The trace and determinant of $\mathbf{\Lambda}$ both provide indications of the size of this cloud. The trace gives the sum of the variances and hence indicates the squared radius of the cloud, to the extent that we can think of such a cloud as having a radius. (More precisely, the trace, divided by the number of dimensions, is the mean of the squares of the semiaxes of the ellipsoid, $\mathbf{x}^T\mathbf{\Lambda}^{-1}\mathbf{x} = 1$.) The determinant gives the product of the variances and is thus proportional to the square of the volume of the cloud. Both of these quantities are invariant under rotation, however, so this information is already available in tr **W** and |**W**|. These observations shed considerable light on the separability measures J_2, J_3, and J_4 presented above, since they are now seen as comparing the sizes of the clouds defined by the inter- and intracluster covariance matrices: J_2 compares the squares of their volumes, J_4 compares the squares of their radii, and J_3 seeks to maximize the intercluster radius while holding the intracluster radius steady.

Maximizing separability In the KL transformation, the focus is entirely on the features and the goal is to uncorrelate them. We now consider a different approach in which the focus is on the interclass variation, rather than on the features themselves. We will again transform the coordinates of the feature space, but this time we will align the directions of *maximum separability* with the axes. This is frequently closer to what we want, since we have not assurance that the uncorrelated variables created by KL are necessarily good discriminants, or that a large variance corresponds to a large F ratio. This process is sometimes known as *discriminant analysis*.

An example will make this clear. Consider the three clusters of features in Fig. 7-4a. The elliptical shapes of the clusters are similar to our example from

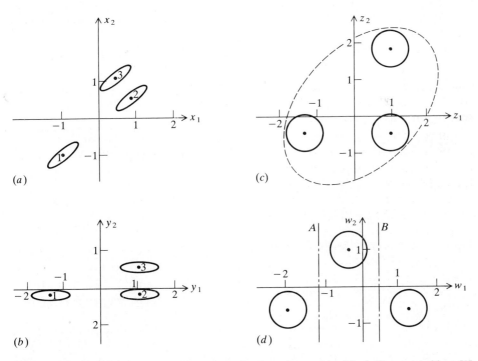

Figure 7-4 Contours of equal probability density for three classes: (*a*) original, (*b*) as rotated by a KL transformation, (*c*) after whitening transformation, (*d*) after rotation of whitened distributions. The final transformation aligns the axes of the dotted ellipse in (*c*) with the coordinate axes; the lines *A* and *B* in (*d*) are decision thresholds.

Fig. 7-3, and the data of Fig. 7-4 have in fact the same **W** matrix. A KL transformation will not do much for us here; the rotated features are plotted in Fig. 7-4*b*, and we see that both components are still significant. What we need is a method that will choose the degree of rotation more intelligently.

We wish, in fact, to rotate the interclass distribution, but to do this properly, we must first neutralize the distracting effect of the individual cluster shapes. We can do this by a scaling transformation which makes the clusters circular, as in Fig. 7-4*c*. (This is called "whitening" the density functions.) Then we can think of the resultant clusters as three samples from an elliptical distribution, as suggested by the dotted ellipse in Fig. 7-4*c*, and it is this ellipse which we now wish to rotate. The transformations that took us from (*a*) to (*c*) in Fig. 7-4 will also transform the interclass covariance matrix **B**; to rotate the dotted ellipse in Fig. 7-4*c*, therefore, we diagonalize the transformed **B**.

The steps in this procedure, if we performed them in sequence, would then be:

1. Diagonalize **W**, finding **Y** such that $\mathbf{Y}^T\mathbf{W}\mathbf{Y} = \mathbf{D}$.
2. Whiten the intraclass clusters by finding $\mathbf{Z} = \mathbf{Y}\mathbf{D}^{-1/2}$. Then $\mathbf{Z}^T\mathbf{W}\mathbf{Z} = \mathbf{D}^{-1/2}\mathbf{D}\mathbf{D}^{-1/2} = \mathbf{I}$. ($\mathbf{D}^{-1/2}$ is the diagonal matrix whose diagonal elements are the reciprocals of the square roots of the corresponding elements of **D**.)
3. Diagonalize $\mathbf{Z}^T\mathbf{B}\mathbf{Z}$, finding **A** such that $\mathbf{A}^T\mathbf{Z}^T\mathbf{B}\mathbf{Z}\mathbf{A} = \Lambda$.

The result of these steps is shown in Fig. 7-4*d*. Here the transformed feature clusters are so disposed that the direction of maximum separability is parallel to the horizontal axis.

In practice, the whitening step can be omitted, and the other two steps consolidated, by finding the eigenvalues and eigenvectors of the product $\mathbf{W}^{-1}\mathbf{B}$. (This will be recognized as the form we used in the separability measures J_1 and J_2.) As before, we find the λ's for which

$$|\mathbf{W}^{-1}\mathbf{B} - \lambda\mathbf{I}| = 0$$

Then for each λ_i, we find a vector $\mathbf{a}_i$ for which

$$(\mathbf{W}^{-1}\mathbf{B} - \lambda_i)\mathbf{a}_i = 0$$

These λ's are identical to the λ's obtained in step 3 above. The transformation matrix **A** is then built up from the column vectors $\mathbf{a}_i$:

$$\mathbf{A} = [\mathbf{a}_1, \mathbf{a}_2, \ldots, \mathbf{a}_n]$$

One difference between this procedure and the KL transformation is that **A** will not diagonalize the product $\mathbf{W}^{-1}\mathbf{B}$, because this product is not symmetric.

As an example of this process, consider the three classes shown in Fig. 7-4.

They have means as follows:

Class 1 $(-0.984, -0.984)$
Class 2 $(0.893, 0.555)$
Class 3 $(0.454, 1.090)$

and they are all assumed to have the same individual densities as the example of Fig. 7-3. Then

$$\mathbf{B} = \begin{bmatrix} 0.64263 & 0.62625 \\ 0.62625 & 0.77291 \end{bmatrix} \qquad \mathbf{W} = \begin{bmatrix} 0.7 & 0.5 \\ 0.5 & 0.5 \end{bmatrix}$$

Except for the substitution of $\mathbf{W}^{-1}\mathbf{B}$ for $\mathbf{W}$, the computations proceed as in the Karhunen-Loève case. The reader should verify that $|\mathbf{W}^{-1}\mathbf{B} - \lambda\mathbf{I}| = \lambda^2 - 2.3611\lambda + 1.0451$; that the resulting transformation matrix is

$$\mathbf{A} = \begin{bmatrix} 0.39826 & 0.81290 \\ -0.91727 & -0.56963 \end{bmatrix}$$

and that $\mathbf{A}^T\mathbf{W}\mathbf{A}$ and $\mathbf{A}^T\mathbf{B}\mathbf{A}$ are both diagonal. Notice, however, that $\mathbf{A}$ does not diagonalize $\mathbf{W}^{-1}\mathbf{B}$:

$$\mathbf{A}^T\mathbf{W}^{-1}\mathbf{B}\mathbf{A} = \begin{bmatrix} 1.77091 & 0.51090 \\ 1.49863 & 0.59119 \end{bmatrix}$$

The improved separability can be seen if the distributions are imagined projected onto the horizontal axis: clearly two decision thresholds, as suggested by the vertical lines A and B in the figure, would be sufficient to separate the classes. Furthermore, the F ratio of the projected distributions is given by λ_1 and, in general, λ_i is equal to the F ratio of the projection of the transformed distributions onto the w_i axis.

Before performing these transformations, however, we can judge the overall quality of our initial feature set by summing these F ratios. We said that these F ratios are given by the eigenvalues λ_1, λ_2, etc. Recall, however, that the sum of the eigenvalues of a matrix is equal to its trace, and that the trace of $\mathbf{W}^{-1}\mathbf{B}$ is invariant under any nonsingular transformation. That is another reason for the separability measure $J_1 = \text{tr}(\mathbf{W}^{-1}\mathbf{B})$: since the trace does not change, that particular piece of information is already available without transforming $\mathbf{W}^{-1}\mathbf{B}$.

The notion of projection onto the horizontal axis brings up an additional point. This transformation has thrown all the irrelevant information onto the other dimension, and we are therefore back to the strategy that we used with the KL expansion: we preserve those combinations which have high F ratios and dismiss as irrelevant those which have low F ratios. In this way, we have again reduced the dimensionality of the space which we must consider. The use of transformations is therefore frequently referred to in the literature as *dimensionality reduction*.

These transformations suffer from three drawbacks:

1. They are computationally expensive. If we have been diligent in searching for features, we may have to diagonalize a very large matrix.
2. The resulting components, although optimal in some senses, are not intuitively meaningful. (There is no absolute requirement that they should be, of course, but most researchers feel distinctly more comfortable when they are.)
3. Although the number of transformed features is minimized, each one is a linear combination of a number of observables. If each combination uses a large number of observables (and there is no guarantee that it will not), then although we have minimized the dimension of the final recognition vector, we may still have a large number of observables to measure.

On the other hand, transformations handle the process of feature selection in a more subtle and flexible way than, for example, the subset selection techniques described previously. If we view feature selection as a process of assigning weights to features, then the knock-out, add-on, and dynamic programming techniques permit only weights of zero or one and yield a single set of features; transformation techniques yield multiple sets of features, in each of which the weights can take on any conceivable value, including negative weights should they prove desirable.

7-5 CLUSTERING

In some cases features may separate classes well enough that the classes occupy essentially nonoverlapping regions in the feature space. In this case it is possible to allow the recognizer to group the training data into categories without supervision. This gives rise to a process known as *clustering*.

Clustering has not seen much use in speech processing until recently, since most recognizers did not achieve high enough accuracies for clustering to be feasible. (Clustering will not make a good recognizer out of a poor one.) It can be useful for other purposes, however. Rabiner *et al.* (1979) investigated a speaker-independent word-recognition system in which multiple templates were permitted for each word. Instead of a single pattern for each word, the pattern library had as many templates as were needed to accommodate different possible pronunciations. During the training phase, a very large number of templates were obtained for each word. Clustering was used to identify groups of similar templates; after clustering the pattern-library entry for each word contained up to five representative templates, these being the means of the corresponding clusters.

Clustering is also closely related to the techniques used to create the codebooks used in vector quantization, a technique to be discussed in Chapter 10.

Duda and Hart (1973) mention another potentially useful application of clustering. Speech data may change slowly with time as the talker's speech habits change. If the recognition classes are well separated to begin with, a clustering process can be used to update the pattern library so that it can track these slowly varying changes.

A number of clustering algorithms have been developed; we will outline some of the more well-known ones here. In all cases, we will assume that there are N data points $\{x_i\}$ to be grouped into K classes $\{C_j\}$. (Each x_i is a vector of features and corresponds to a point in a multidimensional feature space.) N is determined by the size of the training set and K must in most cases be decided by the investigator from some extraneous consideration; e.g., for a digit recognizer, there would naturally be 10 classes.

Reclassification

In this procedure, a preliminary set of clusters is formed by partitioning all of the data. This preliminary clustering is then evaluated by some statistical test—e.g., we could apply our measure J_1, using the pooled intracluster covariance matrices for **W** and the covariance matrix of the cluster means for **B**. Then each data point in turn is considered for reclassification. J_1 is reevaluated for each possible reassignment of the data point. If any improvement results, the point is permanently reassigned to the class which gave the greatest improvement. When all points have been considered, J_1 is recomputed for the entire clustering. This process is repeated until no points are reassigned.

For clarity, we will rephrase this algorithm in pseudo-Pascal:

```
Repeat
    For i := 1 to N do
        begin
        For j := 1 to K do
            Recompute clustering criterion under assumption that point i is
            reassigned to cluster j; let j_opt[i] be the value of j giving greatest
            improvement;
        Reassign point i to cluster j_opt[i]
        end;
until no points reassigned;
```

This can be a very time-consuming process, since the clustering criterion has to be computed NK times on each cycle. There is no way to evade this at the beginning of the process, although, once the clustering has begun to stabilize, it may be feasible to omit considering reassignments to clusters known to be remote from point i.

The K-Means Algorithm

Here the initial clusters are characterized only by their means. (These means are frequently obtained from the first K data points.) Then every data point x_i is assigned to the cluster whose mean is nearest to x_i. After all data points have been assigned, the cluster means are recomputed. This process is repeated until no change in assignments occurs.

In pseudo-Pascal, this algorithm runs as follows:

```
Repeat
    For i := 1 to N do
        Assign point i to class j for which the distance
        (x[i] − μ[j])² is a minimum;
    For j := 1 to K do
        Recompute μ[j] from average of data points assigned to it;
until no further change in assignments;
```

This is a very efficient and very popular clustering technique. We will meet it in another form when we consider vector quantization in Chapter 9. A highly sophisticated and sensitive algorithm, ISODATA, is an elaboration of the K-means algorithm (Ball and Hall, 1965).

A modification of this procedure, useful if the number K of classes is not initially fixed, uses a maximum distance threshold. For each new point, if the minimum distance exceeds the threshold, then the new point is made the nucleus of a new cluster. This modification essentially changes the problem from that choosing a suitable K to that choosing a suitable threshold.

The K-means algorithm does not require a strict distance measure; any measure of dissimilarity, $D(x, \mu)$, will serve, provided it is relevant to the particular application. If a distance is not used, then the mean of the cluster must be defined as the point q which minimizes the average of $D(x_i, q)$ for all points in the cluster.

A weakness of both these algorithms is that their performance can be affected by the choice of the initial clustering. It is known that these algorithms will converge to an optimum clustering, but this optimum may be a local optimum rather than the global optimum. The following two methods attempt to draw the clustering from the data instead of imposing an initial clustering upon them.

Farthest Neighbor

This method starts with a single cluster consisting of one data point. Then the remaining points are tested and the point which is farthest from the initial cluster is chosen as the nucleus of the second cluster. Then the point which is most remote from these two clusters is made the nucleus of the third cluster. This process continues either until the number of clusters is equal to K or until the maximum distance is less than some threshold value. Each of the remaining data points is assigned to the nearest cluster. This algorithm can be used to generate the initial clustering for the reclassification or the K-means algorithm.

Agglomeration

In this algorithm we build clusters by merging smaller clusters. Initially, every data point is a cluster. The entire set of clusters is examined and the two clusters which are nearest are identified and consolidated into a single cluster. This process repeats, each time merging the two nearest clusters, until the number of clusters is equal to K.

PROBLEMS

7-1 Given the following data, find: (a) the means of the classes, (b) the intraclass covariance matrix for each class, (c) the interclass covariance matrix.

Class 1:	x	y		Class 2:	x	y
1	2.90	0.93		1	−0.40	−1.59
2	0.47	1.92		2	0.39	−0.44
3	1.94	0.83		3	0.03	−2.31
4	2.88	0.17		4	−0.71	−1.47
5	0.65	0.47		5	−0.86	−1.12
6	2.26	0.63		6	−0.56	0.36
7	0.85	0.84		7	0.19	−1.47
8	1.04	0.75		8	−0.39	−1.19
9	0.40	2.80		9	1.37	−2.06
10	2.16	2.06		10	0.76	−0.79
11	1.40	1.61		11	−0.68	−1.36
12	0.75	2.27		12	1.19	−2.29
13	0.09	1.63		13	−1.01	−1.28
14	2.36	−0.17		14	−1.98	−0.56
15	1.08	2.54		15	−0.12	−1.81
16	1.14	1.45		16	0.72	−2.34

Class 3:	x	y		Class 4:	x	y
1	0.41	1.90		1	0.53	−0.64
2	−0.03	0.51		2	−0.64	1.67
3	0.95	1.79		3	−1.06	1.22
4	1.24	1.06		4	−0.44	−0.05
5	−0.29	0.90		5	−0.59	1.06
6	0.63	0.61		6	0.47	0.35
7	−1.77	1.69		7	1.30	−1.19
8	−1.84	3.27		8	0.05	−0.06
9	1.22	−0.78		9	1.10	−1.61
10	0.59	−0.15		10	−0.33	0.96
11	0.19	1.70		11	0.73	−1.30
12	1.87	−1.02		12	2.07	−3.28
13	−0.78	3.13		13	1.17	−1.24
14	−1.63	1.77		14	2.68	−1.15
15	−0.36	1.36		15	1.97	−1.70
16	0.31	−0.83		16	0.54	0.42

7-2 Using the results of Prob. 7-1, compute the measures J_1, J_2, and J_4 for the data of Prob. 7-1.

7-3 Find the Mahalanobis distance from each of the following vectors to each of the four classes of Prob. 7-1:
    (a) (0.0, 0.0)   (b) (1.0, 1.0)
    (c) (−1.0, 1.0)   (d) (1.0, 1.5)

7-4 Given three classes with means and covariance matrices as follows:

Class 1: Mean = $(-1.0, 0.4)$

$$\mathbf{W}_1 = \begin{bmatrix} 0.6 & -0.3 \\ -0.3 & 0.5 \end{bmatrix}$$

Class 2: Mean = $(0.5, -0.5)$

$$\mathbf{W}_2 = \begin{bmatrix} 0.7 & -0.5 \\ -0.5 & 0.5 \end{bmatrix}$$

Class 3: Mean = $(0.0, 1.5)$

$$\mathbf{W}_3 = \begin{bmatrix} 0.6 & -0.4 \\ -0.4 & 0.4 \end{bmatrix}$$

Find the pooled intraclass covariance matrix $\mathbf{W}$ and the interclass covariance matrix $\mathbf{B}$; find the transformation $\mathbf{A}$ which diagonalizes $\mathbf{W}^{-1}\mathbf{B}$.

7-5 Write a K-means clustering program and use it to cluster the following data using the euclidean distance measure. Assume four clusters with initial means $(0.7, 0.7)$, $(0.7, -0.7)$, $(-0.7, 0.7)$, and $(-0.7, -0.7)$.

x	y	x	y	x	y
−0.05	2.07	0.36	0.90	3.64	2.48
1.39	2.74	0.98	1.69	1.23	2.49
1.30	0.02	1.53	1.99	1.55	3.00
2.17	−1.14	−1.05	−3.28	−0.46	−0.65
0.91	−0.45	−0.29	−0.09	1.03	1.86
0.62	1.73	−1.27	3.39	1.97	1.56
1.19	−1.42	−1.48	−4.64	1.77	−0.80
1.50	−2.11	0.94	0.29	2.28	−0.65
0.86	1.56	1.77	2.22	2.04	0.59
2.32	0.02	1.34	1.29	1.10	0.22
3.38	2.06	−0.29	−1.47	1.40	−0.37
2.14	0.02	−0.20	0.44	0.68	1.43
1.25	1.71	1.55	1.28	4.33	3.72
1.10	0.75	0.37	−1.74	1.55	−0.91
0.92	1.99	1.30	1.07	2.35	1.12
2.92	0.20	0.72	−0.12	0.27	−3.78
1.66	−1.52	0.01	−2.20	−1.95	−3.96
−0.10	−1.18	−0.07	−3.47	1.55	−1.12
1.92	−0.57	1.55	0.92	3.15	1.79
0.75	0.05	1.39	1.03	1.32	0.89
2.60	0.63	0.94	−0.63	0.77	−0.19

REFERENCES

Andrews, D. R., et al.: The IBM 1975 optical page reader: Part III. Recognition logic development, *IBM J. Res. Develop.*, vol. 12, pp. 364–371, September, 1968. (An excellent essay on the significance and methodology of feature selection.)

Atal, B. S.: Automatic speaker recognition based on pitch contours, Ph.D. Thesis, Polytech. Inst. of Brooklyn, 1968. (Contains a particularly illuminating discussion of the KL transformation.)

Ball, G. H., and D. J. Hall.: ISODATA, a novel method of data analysis and pattern classification, Stanford Research Inst. Tech. Report (NTIS No. AD699616), 1965.

Bricker, P. D., et al.: Statistical techniques for talker identification, *BSTJ*, vol. 50, no. 4, pp. 1427–1454, April, 1971.

Buzo, A. A., H. Gray, Jr., R. M. Gray, and J. D. Markel: Speech coding based on vector quantization, *IEEE Trans.*, vol. ASSP-28, no. 5, pp. 562–574, October, 1980.

Cheung, R. S., and B. A. Eisenstein: Feature selection via dynamic programming for text-independent speaker recognition, *IEEE Trans.*, vol. ASSP-26, no. 5, pp. 397–403, October, 1978.

Chien, Y. T., and K. S. Fu: On the generalized Karhunen-Loève expansion, *IEEE Trans.*, vol. IT-13, no. 3, pp. 518–520, July, 1967.

────── and ──────: Selection and ordering of feature observations in a pattern recognition system, *Information & Control*, vol. 12, pp. 395–414, 1968.

Duda, R. O., and P. E. Hart: *Pattern Classification and Scene Analysis*, Wiley-Interscience, New York, 1973.

Feucht, D.: Pattern recognition—basic concepts and implementations, *Computer Design*, pp. 57–68, December, 1977.

Fukunaga, K.: *Introduction to Statistical Pattern Recognition*, Academic Press, New York, 1972.

Goldstein, U.: Speaker-identifying features based on formant tracks, *JASA*, vol. 59, no. 1, pp. 176–182, January, 1976.

Ho, Y-C., and A. K. Agrawala: On pattern classification algorithms: introduction and survey, *Proc. IEEE*, vol. 56, no. 12, pp. 2101–2114, December, 1968.

Itakura, F.: Minimum prediction residual principle applied to speech recognition, *IEEE Trans.*, vol. ASSP-23, no. 1, pp. 67–72, February, 1975.

────── and S. Saito: A statistical method for estimation of speech spectral density and formant frequencies, *Electron. Commun. Japan*, vol. 53-A, pp. 36–43, 1970.

Kramer, H. P., and M. V. Mathews: A linear coding for transmitting a set of correlated signals, *IEEE Trans.*, vol. IT-2, no. 3, pp. 41–45, September, 1956.

Kullback, S.: *Information Theory and Statistics*, Wiley, New York, 1959.

Levine, M. D.: Feature extraction: a survey, *Proc. IEEE*, vol. 57, no. 8, pp. 1391–1407, August, 1969.

Mahalanobis, P. C.: On the generalized distance in statistics, *Proc. Nat. Inst. Sci. India*, vol. 12, pp. 49–55, 1936.

Marill, T., and D. M. Green: On the effectiveness of receptors in recognition systems, *IEEE Trans.*, vol. IT-9, no. 1, pp. 11–17, January, 1963.

Markel, J. D., and A. H. Gray, Jr.: *Linear Prediction of Speech*, Springer-Verlag, New York, 1976.

Nagy, G.: Classification algorithms in pattern recognition, *IEEE Trans.*, vol. AU-16, no. 2, pp. 203–212, June, 1968.

Nemhauser, G. L.: *Introduction to Dynamic Programming*, Wiley, New York, 1966.

Proceedings of the IEEE, vol. 64, no. 4 (April, 1976). Special issue on man-machine communication.

Rabiner, L. R., et al.: Speaker-independent recognition of isolated words using a clustering technique, *IEEE Trans.*, vol. ASSP-27, no. 4, pp. 336–349, August, 1979.

Sambur, M.: Selection of acoustic features for speaker identification, *IEEE Trans.*, vol. ASSP-23, no. 2, pp. 176–182, April, 1975.

Souza, P. de, and P. J. Thomson: LPC distance measures and statistical tests with particular reference to the likelihood ratio, *IEEE Trans.*, vol. ASSP-30, no. 2, pp. 304–315, April, 1982.

Tou, J. T., and R. C. Gonzalez: *Pattern Recognition Principles*, Addison-Wesley, Reading, Mass., 1974.

Watanabe, S.: Karhunen-Loève expansion and factor analysis: theoretical remarks and applications, *Trans. Fourth (1965) Prague Conf. Info. Theory, Statis. Decision Functions, and Random Proc.*, Academic Press, New York, pp. 635–660, 1967.

PART THREE

APPLICATIONS

We begin our survey of applications with a survey of methods for determining pitch and formant frequencies, since these features are used in many of the other application areas to be discussed.

Voice encoding and synthesis are important wherever voice has to be transmitted or stored digitally; this includes computer-controlled voice-response systems, transmission of voice over digital data channels, voice encryption, and transmission through poor-quality or limited-bandwidth media. The problem is to squeeze the voice into the smallest number of bits with the least loss of intelligibility and quality. There are two general ways of doing this, depending on how faithfully one tries to preserve the actual time function; accordingly one refers to waveform encoding or to vocoders. Since this topic involves a lot of material, we have chosen to divide the material, somewhat summarily, along these lines, and since vocoders and synthesizers share a lot of equipment and some problems, we have grouped the problem of speech synthesis with the material on vocoders.

Speech recognition and speaker recognition are gradually emerging from the laboratory; speech recognition is of particular interest in situations where the hands or the eyes are otherwise occupied, or with the disabled. Speech enhancement has limited applications in forensic work, but it is also important in enabling the previously mentioned processes, most of which were developed on laboratory-quality, "clean" speech, to work with noisy speech in everyday environments.

The literature on these applications has now become so extensive that it is impossible to do justice to even one of these areas in the space available here. This section is therefore limited to brief descriptions of representative efforts in the various subject areas. There seems little point in trying to repeat in detail material which has, for the most part, been adequately covered in the literature. Hence the reader should regard this section as a survey painted in rather broad strokes and not intended to be exhaustive.

CHAPTER
EIGHT

PITCH AND FORMANT ESTIMATION

We are now in a position to apply the theory we have covered to a practical issue in speech processing. Estimates of pitch and formant frequencies have found extensive use in speech encoding, synthesis, and recognition. Determining these parameters from the speech waveform has historically been a major phase of research into speech.

8-1 FUNDAMENTAL FREQUENCY ESTIMATION

Estimating the pitch of voiced speech sounds has been described as the "hardy perennial" among speech-processing problems. It is not obvious why the problem should be so difficult, but a brief historical survey will uncover most of the reasons.

The first method tried was simply to low-pass the speech signal in order to remove all harmonics and then measure the fundamental frequency by any convenient means. This method ran into two difficulties. First, since pitch can easily cover a 2 to 1 range, the filter had to be adaptive in order to be sure of always passing the fundamental and rejecting the second harmonic. The filter frequency was set by tracking the pitch and predicting the forthcoming pitch value; hence any error in one frame of speech could cause the filter to select the wrong cutoff frequency in the next frame and so lose track of the pitch altogether. The second difficulty arose from the fact that in many cases pitch was to be estimated from telephone speech. The frequency response of a voice-grade telephone channel drops off rapidly below 300 Hz; hence for many male voices the fundamental frequency is absent or so weak as to be lost in the system noise.

In the absence of a fundamental, it is customary to search for periodicities in a signal by examining its autocorrelation function. In a periodic function, the autocorrelation will show a maximum at a lag equal to the period of the function. Several problems arise in applying this principle to pitch estimation. First, speech is generally not exactly periodic, because of changes in pitch and in formant frequencies. Hence the maximum may be lower and broader than expected; this causes problems in setting an automatic decision threshold. Second, in some voices, as we observed in Chapter 6, the first formant frequency may be equal to or below the pitch frequency. If it is, and if its amplitude happens to be particularly high, it may cause a peak in the autocorrelation function which is comparable to the peak belonging to the fundamental. Figure 8-1 shows the /ə/ from "the" spoken by an adult female; here there are three dominant peaks. From visual inspection of the waveform, we can determine that the peak at 40 samples corresponds to F_0, which is 200 Hz; but the peak at 20 samples is nearly as big as that for F_0, and it represents a believable pitch for a female talker. It should be clear, even from this relatively well-behaved example, that designing reliable decision logic for such cases is no simple task. Pathological conditions such as these may occur only rarely, but experience has shown that estimation errors tend to occur in clusters, because the condition giving rise to them lasts longer than one frame. A pitch-tracking process can usually ride out a single error, but not a string of (say) half-a-dozen errors.

All of these problems are compounded by the fact that most pitch estimators are also used to indicate presence or absence of phonation. If an acceptable pitch estimate is found, the speech is characterized as voiced with the indicated pitch frequency; if no reasonable pitch estimate can be found, the algorithm indicates unvoiced speech. Hence it is important not only to get accurate pitch measurements but also to avoid spurious responses in the absence of voicing.

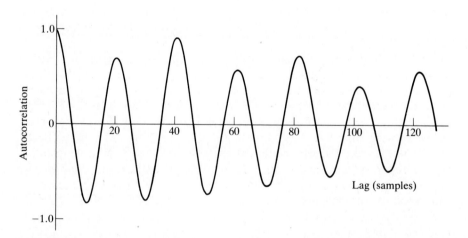

Figure 8-1 Autocorrelation function of [ə] spoken by an adult female. The signal is sampled at 8 kHz.

Methods Using Modified Autocorrelation

The principal problem with autocorrelation is that the first formant may interfere with the fundamental. Hence many investigators have considered ways of flattening the spectrum so all harmonics are essentially the same size; in that case F_1 no longer dominates and autocorrelation should work. The following techniques have been used.

Adaptive filtering In a method reported by Sondhi (1968), the signal is run into a filter bank, as shown in Fig. 8-2. Each filter covers approximately 100 Hz and has its own automatic gain control to keep its output level constant. The combined filter outputs will then have a flat spectrum; these outputs are passed to the autocorrelator for estimating pitch. The autocorrelation function of a spectrum-flattened signal normally shows a prominent peak at pitch period; if no such peak is found, the algorithm reports unvoiced speech. In a refinement of this method, the filter outputs are shifted in phase in order to synchronize them; this is done by assuming the vocal tract transfer function to be minimum-phase and computing its phase function from the spectrum-envelope estimate available from the filter-bank gain settings. The autocorrelator examines a 30-ms segment of speech; a voiced/unvoiced decision is obtained by comparing the largest peak found with a preset threshold.

The SIFT (simplified inverse filter tracking) algorithm (Markel, 1972) is a modernized version of this approach (see Fig. 8-3). Here the signal is spectrum-flattened by passing it through an LPC-derived inverse filter. The speech,

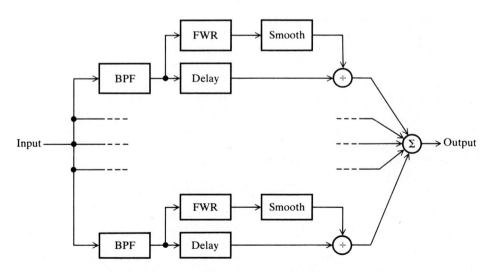

Figure 8-2 Removal of spectrum envelope by means of a filter bank with automatic gain control on each channel. The output amplitude of each bandpass filter (BPF) is estimated by a full-wave rectifier (FWR); the smoothed output of the rectifier is used to control the filter's input to the summer.

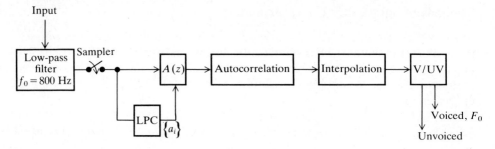

Figure 8-3 Removal of spectrum envelope by LPC-derived inverse filter.

sampled at 10 kHz, is low-pass filtered to 800 Hz, and the predictor computes a fourth-order filter. We have seen in Chapter 6 that the inverse filter is a spectrum-flattening filter; hence the present filter provides us with a simplified (i.e., cheap) spectrum flattener. The prediction error is the input to the autocorrelator. Voicing is determined by comparison against a threshold, as usual, and continuity requirements are imposed to reduce the likelihood of errors.

Generally similar systems are described in Atal and Hanauer (1971) and Maksym (1973).

Nonlinear processing The low-amplitude portions of speech tend to contain most of the formant information and the high-amplitude portions most of the pitch information. Hence any nonlinear processing which deemphasizes or suppresses the low-amplitude portions will improve the performance of the autocorrelator. The appeal of nonlinear processing is that it can be done in the time domain cheaply by hardware. We instance two cases.

Center clipping Here the low-amplitude portions of the signal are removed by means of a center clipper whose clipping point is determined by the peak amplitude of the speech signal, as shown in Fig. 8-4. The clipper is set to reject all portions of the waveform below some threshold level T. The center-clipped speech is then passed to an autocorrelator. The autocorrelation function is typically zero for most lags, with large, sharp peaks at the pitch period and only small secondary peaks. The principal peak can then be identified with very simple logic.

Three such clippers have been investigated in considerable detail. The clipper of Fig. 8-4a has the input-output function

$$C_1(x) = \begin{cases} x - T, & x > T \\ 0, & |x| \leq T \\ x + T, & x < -T \end{cases}$$

The effect on a speech waveform is shown in Fig. 8-4b and c. Using this clipper, with T automatically maintained at 30 percent of the peak amplitude of the speech signal, Sondhi (1968) reports good performance on telephone-bandwidth speech at signal-to-noise ratios as low as 18 dB.

PITCH AND FORMANT ESTIMATION **201**

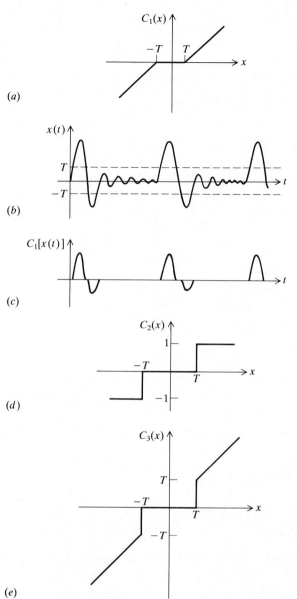

(a)
(b)
(c)
(d)
(e)

Figure 8-4 Removal of low-amplitude portions of the speech signal by means of a center clipper. (a) Clipper's input-output function; (b) input signal; (c) clipper output; (d), (e) clipping functions investigated by Dubnowski.

Two similar clippers have been proposed. The one in Fig. 8-4d (Dubnowski et al., 1976) has the function

$$C_2(x) = \begin{cases} 1, & x > T \\ 0, & |x| \leq T \\ -1, & x < -T \end{cases}$$

and the one in Fig. 8-4e has the function

$$C_3(x) = \begin{cases} x, & x > T \\ 0, & |x| \leq T \\ x, & x < -T \end{cases}$$

In a detailed comparison of all three types, Rabiner et al. (1976) found only minor differences in performance.

Cubing (Atal, 1968)   The speech waveform is passed through a nonlinear circuit whose transfer function is $y(t) = x^3(t)$. Cubing tends to suppress the low-amplitude portions of the speech and has the added advantage that it is not necessary to maintain an adjustable threshold.

Magnitude difference function (Moorer, 1974; Ross et al., 1974)   The point of using the autocorrelation function is to determine the lag at which successive portions of the time waveform most closely resemble each other. There are other measures of similarity than multiplication, however. Moorer and Ross both chose to consider the absolute values of the differences between lagged signal samples, named the AMDF (average magnitude difference function) by Ross:

$$D_k = \frac{1}{N} \sum_n |X(n) - X(n-k)| \qquad (8\text{-}1)$$

This difference function will show a minimum for a lag k equal to the pitch period. Ross et al. compare (8-1) to the standard autocorrelation function and show that D_k is approximately proportional to $[2(R_0 - R_k)]^{1/2}$. Moorer's derivation is particularly appealing: he likens this measure to the output of a variable comb filter, as shown in Fig. 8-5; when the spacing between the teeth of the comb

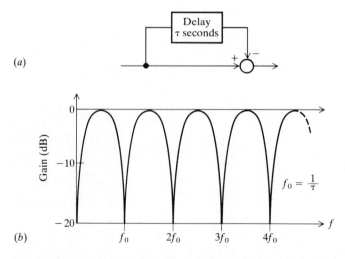

Figure 8-5 Use of lagged differences to determine pitch. (a) Delay followed by subtractor; (b) equivalent comb filter.

matches the spacing between the pitch harmonics, the output will be a minimum. The logic in which the AMDF algorithm is embedded searches for this minimum and outputs either a pitch or a pitch period. The minimum must have a certain depth to be accepted; if no such minimum is found, the algorithm reports absence of voicing. The AMDF pitch algorithm has found wide acceptance in speech-encoding applications for the military.

Un and Yang (1977) applied the AMDF technique to the linear-prediction residual instead of to the speech itself; the resulting function showed much narrower and deeper minima than are obtained with speech itself.

The Cepstrum

The cepstrum of a signal is the Fourier transform of the logarithm of its power spectrum. The cepstrum provides another, very powerful method of spectrum flattening (Noll, 1967). It derives from the excitation-modulation model of the vocal tract. Recall that the spectrum of voiced speech is given by

$$X(f) = G(f)H(f)$$

where $G(f)$ is the glottal excitation spectrum and $H(f)$ is the vocal tract transfer function. If we take the logarithm of the power spectrum, we will transform these multiplicative components into additive ones:

$$T(f) = 2 \ln |X(f)| = 2[\ln |G(f)| + \ln |H(f)|] \qquad (8\text{-}2)$$

A sketch of $T(f)$ is shown in Fig. 8-6a. Note that $T(f)$ consists of two components: a slowly varying component which correspond to the spectrum envelope and a rapidly varying component which corresponds to the pitch-harmonic peaks. These components can be separated by filtering, or by taking a second Fourier transform. If we do the latter, we get the cepstrum:

$$C(q) = F\{T(f)\}$$
$$= 2F\{\ln |G(f)| + \ln |H(f)|\} \qquad (8\text{-}3)$$

[The term "cepstrum" was the coinage of J. R. Tukey (Bogert et al., 1963). It reflects the fact that this transform does not take us back to the time domain, but into a new domain which Tukey named "quefrency." The reversals are intended to reflect the fact that the cepstrum operation, in a sense, turns the spectrum "inside out," and Tukey provides a rich vocabulary of similar reversals for our delectation: cepstrum, alanysis, quefrency, liftering, rahmonic, repiod, darius, gamnitude, saphe and lopar. Of these, cepstrum has found wide acceptance and quefrency, liftering, and rahmonic will be useful to us. Tukey seems to have given up on "rectangular."]

A sketch of $C(q)$ is shown in Fig. 8-6b. The cluster of components near the origin is the transform of the spectrum envelope; the narrow peak at $q = t_0$ is the transform of the harmonic peaks. The separation between the pitch peak and the envelope transform is always great enough that the former can easily be distinguished.

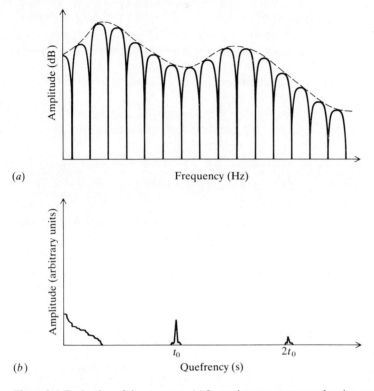

(a)

(b)

Figure 8-6 Derivation of the cepstrum. (*a*) Logged power spectrum showing rapidly varying spectrum of harmonic peaks (solid curve) within slowly varying spectrum envelope (dotted curve). (*b*) Fourier transform of logged power spectrum (idealized): the low-quefrency portion corresponds to the spectrum envelope in (*a*) and the peaks at t_0 and $2t_0$ represent the pitch and its second rahmonic.

When used with noiseless speech, the cepstrum is unparalleled as a pitch extractor, and its performance has long been a standard by which other pitch algorithms have been measured. In the presence of additive noise, however, its performance deteriorates rapidly. Figure 8-7 shows the model of speech with additive noise. Clearly, the signal being analyzed is no longer simply $G(f)H(f)$ but rather $G(f)H(f) + N(f)$. We have thus lost the multiplicative property on

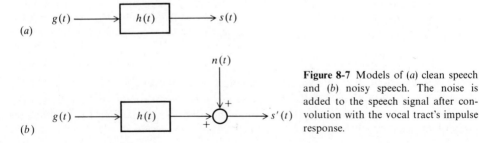

Figure 8-7 Models of (*a*) clean speech and (*b*) noisy speech. The noise is added to the speech signal after convolution with the vocal tract's impulse response.

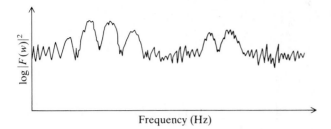

Figure 8-8 Sketch of logged power spectrum of noisy speech. The noise dominates in the low-level regions and obscures the periodicity of the pitch harmonics.

which the cepstrum depends. The effect of noise can be seen in the sketch in Fig. 8-8, which shows the log of the spectrum of noisy speech. Here the low-lying portions of the log spectrum are filled with noise; this means that the input to the cepstrum is no longer purely periodic, and the pitch peak in the cepstrum will be broadened and corrupted by noise. As the noise level increases, the usable portion of the log spectrum becomes smaller and smaller, and the sensitivity of the cepstrum decreases accordingly.

Harmonic-Peak-Based Methods

A number of pitch extractors use the harmonic peaks of the speech spectrum as their primary input. These algorithms all make use of either the fact that the harmonic peaks occur at integer multiples of the pitch frequency or the fact that the differences in the peak frequencies are integer multiples of the pitch frequency. These extractors have two important virtues: they are simple to implement and they are highly resistant to noise. The second fact comes about because as the noise level increases, the peaks are the last parts of the spectrum to be submerged. Some of these extractors will work on as few as three peaks, and so the noise level must be high enough to inundate even these peaks before the extractor breaks down.

Peak-difference extractors Aschkenasy et al. (1974) use the following algorithm. First, a pool is formed of the largest spectrum peaks below 1200 Hz. Then the following steps are carried out:

1. Select the three largest peaks from this pool and compute the frequency differences $d_1 = f_2 - f_1$ and $d_2 = f_3 - f_2$ (Fig. 8-9). Since the peak frequencies are integer multiples of F_0, d_1 and d_2 are likewise multiples of F_0 and probably small multiples. We will assume that $d_2 > d_1$; then d_2 is probably equal to nd_1, where $n = 1, 2,$ or 3.
2. Estimate $n = d_2/d_1$; then $F_0 = (d_1 + d_2)/(n + 1)$. This is our first pitch estimate.
3. Determine the harmonic numbers of the three peaks: $n_i = f_i/F_0$.

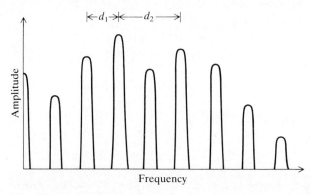

Figure 8-9 Frequency differences between largest spectrum peaks as used in the pitch detector of Aschkenasy et al. (1974).

4. Using these harmonic numbers, refine the pitch estimate:

$$F_0 = \frac{f_1/n_1 + f_2/n_2 + f_3/n_3}{3}$$

The program includes a number of checks for reasonableness and consistency. If these tests fail, the smallest of the three peaks is replaced with the largest peak remaining in the pool and the algorithm repeats. If no consistent results are obtained, the program gives up and reports an unvoiced sound. Since d_1 could have been $2F_0$, the program also tries $F_0/2$ as well.

A closely similar method is due to Snow and Hughes (1969), but it requires that two of the peaks tested be consecutive harmonics. The main weakness of both of these methods is that they require at least three peaks of significant size; hence they tend to fail only on speech signals which are nearly sinusoidal and therefore provide only one usable peak. An example of such a signal is the sound [i] spoken by a female over a telephone system (Sondhi, 1968).

Another peak-based method is described by Seneff (1978). After culling bad peaks with tests based on peak area and proximity to larger peaks, the process enters pitch estimates into a table. The first estimate is based on the two largest spectrum peaks; then successively smaller peaks are incorporated into the estimate and the new values entered in the table. The process terminates when eight nearly equal estimates appear in the table (nearly equal means less than 14 Hz apart); the mean of these eight is taken as the pitch.

Histogram methods Schroeder (1968) investigated three related pitch algorithms: the frequency histogram, the period histogram, and the product spectrum.

Peak-based methods make use of the fact that voice harmonics are harmonic to a high degree of precision. This means that the fundamental frequency can be determined with great accuracy by dividing the frequency of a harmonic peak by its harmonic number. The problem is, of course, that we do not know the harmonic number because we do not yet know the fundamental frequency. It is this problem which gives rise to all of the detective work in Aschkenasy's method. Schroeder escapes from this circle altogether by finding *all* integer submultiples of

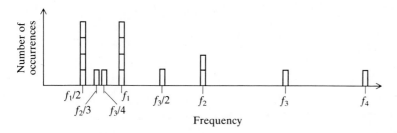

Figure 8-10 A Schroeder histogram plotted on a linear frequency scale.

all the peaks and entering them in a histogram, as shown in Fig. 8-10. Most of these entries will be scattered, but the correct submultiples will all coincide and add up; hence the pitch can be found by locating the highest entry in the histogram. The weakness of this method is that if F_0 is a peak in the histogram, then $F_0/2$ will be an equally high peak. Hence the histogram is scanned from the high-frequency end downwards and threshold tests are used to reject submultiples of the pitch. The HIPEX system (Miller, 1970) is a hardware implementation of the frequency histogram.

In the period histogram, the harmonics are separated by means of a filter bank. If each harmonic is isolated by a filter, then the filter's output will be a sinusoid and we can measure its period. A histogram is now formed from integer multiples of the periods; again, multiples corresponding to the pitch period will coincide. This is clearly nothing more than the time-domain complement to the frequency histogram. Both can be improved by weighting the histogram entries, usually according to the amplitude of the component which gave rise to them, or alternately by the log of the amplitude.

The product spectrum is a more subtle version of the frequency histogram. The peak-finding process is bypassed in this version. Instead of dividing peak frequencies by integers, the entire spectrum is rescaled by compressing its frequency axis by integer scale factors. These compressed spectra are logged and their logs summed. The sum is the log of the product of the compressed spectra:

$$P(f) = \ln \prod_n |X(nf)| \qquad (8\text{-}4)$$

In the product spectrum, there will be a peak at the pitch frequency F_0, resulting, as in the case of the frequency histogram, from coinciding submultiples of the harmonic peaks. The product spectrum is more expensive to compute than the frequency histogram, and special techniques may be required to provide the necessary resolution in the scaled spectra.

Maximum-Likelihood Methods

These techniques are based on unpublished work by D. Slepian (see Noll, 1969); they have been studied by Noll (1969), Wise et al. (1976), and Friedman (1977). They estimate the pitch period by minimizing the error between an estimated "true" periodic signal and the observed speech waveform. If the estimated signal is $s_0(t)$ and the length of the analysis window is T, then the error is the weighted mean-square discrepancy

$$\int_0^T [s(t) - s_0(t)]^2 \, dt$$

Friedman incorporates a time-weighting function $w(t)$ intended to favor the center of the window in order to minimize the effect of pitch changes over the duration of the window.

From this error, a likelihood estimate is obtained as a function of the period t_0 of s_0. Friedman's form of this likelihood is

$$I(t_0) = \int_0^{t_0} \frac{N^2(t)}{D(t)} \, dt$$

where

$$N(t) = \sum_k s(t + kt_0) w(t - kt_0)$$

and

$$D(t) = \sum_k w(t - kt_0)$$

where the sums are over all the apparent periods in the time window. The pitch period is the value of t_0 which maximizes I.

The performance of the maximum-likelihood method is in general similar to that of the Schroeder histogram methods, including great robustness in the presence of noise and a tendency to octave errors.

Time-Domain Analysis

Some investigators have attempted to determine fundamental frequency by detailed analysis of the speech waveform itself.

Gold and Rabiner (1969) devised a parallel-processing detector which found six measurements of the waveform which were then applied to six independent pitch detectors. The final pitch decision was made by majority logic driven by the six detectors. The waveform attributes used were positive and negative peak amplitudes and positions, peak-to-previous-peak, and peak-to-valley measurements. The speech was initially low-pass filtered to 600 Hz, with additional high-pass filtering to remove 60-Hz hum if needed. The measurements were found to be in good agreement with measurements determined by inspection and the process was noise-resistant.

Miller (1975) reasoned that every pitch period should normally be marked by one excursion that is significantly larger than its neighbors. (This is the feature that is usually taken as the starting point by a human pitch detector working with displays of speech waveforms.) These excursions he named principal cycles. His *data-reduction* pitch extractor low-pass filters the speech to 900 Hz and identifies potential principal cycles in the output on the basis of zero-crossing and area criteria. Spurious cycles are then removed by means of a battery of tests based on polarity, proximity, and consistency with pitch estimates obtained elsewhere in the syllable nucleus and in the phrase.

Geçkinli and Yavuz (1977) base their detector on the locations of zero-crossing in speech which has been low-pass filtered to 900 Hz. Zero-crossing locations corresponding to the large initial excursions in a pitch period form a pattern which is consistent from one period to the next. Their program looks for these consistencies in adjacent periods.

Evaluations

Two studies have been made in which a number of the foregoing pitch extractors have been evaluated against objective and subjective criteria. Rabiner *et al.* (1976) obtained accurate pitch data for approximately 120 seconds of speech from seven talkers, using an interactive identification system (McGonegal *et al.*, 1975), and evaluated the following methods with this data base:

AMDF (Ross *et al.*, 1974)
Center-clipping (Dubnowski *et al.*, 1976)
Cepstrum (Schafer and Rabiner, 1970)
Data reduction (Miller, 1975)
LPC (Atal, unpublished)
Parallel processing (Gold and Rabiner, 1969)
SIFT (Markel, 1972)

No one technique was best for all talkers. Generally, spectral methods were best with low-pitched voices, since these voices provided an abundance of harmonics in the analysis range, and time-domain techniques were best with high-pitched voices, since these voices produced many pitch periods over the time windows used. The techniques were also evaluated for accuracy in distinguishing voiced speech from unvoiced; here the results were even less clear-cut. The voiced/unvoiced decision is in most cases a validity test made by comparing the pitch indication against some threshold, and there is a tradeoff between the threshold level and the type of error made. Computationally, Miller's data-reduction method was fastest and the cepstrum, with its repeated Fourier transforms, was slowest.

McGonegal *et al.* (1977) tested the same set of pitch extractors on the basis of subjective evaluations. The pitch measurements and voicing decisions obtained by the various methods were used to control a speech synthesizer, and a jury of eight listeners evaluated the resulting speech. On this basis, the Atal LPC extractor was highest in average rank in all categories and the data reduction ranked lowest. The subjective ranking did not agree well with the objective rankings obtained in the Rabiner *et al.* (1976) study. All automatic extractors ranked well below the semiautomatic process, however, which in turn ranked well below natural speech.

8-2 FORMANT FREQUENCY ESTIMATION

Formants are of interest to us for a number of reasons. They represent the most immediate source of articulatory information and the source most familiar to us by virtue of our use of formant information in speech perception. Hence they have been used extensively as primary features in speech recognition and as the principal information to be transmitted in encoded speech.

Information about formants is contained in the spectrum envelope. Hence all formant estimators either implicitly or explicitly examine the spectrum envelope. Like pitch extraction, formant identification is one of those things which on the surface seem straightforward but which in practice are plagued by a lot of problems. These problems are as follows:

1. *Spurious peaks.* The maxima in the spectrum envelope are normally due only to formants. Spurious peaks, however, do occur; they were particularly prevalent as artifacts in the spectrum-envelope estimators used before linear prediction became the preferred method. Even with linear prediction, they are not unknown: the predictor is given two or three extra poles for increased flexibility, and it may occasionally use them to indulge in spurious peaks. In addition, traditional formant identifiers have trouble finding a suitable niche for the extra formant which appears in nasalized vowels.
2. *Blends.* The frequencies of adjacent formants may actually be too close to resolve. At these points, instead of having excess envelope peaks, we have an apparent deficiency, and considerable practical difficulties are involved in conferring on a formant-extraction algorithm enough intelligence to recognize a blend when it sees one.
3. *High-pitched speech.* The spectrum envelope was traditionally estimated from the sample points provided by the harmonic peaks. High-pitched voices, such as those of women and children, have relatively widely spaced harmonics and thus provide fewer points from which to estimate the spectrum envelope. One would think that this problem would disappear if the envelope were estimated by means of linear prediction, but it has been shown (Makhoul, 1975) that in such speech the LPC envelope peaks tend to be drawn away from their true values and toward the nearest harmonic peaks.

In some procedures, the focus is on the estimation of the envelope itself (especially in techniques antedating linear prediction). In most modern techniques, the emphasis is on finding the maxima in the envelope and assigning them to formants.

Estimation from Filter-Bank Outputs

This is the earliest form of formant extractor. It has lost some popularity to methods based on linear prediction, but since filter banks continue to be used for speech recognition, it is still relevant to us here. In addition, filter banks can be designed to match the estimated frequency sensitivity of the ear more closely than

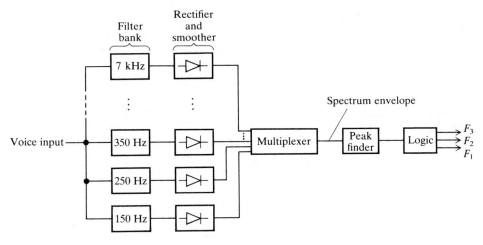

Figure 8-11 Formant estimation by means of a filter bank. (*Adapted from Flanagan, 1956.*)

LPC estimates, and this fact has resulted in continued interest in filter-bank analysis. We cite Flanagan (1956), one of the earliest efforts but still one of the best. The system is sketched in Fig. 8-11. The filters cover an analysis band from 150 to 7000 Hz using the Koenig approximation to the mel scale: 100-Hz bandwidths up to 1 kHz, increasing logarithmically above that frequency. The filter outputs are full-wave rectified and used to provide the spectrum-envelope estimate. Logic is used to identify peaks within appropriate frequency ranges as formants 1, 2, and 3. Peaks are assigned sequentially; each peak is constrained to lie within its known frequency range and above the frequency of the previous formant.

Analysis by Synthesis

The interest of this method is mainly historical, since it has been superseded by methods based on linear prediction. The intent was to duplicate the vocal tract transfer function over the ranges of the first three formants by means of a model consisting of a set of three tunable two-pole filters, and the trick was to find a way of varying the center frequencies and bandwidths of these filters until they matched the observed spectrum envelope. Bell *et al.* (1961) and Paul *et al.* (1964) matched the model to filter-bank outputs; Mathews *et al.* (1961) matched the model to the transform of one pitch period of the waveform. Pinson (1963) carried out the matching in the time domain; Olive (1971) matched all three filters simultaneously instead of sequentially.

Estimation from Cepstrum (Schafer and Rabiner, 1970)

In discussing the cepstrum, we observed that the logging operation and the second transform separated the spectrum envelop from the pitch harmonics. In fundamental-frequency estimation, we were trying to find the pitch harmonics, but clearly the cepstrum can provide us with the spectrum envelope as well. Schafer and Rabiner (1970) removed the pitch peak and its rahmonics by longpass liftering and then recovered the spectrum envelope by an inverse transformation of the cepstrum. Envelope maxima can then be assigned to formants on a system using frequency-dependent thresholds.

LPC-Based Estimates

The ultimate estimator of the spectrum envelope has been, in recent times, the vocal tract filter derived from linear prediction. Since linear prediction gives us a good model of the vocal tract (provided the speech is substantially noise-free), this is clearly a good point of departure for obtaining formant frequencies. The LPC estimate has been faulted because its frequency sensitivity does not match that of the ear (Pisoni, 1985), but for many purposes it is still the cheapest and best method available. There are, in general, two ways to proceed. One is to compute the roots of $A(z)$ by means of any standard complex root-finding program; the other is to find local maxima in the spectrum envelope derived from the predictor, a process known as "peak-picking."

Root-finding The computational expense associated with root-finding is usually prohibitive for real-time speech work, but the process is frequently used in research and we will discuss it briefly here.

Programs for finding the complex roots of a polynomial usually use a Newton-Raphson search algorithm. This algorithm starts with an initial guess at the root and evaluates the polynomial and its derivative at the guess; then it uses these results to find an improved guess. The process usually terminates when the difference between successive guesses is less than some predetermined limit. The polynomial is then "deflated" by dividing it by the factor corresponding to the root just found. If the root is real, the factor is linear; if the root is complex, a quadratic factor can be found from the root and its conjugate. Deflating the polynomial effectively removes the root; the program can then be applied to the deflated polynomial to find a different root. The deflation and root-finding processes are repeated until all roots have been found. Because the roots being removed are not known exactly, deflation always entails some loss of precision, so that successive roots are found less and less accurately. This problem is commonly avoided by doing the final Newton-Raphson iterations for each new root on the undeflated polynomial. [One widely available program along these lines is the subroutine, POLRT, contained in the IBM (1968) Scientific Subroutine Library.]

This type of algorithm will occasionally blow up when the iteration yields a guess for which the value of the polynomial or its derivative is so large as to cause a floating-point overflow error. Because the roots are all concentrated within or very near to the unit circle, the guess in such cases will always be found to be far from the unit circle. This problem can be avoided by modifying the program to restrict guesses to within some reasonable distance from the origin—

for example, 5 units. Since the poles are always within the unit circle for autocorrelation predictors and at worst only a short distance outside for covariance predictors, this limit will not prevent the correct roots from being found.

The computational burden of an iterative complex root-finding algorithm is usually considerable because of the number of iterations required for each root. The program can be speeded up significantly, however, if the initial guesses for each frame are the root locations from the previous frame; generally the frame-to-frame motion of the roots is small enough that the new values converge after relatively few iterations (Sambur, 1979). To start the process on the first frame, the initial guesses can be placed at equal intervals about the unit circle.

If there is a root at some value z_i, as shown in Fig. 8-12, then the corresponding formant frequency and 3-dB bandwidth are given by

$$F_i = \frac{\theta_i}{2\pi T_s} \qquad (8\text{-}5a)$$

$$B_i = -\frac{\ln |z_i|}{\pi T_s} \qquad (8\text{-}5b)$$

where $T_s = 1/f_s$. For example, if a root is found at $z_i = 0.1 + j0.95$, then $|z_i| = 0.955$ and $\theta_i = 1.466$ rad. If the speech was sampled at 8 kHz, this gives a frequency of 1866 Hz and a bandwidth of 117 Hz. Since the poles come in conjugate pairs, only those with a positive imaginary part need be examined. If B_i is negative, the corresponding pole lies outside the unit circle. It is customary to correct this, if necessary, by reflecting the pole inside the unit circle—i.e., by replacing z_i by $1/z_i$; clearly this has no effect on the absolute value of B_i.

Figure 8-13 shows formants for "ten above in the suburbs," from the weather data, as computed from predictor coefficients. A tenth-order autocorrelation predictor was used, and roots were found using a Newton-Raphson root finder modified as described above. This figure should be compared with the spectrogram shown in Fig. 5-2.

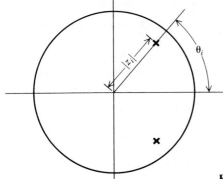

Figure 8-12 Complex pole-pair and polar coordinates.

214 APPLICATIONS

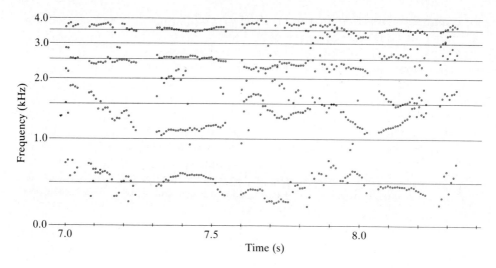

Figure 8-13 Formant values for the phrase "ten above in the suburbs." Time scale in seconds corresponds to time in Figs. 4-5 and 5-34; frequency is plotted using the Koenig approximation to the mel scale.

Peak-picking The other way to obtain formant data from the predictor coefficients is to compute the spectrum envelope $H(z)$ using the method described in Sec. 6-9. The formants can then be found by searching the envelope for local maxima. This approach is clearly cheaper than the root-finding method. Its principal weakness is its vulnerability to formant blends. In a blend, the poles of two adjacent formants are so close together that the spectrum envelope shows only one local maximum instead of two. Hence the peak picker thinks there is only one formant there, and this causes confusion subsequently when peaks are assigned to formants.

Most modern methods for resolving blends do so by reducing the distance from the poles to the contour on which $H(z)$ is evaluated. To obtain the spectrum envelope, we evaluate $A(z)$ on the unit circle, as described in Chapter 6. Clearly, if the function were evaluated on a contour lying inside the unit circle and passing between it and the poles, the resulting envelope would be less likely to show blends. In principle, any blend can be resolved by passing the evaluation contour close enough to the poles.

This technique was initially proposed by Schafer and Rabiner (1970). They did not apply it to $A(z)$ directly, but used a nearly equivalent technique with their cepstrum-based formant extractor. Instead of applying a Fourier transform to the liftered cepstrum, they used an alternate transform whose effect was equivalent to evaluating $A(z)$ on a spiral path, as shown in Fig. 8-14a. (It is not exactly the same, because the envelope obtained from cepstral liftering corresponds to a running average of the log spectrum, where the LPC envelope, as we saw in Sec. 6-6, tends to follow the maxima of the spectrum.) This transform is called the "chirp-Z transform." Where the discrete Fourier transform evaluates $A(z)$ at

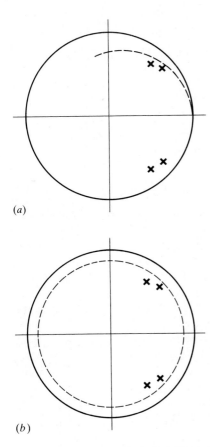

Figure 8-14 Contours for evaluating spectrum envelope using (*a*) the chirp-Z transform and (*b*) the McCandless enhancement.

points $z_i = W^i$, the chirp-Z transform evaluates $A(z)$ at points $z_i = (kW)^i$, where $k < 1$. This path is therefore a logarithmic spiral going inward from (0, 1), as shown in the figure.

An equivalent procedure can be applied to $A(z)$ itself. Here it is easier to choose a circular contour, as shown in Fig. 8-14*b*, rather than a spiral one (McCandless, 1974). Thus instead of evaluating

$$[S(n)]^{-1} = A(z)\bigg|_{z = e^{jn\theta}}$$

we evaluate

$$[S'(n)]^{-1} = A(z)\bigg|_{z = r^{-1} e^{jn\theta}} \tag{8-6}$$

where $r < 1$. In practice, evaluation on this contour is computationally awkward; it is easier to get an equivalent result by adjusting the coefficients $a(i)$ and evaluating the adjusted polynomial on the unit circle. This can be seen by writing (8-6) out in detail:

$$[S'(n)]^{-1} = \sum_{k=0}^{p} a(k)r^{-k}e^{jkn\theta}$$

$$= \sum_{k=0}^{p} a'(k)e^{jkn\theta}$$

where $a'(k) = r^{-k}a(k)$. In making this transformation, we have in effect created a new transfer function whose roots have been moved closer to the unit circle. Usually the new contour will resolve all the formants, although not always: even after modification, one formant may be in the shadow of another.

In a related technique, Kang and Coulter (1976) moved the roots directly onto the unit circle. If the autocorrelation method was used, and if the results of the analysis are at hand, this can be done very easily by setting the final reflection coefficient to unity. It will be recalled that the poles of an autocorrelation filter are never outside the unit circle. From the theory of equations, however, we know that the final coefficient of the polynomial $A(z)$ is equal to the product of the magnitudes of all the roots. This final coefficient is the last reflection coefficient; hence the Kang-Coulter method forces all roots to the unit circle and every pole results in a spectrum peak. (In practice, the poles are not moved all the way to the unit circle; instead, the final reflection coefficient is set to 0.999.) Kang and Coulter call these values "pseudoformants." The problem with this method is that the poles do not migrate along radial paths, and hence the apparent formant frequencies are not exactly the same as the correct values. Kang and Coulter therefore use an iterative method which steps the final reflection coefficient down from 0.999 to the actual value in increments of 0.2. If a formant disappears along the way, the last observed frequency is retained. In this way, all formant values are obtained, and the error in estimating the frequencies of blends is minimized.

It is instructive to compare these two methods by trying them on some specific data. Figure 8-15 shows a spectrum envelope with a blend in which F_3 is

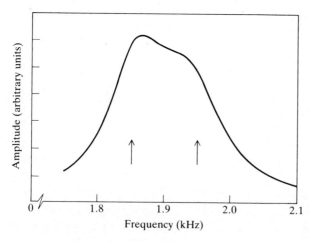

Figure 8-15 Spectrum envelope in the vicinity of a formant blend. The arrows indicate the true formant frequencies as found by root-finding.

hidden beneath the skirts of F_2. The formants and their corresponding pole locations are as follows (we assume a sampling frequency of 10 kHz):

$$F_1 = 475 \text{ Hz, BW} = 50 \text{ Hz;} \quad r_1 = 0.98441, \theta_1 = 17.1°$$
$$F_2 = 1850 \text{ Hz, BW} = 80 \text{ Hz;} \quad r_2 = 0.97518, \theta_2 = 66.6°$$
$$F_3 = 1950 \text{ Hz, BW} = 100 \text{ Hz;} \quad r_3 = 0.96907, \theta_3 = 70.2°$$
$$F_4 = 3150 \text{ Hz, BW} = 200 \text{ Hz;} \quad r_4 = 0.93910, \theta_4 = 113.4°$$

The corresponding transfer function is

$$A(z) = 1 - 2.56696z^{-1} + 4.47145z^{-2} - 5.65310z^{-3} + 5.69656z^{-4}$$
$$- 5.08893z^{-5} + 3.71560z^{-6} - 1.99179z^{-7} + 0.76323z^{-8}$$

In the McCandless enhancement, we evaluate on the contour, $|z| = 0.97615$. (This is the radius of the pole at 1850 Hz, divided by 0.999.) The modified polynomial is

$$A_1(z) = 1 - 2.62969z^{-1} + 4.69266z^{-2} - 6.07774z^{-3} + 6.27413z^{-4}$$
$$- 5.74186z^{-5} + 4.29477z^{-6} - 2.35852z^{-7} + 0.92585z^{-8}$$

The enhanced spectrum is the solid curve in Fig. 8-16. Formant 3 now shows a peak, but it is a relatively small one, even though the contour was deliberately chosen to graze the F_2 pole, and it is easy to imagine a situation in which F_3 would still be invisible. McCandless had a fast processor available and was able to try a large number of contours in relatively small steps. She also obtained satisfactory results, however, using only three contours with radii of 0.96, 0.92, and 0.88.

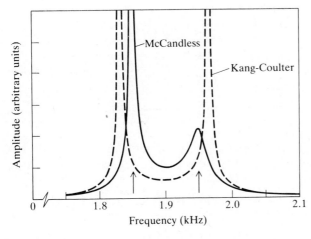

Figure 8-16 The blend of Fig. 8-15 resolved by the McCandless enhancement procedure (solid curve) and the Kang-Coulter "pseudoformant" method. The arrows indicate the locations of the formants.

The Kang-Coulter enhancement proceeds as follows. The final stage of the Levinson recursion which gave rise to $A(z)$ was

$$\begin{bmatrix} 1.0 \\ -2.56696 \\ 4.47145 \\ -5.65310 \\ 5.69656 \\ -5.08893 \\ 3.71560 \\ -1.99179 \\ 0.763235 \end{bmatrix} = \begin{bmatrix} 1.0 \\ -2.50737 \\ 3.91780 \\ -4.23753 \\ 3.23074 \\ -1.85470 \\ 0.72540 \\ -0.07808 \\ 0.0 \end{bmatrix} + 0.763235 \begin{bmatrix} 0.0 \\ -0.07808 \\ 0.72540 \\ -1.85470 \\ 3.23074 \\ -4.23753 \\ 3.91780 \\ -2.50737 \\ 1.0 \end{bmatrix}$$

If this final cycle is repeated with $k_8 = 0.999$, we get the following polynomial:

$$A_3(z) = 1 - 2.58537z^{-1} + 4.64247z^{-2} - 6.09033z^{-3} + 6.45825z^{-4}$$
$$- 6.08799z^{-5} + 4.63928z^{-6} - 2.58294z^{-7} + 0.99900z^{-8}$$

The spectrum envelope corresponding to $A_3(z)$ is the dashed curve in Fig. 8-16. Here all formants are unmistakably visible, but they have been shifted away from the correct positions. (Notice that the McCandless peaks are always directly on top of the correct frequencies.) The Kang-Coulter enhancement unfailingly finds all formant values, but the computational burden may be somewhat higher and the values may not be entirely accurate.

An altogether different solution to the blend problem has been proposed by Christensen et al. (1976). Instead of examining the spectrum itself, they examine the second derivative of the logged power spectrum. Since a merged formant peak is usually visible as a bump on the shoulder of the adjacent peak, the bump should produce a local minimum in the second-derivative spectrum. In addition to that, however, the magnitude of the local minimum provides an indication of the bandwidth of the formant.

This comes about as follows. We can represent the power spectrum of a single pole-pair by

$$H(f) = |A(jf)|^2 = \frac{1}{(f^2 - f_0^2)^2 + b^2 f^2}$$

where f_0 is the center frequency and b is the bandwidth. (The numerator is independent of frequency, and we have set it to unity for simplicity.) After a good deal of manipulation, the second derivative of $L(f) = \log(H)$ can be shown to be

$$\frac{d^2 L}{df^2} = \left[\frac{4(f^2 - f_0^2)f + 2b^2 f}{(f^2 - f_0^2)^2 + b^2 f^2}\right]^2 - \frac{12f^2 - 4f_0^2 + 2b^2}{(f^2 - f_0^2)^2 + b^2 f^2}$$

If we assume that the second derivative reaches its minimum at the resonant frequency, and if we assume that the b is small compared to f_0, so that resonance occurs at $f = f_0$, then the second derivative reduces to

$$\frac{d^2 L}{df^2} = \frac{2b^2 - 8f_0^2}{b^2 f_0^2}$$

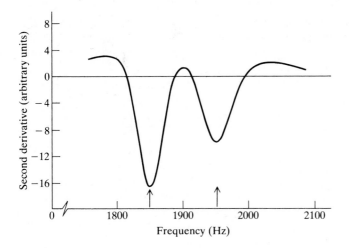

Figure 8-17 Second derivative of the blend of Fig. 8-15. The arrows indicate the locations of the formants.

However, if b is small compared to f, then this reduces further to approximately $-8/b^2$, which is the desired result. In practice, the constant of proportionality depends on details of the implementation (such as the omitted numerator), and the bandwidths are computed using the formula $b = b_0(d/d_0)^s$, where d is the second derivative. In an analysis of two minutes' worth of speech data, Christensen et al. obtained an empirical value of -0.53 for s. It should be borne in mind that this derivation is for an isolated pole and does not take into account interactions between closely spaced resonances.

If we plot the second derivative for our test data, as shown in Fig. 8-17, we find that the minima in the second difference occur at approximately the correct frequencies. The ratio of their amplitudes is 1.69 to 1, corresponding to a bandwidth ratio of 1.32 to 1 comparable to the 1.25 to 1 ratio in the original data. This represents a very attractive modification of the peak-picking method for locating formants.

8-3 TRACKING AND SMOOTHING

All pitch and formant extractors are, as we have seen, subject to errors. One way to reduce the error rate is to require some continuity in the values obtained, on the grounds that wrong estimates will result in irregular values while right ones will not. Continuity requirements may be imposed either by means of a tracker which guides the estimation process while it is going on or by a smoother which edits the data afterwards.

A tracker works by predicting the forthcoming value of the variable being tracked and then encouraging the parameter extraction algorithm to provide a value close to the predicted value. For example, a pitch tracker used in conjunction with the Schroeder histogram might operate by setting limits to the frequency range to be covered by the histogram and thus minimizing the likelihood of octave errors. The predictor is usually fairly simple, and may be no more than a linear projection from the two most recent values. A more finely tuned predictor is of little use, because it is going to be used only to set limits and not to determine a value precisely.

Tracking is a risky procedure, however, because if an error is not eliminated, then the tracker will tend to propagate that error when it uses it to predict the limits on the following values. Also, as we have observed previously, errors in speech tend to cluster, and most trackers are not able to ride out a string of errors; in fact, it is then not generally feasible to enable the tracker to recognize errors as such. A further problem is that both pitch and formants occasionally change abruptly, and a tracker will try to suppress these changes.

It is therefore usually safer to apply a smoothing algorithm over an entire utterance after the raw data have been extracted. In this way, continuity requirements can be used to smooth the data without adversely influencing the decisions made by the feature estimator.

Smoothing can take a number of different forms. In its simplest (and probably safest) version, smoothing simply looks for points that are grossly out of line with adjacent values, as in Fig. 8-18. Such points can be detected by comparing the second difference of the sequence to some suitably determined threshold.

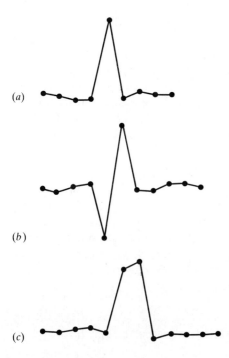

Figure 8-18 One- or two-frame errors which show up as gross discontinuities are easily identified.

Points found to be in error can either be returned to the extraction routine with a request for a better value, or they can be replaced with values interpolated from the adjacent data. This kind of data editing will work only on isolated errors or very short runs, since it is essential to have a large body of reliable data against which to compare the outliers.

The temptation to smooth by means of a running average should be resisted, because averaging tends to wipe out discontinuities. In speech, discontinuities are usually important. In Fig. 8-19a, for example, the talker has lowered his velum at the point marked by the dotted line, and the formant track shown has a discontinuity there. This is important articulatory information which must not be blurred by smoothing, as suggested by the dotted line.

An alternative to smoothing by a running average is *median smoothing* (Tukey, 1974; Rabiner *et al.*, 1975). This is a nonlinear process; it uses a window which slides over the data, just as the window in conventional smoothing does, but the smoothing operation replaces the point at the center of the window by the *median* of the points in the window rather than by their mean or by a weighted average. For example, in the points in Fig. 8-20, the mean value is marked by the hollow circle at A and the median point by the $\times$ at B. Notice that the maverick point influences the mean but not the median. Median smoothing thus tends to suppress small irregularities in pitch and formant data without blurring large discontinuities. This can be seen by comparing the two types of smoothing in the data of Fig. 8-19.

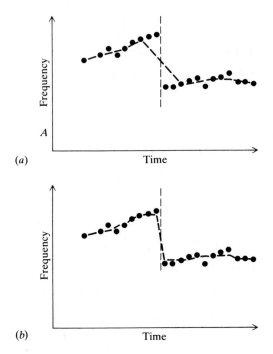

Figure 8-19 Important discontinuity (a) blurred by a running average and (b) preserved by median smoothing.

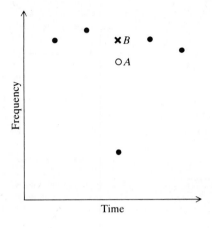

Figure 8-20 Out-of-line value corrected by (A) running average and (B) median smoothing.

PROBLEMS

8-1 Complete the derivation of the Christensen formula for the relation between the second derivative of the log power spectrum and formant bandwidth.

8-2 Suppose a vocal tract transfer function has the following form:

$$A(z) = 1 - 1.2956z^{-1} + 0.7167z^{-2} + 0.6961z^{-3} - 1.3508z^{-4} + 0.5184z^{-5}$$
$$+ (0.1871z^{-6} - 0.1722z^{-7} + 0.0440z^{-8} + 0.1801z^{-9} + 0.0810z^{-10}$$

Use the DFT procedure outlined in Sec. 6-9 to find the spectrum envelope corresponding to this transfer function. In this and the following problems, pad the predictor coefficients with zeros to a length of 512 points in order to get sufficient frequency resolution. Plot the log spectrum in decibels.

8-3 Using the data of Prob. 8-2, carry out the McCandless enhancement procedure, evaluating this polynomial on a contour of radius 0.94. Find and plot the spectrum envelope of the enhanced polynomial.

8-4 Using the results from Prob. 8-2, find and plot the second difference of the log spectrum. Estimate the bandwidths of formants 1, 2, and 3.

8-5 In the transfer function of Prob. 8-2, the reflection coefficient k_{10} is clearly equal to 0.0810. Use the results of Prob. 6-10 to compute the corresponding Kang-Coulter polynomial.

8-6 If you have access to a root-finding program, determine the formant frequencies for the original and modified polynomials in Probs. 8-2, 8-3, and 8-5. Compute the bandwidths of the formants from the roots of the original transfer function and compare them with the estimates from Prob. 8-4.

REFERENCES

Atal, B. S.: Automatic speaker recognition based on pitch contours, Ph.D. Thesis, Polytech. Inst. Brooklyn, 1968.
——— and S. L. Hanauer: Speech analysis and synthesis by linear prediction, *JASA*, vol. 50, no. 2, pp. 637–655, August, 1971.
Aschkenasy, E., *et al.*: Determining vocal pitch from fine-resolution spectrograms, *IEEE Symposium on Speech Recog.*, April, 1974.
Bell, C. G., *et al.*: Reduction of speech spectra by analysis-by-synthesis techniques, *JASA*, vol. 33, pp. 1725–1736, December, 1961.

Bogert, D. P., et al.: The quefrency alanysis of time series for echoes: cepstrum, pseudo-autocovariance, cross-cepstrum, and saphe cracking, in M. Rosenblatt (Ed.), *Proc. Symp. Time Series Analysis*, Wiley, New York, chap. 15, pp. 209–243, 1963.

Christensen, R. L., et al.: A comparison of three methods of extracting resonance information from predictor-coefficient coded speech, *IEEE Trans.*, vol. ASSP-24, no. 1, pp. 8–14, February, 1976.

Dubnowski, J. J., et al.: Real-time hardware pitch detector, *IEEE Trans.*, vol. ASSP-24, no. 1, pp. 2–8, February, 1976.

Flanagan, J. L.: Automatic extraction of formant frequencies from continuous speech, *JASA*, vol. 28, pp. 110–118, 1956.

Friedman, D. H.: Pseudo-maximum-likelihood speech pitch extraction, *IEEE Trans.*, vol. ASSP-25, no. 3, pp. 213–221, June, 1977.

Gallagher, Jr., N. C., and G. L. Wise: A theoretical analysis of the properties of median filters, *IEEE Trans.*, vol. ASSP-29, no. 6, pp. 1136–1141, December, 1981.

Geçkinli, N. C., and D. Yavuz: Algorithm for pitch extraction using zero-crossing interval sequence, *IEEE Trans.*, vol. ASSP-25, no. 6, pp. 559–564, December, 1977.

Gold, B., and L. Rabiner: Parallel processing techniques for estimating pitch periods of speech in the time domain, *JASA*, vol. 46, no. 2, pp. 442–448, August, 1969.

IBM: *System/360 Scientific Subroutine Library, Programmer's Manual*, IBM Corporation, 1968.

Kang, G. S., and D. C. Coulter: 600 bits/second voice digitizer (linear predictive formant vocoder), Naval Res. Lab., 1976.

McCandless, S. S.: An algorithm for automatic formant extraction using linear prediction spectra, *IEEE Trans.*, vol. ASSP-22, no. 2, pp. 135–141, April, 1974.

McGonegal, C. A., et al.: A semi-automatic pitch detector (SAPD), *IEEE Trans.*, vol. ASSP-23, no. 6, pp. 570–574, December, 1975.

———, et al.: A subjective evaluation of pitch detection methods using LPC synthesized speech, *IEEE Trans.*, vol. ASSP-25, no. 3, pp. 221–229, June, 1977.

Makhoul, J. I.: Linear prediction: a tutorial review, *Proc. IEEE*, vol. 63, no. 4, pp. 561–580, April, 1975.

Maksym, J. N.: Real-time pitch extraction by adaptive prediction of the speech waveform, *IEEE Trans.*, vol. AU-21, no. 3, pp. 149–154, June, 1973.

Markel, J. D.: The SIFT algorithm for fundamental frequency estimation, *IEEE Trans.*, vol. AU-20, no. 5, pp. 367–377, December, 1972.

Mathews, M. V., et al.: Pitch-synchronous analysis of voiced sounds, *JASA*, vol. 333, pp. 179–186, 1961.

Miller, N. J.: Pitch detection by data reduction, *IEEE Trans.*, vol. ASSP-23, no. 1, pp. 72–79, February, 1975.

Miller, R. L.: Performance characteristics of an experimental harmonic identification pitch extraction (HIPEX) system, *JASA*, vol. 47, no. 6, pp. 1593–1601, June, 1970.

Moorer, J. A.: The optimum comb method of pitch period analysis of continuous digitized speech, *IEEE Trans.*, vol. ASSP-22, no. 5, pp. 330–338, October, 1974.

Nodes, T. A., and N. C. Gallagher, Jr.: Median filters: some modifications and their properties, *IEEE Trans.*, vol. ASSP-30, no. 5, pp. 739–746, October, 1982.

Noll, A. M.: Cepstrum pitch determination, *JASA*, vol. 41, no. 2, pp. 293–309, February, 1967.

———: Pitch determination of human speech by the harmonic product spectrum, the harmonic sum spectrum, and a maximum likelihood estimate, *Symp. Computer Proc. in Commun.*, Polytech. Inst. of Brooklyn, pp. 779–797, 1969.

Olive, J. P.: Automatic formant tracking by a Newton-Raphson technique, *JASA*, vol. 50, no. 2, pp. 661–670, August, 1971.

Paul, A. P., et al.: Automatic reduction of vowel spectra; an analysis-by-synthesis method and its evaluation, *JASA*, vol. 36, pp. 303–308, 1964.

Pinson, E. N.: Pitch-synchronous time-domain estimation of formant frequencies and bandwidths, *JASA*, vol. 35, pp. 1263–1273, 1963.

Pisoni, D. B.: Speech perception: some new directions in research and theory, *JASA*, vol. 78, no. 1, pt. 2, pp. 381–388, July, 1985.

Rabiner, L. R., et al.: Applications of a non-linear smoothing algorithm to speech processing, *IEEE Trans.*, vol. ASSP-23, no. 6, pp. 552–557, December, 1975.

———, et al.: A comparative performance study of several pitch detection algorithms, *IEEE Trans.*, vol. ASSP-24, no. 5, pp. 399–418, October, 1976.

Ross, M. J., et al.: Average magnitude difference function pitch extractor, *IEEE Trans.*, vol. ASSP-22, no. 5, pp. 353–362, October, 1974.

Sambur, M.: Personal communication, 1979.

Schafer, R. W., and L. R. Rabiner: System for automatic formant analysis of voiced speech, *JASA*, vol. 47, no. 2, pp. 634–648, February, 1970.

Schroeder, M. R.: Period histogram and product spectrum: new methods for fundamental-frequency measurement, *JASA*, vol. 43, no. 4, pp. 829–834, April, 1968.

Seneff, S.: Real-time harmonic pitch detector, *IEEE Trans.*, vol. ASSP-26, no. 4, pp. 358–365, August, 1978.

Snow, T. B., and G. W. Hughes: Fundamental frequency estimation by harmonic identification, *JASA*, vol. 45, no. 1, p. 316(A), January, 1969.

Sondhi, M. M.: New methods of pitch extraction, *IEEE Trans.*, vol. AU-16. no. 2, pp. 262–266, June, 1968.

Tukey, J. W.: Nonlinear (nonsuperposable) methods for smoothing data, *Congress Record, 1974 EASCON*, p. 673, 1974.

Un, C. K., and S.-C. Yang: A pitch extraction algorithm based on LPC inverse filtering and AMDF, *IEEE Trans.*, vol. ASSP-25, no. 6, pp. 565–572, December, 1977.

Wise, J. D., et al.: Maximum likelihood pitch estimation, *IEEE Trans.*, vol. ASSP-24, no. 5, pp. 418–423, October, 1976.

CHAPTER
NINE

SPEECH COMPRESSION

Speech may be encoded digitally for many purposes. It is frequently desirable to store "canned" utterances for automatic playback at certain times; e.g., in telephone call–interception systems. Playback of digitized speech is more flexible and easier to control than playback of analog tape recordings, and since the appearance of cheap memory, it also has the potential of being more economical. Digital signals can also be made more resistant to degradation than analog signals; hence digitized speech is the preferred mode for transmission in noisy channels. It is also necessary to digitize speech for transmission over digital data links and for encryption purposes. (All modern encryption techniques are inherently discrete processes and hence require digitized data.)

If speech is encoded by means of conventional analog-to-digital conversion techniques, a very large number of bits must be transmitted (or stored) per second of speech, as we will see presently. This *bit rate* is usually prohibitive, and "compression" refers to reducing this bit rate in order to render the process economical.

Compressing speech entails a three-way tradeoff among the goals of preserving intelligibility and quality, limiting the bit rate, and keeping the encoding and decoding processes computationally cheap. We will divide speech-compression techniques rather arbitrarily into two general categories. The first attempts to preserve the input waveform, in the sense that the recovered speech signal is essentially the same as the input speech signal. This approach is commonly known as *waveform encoding*. The second approach attempts to provide a signal which will sound like the input speech, without necessarily matching the input waveform. Devices which do this are known as *vocoders* (for "voice encoders").

An encoded waveform is like a phonograph record: the encoded data represent the sound made by the musician, and in principle the waveform presented to the loudspeaker terminals is the same as the waveform at the recording microphone, except for errors introduced in the recording and playback processes. The output of a vocoder is like a player-piano roll: the encoded data consist of instructions for imitating the input waveform, and there is no expectation that the output waveform will match the waveform produced at the recording session in detail.

We have chosen to discuss waveform coding in this chapter and vocoders in Chapter 10. In practice the boundary between these two approaches is not sharply drawn, and there are thus a few exceptions to this organization. In particular, as waveform coding systems go to lower and lower bit rates, the emphasis in design tends to shift toward perceived sound quality over accuracy of waveform reproduction. Further, the channel vocoder is historically a voice encoder, but since most of its modern offshoots are waveform coders, we discuss it in this chapter instead of Chapter 10.

9-1 PULSE-CODE MODULATION (PCM)

Analog-to-digital (A/D) conversion of speech is logically and historically the starting point in digital representation of speech. The steps are similar to any digitization scheme: first the bandwidth of the speech signal is limited to some appropriate value by an antialiasing filter. The signal is then sampled at a frequency at or above the Nyquist rate and the samples are converted to binary numbers proportional to their amplitudes. The binary values are frequently represented by pulses which thus encode the sample amplitudes, and it is this fact that gives rise to the name PCM. At the output, the binary values are applied to a digital-to-analog (D/A) converter and the output is filtered to smooth out the quantization steps.

Telephone bandwidth, from 0.3 to 3.3 kHz, has become a *de facto* standard; the antialiasing filter typically has a corner frequency of approximately 3.5 kHz and the sampling rate is usually 8 kHz with a resolution of 12 bits.

The output filter is designed to cut off at the same frequency as the input filter, but it will also incorporate some high-frequency emphasis. The reason for this is that the output of the D/A converter is not an impulse train but a piecewise rectangular ("boxcar") signal, as shown in Fig. 9-1. It is not difficult to show that the boxcar operation applies a $\sin f/f$ weighting to the spectrum which must be corrected by the output filter in order to restore the frequency balance of the original signal.

The finite step size inherent in quantization causes errors in the encoding of the signal. These errors are heard as noise in the recovered speech. The error in any given sample will be the difference between the input value and the nearest quantization step. Let the quantizer's step size be s. If we assume that the step size is small compared with the signal and that the signal does not exceed the

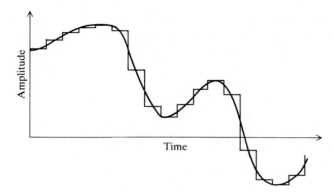

Figure 9-1 Continuous time function estimated by piecewise-rectangular output of a digital-to-analog converter.

range of the quantizer, then the probability density of the error will be rectangular with a width of s and a variance of $s^2/12$. The noise power will be equal to this variance. The signal power, similarly, will be equal to its variance. In practice the signal is scaled so that its variance will be less than that afforded by the saturation level by some margin of safety, in order to minimize the likelihood of overload. This margin is commonly called "headroom."

For any speech encoding scheme, we define its signal-to-noise (S/N) ratio as the ratio of signal power to quantization noise power. If the converter has a word length of B bits, then its range is from -2^{B-1} to $2^{B-1} - 1$ (assuming two's-complement representation) and the saturation level is given by

$$A_{max} = 2^{B-1}s$$

If the headroom factor is h, then

$$X_{rms} = \frac{A_{max}}{h}$$

$$= \frac{2^{B-1}s}{h}$$

The signal-to-quantizing-noise (S/N) ratio is given by

$$S = \frac{X_{rms}^2}{s^2/12}$$

$$= \frac{12 \times 2^{(2B-2)}}{h^2}$$

In decibels, this is

$$S_{dB} = 6B + 4.8 - 20 \log_{10} h \tag{9-1}$$

We can now make some estimates of the bit rate for high-quality speech transmission. Suppose we require an S/N ratio of 60 dB and that a headroom factor of 4 is acceptable. Then the required word length is

$$B = \left\lceil \frac{67.3}{6} \right\rceil = \lceil 11.21 \rceil = 12 \text{ bits}$$

(where $\lceil x \rceil$ is the "ceiling" of x, the smallest number that is greater than or equal to x). If we sample at 8 kHz, then PCM requires $8k \times 12 = 96{,}000$ bits/s.

If this is too high a bit rate to be acceptable, as it usually is, then we must either use a shorter word length or find a more ingenious way to encode.

9-2 WAVEFORM ENCODERS: BASIC TECHNIQUES

There are two general ways to reduce the bit rate required in waveform encoders: either reduce the disturbing effect of the quantization noise or reduce the amount of information which has to be encoded. These two techniques are frequently combined.

The disturbing effects of quantization noise are minimized by concealment: i.e., the noise is redistributed in such a way as to render it less noticeable. There are a number of ways in which this can be done.

Dither

Part of what makes quantizing noise objectionable at very short word lengths is the fact that the quantization error is not uncorrelated with the instantaneous signal value. It has been found that the annoyance can be reduced by eliminating this correlation. This can be done by applying "dither" to the speech signal (Jayant and Rabiner, 1972). Dither is noise deliberately added to the signal, as shown in Fig. 9-2. The noise is generated independently of the speech, usually as pseudorandom noise, and hence it is uncorrelated with the speech signal. The quantizing error now reflects the instantaneous value of the combined signal and

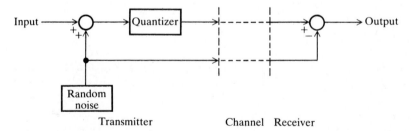

Figure 9-2 Use of random noise ("dither") to remove correlation between input sample values and quantization noise. The dither is removed from the signal at the receiver by subtraction. If the noise is generated by synchronized pseudorandom number generators, it need not be transmitted along with the signal.

noise; if the amplitude of the noise is comparable to that of the speech signal, the error is no longer strongly correlated with the speech. The digital samples transmitted down the line now contain the combined speech and dither. At the receiving end, however, the same noise is subtracted from the D/A-converted speech signal. (The noise can be generated locally, using a matching pseudorandom generator suitably synchronized with the transmitter, so that the dither itself does not have to be transmitted over the channel.) The listener therefore hears the speech signal alone, plus quantizing noise which is no longer correlated with the signal. Note that this technique does not reduce the quantizing noise but only converts it to a form which listeners find less annoying.

Nonuniform Quantizers

From an S/N standpoint, equally spaced levels are appropriate only if all levels are equally likely, and we know from observed probability densities (Chapter 5) that speech signals are heavily concentrated in the low amplitudes (and we know from the center-clipping experiments described in Chapter 3 that this is where the information is). Hence it is a much better strategy to use a nonuniform quantizer in which the steps are densest at the low levels.

It is convenient to visualize such a quantizer as a nonlinear predistortion followed by a uniform quantizer. The predistortion function is designed to give the output signal an approximately uniform (rectangular) probability density. At the receiving end, the D/A-converted signal is passed through a complementary circuit which restores the original amplitudes. (Such a matched compressor/expander set is commonly called a *compandor*.)

It can be shown (Papoulis, 1984) that if a random process with a probability distribution function $F(x)$ is passed through a monotonic, nonlinear function $y = q(x)$, then the probability distribution function of the output will be

$$G(y) = F(q^{-1}(x)) \tag{9-2}$$

In that case, the predistortion function which will convert x to a uniformly distributed function on $(0, 1)$ is simply $q(x) = F(x)$. If we want y to have a rectangular density on $(-1, 1)$, then $q(x) = F(\frac{1}{2}(x + 1))$. For example, if x were gaussian with a variance of unity, then $q(x)$ would be given by

$$q(x) = \text{erf}(x)$$

The probability density function of speech, as we have seen in Chapter 6, approximates a modified gamma density function. The integral of this cannot be expressed in closed form, but Paez and Glisson (1972) have tabulated optimum quantization levels for this density.

In practice, it is not necessary to match the distribution function so nicely. One widely used compandor is the μ-law compandor (Smith, 1957):

$$y = \text{sign}(x) \frac{\log(1 + \mu|x|)}{\log(1 + \mu)} \tag{9-3}$$

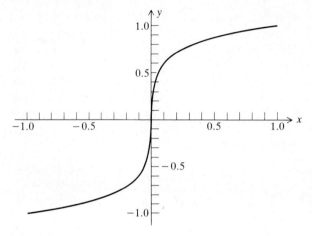

Figure 9-3 Input-output function of a μ-law compressor. The inverse of this function is used at the receiver to restore the linear signal.

where x is the ratio of the input voltage to the A/D saturation level. The input/output characteristic of this compandor is shown in Fig. 9-3. Notice that $\mu = 0$ gives linear operation. Eight-bit compandors are now available as integrated circuits; using a value of $\mu = 255$, they can encode telephone-quality speech with a fidelity comparable to that of a 12-bit uniform quantizer.

Finally, performance can be improved by making the quantizer adapt its step sizes in response to the signal, as shown in Fig. 9-4. In a system described by Jayant (1973) the adaptation logic simply multiplies the previous step size by a factor determined by the magnitude of the previous code word. If at time $t = k$ an input sample y_k and a step size s_k produced a code word H_k, then at $t = k + 1$, the new step size is the product of M times the old step size, where M is a function of the magnitude of H_k:

$$s_{k+1} = s_k M(|H_k|)$$

The multiplication rule is usually determined empirically, and it is designed to provide rapid increases in step size and relatively slow decreases. This is necessary because the noise due to overload is potentially much greater than that due to insufficiently fine sampling.

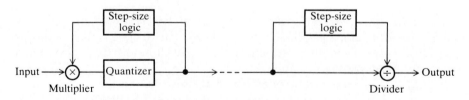

Figure 9-4 Use of adaptive step size to improve quantizer performance. If the step-size logic is driven from the quantizer output, as shown, the identical logic can be used at the receiver to restore the signal.

Differential Quantization

The second way of decreasing the required bit rate is to reduce the amount of information that must be encoded. This is done by taking advantage of the very considerable amount of redundancy in the speech signal.

We saw in Chapter 5 that there is a significant correlation between successive speech samples (Fig. 5-33). We should be able to take advantage of the redundancy implied by this correlation to reduce the amount of information we have to transmit. For example, if we take the difference of the signal, $\Delta x(n) = x(n) - x(n-1)$, this will have a lower variance (and hence lower power) than x itself. If the power is reduced, then we should be able to encode the signal with fewer bits and thereby reduce the bit rate required.

To see what the reduction in variance is, assume $x(t)$ stationary and let $y(t)$ be the differenced signal $x(t) - x(t-1)$. Then

$$E\{y^2(t)\} = E\{x^2(t) - 2x(t)x(t-1) + x^2(t-1)\}$$

$$= 2r_0\left(1 - \frac{r_1}{r_0}\right) \qquad (9\text{-}4)$$

Since the variance of x is r_0, we see that differencing reduces the output power in any signal in which $r_1/r_0 > 0.5$. In speech, the long-term average of this ratio is typically 0.85 or more.

The basic principle is illustrated in simplified form in Fig. 9-5. The circuit at the transmitter computes $x(n)$; this difference is transmitted through the channel to the receiver, where it is integrated in the feedback loop and the original signal is restored. Using Z-transform notation,

$$E(z) = X(z)(1 - z^{-1})$$

$$Y(z) = \frac{E(z)}{1 - z^{-1}} = X(z)$$

This scheme, called differential PCM (DPCM), requires several refinements to make it practical. First, it is not realistic to omit the effect of quantization noise. We will represent the quantizer, in fact, by a source of additive, uncorrelated noise, as shown in Fig. 9-6. If we quantize the difference signal,

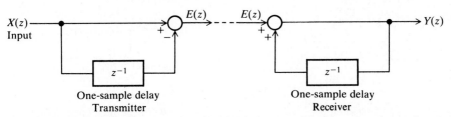

Figure 9-5 Differential quantization, simplified form. A one-sample delay saves the previous sample for subtraction at the transmitter and for addition at the receiver.

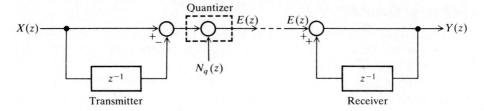

Figure 9-6 Differential quantization with quantization of the difference signal. The quantization noise is modeled by additive noise $N_q(z)$.

however, as shown here, we find that the quantization noise makes a disproportionate contribution to the recovered signal, for if the quantization noise $N_q(z)$ is additive and uncorrelated, then

$$E(z) = X(z)(1 - z^{-1}) + N_q(z)$$

and

$$Y(z) = X(z) + \frac{N_q(z)}{1 - z^{-1}}$$

Thus the quantization noise is integrated at the receiver, and this buildup of noise is found to be more disturbing than the same noise would have been had it been merely added to the original speech signal.

We can avoid this problem by using the configuration of Fig. 9-7. At the transmitter,

$$E(z) = X(z) + C(z) + N_q(z) \tag{9-5}$$

Because of the feedback loop,

$$C(z) = \frac{E(z)z^{-1}}{1 - z^{-1}}$$

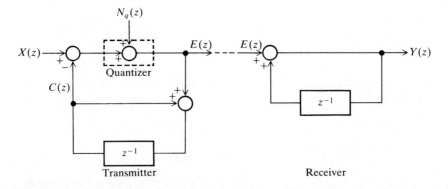

Figure 9-7 Differential quantization with the quantizer inside a feedback loop at the transmitter.

Substituting this in (9-5), we have

$$E(z) = [X(z) + N_q(z)](1 - z^{-1}) \tag{9-6}$$

Here the quantization noise is being differenced along with $x(n)$, and at the receiver,

$$Y(z) = X(z) + N_q(z)$$

The next refinement is to recognize that simple differencing does not minimize the error of the output. From the theory of linear prediction, we already know that if the correlation between adjacent samples is given by $r_1 = \langle x(n)x(n-1) \rangle$, then the optimum gain in the delay path is $a = -r_1/r_0$. We also know that the output power is given by

$$E\{y^2(t)\} = E\{x^2(t)\}(1 - a^2)$$

Notice that while simple differencing reduced the output power only if r_1/r_0 was greater than 0.5, the optimum predictor reduces variance for any signal in which $r_1 \neq 0$.

From here it is a short step to replace the simple differencer by a full pth-order linear predictor, as in Fig. 9-8. Since the DPCM schemes discussed so far are nonadaptive, a fixed set of predictor coefficients is used. We will use $P(z)$ to represent the predictor function. In the notation of Chapter 6,

$$P(z) = A(z) - 1$$

In this case,

$$C(z) = \frac{E(z)P(z)}{1 - P(z)}$$

and

$$E(z) = [x(z) + N_q(z)][1 - P(z)] \tag{9-7a}$$

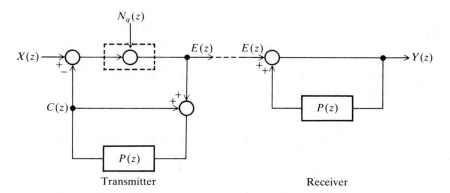

Figure 9-8 Differential quantization with a fixed predictor in place of the simple differencer of Figs. 9-5 to 9-7.

Then, at the receiver,

$$Y(z) = X(z) + N_q(z) \tag{9-7b}$$

as before.

We can obtain the predictor coefficients by using autocorrelation values averaged over a large body of speech data, such as the values shown in Fig. 5-33. The variance of the residual is given by the prediction error

$$E = r_0 \prod_{i=1}^{p}(1 - k_i^2)$$

Using such a predictor, Noll (1972) reports a reduction in variance of 6 dB relative to PCM for a second-order predictor. For higher-order predictors, S/N increases slowly to approximately 9 dB for $p = 10$. Since the autocorrelation function of speech varies from moment to moment and an overall average must necessarily be approximate, this is not surprising. If the reduction in variance is 6 dB, this means that, from Eq. (9-1), we can use one less bit in quantizing the residual than would be required if the original signal were sent.

9-3 APPLICATION OF LINEAR PREDICTION: ADAPTIVE DPCM

The compression ratio of DPCM can be further improved either by adaptive quantization or by adaptive prediction. Adaptive quantization will allow for changes in the variance of the predictor error, while adaptive prediction will follow changes in the autocorrelation function of the input speech. Adaptive quantization of the DPCM residual is in principle similar to adaptive quantization of PCM.

Adaptive prediction (adaptive DPCM, or ADPCM) in its simplest form is simply linear prediction as described at length in Chapter 6. The speech data stream is segmented into contiguous frames of typically 10 to 20 ms and the predictor coefficients (or equivalent information) are transmitted, along with the residual, as shown in Fig. 9-9. At the receiver, an inverse filter controlled by the predictor coefficients reconstructs the speech. Note that Eqs. (9-7) apply to this system as well, except that now $P(z)$ changes adaptively to match the signal. Noll (1972) reports an S/N improvement of more than 12 dB for a tenth-order linear predictor. (An alternative application of linear prediction omits the residual and transmits pitch and voicing information instead. Since this technique does not attempt to preserve the waveform in detail, we have deferred it until Chapter 10 on vocoders.)

The reduction in bit rate is offset by the need to transmit the predictor parameters as well, since these now change from frame to frame of the input speech. The predictor parameters, and any other ancillary data which must be sent in addition to the residual, are commonly known as *side information*.

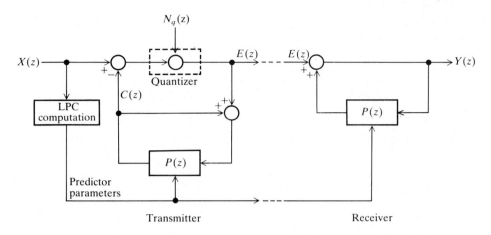

Figure 9-9 Adaptive DPCM. The predictor is controlled by the input signal and its parameters, computed by an LPC algorithm, are transmitted as side information along with the prediction residual $E(z)$.

Various techniques have been devised to minimize the number of bits required by the predictor description. In general, the predictor coefficients themselves are not transmitted, since quantization errors could produce an unstable filter at the receiving end. Instead, the reflection coefficients are usually transmitted. It is a simple matter to ensure that the quantized values fall within the range $(-1, 1)$ and hence result in a stable filter. The reflection coefficients are converted back to predictor coefficients by Levinson recursion. This is done even if (as is usually the case) the predictor is a covariance predictor. The alternative would be to solve the system of (6-54b), repeated here:

$$\mathbf{U}\mathbf{a} = \mathbf{\kappa} \qquad (6\text{-}54b)$$

However, this would require transmitting the $\mathbf{U}$ matrix as side information in addition to the (generalized) reflection coefficients, which would be prohibitive. Another recourse is to compute the true reflection coefficients from the Choleski decomposition using Atal's method (Atal, 1977; Atal and Schroeder, 1979) given in Eqs. (6-59), in which case the Levinson recursion can properly be used to recover the predictor coefficients.

For the equations (9-7) to remain valid, the transmitter and receiver must both use the same $P(z)$. However, the encoding/decoding process will inevitably introduce some quantization error into the predictor parameters. Hence at the transmitter it is necessary not only to encode the filter parameters for transmission but also to decode them locally for use in the predictor. In this way the transmitter and receiver will have identical, if imperfect, predictors. The slight increase in residual power resulting from imperfect prediction is less undesirable than the discrepancies which could result from using nonidentical predictors in the transmitter and receiver.

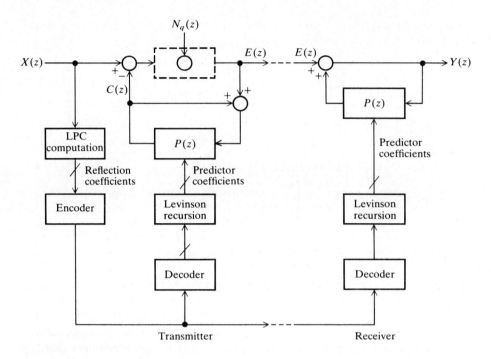

Figure 9-10 A realistic ADPCM system. To ensure faithful reproduction of the input, the parameters controlling the predictor at the transmitter are identical to those used at the receiver.

If we put all these pieces together, the transmitter looks like Fig. 9-10. If a covariance predictor is used, then the LPC computations consist of the first half of the Choleski decomposition,

$$\mathbf{L}\boldsymbol{\kappa} = \mathbf{c} \qquad (6\text{-}54a)$$

and possibly Atal's reflection-coefficient conversion. In either case, the reflection coefficients are quantized for transmission. Matching decoders at transmitter and receiver recover the coefficients, which are then converted to predictor coefficients as indicated by the boxes labeled "Levinson recursion." The rest of the transmitter and receiver are essentially the same as in Fig. 9-9.

It has been found that in quantizing, the reflection coefficients do not all require the same resolution, so different numbers of bits may be used for different coefficients. Gray and Markel (1976) made an exhaustive study of quantization and bit allocation of reflection coefficients. Their criterion for fidelity was the mean square error in spectrum shape, where the comparison was made between the frequency response of the original filter and that of the filter reconstructed from the encoded coefficients. On the basis of this study, the nonlinear quantizations preferred were log-area ratios and the inverse sine function.

Log-area ratios refers to the cylindrical model of the vocal tract. Recall that at the junction between cylindrical sections, the reflection coefficient was given by

$$k_i = \frac{S_n - S_{n-1}}{S_n + S_{n-1}}$$

where S_n and S_{n-1} are the areas of the two sections. Then the area ratio is

$$\frac{S_n}{S_{n-1}} = \frac{1 + k_n}{1 - k_n}$$

and the log-area ratio is the log of S_n/S_{n-1}. Inverse sine coding uses the transformation

$$\lambda_i = \sin^{-1}(k_i)$$

It has been shown (Viswanathan and Makhoul, 1975) that the spectral sensitivity is greatest for those reflection coefficients whose magnitude is close to unity. Hence one reason for the success of both of these transformations is clearly that they provide the greatest resolution for values of k_i near ± 1.

In studying the bit-allocation problem, Gray and Markel found empirically that the standard deviation of reflection coefficients decreased almost uniformly from k_1 (0.43) to k_{10} (0.14), that nonlinear quantization of k_1 and k_2 gave superior results, and that the manner of quantizing the remaining coefficients was not critical. For a maximum spectral deviation of 3 dB, they determined that the bits allocated for the coding of each reflection coefficient could be decreased almost linearly from 8 bits for k_1 to 4 bits for k_{10}. Their results are summarized in Table 9-1.

Table 9-1 Means, standard deviations, and bit assignments for reflection coefficients†

Coefficient number	Mean	Standard deviation	Bits‡
1	−0.40630	0.4334	8
2	0.26920	0.4219	7
3	−0.17430	0.2721	7
4	0.18550	0.2819	6
5	0.05539	0.2470	6
6	0.28130	0.2517	6
7	0.05886	0.2487	6
8	0.07080	0.2121	5
9	−0.02784	0.1801	4
10	0.03665	0.1366	4

† After Gray and Markel (1976). © 1976, IEEE.

‡ Required for maximum spectral deviation < 3 dB. Exact numbers differ between log-area and inverse sine methods but round off to the same integers.

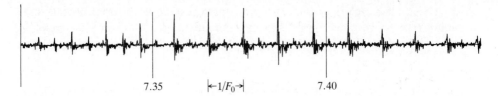

7.35 |←1/F_0→| 7.40

Figure 9-11 Prediction residual of a portion of the [ə] from "above" (tenth-order covariance predictor; speech differenced before prediction). The residual shows a marked periodicity corresponding to the pitch period.

These results do not take into account the probability densities of the reflection coefficients. In a later study, Markel and Gray (1980) showed that the number of bits for parameter coding could be further reduced if the quantization levels for each parameter were tailored to its probability density. Using a spectral-distortion criterion, backed up by listening tests, they found that the total bit requirements could be further reduced by approximately 9 to 10 bits per frame with no significant difference in quality.

An added improvement in the S/N ratio can be obtained by means of a second predictor to remove the periodicity due to pitch. For voiced speech, the prediction residual takes the form of a series of pulses at the pitch frequency, as shown in Fig. 9-11. The shapes of consecutive pulses tend to be similar. This consideration has led a number of researchers (Kimme and Kuo, 1963; Atal and Schroeder, 1970; Makhoul and Berouti, 1979) to incorporate a second predictor which removes pitch periodicity by estimating each new residual pulse from the preceding one. If the pitch period is T_0, then this predictor takes the form

$$P_2(z) = r_T z^{-T_0}$$

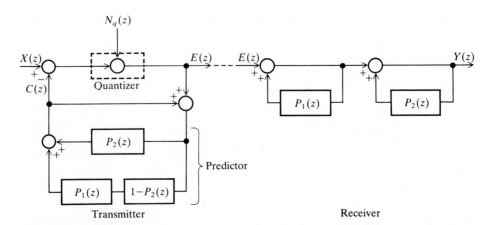

Figure 9-12 Adaptive DPCM system incorporating pitch-period prediction. (*Adapted from Atal and Schroeder, 1970.*)

where r_T is the normalized autocorrelation of the residual at a lag T_0. The predictor function is thus $[1 - P_2(z)]$. If the regular predictor is represented by $P_1(z)$, then the overall predictor will be $[1 - P_1(z)]$ cascaded with $[1 - P_2(z)]$, or $[1 - P_1(z) - P_2(z) + P_1(z)P_2(z)]$. This function is implemented by the system shown in Fig. 9-12.

Since the pitch period will generally not be an integer number of samples, a three-tap filter is sometimes used to remove pitch periodicity. The delays are $T - 1$, T, and $T + 1$, where T is the lag nearest to the pitch period.

Atal and Schroeder (1970) implemented a predictor similar to Fig. 9-12 as a computer simulation, using speech sampled at 6.67 kHz and a 1-bit quantizer for the residual. The system was evaluated by comparing the output speech with μ-law encoded speech sampled at the same rate. The output was subjectively judged better than 5-bit μ-law speech but inferior to 6-bit μ-law speech; this corresponds to an S/N ratio between 21 and 27 dB.

Residual Compression

In ADPCM, most of the channel capacity is still taken up by the residual. If the speech was initially coded with a 12-bit word length, then 24 dB of compression reduces the necessary word length by only 4 bits. The bit rate is then reduced only by a third; indeed, the overall reduction is less than this, because extra bits will be needed to transmit the side information. Hence, if further compression is required, we must examine ways to compress the residual itself.

This problem has been studied by Atal, Schroeder, and Remde (Atal and Schroeder, 1980; Schroeder and Atal, 1981; Atal and Remde, 1982). Their chief finding has been that, in contrast to the speech signal itself, the parts of the residual which are most important to speech quality are the high-amplitude portions. In addition, they have found:

1. Peak clipping of the residual produces audible distortion.
2. It is important to quantize the high-amplitude portions of the residual accurately.
3. The residual can be severely center-clipped with little or no distortion of the recovered speech.

Center clipping is done by comparing each residual sample to a threshold and setting its value to zero if its absolute amplitude is less than the threshold. The threshold is typically normalized to the overall signal level, e.g., by making it proportional to the rms value of the residual. Center clipping is a particularly useful compression device because much of the prediction residual tends to be of low amplitude. Atal (1982) reports that as much as 90 percent of the residual can be removed by center clipping with "fairly good" output speech. If ADPCM has enabled coding the residual with 8 bits per sample and center clipping has wiped out 90 percent of the residual, then in principle the average effective bit rate is now 0.8 bit/sample. (Since it is still necessary to indicate which samples are zeros and which nonzero, the actual bit rate will be somewhat higher than this.)

The fact that the residual quantizer is inside a feedback loop complicates the problem of determining the step size. This is because we would like to scan the entire quantized residual to see what the maximum value will be and at what level to place the center-clipping threshold. However, the residual cannot be quantized until these values are known.

One partial solution to this problem is to use the somewhat more complicated structure shown in Fig. 9-13. Here the quantization is done outside the loop, and the quantization noise, isolated by subtracting the quantizer input from its output, is processed by a second filter $F(z)$. In this case,

$$E(z) = X(z)[1 - P(z)] + N_q(z)[1 - F(z)] \qquad (9\text{-}8)$$

If $F(z)$ is made identical to $P(z)$, then we have the same result as in (9-7b). [There is another reason for moving $P(z)$ out of the loop, which will become apparent when we discuss noise shaping below.]

This structure gives us a chance to estimate the quantized residual by viewing the unquantized residual at point A. If we can assume that the actual statistics of the quantized residual are some multiple of those estimated from the unquantized residual, we can then proceed with our scaling. In practice, this multiple changes, especially as we go from vowels to fricatives, and a certain amount of peak clipping is unavoidable.

Atal and Schroeder (1980) added a pitch-period predictor to this structure, resulting in the system of Fig. 9-14. This system takes the initial center-clipping threshold from the unquantized residual but then updates it on a sample-by-sample basis as the modified residual samples at point B are applied to the quantizer. If the unquantized residual is $v(n)$ and the input to the quantizer is $q(n)$, then the threshold for sample n is given by

$$\theta(n) = \theta(0) \sqrt{\frac{100\mu(n)}{\gamma} \frac{\overline{|q(n)|}}{\overline{|v(n)|}}} \qquad (9\text{-}9)$$

where $\theta(0)$ is the initial threshold estimated at the beginning of the frame, $\mu(n)$ is the actual number of samples zeroed by center clipping, and γ is the number

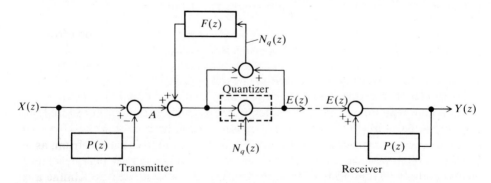

Figure 9-13 Adaptive DPCM system modified to make the unquantized residual available (at point A) for determining step size. (*After Atal and Schroeder, 1979; original © 1979, IEEE.*)

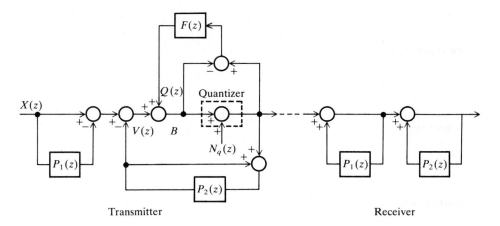

Figure 9-14 The adaptive DPCM system of Fig. 9-13 with a pitch-period predictor added. (*After Atal and Schroeder, 1980; original © 1980, IEEE.*)

required. The averages $|q(n)|$ and $|v(n)|$ are estimated by means of a "leaky" integrator with a time constant of 5 ms. The quantizer incorporates the center clipper and has a variable step size as well.

Makhoul and Berouti (1979) took a different line entirely. Their strategy was to use a conventional quantizer inside the loop with an essentially unlimited range and to reduce the bit rate using a technique based on the concept of entropy coding. In entropy coding, the bit patterns are not simple binary representations of the signal levels; instead, variable-length codes are used, assigning the shortest code words to the most frequently occurring values. Since the residual spends most of its time in the low-amplitude range, the short words correspond to these amplitudes. Makhoul and Berouti's coding simply used lengths which increased monotonically with increasing residual amplitude, assigning an even number of bits to negative samples and an odd number to the others. This results in a very economical representation of the residual, without clipping on occasional large residual samples. While the efficiency of this codebook is slightly lower than that of a Huffman code, it has the virtue of being simple and of allowing the receiver to resynchronize quickly in the event of a transmission error. No pitch prediction or center clipping was done in this scheme.

Noise Shaping

When we can no longer reduce the noise caused by quantizing the residual, we can still render it less noticeable by shaping its frequency spectrum. If we can get the noise spectrum to follow the spectrum envelope of the speech spectrum, as in Fig. 9-15, then the frequency components in the speech formants will tend to mask the quantization noise. This recourse has been investigated by Kimme and Kuo (1963), Berouti and Makhoul (1978), Makhoul and Berouti (1979), and Atal and Schroeder (1979, 1980).

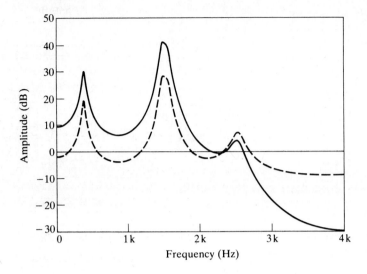

Figure 9-15 Noise shaping. The solid line is the spectrum envelope as estimated by the linear predictor; the solid line is the spectrum of the noise-shaping filter.

Refer to Fig. 9-13 again, and consider the case where $F(z)$ is different from $P(z)$. Then in the recovered speech,

$$Y(z) = X(z) + N_q(z) \frac{1 - F(z)}{1 - P(z)} \tag{9-10}$$

and the noise spectrum will be shaped by the ratio of the two filter functions. If $F(z)$ is so designed that the roots of $[1 - F(z)]$ correspond to those of $[1 - P(z)]$, but lie closer to the origin, then there will be incomplete cancellation and the noise spectrum in the recovered speech will follow the spectrum envelope of the speech itself. This is easily done. If

$$P(z) = \sum_{i=1}^{p} a(i) z^{-i}$$

then we can move all of the roots of $[1 - P(z)]$ closer to or farther from the origin by multiplying each $a(i)$ by a factor α^i. Therefore we form $F(z)$ from $P(z)$ as follows:

$$F(z) = \sum_{i=1}^{p} \alpha^i a(i) z^{-i}$$

Atal (1982) reports that a value of $\alpha = 0.73$ produces satisfactory results. The curves in Fig. 9-15 were obtained with this factor. Notice that in the neighborhood of the formants, the incomplete cancellation causes the noise spectrum to peak; in between formant peaks, the cancellation is more nearly complete and the noise spectrum tends to be approximately flat.

Multipulse

In the foregoing material we have seen a series of developments in the course of which more and more of the residual has been deleted before transmission. As the amount of residual transmitted decreases, it becomes necessary to choose what will be transmitted very carefully so that the little bit that reaches the receiver will produce as high quality an output as possible.

Another approach to residual editing has been investigated by Atal and Remde (1982). Instead of deleting residual samples according to some rule, their system starts with nothing at all and builds up the residual sample by sample.

This scheme works as follows. Compute the predictor parameters and build the filter. Apply a single pulse and set its amplitude and location for the best match between the filter response and the original signal. Then apply a second pulse, selecting its amplitude and location on the same basis. Continue applying pulses, locating and scaling each one individually for the best match between the filter output and the original signal, until some distortion criterion has been met or until the maximum permitted number of pulses has been assigned.

Atal and Remde report "little audible distortion" with as few as 8 pulses per 10 ms of speech. (At a sampling rate of 8 kHz, this corresponds to removal of 90 percent of the residual.) Note that if we started with the problem of finding the optimum set of eight pulses, given the predictors and the original signal, we would be able to find the optimum combination, but at a computationally formidable cost. Atal and Remde, by building their residual one pulse at a time, have produced a suboptimal solution which is computationally cheap.

The pulses are selected using the analysis-by-synthesis procedure illustrated in Fig. 9-16. The error signal is found by subtracting the synthesized speech from the input, as usual. (Before any residual pulses have been assigned, the synthesized speech consists only of the samples remaining in the filter from the previous time segment.) This error is then passed through a filter which emphasizes those

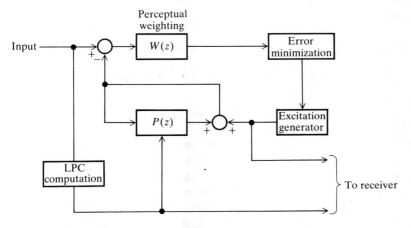

Figure 9-16 Simplified block diagram of the multipulse residual generation of Atal and Remde (1982).

frequency ranges in which the ear is particularly sensitive to distortion and deemphasizes those ranges in which it is not. Thus the actual minimization is done on an error signal which has been weighted according to our knowledge of human perception. The box labeled "error minimization" represents the search for the best location and size of the next pulse to be added to the residual. The loop is closed when the new excitation is applied to the LPC filter and the output compared with the incoming speech.

Each new pulse is found as follows: given a specific location, the weighted mean square error can be expressed as a function of the pulse amplitude, and this error can be minimized by setting its derivative to zero. In this way, an optimum pulse amplitude and residual error can be found for every available location. The location chosen for the new pulse is that for which the resultant error is a minimum.

9-4 DELTA MODULATION

Delta modulation can be thought of as DPCM with a one-bit quantizer. The basic scheme is shown in Fig. 9-17a. The quantizer output is a 1 if the difference is positive and 0 if it is negative. At the receiver, the bit stream is used to control an up/down counter; as a result, the signal is approximated by an ascending or descending staircase, as shown in Fig. 9-17b.

The appeal of delta modulation is its simplicity. As usual, it takes a considerable amount of refinement to make it work. It requires a sampling rate well above the Nyquist value so the maximum slew rate does not exceed one quantization step per sampling period. If the rate of change exceeds this limit, the

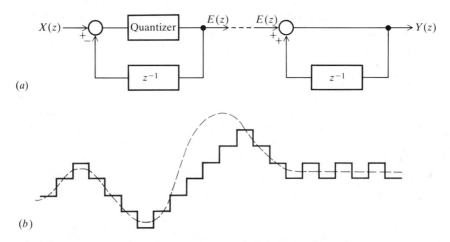

Figure 9-17 Delta modulation. (a) System block diagram; (b) input (dotted) and output (solid) waveform, showing slope overload and granular noise.

encoder cannot keep up with it and the signal is distorted. This condition is called *slope overload*; in practice, a limited probability of overload is accepted. Since the coding scheme does not allow for a steady state, a constant input can only be encoded as a string of alternating ones and zeros; this gives rise to *granular noise*. The trick in delta modulation is to find a step size which minimizes these two kinds of distortion.

To minimize slope overload, the step size should be made large; to minimize granular noise, it should be made small. This suggests that there is an optimum step size for any given sampling rate. Abate (1967) found empirically that at the optimum step size,

$$\frac{\text{Maximum slew rate of system}}{\text{RMS slew rate of signal}} = \ln \frac{\text{sampling frequency}}{\text{signal bandwidth}} \qquad (9\text{-}11a)$$

If the slew rates are normalized with respect to the sampling frequency, this is

$$s_{\text{opt}} = \sigma_\Delta \ln 2B \qquad (9\text{-}11b)$$

where σ_Δ is the rms value of the difference between successive samples and B is the ratio of the sampling frequency to the Nyquist rate. Abate also found that the maximum S/N ratio varied approximately as the cube of B. Using gaussian noise as a model signal, Abate obtained a maximum S/N ratio of approximately 20 dB at a sampling rate 8 times the Nyquist value. For telephone speech, this translates to a bit rate of approximately 64k bits/s.

Adaptive Delta Modulation; CVSD

It should be possible to improve the performance of delta modulation by matching the step size to the signal, as was done with PCM and DPCM. In those cases, the adaptation rule was based on the magnitude of the previous encoded sample. With delta modulation, however, the magnitude of the previous sample is always unity; hence it is necessary to inspect a number of samples of the output sequence to estimate whether slope overload or granular noise is about to occur. Since the system has to respond quickly, particularly to the presence of slope overload, the number of output samples examined before reaching a decision must be kept small. Hence the adaptation logic is of necessity crude and inclined to overreact.

In a system due to Jayant (1970), the step size is allowed to range between limits d_{min} and d_{max} under the control of a variable multiplier M. On each new sample, the step size is M times its previous value. M is controlled by the history of the output bits. If the bits are the same, overload is considered imminent and M is increased; if they are different, granular noise is considered imminent and M is decreased. A typical rule is

$$M = \begin{cases} 2, & e(n) = e(n-1) \\ \tfrac{1}{2}, & e(n) \neq e(n-1) \end{cases} \qquad (9\text{-}12)$$

Greefkes (1970) has proposed a somewhat more flexible scheme known as continuously variable-slope delta modulation (CVSD). Here a sequence of three identical samples indicates overload; the adaptation rule is

$$s(n) = \begin{cases} ks(n-1) + P, & e(n) = e(n-1) = e(n-2) \\ ks(n-1) + Q, & \text{otherwise} \end{cases} \quad (9\text{-}13)$$

P is a large constant which enables the system to respond to overloads. The factor k is less than 1; in the absence of overload, the step size gradually decays to a minimum determined by k and Q together. By varying k, the modulator can be made to respond slowly or quickly, as desired.

9-5 FILTER-BANK CODERS

Coders in this category divide the frequency content of the speech into contiguous frequency bands by means of a bank of filters and then transmit the contents of these bands. The different types vary principally in the fidelity with which these bands, or channels, are encoded. At the simplest level, the channel vocoder preserves only the general spectrum envelope and as such properly belongs in the following chapter, but it has given rise to a number of other types which preserve the waveform with a high degree of fidelity.

The Channel Vocoder

This is the earliest form of vocoder to be widely used (Dudley, 1939; Schroeder, 1966; Gold and Rader, 1967). The transmitter provides a coarse spectrum analysis of the input speech and the receiver generates a signal whose frequency content matches that specified by the transmitter.

A channel vocoder is shown in Fig. 9-18. At the transmitter, the speech is applied to a bank of filters and to a pitch extractor. The filters divide the frequency range of the voice into a number of contiguous bands, or channels. The number of filters varies in different implementations from 14 to more than 20, and the frequency range covered is typically telephone bandwidth, i.e., from 300 Hz or below to approximately 3.3 kHz. The output of any one filter has an envelope which reflects the moment-to-moment variation in the amount of power in that filter's frequency band. The envelopes of all of the filter outputs thus provide an approximation to the spectrum envelope of the speech.

Since this envelope changes at a rate much slower than that of the speech waveform itself, it can be sampled at very low rates. Hence the filter outputs are envelope-detected, usually by means of a full-wave rectifier and a low-pass filter, and sampled at typically 50 samples per second. These envelope samples are multiplexed and transmitted to the receiver. (The multiplexing and demultiplexing operations have been omitted from Fig. 9-18 for simplicity.)

The pitch extractor determines the fundamental frequency of the voice and indicates whether voicing is in fact present; in most cases, if the frequency is well

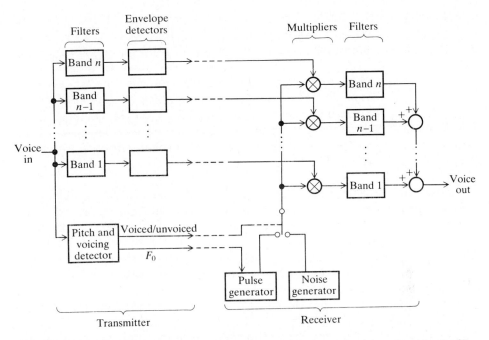

Figure 9-18 A channel vocoder. The amplitude spectrum of the input signal is analyzed by the filter bank shown, and the channel amplitudes are used to control a matching filter bank at the receiver.

defined and passes some validation test, the sound is characterized as voiced, and if the test fails, then the speech is considered unvoiced. The pitch and voicing information is likewise sampled and transmitted along with the filter output levels.

The receiver is a synthesizer which is driven by the specifications arriving from the transmitter. The voiced/unvoiced signal from the transmitter is used to select an excitation function which is either a pulse train for voiced speech or wideband noise for unvoiced speech. If the pulse train is selected, then the pitch information is used to determine the repetition rate of the train. The excitation is then applied to the inputs of a filter bank which matches the filter bank in the transmitter. The amplitude of each filter's output is determined by a multiplier which controls the level of excitation applied to the filter's input. The gain of each multiplier is set by the corresponding envelope samples received from the transmitter. The modulators and filter bank thus attempt to recreate the filter outputs which were obtained at the transmitter. The output speech is derived by summing the outputs of all the filters.

The channel vocoder is a reasonable solution of the coding problem, given the hardware resources of the era in which it was developed. In evaluating its performance we must distinguish between voice quality and intelligibility. Quality is a relatively subjective attribute indicating generally how pleasant the speech sounds and how long it can be listened to without undue fatigue; intelligibility is a relatively objective measure indicating how accurately the speech is heard by the listener. (The qualifier, "relatively," is used because both quality and intelligibility can be measured and quantified by means of proper psychometric techniques.) The output speech of a channel vocoder is typically poor in quality but can be made to be high in intelligibility. The channel vocoder is also generally resistant to degradation by background noise and in general is more robust than many of the more modern systems that have supplanted it. This combination of robustness and high intelligibility made the channel vocoder the standard for military use for many years. Indeed, interest in the channel vocoder continues (Gold, 1979; Gold et al., 1981).

Variants of the channel vocoder The channel vocoder went through a long evolution. Different types of filter were investigated and different numbers of filters were used in the filter bank. The filter bandwidths were usually uniform, but occasionally were made narrower for low frequencies and wider for high frequencies. The sampled filter outputs were usually time-multiplexed but occasionally frequency-multiplexed. The similarity between the filter banks used in the channel vocoder and those in subband coders (discussed below) has been exploited to produce multiple-rate encoders in which the high rate used subband coding and the low rate channel vocoding (Gold et al., 1981).

If the outputs of the filters are to add smoothly at the receiver, then the filters must be designed with some care. Any bandpass filter will delay the signal by a certain amount; for good performance the delays of the filters should be equal. The filters must also have sharp cutoffs in order to obtain good separation between bands; but sharp-cutoff filters frequently have a long impulse response, and the resultant ringing can obscure temporal changes in the speech and impart a reverberant quality to the output. Hence the tradeoff between cutoff and impulse response must be considered carefully.

It was determined relatively early (Schroeder, 1966) that the quality of the received voice was greatly affected by the excitation signal used. (We will find that this is also true of the LPC vocoder.) A lot of research has therefore gone into improving the excitation. Two schemes are of particular interest.

Spectrum flattening is used to ensure that the input levels at the receiver filters are all equal. Figure 9-19 shows a typical implementation for one channel at the receiver. The excitation for each band is filtered and then hard-limited before being applied to the second filter. [In a hard limiter, or infinite clipper, the output and input are related by $y(t) = x(t)/|x(t)|$.] The filter restricts the excitation to a band matching that of the output filter; in the case of voiced speech, this is ideally a sine wave of a frequency equal to the pitch harmonic falling within the filter's passband. The hard limiter changes this to a square wave of controlled amplitude. This square wave is applied to the multiplier and the multiplier output filtered by the second filter. The use of spectrum flattening improved performance somewhat, although with low-pitched voices there will sometimes be more than one pitch harmonic present in a channel, in which case the input to the limiter will not be a sine wave and its output may contain significant out-of-

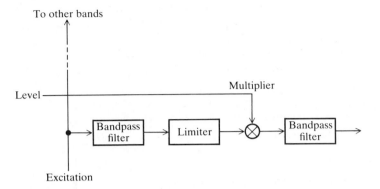

Figure 9-19 One channel in the receiver of a channel vocoder employing spectrum flattening. Matched limiters in all channels make the inputs to the multipliers uniform.

band components. For a discussion of the merits of spectrum flattening, see Gold and Rader (1967).

Voice excitation (David et al., 1962) does away with the pitch extractor and voicing detector altogether. In lieu of pitch and voicing information, a low-pass filtered version of the voice itself is transmitted. This signal, called the baseband, has a bandwidth of approximately 600 to 1000 Hz. (A baseband is, strictly, the modulation carried by a narrowband signal, but the term is also occasionally used loosely to refer to a signal obtained from a wideband signal by low-pass filtering, as here.) At the receiver, a wideband excitation signal is generated by passing the baseband signal through a nonlinear distortion element, as shown in Fig. 9-20. The nonlinear element generates harmonic products throughout the speech spectrum and this spectrum-broadened signal is used to generate the excitation. The distorted signal is applied to a filter/limiter combination similar to the spectrum-flattening vocoder described above and shown in Fig. 9-19. (This process of generating a wideband excitation from the baseband signal is also known as spectrum flattening.)

Voice excitation has the advantage of avoiding two of the most difficult problems in vocoder design: pitch determination and voicing determination. Clearly, the pitch information is still present in the baseband of voiced speech, since the bandwidth is wide enough to carry at least one or two harmonics, even in telephone-bandwidth speech. Since these pitch elements generate the excitation directly, the errors associated with conventional pitch detectors never occur.

Voice excitation also evades a persistent problem with any conventional voicing detector: the fact that normal speech contains many stretches in which it is not at all clear whether voicing is present or not, and where an excitation consisting of some kind of mixture of the two would be most desirable. The procrustean decision of the standard voiced/unvoiced detector is always detrimental to speech quality at these points. The existence of these uncertain areas in speech is also a strong element in the motivation of Atal and Remde's multipulse system. Both multipulse and voice excitation avoid any specific decision about pitch or

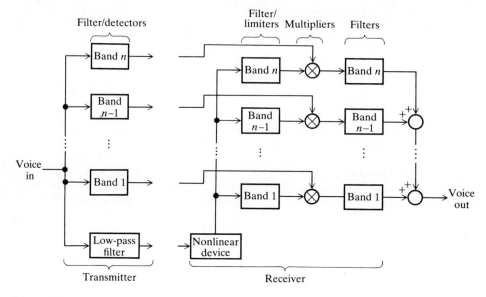

Figure 9-20 A voice-excited channel vocoder. A low-pass filtered version of the input takes the place of the pitch and voicing information of the regular channel vocoder.

voicing, and both are able to preserve the character of these indeterminate sounds well enough to produce natural-sounding speech.

The disadvantage of voice excitation is that it requires a higher bit rate and thus does not permit the high compressions afforded by other types of channel vocoder. The bandwidth of the baseband is a significant fraction of the original signal's bandwidth, and hence the overall compression cannot be higher than approximately 4 to 1.

The Formant Vocoder

In the *formant vocoder* (Schroeder, 1966; Flanagan, 1972b), the transmitter uses a formant extractor instead of a filter bank, and the transmitted parameters are the frequencies and bandwidths of F_1, F_2, F_3, and possibly F_4. Formant frequencies and bandwidths are estimated using one of the techniques described in Chapter 8. The transmitter also provides pitch and voicing information as usual. The receiver contains three or four variable filters which are controlled by the formant parameters received from the transmitter. The formant filters can be either parallel, as shown in Fig. 9-21, or cascaded, similar to the terminal-analog formant synthesizers which will be illustrated in Sec. 10.3 below. Since only three or four frequencies and bandwidths are required to characterize the spectral content of the speech, very low bit rates are possible with this system. The weakness of the formant vocoder originally lay in the difficulty of implementing reliable and robust formant estimators; with the modern techniques described in Chapter 8, this problem has been ameliorated but not eliminated.

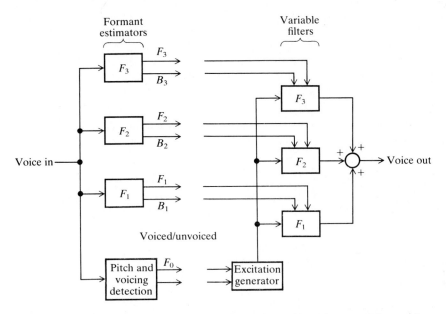

Figure 9-21 A formant vocoder. The filter banks are replaced by estimators of formant frequency and bandwidth at the transmitter and, at the receiver, by a set of variable filters.

The Phase Vocoder

The output of any filter in the channel vocoder can be viewed as a sinusoid of frequency f_0 (where f_0 is the center frequency of the filter's passband) modulated by some slowly varying function $p(t)$. In the channel vocoder, envelope detection of the filter's output extracts the amplitude of $p(t)$ for transmission. In the phase vocoder (Flanagan and Golden, 1966), the phase of $p(t)$ is also transmitted.

To see the reason for this, let us take another look at the channel vocoder's filter bank. These filters partition the input signal into a set of contiguous frequency bands. If the filters are designed with care (i.e., with flat response, linear phase, and uniform delays), it should be possible to sum their outputs and get a result which is substantially the same as the input. Hence we should be able to do away with the excitation signal and make a vocoder as shown in Fig. 9-22. (Notice that, after the formant vocoder, which represented the furthest remove from pure waveform reproduction, the phase vocoder takes us back into the domain of waveform encoding.)

Here there is no envelope detection; to make this scheme work, we have to transmit the actual filter outputs and not just their envelopes. To do this economically, we would like to represent each filter by the combination of an equivalent low-pass filter and a center frequency f_0. We will need only transmit this equivalent low-pass output for each filter, since its center frequency is known. The equivalent low-pass output can be represented by its amplitude and phase. This output, shifted back to f_0 at the receiver, will be our desired channel signal.

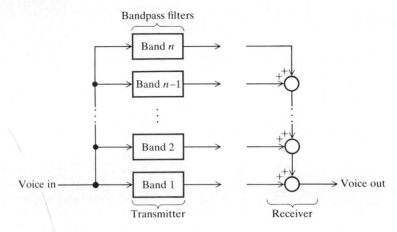

Figure 9-22 The principle of the phase vocoder. The outputs of an ideal filter bank should sum to a duplicate of the input signal.

These reconstructed channel signals can then be summed to generate the required speech as before.

If the channel is shifted down to the dc component, however, the frequency-shifted signal will be complex, not real. This is because the half of the channel below f_0 maps onto negative frequency, as shown in Fig. 9-23b, and the half above f_0 maps onto positive frequency. For the signal in Fig. 9-23b to be real, however, the negative-frequency components must be the complex conjugates of the corresponding positive-frequency components, which would require a similar symmetry in the original channel, and such a symmetry will not be found. If the baseband signal is complex, then its samples will have both amplitude and phase, and both amplitude and phase must be transmitted.

For the low-pass signal to include the phase information, we must replace each filter by the rather complicated structure shown in Fig. 9-24. Here, ω_0 is $2\pi f_0$, and the multiplier-filter combinations shift the center frequency of the bandpass filter's output down to the dc component. The outputs $x(t)$ and $y(t)$ are

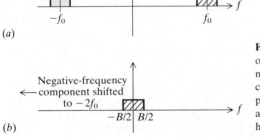

Figure 9-23 Effect of heterodyning the output of the filter at f_0 to zero. In (a), the negative-frequency components are the complex conjugates of the corresponding positive ones. In (b), the band at f_0 is centered about zero, but the negative-frequency band has been shifted from $-f_0$ to $-2f_0$.

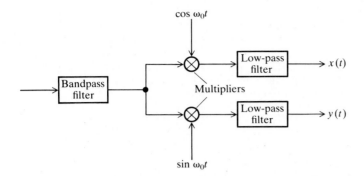

Figure 9-24 Synchronous quadrature detector used to replace heterodyning in the phase vocoder. Outputs $x(t)$ and $y(t)$ are amplitude envelopes of real and imaginary components of the baseband signal.

now baseband signals containing all information about the original filter output except its center frequency, which, being known, does not have to be transmitted. (Readers with experience in communications or radar will recognize the process shown in Fig. 9-24 as synchronous quadrature detection.)

The amplitude of $p(t)$ is now given by $A(t) = x^2(t) + y^2(t)$ and the phase by $\Phi(t) = \arctan[y(t)/x(t)]$. At the receiver, we can reconstitute the original filter output in two steps: first phase-modulating a sinusoid at the frequency f_0 with $\Phi(t)$ and then amplitude-modulating the result with $A(t)$. Before we put this all together, however, one other detail must be considered. $A(t)$ will vary at roughly the same rate as the envelope of the filter output, and we know from channel vocoder experience that it can be sampled at a relatively low rate. It is not at all clear how we are to sample or even economically compute $\Phi(t)$, since it is essentially unbounded. Flanagan and Golden chose instead to compute and sample the derivative, $\Phi'(t)$. It is not difficult to show that

$$\Phi'(t) = \frac{x(t)y'(t) - y(t)x'(t)}{x^2(t) + y^2(t)} \qquad (9\text{-}14)$$

Bernstein's inequality (Papoulis, 1968) states that the derivative of a bounded, band-limited signal is bounded; hence $x'(t)$ and $y'(t)$ are bounded and so likewise is $\Phi'(t)$.

One channel of the complete phase vocoder is shown in Fig. 9-25. This system was implemented by Flanagan and Golden as a computer simulation with 30 channels, each 100 Hz wide, covering a range of 50 to 3050 Hz. Since $A(t)$ and $\Phi'(t)$ are slowly varying signals, they can also be low-pass filtered to reduce the bandwidth required for transmission. In the simulation, low-pass filters cutting off at 25 Hz were used. The total bandwidth required was thus 30×25 Hz, or 1500 Hz; this corresponds to a bandwidth reduction of 2 to 1. Spectrograms of the output speech showed good preservation of pitch and voicing information as well as formant frequencies, and the quality was described as "considerably surpassing" that of conventional channel vocoders.

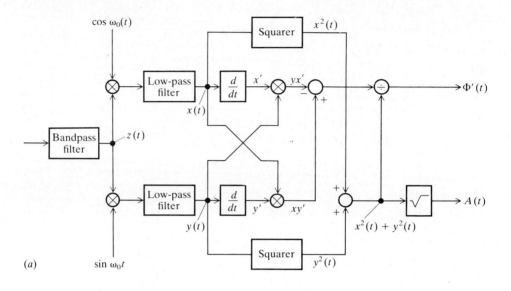

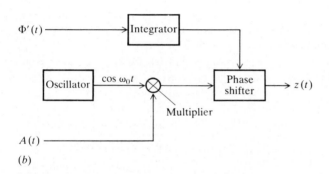

Figure 9-25 One channel of the phase vocoder: (a) at transmitter; (b) at receiver. (*After Flanagan and Golden, 1966.*)

This seemingly cumbersome structure can be realized economically using digital processing techniques. Schafer and Rabiner (1973) pointed out that the multiplication and low-pass filtering operations of Fig. 9-25 could be replaced by Fourier transformation of a suitably modified input signal. Using an implementation based on the FFT, with 28 channels and no quantization of $A(t)$ and $\Phi(t)$, they obtained essentially unchanged speech at the output of the system. Two quantization schemes were tried; using adaptive delta modulation, they got good performance at rates down to approximately 28k bits/s; with PCM coding, they were able to operate as low as 16k bits/s. The input sampling rate was 12 kHz, corresponding to a bit rate of 144k bits/s, assuming 12-bit sampling; hence the compression ratios obtained were 5 to 1 for ADM and 9 to 1 for PCM.

The Subband Vocoder

In spite of its complexity, the phase vocoder has a number of attractive features. It promises, in general, better reproduction of the input speech than does the channel vocoder. Furthermore, quantization noise in any one channel will not spill over into other channels and mask their contents, and, in fact, since channel amplitudes will generally differ, each channel can be quantized with a step size matched to its level. Indeed, adaptive bit assignments matched to changing levels of each channel can further reduce the overall bit rate.

Two changes can be made to simplify the phase vocoder scheme: we can reduce the number of channels and we can use a frequency-shifting technique which will yield real baseband signals. Vocoders designed around these principles are called subband coders; where the phase vocoder literature refers to channels, we now refer to subbands.

To obtain a real output for each frequency-shifted subband, we need to consider the negative-frequency portion of the original subband. When we did the shift shown in Fig. 9-24, the negative-frequency portion was shifted down to $-2f_0$, after which it was wiped out by the filtering which followed the shift. Since this negative-frequency part was in fact derived from a real signal, it and the positive-frequency part together have the symmetry we are after. If we could simultaneously shift the positive-frequency part down and shift the negative-frequency part up, as shown in Fig. 9-26, the resulting baseband signal would be real.

Crochiere et al. (1976) give the following steps for accomplishing this shift. (1) Shift the positive band down to the dc component by multiplying by $\cos \omega_0 t$ and $\sin \omega_0 t$, exactly as was done in the phase vocoder. (2) Low-pass filter the shifted signal and (3) down-sample. (4) Shift the signal back up by $B/2$, where B is the original subband bandwidth. Call this signal $X(f)$, as in Fig. 9-26. (5) Shift the negative band up to the dc component; (6) low-pass filter this shifted sample and (7) down-sample. (8) Shift this signal back down by $B/2$; call this signal $Y(f)$. (9) Sum $X(f)$ and $Y(f)$. Crochiere et al. show that these steps can be combined and economically implemented; in particular, by strategic selection of the lower sampling rate, the final shifts by $\pm B/2$ can be done using multiplications of 0 and

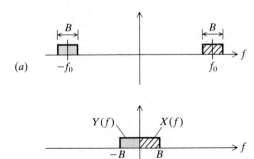

Figure 9-26 Preservation of complex-conjugate symmetry in the subband vocoder. The original filter output is shown at (a); the positive band is shifted down in frequency, and the negative band is shifted up, until their edges meet at the d-c component, as shown in (b).

±1. A byproduct of this scheme is that the initial bandpass filter can be eliminated and the low-pass filter used to determine the subband size.

This process is done for each subband. At the receiver, the shifting process is reversed to recover the subbands, which are then added together to reconstruct the speech signal.

If the subbands are all of equal size, and if they all begin at integer multiples of B, then the frequency shifts can be managed even more cheaply (Crochiere et al., 1976; Crochiere, 1977); the initial bandpass filter is retained and the output is immediately down-sampled to a rate equal to $2B$. The filter output is thus undersampled, and the desired baseband signal can be obtained from the aliased images of the positive- and negative-frequency components, as shown in Fig. 9-27. At the receiver, each subband is restored by "up-sampling." If the down-sampling was done by a factor of k, then up-sampling is done by inserting $(k-1)$ zero samples after each incoming sample. A bandpass filter is then used to select the image falling in the desired subband. In this way, all multiplications by $\cos \omega_0 t$ and $\sin \omega_0 t$ are avoided. This process is known as *integer-band sampling*.

Esteban and Galand (1977) generate subbands by first dividing the entire speech band into two equal parts; then these subbands are similarly split to yield four subbands. This process can be repeated as required to generate any 2^k subbands. The filters used for this division are a type known as *quadrature mirror filters*; these have the property that the filter for the upper subband has a frequency response which is the mirror image of that of the filter for the lower subband:

$$|H_1(e^{j\omega T})| = |H_2(e^{j(\omega_s/2 - \omega)T})|$$

Such a pair of filters can be implemented using FIR digital filters; H_2 is obtained from H_1 by reversing the sign of every other sample of the impulse response of H_1. Each stage of splitting is followed by down-sampling by a factor of 2. At the receiver, the incoming samples are up-sampled by interpolation, exactly as in the integer-band system, and bandpass-filtered using pairs of filters which match the corresponding filters at the transmitter. Esteban and Galand (1977) show that this process results in perfect reconstruction of the input signal, provided the filters H_1 and H_2 are of even order.

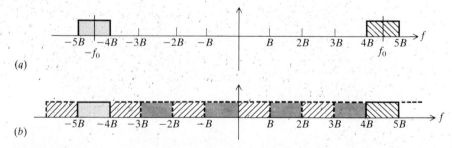

Figure 9-27 Integer-band sampling. The shift of Fig. 9-26 is implemented by suitably undersampling the filter outputs; this produces interleaved replications of the filter bands, as shown, and the images adjacent to the d-c component are selected by the output filter frequency.

9-6 ADAPTIVE TRANSFORM CODING

Let us return to the problem of reducing the redundancy among nearby sample values. We have seen the use of prediction to reduce redundancy; another way to reduce redundancy is to transform the signal by a mathematical operation that produces independent samples. The general scheme is illustrated in Fig. 9-28. The speech stream is divided into contiguous frames; each frame is transformed by the operation A and the transformed values are encoded and transmitted. At the receiver the original speech is recovered by the inverse transformation A^{-1}.

Since each sample now carries no redundant information, it can be quantized with fewer bits than would have been required for x. Furthermore, if the variances of the transformed samples show a consistent pattern, we will see that we can improve the tradeoff between bit rate and speech quality by assigning fewer bits to the samples with small variances or even, in extreme cases, by omitting some samples altogether.

The problem is clearly to come up with a transformation that will do all these things for us. It is generally impossible to find an invertible transform that will yield independent samples (Huang and Schultheiss, 1963). Uncorrelated samples can be found, however, and we will be content with these. Let us represent a block of speech samples by the vector $\mathbf{x}$:

$$\mathbf{x} = \begin{bmatrix} x_1 \\ x_2 \\ x_3 \\ \vdots \end{bmatrix}$$

We will assume throughout that our signal has a mean value of zero. Then the covariance matrix of $\mathbf{x}$ is given by

$$\mathbf{R}_{xx} = E\{\mathbf{x}\mathbf{x}^T\}$$

If the samples x_i were uncorrelated, $\mathbf{R}_{xx}$ would be a diagonal matrix. Hence if we wish to generate uncorrelated samples by transforming $\mathbf{x}$, our problem is to find a transformation $\mathbf{A}$,

$$\mathbf{y} = \mathbf{A}\mathbf{x}$$

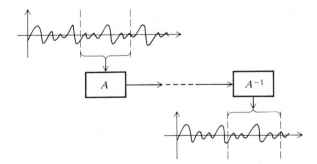

Figure 9-28 General scheme of adaptive transform coding.

such that $\mathbf{R}_{yy}$ is a diagonal matrix. Call this matrix $\Lambda = \text{diag}(\lambda_1, \lambda_2, \ldots)$. Then

$$\begin{aligned}\Lambda &= E\{\mathbf{y}\mathbf{y}^T\} \\ &= E\{\mathbf{A}\mathbf{x}\mathbf{x}^T\mathbf{A}^T\} \\ &= \mathbf{A}\mathbf{R}_{xx}\mathbf{A}^T\end{aligned} \qquad (9\text{-}15)$$

We recognize this as the diagonalization procedure outlined in Chapter 8. In the present context $\mathbf{A}$ is known as the discrete Karhunen-Loève transformation (KLT). [It is also occasionally known (Wintz, 1972) as the Hotelling transform, but this name does not seem to have caught on.] As we saw in Chapter 8, $\mathbf{A}$ can be assembled from the normalized eigenvectors of $\mathbf{R}_{xx}$.

The main difficulty with this approach is that the matrix $\mathbf{A}$ must be recomputed for each new frame of speech, since the speech signal, as we have seen, is not stationary. It is therefore necessary to transmit the autocorrelations of $\mathbf{x}$ as side information and to have the receiver compute $\mathbf{A}^{-1}$ for each new frame. This is computationally burdensome: a KLT transformation for a vector of length N requires $O(N^4)$ computations (Wintz, 1972). Hence a good deal of research has gone into finding fast, data-independent transformations whose performance is comparable to that of the KLT.

The principal candidates have been the DFT, the Walsh-Hadamard transform, and the discrete cosine transform (DCT), since there are simple and fast methods for computing all of these (Campanella and Robinson, 1971; Zelinski and Noll, 1977). Of these, the DCT has been shown to yield performance typically within 1 to 2 dB of the KLT; the other transforms are considerably inferior. A number of arguments have been given to explain the performance of the DCT; probably the most persuasive is that its basis vectors are good approximations to the eigenvectors of a variety of Toeplitz matrix resembling the covariance matrices of speech signals (Ahmed and Rao, 1975).

The DCT of an M-point sequence is defined as follows (Ahmed, Natarajan, and Rao, 1974):

$$X(k) = c(k) \sum_{i=0}^{M-1} x(n) \cos \frac{(2n+1)k\pi}{2M} \qquad (9\text{-}16a)$$

and its inverse is given by

$$x(n) = \frac{1}{M} \sum_{i=0}^{M-1} X(k)c(k) \cos \frac{(2n+1)k\pi}{2M} \qquad (9\text{-}16b)$$

where

$$c(k) = \begin{cases} 1, & k = 0 \\ \sqrt{2}, & \text{otherwise} \end{cases}$$

Ahmed, Natarajan, and Rao (1974) have observed that the DCT is related to the DFT of the $2M$-point function obtained by padding x with M zeros. Let $y(n)$ be the padded version of x; then the DFT of y is

$$Y(k) = \sum_{n=0}^{M-1} y(n) W^{nk}$$

where $W = \exp(-j2\pi/2M)$ and the sum stops at $M-1$ because of the zero padding. Then

$$Y(k) = W^{-k/2} \sum_{n=0}^{M-1} y(n) W^{(n+1/2)k}$$

The real part of the sum, for real y, is

$$\sum_{n=0}^{M-1} y(n) \cos \frac{(2n+1)k\pi}{2M}$$

Hence the DCT of x is

$$X(k) = c(k) \operatorname{Re} \{W^{k/2} Y(k)\} \tag{9-17}$$

This relation can be used to obtain a fast algorithm for computing the DCT. It also means that information about the spectrum envelope can be obtained from the DCT.

The transform samples $X(k)$ are computed by the transmitter and quantized. Because the DCT produces approximately uncorrelated samples, the samples can be quantized with fewer bits than the input samples would require. At the receiver, $x(n)$ is reconstructed from the coefficients. In practice, however, further compression is obtained by making the bit-assignment rule depend on the spectral shape of $X(k)$. This allows us to shape the frequency distribution of the quantization noise in order to mask it with the formants, as described earlier. Zelinski and Noll (1977) obtain the spectral information from a smoothed version of the DCT; a more elaborate system by Tribolet and Crochiere (1979) finds the spectrum envelope by linear prediction. Since the spectrum is continually varying, the bit-assignment rule is also continuously changing; hence the side information transmitted along with the components must include either the bit assignments or information from which the bit assignments can be inferred.

PROBLEMS

9-1 The "boxcar" effect at the output of the D/A converter can be modeled as a convolution of an impulse train with a rectangular pulse whose width is equal to the sampling interval. Using this fact, show that the "boxcar" effect multiplies the spectrum of the output signal by a sin f/f function.

9-2 Using the definition of the probability distribution function, prove Eq. (9-2).

9-3 Prove that the compander function, (9-3), approaches the linear function $y = x$ in the limit as $\mu \to 0$.

9-4 Suppose a three-tap filter is used to remove the pitch periodicity from a residual. Let the predictor be

$$\hat{y}(n) = -[b_1 y(n-T+1) + b_2 y(n-T) + b_3 y(n-T-1)]$$

(T is assumed known). Derive the equations for computing the coefficients b_1, b_2, and b_3.

9-5 The following formulation of the DCT is due to Chen et al. (1977). Let $y(n)$ be a $2M$-point vector consisting of the **x** vector and its reflection: $y(n) = x(n)$ for $0 < n \le M - 1$ and $y(n) = x(2M - 1 - n)$ for $n > M - 1$. Let $Y(k)$ be the $2M$-point DFT of $y(n)$. Show that the DCT of x is given by $X(k) = c(k) \exp(-jk\pi/2M)Y(k)$.

9-6 Use (9-17) to show that the envelope of the DCT of $x(n)$ is identical to that of the DFT.

REFERENCES

Abate, J. E.: Linear and adaptive delta modulation, *Proc. IEEE*, vol. 55, pp. 298–308, March, 1967.

Ahmed, N., T. Natarajan, and K. R. Rao: Discrete cosine transform, *IEEE Trans.*, vol. C-23, pp. 90–93, January, 1974.

——— and K. R. Rao: *Orthogonal Transforms for Digital Signal Processing*, Springer-Verlag, New York, 1975.

Atal, B. S.: Linear prediction of speech—recent advances with applications to speech analysis, in D. R. Reddy (Ed.), *Speech Recognition*, Academic Press, New York, pp. 221–230, 1975.

———: Predictive coding of speech at low bit rates, *IEEE Trans.*, vol. COM-30, no. 4, pp. 600–614, April, 1982.

——— and J. R. Remde: A new model of LPC excitation for producing natural-sounding speech at low bit rates, *ICASSP-82*, pp. 614–617, 1982.

——— and M. R. Schroeder: Adaptive predictive coding of speech signals, *BSTJ*, vol. 49, pp. 1973–1986, October, 1970.

——— and ———: Predictive coding of speech signals and subjective error criteria, *IEEE Trans.*, vol. ASSP-27, no. 3, pp. 247–254, June, 1979.

——— and ———: Improved quantizer for adaptive predictive coding of speech signals and low bit rates, *ICASSP-80*, pp. 535–538, 1980.

Beddoes, M. P., and T. K. Chu: Direct sample interpolation (DSI) speech synthesis: an interpolation technique for digital speech data compression and speech synthesis, *IEEE Trans.*, vol. ASSP-30, no. 6, pp. 825–832, December, 1982.

Berouti, M., and J. Makhoul: High quality adaptive predictive coding of speech, *ICASSP-78*, pp. 303–306, April, 1978.

Campanella, S. J., and G. S. Robinson: A comparison of orthogonal transformations for digital speech processing, *IEEE Trans.*, vol. COM-19, pt. 1, pp. 1045–1049, December, 1971.

Chen, W., et al.: A fast computational algorithm for the discrete cosine transform, *IEEE Trans.*, vol. COM-25, pp. 1004–1009, September, 1977.

Crochiere, R. E.: On the design of sub-band coders for low bit-rate speech communications, *BSTJ*, vol. 56, pp. 747–770, May-June, 1977.

———, et al.: Digital coding of speech in sub-bands, *BSTJ*, vol. 55, pp. 1069–1085, October, 1976.

David, Jr., E. E., et al.: Voice-excited vocoders for practical speech bandwidth reduction, *IRE Trans.*, vol. IT-8, pp. S101–105, September, 1962.

Dudley, H.: The vocoder, *Bell Laboratories Record*, vol. 18, pp. 122–126, December, 1939.

Esteban, D., and C. Galand: Application of quadrature mirror filters to split band voice coding schemes, *Proc. ICASSP*, pp. 191–195, 1977.

Flanagan, J. L.: Voices of men and machines, *JASA*, vol. 51, no. 5(1), pp. 1375–1387, May, 1972(a).

———: *Speech Analysis, Synthesis, and Perception*, Springer-Verlag, Berlin, 1972(b).

——— and R. M. Golden: Phase vocoder, *BSTJ*, vol. 45, pp. 1493–1509, November, 1966.

Gold, B.: Channel vocoder quality improvements, *Speech Communication Papers: 97th Meeting of the Acoust. Soc. Amer.*, pp. 385–390, 1979.

——— and C. M. Rader: The channel vocoder, *IEEE Trans.*, vol. AU-15, no. 6, pp. 148–161, December, 1967.

———, et al.: New applications of channel vocoders, *IEEE Trans.*, vol. ASSP-29, no. 1, pp. 13–23, February, 1981.

Gray, Jr., A. H., and J. D. Markel: Quantization and bit allocation in speech processing, *IEEE Trans.*, vol. ASSP-24, no. 6, pp. 459–473, December, 1976.

Greefkes, J. A.: A digitally companded delta modulation modem for speech transmission, *Proc. IEEE Int. Conf. on Communications*, pp. 7-33–7-48, June, 1970.

Huang, J. J. Y., and P. M. Schultheiss: Block quantization of correlated gaussian random variables, *IEEE Trans.*, vol. CS-11, pp. 289–296, September, 1963.

Jayant, N. S.: Adaptive delta modulation with a one-bit memory, *BSTJ*, pp. 321–342, March, 1970.

———: Adaptive quantization with a one-word memory, *BSTJ*, pp. 1119–1144, September, 1973.

———: Digital coding of speech waveforms: PCM, DPCM, and DM quantizers, *Proc. IEEE*, vol. 62, no. 5, pp. 611–632, May, 1974.

——— and P. Noll: *Digital Coding of Waveforms*, Prentice-Hall, Englewood Cliffs, 1984.

——— and L. R. Rabiner: The application of dither to the quantization of speech signals, *BSTJ*, pp. 1293–1304, July-August, 1972.

Kimme, E. G., and F. F. Kuo: Synthesis of optimal filters for a feedback quantization system, *IEEE Trans.*, vol. CT-10, pp. 405–413, September, 1963.

Makhoul, J., and M. Berouti: Adaptive noise spectral shaping and entropy coding in predictive coding of speech, *IEEE Trans.*, vol. ASSP-27, no. 1, pp. 63–73, February, 1979.

Markel, J. D., and A. H. Gray, Jr.: *Linear Prediction of Speech*, Springer-Verlag, New York, 1976.

——— and ———: Implementation and comparison of two transformed reflection coefficient scalar quantization methods, *IEEE Trans.*, vol. ASSP-28, no. 5, pp. 575–583, October, 1980.

Oliver, B. M., et al.: The philosophy of PCM, *Proc. IEEE*, vol. 36, no. 11, pp. 1324–1331, November, 1948.

Paez, M. D., and T. H. Glisson: Minimum mean-squared-error quantization in speech PCM and DPCM systems, *IEEE Trans.*, vol. COM-20, pp. 225–230, April, 1972.

Papoulis, A.: *Systems and Transforms with Applications in Optics*, McGraw-Hill, New York, 1968.

———: *Probability, Random Variables, and Stochastic Processes*, McGraw-Hill, New York, 1984.

Schafer, R. W., and L. R. Rabiner: Design and simulation of a speech analysis-synthesis system based on short-time Fourier analysis, *IEEE Trans.*, vol. AU-21, no. 3, pp. 165–174, June, 1973.

Schroeder, M. R.: Vocoders: analysis and synthesis of speech, *Proc. IEEE*, vol. 54, pp. 720–734, May, 1966.

——— and B. S. Atal: Rate distortion theory and predictive coding, *ICASSP-81*, pp. 201–204, 1981.

Shannon, C. E.: A mathematical theory of communication, *BSTJ*, vol. 27, pp. 379–423, 623–656, 1948.

Smith, B.: Instantaneous companding of quantized signals, *BSTJ*, pp. 653–709, 1957.

Tribolet, J. M., and R. E. Crochiere: Frequency domain coding of speech, *IEEE Trans.*, vol. ASSP-27, no. 5, pp. 512–530, October, 1979.

Viswanathan, R., and J. Makhoul: Quantization properties of transmission parameters in linear predictive systems, *IEEE Trans.*, vol. ASSP-23, no. 3, pp. 309–321, June, 1975.

Wintz, P. A.: Transform picture coding, *Proc. IEEE*, vol. 60, pp. 980–820, July, 1972.

Zelinski, R., and P. Noll: Adaptive transform coding of speech signals, *IEEE Trans.*, vol. ASSP-25, no. 4, pp. 299–309, August, 1977.

CHAPTER
TEN

VOICE ENCODING AND SYNTHESIS

In the previous chapter, we considered coding systems based on a more or less faithful reproduction of the input waveform. The existence of the speech-production model described in Chapter 5, and reproduced here as Fig. 10-1, however, suggests that speech could be more economically transmitted if the receiver implemented this model and the information transmitted were simply the directions for making the model talk.

There is another application area, however, whose goal is also that of making the model talk; this is speech synthesis. (Voice-response systems which use simple waveform coding are an exception to this.) Synthesis and encoding are intimately related, and in some applications, such as voice-response systems, the only difference is that the channel between transmitter and receiver is replaced by a storage medium. Hence we have chosen to consider these applications together, and this chapter is, in a sense, about the applications of the model of Chapter 5. Synthesizers based on this model are called *terminal-analog* synthesizers; one might well refer also to terminal-analog vocoders, although it is not customary to do so.

A basic property of this model is the separation of excitation and modulation, and this separation is a property of all the systems to be described here, except waveform-coded voice-response systems. As suggested by Fig. 10-1, the excitation portion of the model generally consists of a choice between random noise and a periodic function which may be a simple pulse train. The main exceptions to this are the voice-excited and residual-excited vocoders. The modulation portion consists of one or more variable filters. In the earliest systems, these filters were a filter bank; the filter-bank realization gave rise to the first and most durable of all vocoders, the channel vocoder, which we have already discussed in Chapter 9. Another variable filter is, inevitably, the LPC vocal tract model of Sec. 5-6, and closely related to this are the formant vocoders and synthesizers, which use three or four filters to reproduce the formant resonances.

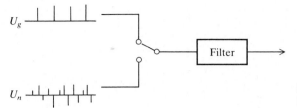

Figure 10-1 The excitation-modulation model of speech generation.

10-1 LINEAR-PREDICTION VOCODERS

Vocoders using linear prediction differ from the linear-prediction waveform encoders described in Chapter 9 in that the residual is no longer available to the receiver. The receiver is therefore intended to synthesize the transmitted speech without actually duplicating the input waveform in detail. This is clearly an artificial distinction, and there are a number of systems which straddle it. Some kind of excitation information, no matter how sketchy, must always be transmitted, and it is simply a matter of deciding how tenuous this information is to be before we put the system into the other category. We have, in fact, already met one such borderline system: Atal and Remde's multipulse system, which in one sense represents the last of a sequence of attritions of the residual, is in another sense a system in which we seek only a perceptually plausible approximation to the input spectrum.

Using the receiver as a synthesizer puts a heavier responsibility on the LPC computations. In a waveform encoder, after all, any system of the sort shown in Fig. 10-2 will reproduce the input exactly (provided $1/[1 - A(z)]$ is stable), and our only concern in choosing $A(z)$ is to permit $E(z)$ to be transmitted economically with negligible distortion. In a vocoder, however, there is no $E(z)$ as such, and we are back to the synthesis model of Fig. 10-1. In introducing linear prediction in Chapter 6, we pointed out the dual rôle of LPC as predictor and as model. In waveform coders, the predictive rôle is uppermost; in vocoders, the modeling rôle is uppermost. It is for this reason that vocoders have been grouped with synthesizers here, for a vocoder can legitimately be viewed as a remotely controlled synthesizer.

This has the following consequences:

1. It is of critical importance to have a good match between $1/A(z)$ and the vocal tract transfer function, and the system is more vulnerable than a waveform

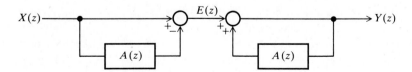

Figure 10-2 Waveform encoding and decoding by means of an arbitrary filter and its inverse.

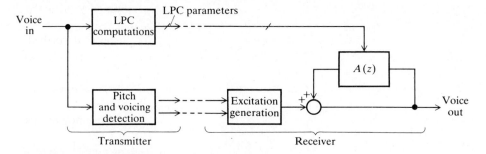

Figure 10-3 A typical linear-prediction vocoder. This system differs from an adaptive DPCM encoder in that pitch and voicing parameters are transmitted instead of a residual. At the receiver, these control an excitation generator, as in the channel vocoder.

encoder to anything which may spoil this match—in particular, to interfering noise.
2. The excitation must be believable. It cannot equal $E(z)$, but it should at least equal something which $E(z)$ might well be.

A typical linear-prediction vocoder is shown in Fig. 10-3. The transmitter has two main subsystems, one for LPC computation and one for the pitch and voicing decision. The incoming voice is divided into contiguous frames typically 20 ms long, and the predictor coefficients and other parameters for each segment are computed, encoded, and transmitted. At the receiver, an excitation generator is controlled by the pitch/voicing signal. The excitation generator produces either a sequence of random pulses or else a pulse train spaced at the pitch period, just as in the channel vocoder. The amplitude of this excitation is determined by the gain input. The excitation is then applied to the inverse filter derived from the predictor coefficients, and the output of this filter is the received voice.

An Autocorrelation Vocoder

To provide a specific example, we will cite details from an implementation by Markel and Gray (1974). In this system, the voice is sampled at 6.5 kHz, and a tenth-order LPC analysis is performed on 128-point frames. Because the autocorrelation method is used, the frames are Hamming-weighted before analysis. Markel and Gray found that the antialiasing filter had to cut off rapidly at the Nyquist frequency; they found that otherwise the autocorrelation predictor wasted some of its poles trying to compensate for the rolloff of the filter. Preemphasis is applied to the input signal in order to enhance the high-frequency content before analysis. The preemphasis function is $(1 - \mu z^{-1})$; for maximal spectral flatness, the optimum μ is given by $\mu = -r(1)/r(0)$. This optimum varies considerably depending on whether the speech sounds are vocoids or fricatives. If μ is allowed to vary, however, then its value must be included in the transmitted data. For parsimony, μ is forced to zero (i.e., the filter is effectively removed) if the optimum value is less than 0.6 and to 0.9 otherwise. Thus presence or absence of the filter can be indicated by one bit in the transmitted data.

The pitch-detection algorithm is a version of the SIFT process described in Chapter 8. Pitch detection is an independent process which runs in parallel with the LPC computation. The input to SIFT is the speech data, low-pass filtered to 900 Hz and down-sampled by a factor of 3. The dc component is removed before analysis and the results are required to exceed a minimum threshold in order to avoid responding to 60-Hz hum as voicing. Various tests for consistency are used to remove remaining errors.

The parameters transmitted are the reflection coefficients, the pitch/voicing information, the residual power, and the preemphasis information.

The receiver uses the reflection coefficients directly in a lattice structure of the type shown in Fig. 6-9. The excitation is chosen on the basis of the pitch/voicing information and the output is deemphasized with a filter matching the input preemphasis filter.

In any vocoder of this sort, optimum performance is obtained when the predictor parameters are held constant over an entire pitch period. That is, once the excitation pulse has been emitted, the filter coefficients are not allowed to change until the entire pitch period begun by that excitation pulse has been synthesized. This is known as pitch-synchronous synthesis. For economy of implementation, however, a fixed frame size is assumed, and the boundaries of this frame will in general not coincide with those of the pitch period. This inconsistency can be resolved in two ways: either the pitch cycle boundaries can be determined at the transmitter and the LPC analysis performed over a subframe embracing a single pitch period, or the receiver can recompute the filter coefficients at the beginning of each pitch period. Gray and Markel chose the second alternative, and the filter coefficients (and also the pitch and amplitude) are obtained by linear interpolation between the windows comprised by the pitch period.

Voice Excitation

As with the channel vocoder, it was found that the quality of the output speech depended critically on the quality of the excitation function provided at the receiver. There are a number of problems here: (1) pitch uncertainties are just as detrimental in the LPC vocoder as they were in the channel vocoder; (2) inaccuracies in the voicing decision, combined with the inability to represent semivoiced sounds like [v], degrade the quality of the output speech; and (3) the impulse-train excitation gives the output voice an "electrical accent" which most users find disagreeable and which makes it difficult to recognize the talker.

As with the channel vocoder, one solution to these problems is voice excitation (Weinstein, 1975). The details of this voice-excited linear-prediction (VELP) vocoder are similar to those of the voice-excited channel vocoder, as can be seen from Fig. 10-4. The input voice is low-pass filtered, and the filter output is down-sampled to its Nyquist rate. This baseband signal is transmitted to the receiver in lieu of the pitch/voicing signal. At the receiver, a wideband excitation is derived

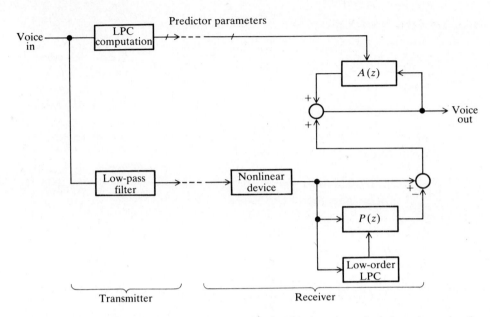

Figure 10-4 A voice-excited linear-prediction vocoder. As with the voice-excited channel vocoder, the pitch and voicing information is replaced by a baseband signal derived from the input.

from the baseband by a nonlinear operation. The wideband excitation is then spectrally flattened. In the channel vocoder, this flattening was done by a combination of filters and hard limiters; here a low-order autocorrelation LPC analysis is applied to the excitation. The excitation is then passed through the filter composed of $P(z)$ and the subtractor. Since LPC filters have the effect of flattening the spectrum of the signal passed through them, this is in a sense the optimum way to proceed. The flattened excitation is then passed through an inverse filter derived from the transmitted predictor parameters, as in any LPC receiver.

The residual-excited linear-prediction (RELP) vocoder, investigated by Un and Magill (1975), is similar. Here it is the residual that is low-pass filtered and transmitted as a baseband instead of the voice. Un and Magill used a corner frequency of 800 Hz and transmitted the baseband using adaptive delta modulation. Spectral flattening at the receiver is apt to be somewhat less critical, since the residual from which the baseband was taken has already been flattened by the linear predictor. Makhoul and Berouti (1979) describe a baseband vocoder in which the high-frequency portions of the excitation are supplied by replicating the spectrum of the baseband excitation signal; this technique does not require a nonlinear element or spectrum flattening.

These systems require a higher bit rate than conventional, pitch-excited vocoders, because of the extra bits required to encode the baseband signals, even at their reduced sampling rate. Un and Magill achieved a transmission rate between 6.5 and 9.6 kbits/s, with speech quality at 9.6 kbits/s described as "quite good."

Variable-Rate Encoding

Another way to reduce the bit rate required for speech coding is to take advantage of the redundancy of the speech signal over time. Since vowels and fricatives, in particular, tend to have regions in which they change slowly, it should not require as much information to describe these portions as to describe rapidly varying regions, such as glides and plosive consonants.

Accordingly, Magill (1973) investigated a system in which a new reflection-coefficient vector was transmitted only when it showed a significant change from the previously transmitted value. The measure of difference was similar to the Itakura log-likelihood measure described in Chapter 8. Makhoul et al. (1974) and Viswanathan et al. (1978) reconstructed the missing parameters by linear interpolation between the transmitted frames. They found that at low frame rates, the choice of frames to be transmitted greatly influenced the quality of the recovered speech, and Viswanathan et al. (1977) describe an automatic scheme for selecting frames whose performance is comparable to the results of manual selection.

Papamichalis and Barnwell (1983) proposed a very flexible system in which the alternatives for each frame were to transmit all, none, or a subset of the reflection coefficients. Their basic LPC system used a tenth-order predictor; to keep computational costs down, they considered only subsets of four or eight coefficients. In this scheme, 16 consecutive frames were parametrized, and dynamic programming techniques were used to determine the optimum choice for each frame, using a cost function which reflected the cost in terms of bit rate and distortion. Using listening tests, they found that variable-rate encoding systems transmitting at 1200 bits/s were judged as good as a fixed-rate system operating at 2400 bits/s.

The LPC-10 Algorithm

We conclude with a summary of a representative 2400-bit/s LPC vocoder algorithm. This description is based on Appendix C of Kang et al. (1979); another summary is to be found in Tremain (1982).

The input speech is sampled at 8 kHz and digitized as 12-bit two's-complement words. The incoming speech is partitioned into 180-sample frames, resulting in a frame rate of 44.44 frames/s. A tenth-order covariance linear predictor is used to compute the vocal tract filter parameters. Pitch and voicing are determined using the AMDF algorithm.

The LPC analysis is preceded by a preemphasis filter with a corner frequency at approximately 80 Hz. The covariance matrix is computed iteratively in a fashion similar to the matrix computation in our program, LPCC, in Appendix B. Fixed-point or block floating-point arithmetic is used throughout. (Block floating point is floating point in which all elements of the block have the same exponent.) The elements of the covariance matrix are represented by 29-bit fixed-point numbers, in order to accommodate the summing of one hundred and twenty 23-bit products. The covariance equations are solved using the Cholesky decomposition of Eqs. (6-55). Intermediate results are scaled to 16 bits. Computation is halted if an unstable filter appears likely to result—i.e., if any column of the covariance matrix underflows, if any main-diagonal element is negative, or if the magnitude of any generalized reflection coefficient exceeds unity. In such a case, the coefficients from the previous frame are reused. The generalized reflection coefficients [i.e., the **κ** vector of (6-54)] are encoded for transmission. The first two coefficients are encoded as log-area ratios and the rest are encoded linearly. The bit assignments used are: 5 bits each for κ_1 through κ_4, 4 bits each for κ_5 through κ_8, 3 bits for κ_9, and 2 bits for κ_{10}. When the speech is unvoiced, only the first four generalized reflection coefficients are coded and the bits normally allocated to the remaining coefficients are used for error protection. The RMS amplitude of the speech is computed from the (0, 0) element of the covariance matrix.

The LPC analysis is what is termed "semipitch synchronous." The basic speech frame is 180 samples long, corresponding to a time duration of 22.5 ms. The LPC analysis system is slaved to the pitch detector, however, and from each 180-sample frame a 130-sample window is selected starting at the beginning of a pitch period. In this way every pitch period is encoded (and, at the receiver, reconstructed) using a single set of predictor coefficients.

Pitch is computed using the AMDF algorithm described in Chapter 8. The speech is low-pass filtered to approximately 1000 Hz and effectively downsampled by a factor of 4. The AMDF is computed for lags ranging from 20 to 156 samples, corresponding to a pitch range from 400 to 51 Hz. A semilogarithmic pitch scale is used to cover this 8 to 1 range in 60 steps. AMDF minima are candidates for the pitch period; the actual period is determined by considering these minima in the light of continuity requirements from frame to frame. The voiced/unvoiced decision is based primarily on the energy in the low-pass filtered speech with reference to estimated background noise. The initial decision is a "yes/no/maybe" result which is then refined by comparing with (1) zero-crossing counts and reflection-coefficient values and (2) results for the adjacent frames. Pitch and voicing are so coded as to prevent single-bit transmission errors from causing gross pitch and voicing errors.

In the transmitted bit stream, 41 bits are used for the reflection coefficients, 7 bits for pitch and voicing, and 5 bits for amplitude. One bit is used for synchronization, giving a total of 54 bits per frame. Since there are 44.44 frames/s, this gives an overall bit rate of 2.4k bits/s. Detailed coding information is given in Tremain (1982).

At the receiver, the bit stream is dissected into its constituent codes and the pitch/voicing, amplitude, and reflection-coefficient values are decoded. Since only one set of parameters is transmitted per frame of speech, it is necessary to interpolate the received values to account for the presence of more than one pitch period in a frame. Pitch is interpolated linearly on the basis of the position of the period within the frame, and amplitude is interpolated logarithmically. In the case of reflection coefficients, the values from the previous frame are saved and, depending on the location of the pitch period within the frame, the old values, the new values, or the average of the two sets are used.

The pitch/voicing code is used to determine the excitation function to be used. If the speech is unvoiced, pseudorandom numbers are generated and used for the excitation; if the speech is voiced, then a locally stored waveform, representing one cycle of a plausible prediction residual, is used as the excitation. This stored waveform is 40 samples long; it is truncated or padded out with zeros as required to match the current pitch period.

The reflection coefficients are converted to predictor coefficients by the Levinson recusion of Eq. (6-19a) or Eq. (6-19b). The inverse filter is a direct-form digital filter. The output is corrected for amplitude, deemphasized, and converted to analog form.

10-2 VECTOR QUANTIZATION

Vector quantization addresses a more general problem than any we have looked at so far: given any input data to be encoded, what is the most economical possible coding scheme? When Shannon (1948) proved that signals from an information source could be coded at a bit rate no greater than the entropy of the source, he showed that this would be achieved, not by coding individual samples but by collecting samples into groups and encoding the groups.

Shannon's model is built around a *codebook*. In the simplest case, this is a collection of S possible messages, with each entry indexed by a k-bit number. The transmitter selects a message from the codebook and transmits its k-bit address; the receiver enters its copy of the codebook at this address and recovers the message. The information rate is $R = (\log_2 S)/k$. This is because if all messages are assumed equally likely, each message passes $\log_2 S$ bits of information to the receiver at a cost of k bits; hence the amount of information per bit is $(\log_2 S)/k$.

Note that we can increase k without penalty. For example, if we double k, each message is twice as long, but we can now expand the codebook to accommodate S^2 messages, in which case the new rate will be $R' = (2 \log_2 S)/(2k) = R$.

Implicit in the idea of a codebook, however, is the idea that each message is much more than a single sample. If we consider a sequence of samples as a vector, then Shannon says that the codebook entries should be vectors rather than individual samples; furthermore, the longer the vector, the better. This is the basis of vector quantization. Notice that the focus of vector quantization is quite different from the issues we have been considering so far: it is not a question of waveform coding *versus* voice coding, but of how the coding, once chosen, shall be done. Vector quantization has been applied to waveforms (Abut, Gray, and Rebolledo, 1982) as well as to predictor parameters (e.g., Buzo et al., 1980). Initially, we will assume that the samples are taken from the speech waveform itself, but we will also address the encoding of predictor parameters.

Vector Quantization of Speech Waveforms

A vector quantizing scheme involves an encoder, a decoder, and a codebook, as shown in Fig. 10-5. The codebook is a lookup table with a k-bit address and 2^k entries. Each entry in the table is a vector of samples; let us call the ith entry $C(i)$. Both the encoder and the decoder have copies of the codebook.

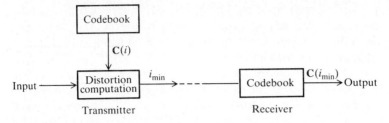

Figure 10-5 A vector quantization (VQ) scheme. Input vectors are compared with entries in a vector codebook; the number of the codebook entry which is the best match (i.e., shows the smallest distortion when compared with the input) is selected for transmission.

The encoder looks at each incoming vector of samples **x** and selects the codeword **y** = **C**(*i*) which is the best match to **x**. Formally, let $d(\mathbf{x}, \mathbf{y})$ be a measure of the error in representing **x** by **y**; $d(\mathbf{x}, \mathbf{y})$ is termed the distortion measure. The euclidean distance $(\mathbf{x} - \mathbf{y})^T(\mathbf{x} - \mathbf{y})$ is a frequently used measure, but any positive-definite quadratic form in $(\mathbf{x} - \mathbf{y})$ will serve.

The reader should notice the distinction between distortion and distance. As we saw in Chapter 7, a distance measure requires (1) dist (**x**, **y**) ≥ 0 with equality for **x** = **y**; (2) dist (**x**, **y**) = dist (**y**, **x**), and (3) dist (**x**, **z**) ≤ dist (**x**, **y**) + dist (**y**, **z**). The concept of distortion is looser and requires only property 1. Thus we do not have to use distances as distortion measures, although we frequently do, primarily because they are well understood and readily computed. The main requirement is that the distortion measure be perceptually meaningful, i.e., that low distortion correspond to a good-sounding output. In speech work, the Itakura and Itakura-Saito errors are frequently used when encoding LPC data.

The encoder transmits that *i* for which $d(\mathbf{x}, \mathbf{C}(i))$ is a minimum (i_{min} in Fig. 10-5). If we are using a euclidean distance as our distortion measure, this amounts to a nearest-neighbor choice.

The decoder receives *i* and presents **C**(*i*) as its output. Clearly the success of this technique depends on having a well-chosen codebook, and the design of a vector quantizer centers as much around the compilation of a suitable codebook as around the selection of an appropriate distortion measure.

This codebook is, in general, not complete: i.e., the number of vectors in the codebook is finite, while the number of possible vectors is usually, for all practical purposes, infinite. The distortion we must live with is, in most applications, that which arises from assigning an incoming vector to a codebook entry that does not quite match.

Vector quantization does not commit the user to any specific model or to any specific distortion measure. The quantization process is reduced to a simple search-and-compare procedure; there are no feedback loops at the transmitter or receiver; hence stability is not an issue and transmission errors will not propagate beyond the vector in which they occur. Indeed, we will see that the chief difficulty in implementing vector quantizers is simply the time required to search a very large codebook.

Lloyd's algorithm The procedure for designing a codebook was developed by Lloyd (1957). The algorithm was designed as a clustering technique for use in pattern recognition and allied fields. It was extended to vector quantization by Linde, Buzo, and Gray (1980) and is therefore sometimes called the LBG algorithm. The algorithm consists of an iterative technique for refining an initial codebook. It will always yield an optimum codebook, but the reader should be warned that the universe of all possible codebooks typically contains many local optima which may be significantly poorer than the global optimum. Lloyd's algorithm will home in on the local optimum nearest to the initial codebook; this optimum may or may not be the global one, depending on how the initial codebook was set up. It may occasionally be necessary to try several initial codebooks.

The algorithm starts with the preliminary codebook and refines it iteratively. The process continues until the performance of the system meets the user's requirements or until no significant further improvement is possible. The algorithm is as follows:

1. Encode a selection of test data with the current codebook and measure the average distortion. If the distortion is small enough, the algorithm terminates.
2. For each address i in the codebook, find the centroid of all the input vectors which were mapped into i and make this centroid the new $C(i)$. Go to step 1.

The test data used in this process are referred to as the training set. Each word in the codebook is used to represent a cluster of possible input vectors from this set.

In this algorithm, step 1 compares each input vector to the entries $\{C\}$ in the existing version of the codebook and associates the vector with that codebook entry $C(i)$ which was the best match—i.e., for which the distortion is a minimum. This step also accumulates these minimum distortions and computes the average distortion at the end.

Step 2 examines the encoding results and asks whether each $C(i)$ is truly representative of the input vectors which were assigned to it. This is a reasonable question, since in some cases vectors may have been assigned to an entry simply because all other alternatives were worse. Replacing the previous $C(i)$ with the centroid makes the entry representative of those choices. When the codebook has been rewritten, however, the encoder has a new menu of codes from which to choose, and so it is necessary to repeat step 1 and see whether some of the input vectors might now find better accommodation elsewhere. This will cause the centroids to shift, necessitating a rerun of step 2.

The word "centroid" is a shorthand way of describing that vector $\mathbf{v}$ which minimizes the average distortion $d(\mathbf{x}, \mathbf{v})$ for all of the vectors $\mathbf{x}$ being considered. (It is in this sense that we say the centroid is "representative" of the $\mathbf{x}$ vectors.) In the case of a euclidean distortion measure, this is a centroid in the usual sense. This is also true if the Mahalanobis distance is used (Abut, Gray, and Rebolledo, 1982). If the $\mathbf{x}$'s are vectors of predictor coefficients, the "centroid" is the set of predictors obtained by averaging the autocorrelation matrices from which the vectors $\mathbf{x}$ were obtained.

Vector Quantization of Predictor Parameters

We will illustrate these principles by considering the vector quantization of linear-prediction parameters, as described in the classic paper by Buzo et al. (1980). We will discuss their choice of a distortion measure, and its consequences, here, and will address the construction of their codebook in a later section.

Their application was a linear-prediction encoder of the type described in the preceding section. In this type of encoder, the pitch and voicing parameters can be expressed very compactly, and so the bulk of the transmitted data is devoted to the predictor parameters. Therefore, their starting point was a codebook in which each entry $\mathbf{C}(i)$ was a vector of predictor parameters, $[\sigma_i, a_i(1), a_i(2), \ldots]$. Their choice of a distortion measure, however, led them ultimately to a much more efficient representation.

The distortion measure used was the Itakura-Saito measure mentioned in Chapter 8:

$$d(\mathbf{x}, \mathbf{a}) = \frac{E}{\sigma^2} + \ln \frac{\sigma^2}{E_\infty} - 1 \tag{10-1}$$

Here $\mathbf{x}$ is the input signal and $\mathbf{a}$ is the model used to represent it; σ is the gain of the model and E is the prediction-error power resulting from applying that model to $\mathbf{x}$. We will use $\mathbf{a}_p$ to represent the particular pth-order model which matches the input $\mathbf{x}$ (that is, $\mathbf{a}_p$ is the optimum autocorrelation predictor derived from the statistics of $\mathbf{x}$). The gain factor associated with this predictor is σ_p, and we saw in Chapter 6 that $\sigma_p^2 = E_p$. Finally, E_∞ is the limit of E_p as $p \to \infty$. (Notice that since $\mathbf{a}_p$ is determined by $\mathbf{x}$, E_∞ depends only on $\mathbf{x}$.) For the optimum model, then, $E_p/\sigma_p^2 = 1$ and

$$d(\mathbf{x}, \mathbf{a}_p) = \ln \frac{E_p}{E_\infty} \tag{10-2}$$

The structure of the transmitter is shown in Fig. 10-6. Here the prediction and quantization steps are shown separately; the input signal is $\mathbf{x}$, the pth order predictor parameters are $\mathbf{a}_p$ and the vector-quantized parameters are $\hat{\mathbf{a}}$. The distortion inherent in the model is $d(\mathbf{x}, \mathbf{a}_p)$, and that resulting from quantizing $\mathbf{a}_p$ is $d(\mathbf{a}_p, \hat{\mathbf{a}})$. The overall distortion introduced by the transmitter is $d(\mathbf{x}, \hat{\mathbf{a}})$, as shown. Buzo et al. show that if the Itakura-Saito measure is used, these distortions are additive: that is,

$$d(\mathbf{x}, \hat{\mathbf{a}}) = d(\mathbf{x}, \mathbf{a}_p) + d(\mathbf{a}_p, \hat{\mathbf{a}}) \tag{10-3}$$

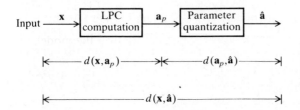

Figure 10-6 The transmission end of a system for vector quantization of LPC parameters, showing the distortion measures used in the analysis of Buzo et al. (1980).

This additive property is the key to the design of the transmitter; it is not at all obvious and the proof is difficult. We will outline the proof here. For any predictor, the output error power is

$$E = \sum_{n=-p}^{p} r_x(n) r_a(n) \tag{10-4}$$

where r_x and r_a are the autocorrelations of $\mathbf{x}$ and the predictor. (This was shown in Chapter 2; in our case, $\mathbf{a}$ is a finite-impulse-response system, so the limits on the sum are $-p$ and p. We write r_x and r_a here instead of r_{xx} and r_{aa} for brevity.) So

$$d(\mathbf{x}, \hat{\mathbf{a}}) = \frac{1}{\sigma_{\hat{a}}^2} \sum_{n=-p}^{p} r_x(n) r_{\hat{a}}(n) + \ln \frac{\sigma_{\hat{a}}^2}{E_\infty} - 1$$

If we substitute the output of the optimum predictor for $\mathbf{x}$, we have

$$d(\mathbf{a}_p, \hat{\mathbf{a}}) = \frac{1}{\sigma_{\hat{a}}^2} \sum_{n=-p}^{p} r_{a_p}(n) r_{\hat{a}}(n) + \ln \frac{\sigma_{\hat{a}}^2}{E_p} - 1$$

(The reason why E_p corresponds to E_∞ may be found in Markel and Gray, 1976.) We saw in Chapter 6, however, that the autocorrelation predictor matches $r_a(n)$ and $r_x(n)$ for $n = 0, 1, \ldots, p$. Hence the two summations are equal, and if we subtract the two distortions, we have

$$d(\mathbf{x}, \hat{\mathbf{a}}) - d(\mathbf{a}_p, \hat{\mathbf{a}}) = \ln \frac{E_p}{E_\infty} \tag{10-5}$$

The right-hand side of (10-5) is just $d(\mathbf{x}, \mathbf{a}_p)$, however, and so the additive property is proved. (The authors call this the "triangle equality.")

Now, $d(\mathbf{x}, \mathbf{a}_p)$ is a function of the input signal and the order of the predictor; hence there is nothing the quantizing process can do to change that. In that case, minimizing $d(\mathbf{a}, \hat{\mathbf{a}})$ is equivalent to minimizing

$$d(\mathbf{x}, \hat{\mathbf{a}}) = \frac{E_{\hat{a}}}{\sigma_{\hat{a}}^2} + \ln \sigma_{\hat{a}}^2 - \ln E_\infty - 1$$

However, E_∞ is a characteristic of the input signal $\mathbf{x}$ and cannot be minimized. Hence it is sufficient to minimize

$$D_i = \frac{E_{\mathbf{a}(i)}}{\sigma_{\mathbf{a}(i)}^2} + \ln \sigma_{\mathbf{a}(i)}^2 \tag{10-6}$$

over all models $\mathbf{a}(i)$ in the codebook.

At the transmitter, then, we examine every codebook entry and compute D for each entry and the input signal. However, $\sigma_{\mathbf{a}}^2$ depends only on the model, so for computational efficiency, we will store $\ln \sigma_{\mathbf{a}}^2$ in the codebook. We will use (10-4) to compute the error power. Thus instead of going through a linear-prediction computation for each input signal, we need only compute $r_x(n)$ for the required lags. Similarly, for every filter in the codebook, we will store, not the

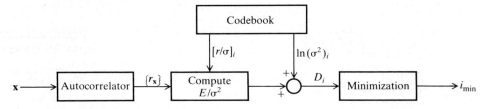

Figure 10-7 The transmitter of the Buzo VQ scheme in its final form.

predictor parameters, but the autocorrelations $r_a(n)$. In fact, to minimize computation time when searching the codebook, we will store $r_a(n)/\sigma_a^2$. Each codebook entry will thus consist of $[\ln \sigma_a^2, r_a(0)/\sigma_a^2, r_a(1)/\sigma_a^2, \ldots, r_a(p)/\sigma_a^2]$.

The final form of the transmitter is shown in Fig. 10-7. The quantizer computes $r_x(n)$ and then selects the codebook entry for which D_i is a minimum; the address of this entry is transmitted through the channel, along with pitch and voicing information. At the receiver, the codebook address is used to retrieve the filter parameters and the voice is reconstructed.

Forming the Initial Codebook

We naturally want to start out with a codebook that is already fairly representative of the data to be encoded. One way to do this is simply to take actual input vectors as the codewords. In quantizing speech waveforms, where adjacent portions of the signal are highly correlated, it will be preferable to space the sample vectors far enough apart that their intercorrelations are negligible.

The algorithm as stated assumes that the codebook has a fixed size. We could start with a small codebook, however, and expand it gradually until it reaches final size. For example, we could examine specific cases of notably poor matches and create new codebook entries for these inputs. This is an attractive possibility if it is important to impose some limit on the maximum distortion instead of, or in addition to, minimizing the average.

Splitting Another way to grow a codebook is to split an existing cluster into two smaller clusters and assign a codebook entry to each (Linde, Buzo, and Gray, 1980). This approach can be used to build the entire codebook, as follows. Create an initial cluster consisting of the entire training set. The initial codebook thus contains a single entry corresponding to the centroid of the entire set. Split this cluster into two subclusters and assign a 0 to one cluster and a 1 to the other. The codebook now contains two entries, one at $i = 0$ and one at $i = 1$. Now split each cluster again and concatenate a 0 to the address of one subcluster and a 1 to the address of the other. The codebook now has four entries, numbered 00, 01, 10, and 11. This process can be repeated until the codebook has the desired size.

Splitting can be done in a number of ways. The ideal would be to divide each cluster by a hyperplane normal to the direction of maximum distortion, in order to ensure that the maximum distortions of the two new clusters will be smaller than that of the original. As the number of table entries increases, however, the computational expense rapidly becomes prohibitive. Some authors perturb the centroid to generate two different points. If the centroid is **x**, then two new centroids can be created by forming $\mathbf{x} + \boldsymbol{\delta}$ and $\mathbf{x} - \boldsymbol{\delta}$, where $\boldsymbol{\delta}$ is a small perturbation vector. In the LPC quantizer described above, Buzo et al. (1980) multiply the reflection coefficients by 0.99 to create one new subcluster and by 1.01 to create the other. Another alternative is the worst-match technique above: for each cluster, find the vector **x** which is the worst match and make this vector the centroid of the new cluster.

Product codes If the speech waveform itself is to be quantized, then the codebook vectors can be pieces of waveform of any convenient length. In that case, the codebook size can be increased by forming product codes (Abut, Gray, and Rebolledo, 1982). A product code is a code made up of smaller codes by concatenation. Here both the vectors and the codebook grow concurrently. We start with vectors of length 1—i.e., scalars. These might be, for example, the output samples of a conventional PCM quantizer. If this is a k-bit quantizer with 2^k values, then the initial codebook contains these 2^k values and its bit rate is just k. We start by optimizing this codebook with Lloyd's algorithm. Call this optimized codebook C_0 and its bit rate k_0; thus C_0 comprises 2^k samples. We then form a new codebook consisting of all possible concatenations of two codes from C_0. (This is customarily written $C_0 \times C_0$.) For example, suppose $k_0 = 2$ and the codebook values are $\{a, b, c, d\}$. Then C_1 contains the 16 values $\{aa, ab, ac, ad, ba, bb, bc, bd, ca, cb, cc, cd, da, db, dc, dd\}$ and $k_1 = k_0 + k_0$. We then optimize C_1 with Lloyd's algorithm. That is, we quantize the training set with the new codebook, update the centroids, requantize, etc., until the minimum distortion is obtained. Then in all subsequent expansions of the codebook, we form $C_i = C_{i-1} \times C_0$, having a word length $k_i = k_{i-1} + k_0$. The constituents of this codebook are the codes from the optimized C_{i-1} and the original codebook C_0. After each expansion, we optimize with Lloyd's algorithm; when the word length r equals the design value, the process terminates.

Controlling Complexity

We have said that Shannon's theory tells us that we get the best performance for large vector lengths. This means using a large codebook, and a large codebook, besides requiring a large amount of memory, will require significant amounts of time to search. Since there is no linear ordering implicit in the codes, it is not feasible to use any of the classic methods of speeding up the search. Even if an ordering were found for the codes, most efficient searches (e.g., binary search, tree search) rely on getting a signed error: the current entry is higher, or lower, than the input value. A distortion measure is by definition nonnegative, so all we learn from a miss is that it was not a hit. Hence with the codebook organized as we have described it so far, the search must be made linearly through the book from start to finish. For every entry to be examined, we must compute $d(\mathbf{x}, \mathbf{C}(i))$, which is typically a quadratic form. If the encoding process is to be performed in real time, this process may be prohibitively slow for large-sized codebooks. Hence a good deal of research has gone into finding ways of speeding up the search. There are two general ways of doing this: (1) impose a structure on the codebook that expedites the search or (2) embed the VQ in some other process which simplifies the data to be coded so we can get by with a smaller codebook.

Tree-searched codebooks One way in which a tree search can be implemented is by means of auxiliary codebooks (Buzo et al., 1980). We divide the main codebook into two halves, and the auxiliary codebook A contains two entries. We enter the auxiliary codebook with the input vector and find the better match. If this is $A(0)$, we then search the first half of the main codebook; if it is $A(1)$, we search the second half. We have thus divided the search time by two at the cost of two auxiliary codebook entries.

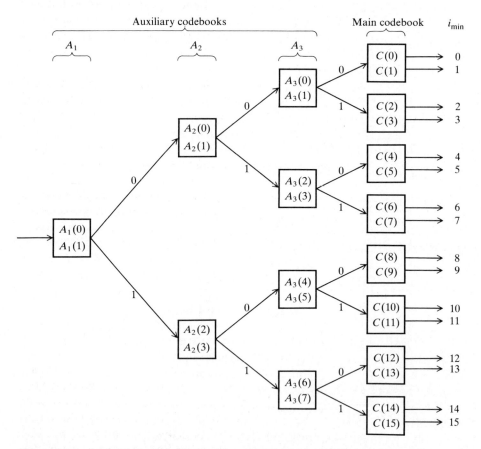

Figure 10-8 A tree-searched codebook. At each stage, the quantizer is directed to the correct auxiliary codebook by the result obtained from the previous stage.

We can easily extend this principle. Instead of one auxiliary codebook, we can have two. A search of A_1 tells us which half of A_2 to search, and a search of that half of A_2 tells us which quarter of the main codebook to use. This principle leads us ultimately to $k-1$ auxiliary codebooks for a main codebook of 2^k entries, structured as a binary tree as shown in Fig. 10-8 for $k = 4$. Here each block contains two codewords; the outcomes direct the encoder to the correct block of the subsequent codebook until the main codebook is reached.

If the main codebook was grown by splitting, then the auxiliary codebooks can be generated as part of the process. The two optimized centroids generated from the first split are used as A_1, the four centroids from the next split become A_2, and so on. This can only be done, however, if $A_2(0)$ and $A_2(1)$ are formed solely from the vectors that went into $A_1(0)$ and $A_2(2)$ and $A_2(3)$ are formed solely from the vectors that formed $A_1(1)$. This means that the A_2 book may be less than optimal, if it should happen that a few elements from $A_1(1)$ really fit better in $A_2(0)$ or $A_2(1)$. In practice, the loss in performance is more than made up by the increase in speed, particularly if it permits a larger codebook than would have been feasible under a linear search. A more serious problem is the increase in storage requirements: a codebook of 2^k vectors requires a tree which itself contains $2^k - 1$ vectors, and this near-doubling in size is frequently unacceptable.

Multiple-stage encoders A way to reduce both the size and the search time is to use a small codebook A to generate a rough approximation to the input vector and then to use a second small codebook B to encode the error left by A (Juang and Gray, 1982). The input vector $\mathbf{x}$ is matched against A and an address i is obtained. Then B is searched for the best match to $\mathbf{x} - A(i)$. If the best match is $B(j)$, then the transmitter sends i and j and the receiver outputs $A(i) + B(j)$.

Product-code quantizers The multiple-stage encoder represents the input vector as the sum of two codewords, a coarse approximation and a fine approximation. The signal can also be represented as the product of an amplitude and a vector that is in some sense normalized to unity. Quantizers based on this principle have been investigated by Buzo *et al.* (1980) and by Sabin and Gray (1984), who have termed them shape-gain quantizers. In the case of LPC quantizers, the gain is the numerator of the model given in (6-34) and the shape is the denominator.

10-3 SPEECH SYNTHESIS

Of the two problems of speech synthesis and speech recognition, synthesis is undoubtedly the easier problem. We still have no general theory of how the brain recognizes speech or speakers, and if we did have such a theory, there is no assurance that simply aping the process on the computer would be the best way to proceed, or that it would even be feasible (although this possibility has not been ruled out and is still being explored). The acoustics of speech generation, however, are well understood, as we have seen in Chapter 5. With modern digital signal-processing techniques, and especially with the lattice-filter structure of linear prediction, the mechanism is quite easy to duplicate. What are not well understood are the mental processes by which phonemes are transformed into speech sounds. Even these, however, have been simulated with considerable success.

We will discuss three topics here: synthesis hardware, voice-response systems, and synthesis algorithms—in particular, synthesis by rule. Of these, the first two require the least amount of detail. Synthesis hardware ranges from simple digital-to-analog converters to fairly elaborate implementations of the speech-production model. These systems use techniques which have already been covered in earlier chapters. In voice-response systems, there is a fixed repertoire of words or phrases to be spoken, prepared in advance, and stored in the machine. In such a system, the synthesizer is merely a storage and playback device using one or another of the waveform-encoding techniques discussed in Chapter 9.

Synthesis by rule is much more ambitious; the vocabulary is usually not determined in advance and the problem to be solved is to accept a phonemic representation (or, ultimately, an ordinary written text with all the peculiarities of English spelling and punctuation) as input and deliver an acceptable, natural-sounding spoken output, usually in real time. We will discuss synthesis hardware and voice-response systems briefly here and devote the bulk of this section to synthesis by rule.

Hardware

Synthesis hardware takes two general forms: (1) digital waveform coding and (2) terminal-analog synthesizers. These two categories correspond to waveform coders and vocoders.

Digital waveform coders These correspond to the playback end of the various coding systems covered in Chapter 9, and they are of greatest interest in voice-response systems where the material to be spoken has been prepared and stored in advance. At the simplest level, such systems are no more than digital-to-analog converters interfaced to a storage medium and some sort of controller for selecting what is to be played back. A telephone-call interception system requires no more than this. If a very large body of material is to be stored, then some sort of compression must be used, in which case the playback hardware will have to incorporate the decoding process as well.

Terminal-analog synthesizers These are so called because their terminal characteristics are an analog of the organs of speech. They are essentially a realization of the engineering model of speech production, shown once more in Fig. 10-9. The filter usually realize the all-pole approximation of the vocal tract transfer function

$$H(z) = \frac{\sigma}{A(z)} \qquad (10\text{-}7)$$

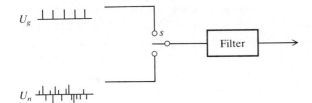

Figure 10-9 The excitation-modulation model of speech generation, here used as a general terminal-analog synthesizer.

The existence of cheap, high-speed digital filtering hardware makes this very easy to implement. The filter can be one of two kinds.

Formant controlled Here $A(z)$ is computed from formant values. Each formant corresponds to a pole-pair and thus contributes a quadratic factor to $A(z)$. For a sampling frequency F_s, a formant frequency f, and a bandwidth b, the corresponding quadratic factor is

$$1 - 2 \exp\left(-\frac{\pi b}{F_s}\right) \cos \frac{2\pi f}{F_s} z^{-1} + \exp\left(-\frac{2\pi b}{F_s}\right) z^{-2} \qquad (10\text{-}8)$$

It is not excessively expensive to compute these factors from formant frequencies and bandwidths. In many cases fixed bandwidths can be assumed, one for each formant, in which case only the $\cos(2f/F_s)$ term need be computed for each new formant frequency. The quadrant factors can be used directly to control parallel second-order resonators, as shown in Fig. 10-10a, or cascaded resonators, as in Fig. 10-10b; alternatively, they can be multiplied together to form $A(z)$, which is then used to control a direct-form all-pole digital filter.

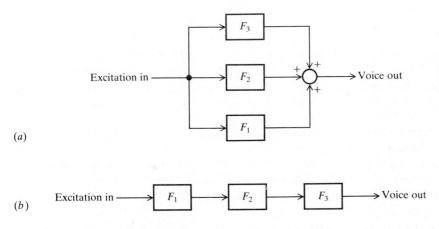

Figure 10-10 Formant-controlled filters for terminal-analog synthesizers: (a) parallel form; (b) series form.

LPC controlled We have already seen that the predictor coefficients computed in linear prediction of speech provide us with a model of the vocal tract. Hence in voice-response systems, the filter coefficients can be computed by applying linear-predictive coding to the voice at the time it is recorded. If the amount of speech to be stored is small, or if there is no shortage of memory, the coefficients can be used as computed. Where storage must be minimized, however, filter coefficients may be stored only for key points within the word and other values interpolated. In this case, the reflection coefficients are usually stored, since these can be interpolated without danger of creating an unstable filter. The reflection coefficients can be converted to predictor coefficients in the program, or they can be applied directly to a lattice filter. There are a number of integrated circuits available which incorporate the entire lattice filter, as well as a considerable amount of control circuitry, and terminal-analog synthesizers are within easy reach of the hobbyist as well as the professional (Ciarcia, 1984).

Voice-Response Systems

In a voice-response system, the vocabulary is decided upon in advance and stored in memory. The principal tradeoffs are among memory size, complexity of the decoding hardware, and the quality of the synthesized voice. Digital coding requires large amounts of memory and a relatively simple decoder and generally provides high-quality voice. A terminal-analog synthesizer is a fairly complex piece of hardware requiring relatively small amounts of memory; the quality of the voice depends on the particular encoding system used but is usually inferior to waveform-encoded speech, just as vocoders, most of which are terminal-analog devices, are inferior to waveform encoders. The choice of system is in fact most frequently influenced by the required quality of the synthesized voice. The standard for voice-response systems is customarily higher than for communications systems, although the nature of the application and its intended market also influence fidelity requirements: the voice used in a talking database system must obviously be better than that used by a talking toy.

With steadily declining memory and mass storage costs, digital coding with minimal compression is obviously very attractive, provided the amount of material to be stored is not very large. At this writing, costs of hard-disk systems with capacities on the order of 50 to 100 megabytes are very reasonable. Using 8-bit μ-law encoded speech and an 8-kHz sampling rate, we can store two hours of speech on a 60-megabyte disk. If compression is to be used, the principal practical difference from communications applications is that the encoding end of the process does not have to be done in real time; hence analysis techniques involving considerable exploration of the speech, with possible backtracking and editing phases, are feasible. Because voice-response systems with extremely large data bases are a relatively new concept with (so far) relatively few users, this is an aspect of voice compression which has received relatively little study.

The most popular method of compression divides the utterances into parts which can then be reassembled into a variety of sentences. (We will see, in fact, that this is a fundamental concept running all through voice synthesis.) Reconstruction from component parts is particularly convenient when there is a large potential repertory of sentences differing only in names and numbers; for example,

$$\left\{\begin{array}{l}\text{United Airlines'}\\ \text{Air Canada's}\\ \text{American Airlines'}\\ \ldots\end{array}\right\} \text{Flight number} \left\{\begin{array}{l}111\\ 112\\ 113\\ \ldots\end{array}\right\} \text{to} \left\{\begin{array}{l}\text{Atlanta}\\ \text{Chicago}\\ \text{Dallas}\\ \ldots\end{array}\right\}$$

The main problem with such techniques is tailoring vocabulary and phrases so that inflection and timing sound natural even with varied content. In some cases the material may be hand-edited on the basis of listening tests; the chief engineering requirement may be to develop an interactive editing system which lends itself to this type of process. (Interactive editing and listening are another repeated theme in speech-synthesis research.) Multiple copies of some words are usually necessary for use in different parts of the sentence. Telephone-call intercept systems and the Texas Instruments' "Speak and Spell" are good examples of these techniques. The intercept system provides multiple recordings of the digits for use in different positions in the phone number; "Speak and Spell" uses a small number of standard sentence skeleta into which a large vocabulary of words can be inserted. (The usually limited vocabulary and large storage capacities of the typical call intercept system permit relatively simple waveform coding; "Speak and Spell" has a large vocabulary compared to its storage size and must use LPC techniques.)

Synthesis by Rule

The most demanding synthesis process starts with written text as input and produces acceptable speech as output. The written text can be a phonemic representation of the speech or, in the most ambitious systems, conventional written language. The latter process can be broken down into two subprocesses: grapheme-to-phoneme translation and phoneme-to-speech translation. Solutions to both of these problems rely heavily on rules found empirically, and considerable effort has gone into developing systems in which proposed rules can be easily implemented and tried out. In general, the higher the required output quality is, the more complicated the synthesis rules will be. Since phoneme-to-speech translation is the more general problem, we will discuss it first.

Conversion of phonemes to speech This process involves the following three problems:

1. Selecting proper allophones
2. Joining adjacent phones naturally
3. Providing proper pitch, stress, and rhythm over the sentence

Conversion of phones to allophones is a matter of rules, most of which can be applied at the word level, since most allophone choices are determined by context within the individual word. In some very simple systems it is left to the user to specify the allophones.

Suitable joints between phonemes are necessary to reproduce the fluency of human speech. Clearly we must supply formant transitions adjacent to consonants in order to provide articulatory information. The concept of the articulatory locus, which we encountered in our study of formant transitions, is helpful here, since the locus is in most cases a function only of the point of articulation. In addition, formant 1 contours and suitable control of the voiced/unvoiced switch can indicate the manner of articulation. The transition from the locus to the steady state is usually generated by some suitable interpolation process.

An additional complication, however, is the fact that in natural speech true steady states are rare. The set of formant frequencies for each vowel should actually be regarded as a target toward which the actual formants move, but which they rarely reach, since we change targets at a rate comparable to the time scale in which the shifts occur.

Because we are used to hearing these continually shifting formants, artificial speech which does not include them is not only not acceptable but in many cases is not intelligible. On paper, a pattern such as that shown in Fig. 10-11a may be recognizable as "we were away," but to be understandable when played through a synthesizer, it must have smooth formant tracks, as shown in Fig. 10-11b. We therefore have an additional set of formant transitions to consider. There are not only those transitions which convey articulatory information about the adjacent consonants but also transitions which arise simply from the continuous motion of the vocal organs from target to target.

It seems likely that the motions of the speech organs which give rise to these smooth tracks are governed by their dynamics, and in particular by their masses, dissipations, and compliances, and by the muscular forces driving them. Rabiner (1968) implemented transitions between consecutive formant frequencies using critically damped exponentials with time constants which were chosen for each possible sequence of vowels. Given the complexity of the relationship between tongue position and formant frequencies, there is no reason to expect the dynamics of the vocal organs to be mirrored by those of the formant transitions, and Rabiner chose to use damped exponentials (1) because they matched observed transitions rather well and (2) because they were easy to specify, and not because of any underlying theory about vocal tract dynamics.

Coker (1976) has developed a detailed model of the dynamics of the vocal tract. This model includes variables, including the position of the center of the tongue, the position of the tip of the tongue, closure and rounding of the lips, the position of the velum, the motion of the arytenoid cartilages, the tension on the vocal cords, and subglottal air pressure. He assumes an underlying system of independent variables of which the observed solution is a linear combination. That is, the underlying system has an input/output relation of the form, $\mathbf{R} = \mathbf{DC}$, where $\mathbf{R}$ and $\mathbf{C}$ are vectors and $\mathbf{D}$ is a diagonal matrix, and there is a transform-

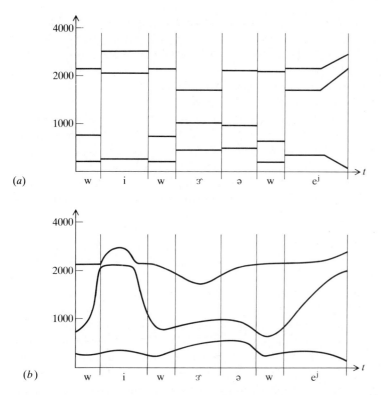

Figure 10-11 Formant tracks of synthesized speech (a) without smooth joins between phonemes; (b) with smoothing to produce more natural-sounding speech.

ation **P** relating the observed and underlying variables, so that if the observed input/output relation is $\mathbf{T} = \mathbf{HX}$, then $\mathbf{X} = \mathbf{PC}$, $\mathbf{Y} = \mathbf{PR}$, and $\mathbf{H} = \mathbf{P}^{-1}\mathbf{DP}$. **P** is approximated by a constant matrix, which means that the dynamic behavior of the speech organs is described entirely by **D**. Since most of the observed variables are essentially independent (e.g., the tip of the tongue and the velum do not interact significantly), the transformation matrix **P** will have few nonzero off-diagonal elements. Coker starts by making an initial guess, $\mathbf{P} = \mathbf{I}$, and introduces off-diagonal elements as the need for them becomes apparent. His primary observations are taken from x-ray photographs; in addition, some time constants for motions of specific organs are estimated from spectrograms. The links between spectrographic data and articulatory positions are the correspondence between formant frequencies and the vowel diagram and the phenomenon of formant transitions, both of which were discussed in Chapter 5. Many of his variables are also related to distinctive features; e.g., lip rounding clearly corresponds to the *rounding* feature, and glottal width to the *voiced/voiceless* feature.

This model has been incorporated in a synthesizer (Coker et al., 1973; Coker, 1976; Umeda, 1976). The synthesizer consists of the dynamic model and an articulatory controller which issues commands, corresponding generally to nerve impulses, to the model. As usual, a set of rules manages the translation from phonemes to the articulatory commands. One of the more interesting problems encountered in this approach arises from the fact that the speech organs are sluggish: i.e., their dynamics cause a time delay from the start of the control pulse to their arrival at the required position. As a consequence, the rules must include a system of priorities, so that, for example, a command for labial closure will be issued far enough in advance to ensure that the lips will in fact close at the required time. It is hard to picture a system of such complexity being deployed as a commercially available synthesizer, but this system is unparalleled for its ambition, boldness, and breadth of scope, and it represents an articulatory research tool *par excellence*, of a theoretical importance comparable to that of the sound spectrograph.

Diphones, dyads, and demisyllables Another approach to the transition problem has been to break the speech stream at midphone instead of between phones. Instead of dividing a word like /əgo/ into /#/ + /ə/ + /g/ + /o/ + /#/ (where the symbol /#/ denotes the silence before and after the word or, alternatively, the boundary between words), we divide it into /#ə/ + /əg/ + /go/ + /o#/. Since each unit combines two elements, the number of descriptions to be stored is significantly larger; on the other hand, the transitions between phones are included in the description and do not have to be estimated. Furthermore, the strongest coarticulation effects are those between adjacent phones, and these two-phone units can incorporate such coarticulations as a matter of course.

Three instances of this concept are diphones (Dixon and Maxey, 1968), the dyads proposed by Peterson *et al.* (1958), and the demisyllables of Fujimura (1976). A diphone is a piece of speech which cannot be shortened or lengthened by extrapolation or excision (Dixon and Maxey, 1968), or simply a piece from the middle of one phoneme to the middle of the next (Schwartz *et al.*, 1979). Dyads are formed by breaking the speech stream at "the phonetically most stable position" of each phone (Peterson *et al.*, 1958), and in the middle of each dyad is a transition between two phones. Demisyllables, as their name suggests, are formed by breaking an individual syllable into two parts; the division is located so as to place most of the vowel in the second demisyllable.

The synthesis system developed by Olive and others is an example of a dyadic synthesizer. Their starting point was the discovery that LPC-coded speech can be acceptably smoothed by simple straight-line interpolation of the log-area parameters between adjacent dyads (Olive and Spickenagel, 1976). On the strength of this finding, they reduced the dyad to the transitional portion alone and replaced the phonetically stable portion by straight-line interpolation between adjacent dyads, as shown schematically in Fig. 10-12*a* and *b*. In a further simplification, they also replaced the transitional portion by a straight-line interpolation; the dyad was thus reduced to a pair of points to be joined to each other and to adjacent dyads, as sketched in Fig. 10-12*c*.

The synthesizer built around this concept (Olive, 1977) used a pronouncing

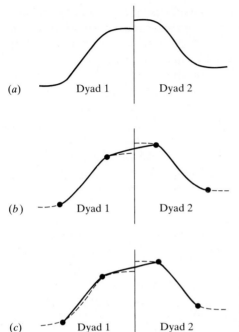

Figure 10-12 Synthesis of speech from dyads: (a) two adjacent dyads; (b) same dyads joined by linear interpolation of phonetically stable parts; (c) same dyads with transitions replaced by straight-line interpolations.

dictionary, to go from text to phonemes and to provide timing information and some prosodic information, and a dyad dictionary, giving corner points for vowel-vowel, consonant-vowel, and vowel-consonant transitions. The dyad dictionary took the form of a matrix which could be entered with the required vowel and consonant and which provided log-area parameters for each corner point. These dictionaries were used in conjunction with a set of rules for concatenating dyads of various types and a set of prosodic rules for determining amplitude (i.e., stress) and pitch. The synthesizer scanned the input text and looked it up in the pronouncing dictionary to find which vowel and consonant phonemes were involved. The dyad matrix was entered with these vowel and consonant values and log-area parameters for the corner points were obtained. The dyad corner points were spaced according to the timing information provided by the pronouncing dictionary and connected by straight-line interpolation, except for adjacent consonants, whose parameters were abutted without smooth transitions. The speech produced by this system was found to be intelligible but lacking in voice quality.

In a subsequent development (Olive and Liberman, 1979), the phones making up dyads were broken down into a larger variety of classes: vowel, liquid/glide, nasal, voiced stop, unvoiced stop, voiced fricative, unvoiced fricative, and silence. Treatment of each class was different, and some classes had a third set of parameters. For example, voiced stops followed by continuants had one set of parameters for the burst and two sets to describe the transition into the following sound. As this synthesis approach evolved, more information was put into the dyad tables, which ultimately (Olive, 1980) became a sizable data structure with variable-length entries which were accessed by a smaller table which served as a directory.

Conversion of unrestricted text to phonemes Most systems for translating text to phonemes use a combination of one or more dictionaries and a set of rules. A number of such sets of rules have been developed; two of the more widely cited ones are the rules developed at the Naval Research Laboratories (the NRL rules) by Elovitz *et al.* (1976) and the text-to-speech rules used in the MITalk system (Allen, 1976).

Such rules operate primarily (1) on words or parts of words and (2) on individual letters or small groups of letters. These two categories correspond, as Allen has pointed out, to the two ways in which humans read alphabetical text: we identify full words or dissect the word into recognizable parts (e.g., *programming = pro + gram + ing*), and when this fails, we sound the word out letter by letter. Rules of type 1 tend to be very numerous and to give high-quality output where they are applicable; rules of type 2 can be reduced to a relatively small set, particularly when the exceptional cases have been already covered by type 1 rules.

The NRL letter-to-sound rules The goals of the NRL project were a small set of rules that would be easy to implement. Their rules take the form of character strings and are written in the following format:

$$A[B]C = D$$

where B is the letter or set of letters under consideration, A and C are the left and right contexts, if any, and D represents the phoneme(s) by which B is replaced in the given context. (D is written in ARPAbet characters.) The context is sometimes one or more specific letters, but it may also be one of a class of letters. Special symbols are used for these classes; for example, # is the code for one or more vowels, + means a front vowel (e, i, y), ^ means a single consonant, and : means zero or more consonants. Word boundaries are indicated by blanks (indicated here by underscores), and a null string means that the replacement is made regardless of the corresponding context, provided all other conditions are met. For example, '[IGN]_ = /AY N/' means that *ign* at the end of a word (right context a blank) is rendered by /AY N/ regardless of what precedes it (left context the null string); and 'E[NG]+ = /N JH/' means that *ng* is pronounced /N JH/ when preceded by *e* and followed by a front vowel. The NRL program scans the incoming character string from right to left and finds the appropriate rule for each character. The rules are tried in order of their appearance, and so the priority of a rule can be set by locating it appropriately in the list. As an example of the operation of the rules, let us take the word " precision." The rules applied are as follows:

[P] = /P/ Default rule for P
[R] = /R/ Default rule for R
_:[E] = /IY/ E following initial consonants
[C]+ = /S/ C followed by front vowel
[I]^+:# = /IH/ I followed by one consonant, a front vowel, zero (or more) consonants, and one or more vowels
#[SION] = /ZH AX N/ SION preceded by one or more vowels

The system as described in Elovitz et al. (1976) does not include provision for stress, intonation, or rhythm. A few of the letter-to-sound rules can be used to derive reliable stress information; e.g., any vowel that is converted to /AX/ (the schwa) is likely to be unstressed. Since listeners found monotone speech fatiguing to listen to, a simple stress algorithm based on applicable letter-to-sound rules was tried; predictably, listeners liked the results better than monotone speech but less than speech in which the stresses had been hand-edited. The study did not address prosodic considerations like stress and intonation patterns over an entire sentence.

The MITalk rules The text-to-phoneme rules in MITalk analyze both words, or parts of words, and letters. Words are composed of one or more morphs. These include roots, prefixes, and suffixes. For example, *disorderliness* consists of the four morphs, *dis + order + ly + ness*; *dis* is a prefix, *order* the root, and *ly* and *ness* are suffixes. Hence words may be analyzed if their constituent morphs can be found. Again, this is the way a reader will deal with an unfamiliar word, trying to decompose it into its morphs and determine its meaning and pronunciation from this analysis. Hence text-to-phoneme conversion by computer also attempts to do a similar decomposition (Allen, 1973, 1976). When morphemic analysis fails, the reader will try to sound the word out from its individual letters, and similarly MITalk has a backup procedure which uses a set of letter-to-sound rules.

The system uses a morph dictionary for morph-to-phoneme conversion. An algorithm by Lee (1968) analyzes the word into morphs by starting from the end of the word and working backwards, finding the longest matching morph with the aid of the dictionary and analyzing the remainder of the word recursively. Allen (1970) found that better performance required an analysis which found all possible decompositions into morphs and then selected the optimum analysis by a set of priorities. He instances the analysis of *scarcity* into *scar + city*, *scarce + ity*, and *scar + cite + y*; *scarce + ity* is chosen because it is formed by adding the suffix *-ity* while the other possibilities use compounding, and the rules give affixation preference over compounding. (A rule choosing only the longest final morph would have found only *scar + city*.)

The morph dictionary which makes this work is a collection of 12,000 morphs obtained from the "Brown Corpus" (Kucera and Francis, 1967). Morph analysis also accounts for the irregularities associated with many high-frequency words; e.g., the NRL rule, '_:[A]^+_=/EY/', which gives us *hale, space, wave, ace*, makes *have* rhyme with *behave*; in MITalk, *have* is an entry in the morph dictionary and hence is exempt from the letter-to-sound rules.

The pronunciation of each morph is given by the morph dictionary; the pronunciation of the entire word is pieced together from its morphs with the aid of a set of morphophonemic rules which determine how adjacent morphs influence each other. The rules modify the phonemic representation of the morphs and determine the stress pattern of the word. Phonemic effects are most noticeable in affixes; e.g., the morph ⟨past⟩, applied to verbs, is picked up by the morph analyzer from the suffix *-ed*; the morphophonemic rules determine whether this shall yield /ɨd/ (as in *padded*), /d/ (as in *zoned*), or /t/ (as in *packed*). Stress rules in English have been analyzed by Chomsky and Halle (1968); coded forms of these rules are used to place the stress in the assembled word. These stress decisions are usually final, although some words may have to await phrase-level analysis for final adjustment.

Morph analysis fails when it cannot find a decomposition into morphs which accounts for all parts of the given word; in this case, letter-to-sound rules are applied instead. Initially, the letter-to-sound procedure attempts to identify and remove affixes. A number of constraints can be used to minimize the errors in identifying affixes. Certain combinations are phonetically impossible in English; hence *corpulent* will not be analyzed as *co + rpulent* because English does not permit an initial *rp*, and it will not be analyzed as *cor + pulent*, because the prefix *cor-* may only be attached to roots beginning with *r*. Other combinations can be ruled out as syntactically impossible, since some suffixes may be attached only to certain parts of speech. Thus *scandalous* can be decomposed only as *scandal + ous* and not as *scand + al + ous*, because the suffix *-al* forms adjectives and the suffix *-ous* can only attach to nouns. After removal of affixes, the remaining part of the word is sounded out with a set of context-dependent rules similar to the NRL rules but more numerous.

MITalk uses syntactic analysis to determine the pitch and stress contours over groups of words. Mechanized analysis of natural-language sentences is extremely difficult, because of the richness and complexity of natural-language grammars and the occasional occurrence of ambiguous sentences. Allen (1968) has shown that while sentence-level analysis is not generally feasible, phrase-level analysis can be carried out easily and provides enough information to determine prosodic features like pitch contours, stress patterns, and rhythm.

REFERENCES

Abut, H., R. M. Gray, and G. Rebolledo: Vector quantization of speech and speech-like waveforms, *IEEE Trans.*, vol. ASSP-30, no. 3, pp. 423–435, June, 1982.

Allen, J.: Machine-to-man communication by speech. Part II: Synthesis of prosodic features of speech by rule, *Proc. 1968 Spring Joint Computer Conf.*, pp. 339–344, 1968.

———: Development of a dictionary for speech synthesis, *JASA*, vol. 49, p. 93, Fall, 1970.

———: Reading machines for the blind: the technical problems and the methods adopted for their solution, *IEEE Trans.*, vol. AU-21, no. 3, pp. 259–264, June, 1973.

———: Synthesis of speech from unrestricted text, *Proc. IEEE*, vol. 64, no. 4, pp. 433–442, April, 1976.
Brantingham, L.: Single-chip LPC speech synthesizer and companion 131k bit ROM, *IEEE Trans.*, vol. CE-25, no. 2, pp. 193–197, May, 1979.
Buzo, A. A., H. Gray, Jr., R. M. Gray, and J. D. Markel: Speech coding based on vector quantization, *IEEE Trans.*, vol. ASSP-28, no. 5, pp. 562–574, October, 1980.
Chomsky, N., and M. Halle: *The Sound Pattern of English*, Harper & Row, New York, 1968.
Ciarcia, S.: Build a third-generation phonetic speech synthesizer, *Byte*, vol. 9, no. 3, pp. 28–41, March, 1984.
Coker, C. H.: Synthesis by rule from articulatory parameters, *Proc. 1967 Boston Conf. Speech Commun.*, Paper A9, pp. 52–53, 1967.
———: A model of articulatory dynamics and control, *Proc. IEEE*, vol. 64, no. 4, pp. 453–460, April, 1976.
———, et al.: Automatic synthesis from ordinary English text, *IEEE Trans.*, vol. AU-21, no. 1, pp. 293–298, February, 1973.
Dixon, N. R., and H. D. Maxey: Terminal analog synthesis of continuous speech using the diphone method of segment assembly, *IEEE Trans.*, vol. AU-16, no. 1, pp. 40–50, March, 1968.
Elovitz, H. S., et al.: Letter-to-sound rules for automatic translation of English text to phonetics, *IEEE Trans.*, vol. ASSP-24, no. 6, pp. 446–459, December, 1976.
Flanagan, J. L.: Note on the design of "terminal-analog" speech synthesizers, *JASA*, vol. 29, pp. 306–310, 1957.
———: Voices of men and machines, *JASA*, vol. 51, no. 5(1), pp. 1375–1387, May, 1972(a).
———: *Speech Analysis, Synthesis, and Perception*, Springer-Verlag, Berlin, 1972(b).
Fujimura, O.: Syllables as concatenated demisyllables and affixes, *JASA*, vol. 59, p. S55, Spring, 1976.
Gersho, A., and V. Cuperman: Vector quantization: a pattern-matching technique for speech coding, *IEEE Communications Magazine*, vol. 21, no. 9, pp. 15–21, December, 1983.
Gray, R. M.: Vector quantization, *IEEE ASSP Magazine*, vol. 1, no. 2, pp. 4–29, April, 1984.
Harris, C. M.: A study of the building blocks of speech, *JASA*, vol. 25, pp. 962–969, 1953.
Holmes, J. N., et al.: Speech synthesis by rule, *Language and Speech*, vol. 7, pp. 127–143, 1964.
Juang, B.-H., and A. H. Gray, Jr.: Multiple stage vector quantization for speech coding, *Proc. ICASSP*, pp. 597–600, April, 1982.
Kang, G. S., et al.: Multirate processor (MRP) for digital voice communications, Naval Research Laboratory Report 8295, March, 1979.
Kucera, H., and W. N. Francis: *Computational Analysis of Present-Day American English*, Brown University Press, Providence, 1967.
Lee, F. F.: Machine-to-man communication by speech. Part I: Generation of segmental phonemes for text, *Proc. 1968 Spring Joint Computer Conf.*, pp. 333–338, 1968.
Liberman, A. M., et al.: Minimal rules for synthesizing speech, *JASA*, vol. 31, no. 11, pp. 1490–1499, November, 1959.
Linde, Y., A. Buzo, and R. M. Gray: An algorithm for vector quantizer design, *IEEE Trans.*, vol. Com-28, no. 1, pp. 84–95, January, 1980.
Lloyd, S. P.: Least squares quantization in PCM, Bell Laboratories Technical Note, 1957; reprinted in *IEEE Trans.*, vol. IT-28, no. 2, pp. 129–137, March, 1982.
Magill, D. T.: Adaptive speech compression system for packet communication systems, *Telecomm. Conf. Record*, 1973.
Makhoul, J., et al.: Natural communication with computers: speech compression research at BBN, BBN Report No. 2976, vol. 2, Bolt Beranek and Newman, 1974.
——— and M. Bernouti: High-frequency regeneration in speech coding systems, *ICASSP-79*, pp. 428–431, 1979.
Markel, J. D., and A. H. Gray, Jr.: A linear prediction vocoder simulation based upon the autocorrelation method, *IEEE Trans.*, vol. ASSP-22, no. 2, pp. 124–134, April, 1974.
——— and ———: *Linear Prediction of Speech*, Springer-Verlag, New York, 1976.
Olive, J. P.: Speech synthesis by rule, *Preprints of the SCS*, vol. 2, pp. 255–260, 1974.
———: Rule synthesis of speech from dyadic units, *ICASSP-77*, pp. 568–570, 1977.

———: A scheme for concatenating units for speech synthesis, *ICASSP-80*, pp. 568–571, 1980.

——— and M. Y. Liberman: A set of concatenative units for speech synthesis, *Speech Communication Papers: 97th Meeting of the Acoust. Soc. Am.*, pp. 515–518, 1979.

——— and N. Spickenagel: Speech resynthesis from phoneme related parameters, *JASA*, vol. 59, no. 4, pp. 993–996, April, 1976.

Papamichalis, P. E., and T. P. Barnwell III: Variable rate speech compression by encoding subsets of the PARCOR coefficients, *IEEE Trans.*, vol. ASSP-31, no. 3, pp. 706–713, June, 1983.

Papoulis, A.: *Systems and Transforms with Applications in Optics*, McGraw-Hill, New York, 1968.

Peterson, G. E., *et al.*: Segmentation techniques in speech synthesis, *JASA*, vol. 30, pp. 739–746, 1958.

Rabiner, L. R.: Speech synthesis by rule: an acoustic domain approach, *BSTJ*, vol. 47, pp. 17–37, 1968.

———, *et al.*: A hardware realization of a digital formant speech synthesizer, *IEEE Trans.*, vol. COM-19, pp. 1016–1020, 1971.

Sabin, M. J., and R. M. Gray: Product code vector quantizers for waveform and voice coding, *IEEE Trans.*, vol. ASSP-32, no. 3, pp. 474–488, June, 1984.

Schwartz, R., *et al.*: Diphone synthesis for phonetic vocoding, *ICASSP-79*, pp. 891–894, April, 1979.

Shannon, C. E.: A mathematical theory of communication, *BSTJ*, vol. 27, pp. 379–423, 623–656, 1948.

Tremain, T. E.: The government standard linear predictive coding algorithm: LPC-10, *Speech Technology*, vol. 1, no. 2, pp. 40–49, April, 1982.

Tribolet, J. M., and R. E. Crochiere: Frequency domain coding of speech, *IEEE Trans.*, vol. ASSP-27, no. 5, pp. 512–530, October, 1979.

Umeda, N.: Linguistic rules for text-to-speech synthesis, *Proc. IEEE*, vol. 64, no. 4, pp. 443–451, April, 1976.

Un, C. K., and D. T. Magill: The residual-excited linear prediction vocoder with transmission rate below 9.6 kbits/s, *IEEE Trans.*, vol. COM-23, no. 12, pp. 1466–1474, December, 1975.

Viswanathan, R., *et al.*: Speech compression and evaluation, BBN Final Report 3794, Bolt Beranek and Newman, 1978.

———, *et al.*: The application of a functional perceptual model of speech to variable-rate LPC systems, *ICASSP-77*, pp. 219–222, 1977.

Weinstein, C. J.: A linear prediction vocoder with voice excitation, *Proc. EASCON*, 1975.

CHAPTER
ELEVEN

SPEECH RECOGNITION

The dream of the 1950s was the "phonetic typewriter." Knowing about formants, transitions, and acoustics of consonants, researchers believed that the process of phonetic transcription could be mechanized and that conversion to phonemic and finally *graphemic* (i.e., written and conventionally spelt) form would follow as a matter of course. This dream has still not come about. Speech-recognition hardware is now commercially available, but the phonetic typewriter is not. The reasons for this provide a good introduction to the realities of speech recognition.

The problems encountered in practical speech recognition can be summarized as follows:

1. Talker variations. No two people sound alike (e.g., the F_1/F_2 loci for vowels vary from talker to talker); the speech signal contains talker-dependent variables as well as phonetic information and it is not always easy to separate them. (*Note.* Because "speaker" is often used to mean "loudspeaker," many authors prefer the word "talker." We will use the two terms interchangeably.)
2. Ambiguity. Acoustical variables are not mapped one to one onto phonemic variables. Human listeners handle this by drawing on their knowledge of the language being spoken and of the subject of the conversation. (Recall that even in good listening conditions and careful enunciation, we frequently have to ask to have proper names spelled.)
3. Variations in individual speech. These are present even in careful reading by trained talkers. They include:
    a. Carelessness. People do not talk any more distinctly than necessary. Short words like "and" or "the" are frequently reduced to grunts. Syllable

breaks are often obscured: digit recognizers have to be able to treat "seven" as a word of either one or two syllables. Careful pronunciation mitigates but does not solve the problem.

    b. Phonetic variations. Formant frequencies, as well as loci and duration of formant transitions, may change over time. It is advantageous for recognizers to include provision for updating pattern libraries so they can track long-term variations in an individual's speech.

    c. Coarticulation. Phonetic characteristics of speech sounds are affected by context. Most of these influences are explained as allophones. For example, since nasalization of vowels is not phonemic in English, we are at liberty to nasalize vowels or not. As a result, vowels in a nasal context usually are nasalized: "man" is pronounced [mæ̃n] (where the tilde indicates nasalization), not [mæn].

    d. Temporal variations. The duration of a word may change, or the timing of its parts. The process must be able to cope with temporal misalignments if the master template contains time-dependent variables (as it usually does).

4. Noise and interference. Humans can recognize speech at poor signal-to-noise ratios and in the presence of interfering speech. A large part of this capability depends on our ability to use binaural input, a process which is still imperfectly understood. Noise degrades the performance of any speech-recognition program. Wideband noise masks weak fricatives, causes linear predictors to produce incorrect parameter estimates, and makes it harder to identify the beginnings and endings of words. Most recognition programs are designed for use with "clean" speech—i.e., speech recorded in nearly noise-free and reverberation-free surroundings.

There is an enormous body of literature on the subject of speech recognition, and we cannot hope to give it all adequate coverage here. In this chapter, we will describe the particular problem areas in each type of speech recognizer and describe some of the more important techniques. For a more detailed introduction, the reader is referred to the survey papers and collections listed in the References.

Types of Recognizer

Recognition problems are conveniently divided up into the following categories. The sequence is in order of increasing difficulty.

1. Isolated-word recognition. Recognition of words separated by pauses.
2. Word spotting. Detection of occurrences of a specified word in continuous speech.
3. Connected speech recognition. Recognition of words without pauses in between.
4. Speech understanding. An elaboration of category 3; creates a pool of information about the utterance and draws on stored information about the language being spoken. The intent is to ease accuracy requirements at lower

levels while still enhancing performance. Ideally, a speech-understanding system will extract the meaning of an utterance, even if it is ungrammatical or incomplete.

In all of these, the system may be talker dependent (i.e., trained for a particular user) or talker independent. At any level, talker-independent systems are much more difficult to implement and show poorer performance than talker-dependent systems. In all cases, performance deteriorates with increasing vocabulary. Current commercially available recognizers are mostly talker-dependent, isolated-word systems.

11-1 ISOLATED-WORD RECOGNITION

We will begin by discussing systems for recognizing isolated words, because these present the fewest problems and because many of the techniques developed for isolated words have been carried over into word-spotting and continuous-speech recognition. Pauses between words simplify recognition because they make it relatively easy to identify endpoints (i.e., the start and end of each word), and they minimize coarticulation effects between words. In addition, isolated words tend to be pronounced somewhat more carefully, since the need to pause between words impedes fluency, which would otherwise tend to encourage a more natural and hence more careless pronunciation.

Features

The choice of features depends on the individual system, but the following selection is typical:

1. Amplitude (or power) versus time
2. Zero-crossing rate
3. Gross spectrum balance (high-frequency versus low-frequency energy)
4. Fine spectral detail in some form or other, e.g.,
   a. DFT spectrum
   b. F_1, F_2, F_3
   c. LPC parameters (predictor or PARCOR coefficients)
   d. Filter-bank outputs (popular because computationally cheap and fast)

Amplitude is the primary source of endpoint information; it is also useful for vowel/consonant discrimination. The zero-crossing rate also helps characterize fricatives and sibilants, as does spectrum balance. Higher-resolution spectral information (i.e., formants, LPC parameters, or filter-bank outputs) provide formant and formant-transition information or its equivalent. The tracks of consecutive predictor coefficients are highly correlated, and predictor coefficients are sometimes subjected to KL transformation to obtain compressed data and greater sensitivity.

The emergence of FFT and LPC techniques initially caused filter-bank methods to fall out of favor, but a classic comparison by White and Neely (1976) showed comparable performance between systems using LPC and $\frac{1}{3}$-octave filter-bank data, and most commercial recognition systems use filter banks. A more recent study by Dautrich et al. (1983), however, found that LPC data yielded better results than filter-bank data. They explained this discrepancy in two ways. First, filter banks inevitably represent a fixed quantization of the frequency range, while linear prediction is adaptive. If a significant energy concentration in some word falls on the boundary between two filters, it may land in one filter's band during training and in the adjacent filter's band during recognition. Thus a small difference in a pole location can cause an exaggerated distance measure between two versions of the same word and can thereby lower recognition accuracy. A linear predictor, on the other hand, will place its poles where they belong in either case, and a small shift in the pole's location will not greatly increase a distance measure such as the Itakura residual. Furthermore, Dautrich's results were obtained with telephone-bandwidth speech. (Their filter banks covered a range from 200 to 3200 Hz.) Most commercial recognition systems, however, are not intended for use with telephone speech, and their filter banks typically cover a frequency range twice as wide. The additional information provided by filters in the range above 3200 Hz offsets any degradation due to the quantization of the frequency range.

Patterns may take the form of collections of features based on some sort of feature-by-feature segmentation of the word, in which case each segment is associated with some expected set of characteristic feature values. For example, in a digit-recognition system, Sambur and Rabiner (1975) used the variation of power over time to segment each digit into initial, medial, and final regions, and then used selected groups of features to characterize the phonetic content of each region. On the other hand, patterns may be represented as time functions which span the entire word, with no attempt at explicit subdivision into smaller elements. For example, in a system which characterizes words by formant frequencies, each pattern may consist of a matrix of formant frequencies, giving F_1, F_2, and F_3 values for a series of samples over the duration of the word. In such cases, the reference pattern is termed a *template*, and in recognition, each template is compared with the corresponding feature matrix of the unknown word.

Vector-quantization techniques, originally developed for speech compression, have also been used as recognition features (Martinez et al., 1982; Shore and Burton, 1982; Burton, Shore, and Buck, 1983; Rabiner et al., 1983). We have seen that codebook entries are associated with centroids of sets of parameter vectors. If an unknown word is a good match to some library pattern, then its parameter vectors should fall near the centroid of the library word, and so its codebook entries should agree substantially with those for the library pattern. Recognition can be done by a simple match of codebook indices or a distance measure can be based on the distances from the unknown's parameters from the centroids of the library word's codebook entries. Vector quantization has found significant application in recognizers based on the hidden Markov model.

Recognition Strategy

An isolated-word recognizer usually treats the word as the unit of recognition. That is, the patterns in the library are for entire words rather than for phonemes or other constituents. Recognition is usually bayesian (i.e., based on a maximum-likelihood measure). Likelihood is computed from a number of distance measures. The Itakura prediction residual is a favorite measure for LPC-based recognizers. In recognizers built around the time-warping process (described below), the minimum $D(C)$ found by the warping process itself provides the distance measure. In systems where a number of distance measures are accumulated, it is usually possible to minimize the time wasted on incorrect words by terminating the process early if the accumulated distance becomes unreasonably great, or if it exceeds the best distance obtained so far.

In large-vocabulary recognizers, the time required to search the entire pattern library and compute distance measures for each possible word can be prohibitive. The process can be made to run faster if obviously wrong choices can be eliminated in a preliminary pass. Kaneko and Dixon (1983) search the entire pattern library in a preliminary pass using only duration and two or three averaged spectra. This initial pass narrows the number of possibilities where recognition can be done with a full feature set on the surviving candidates.

Endpoint Detection

A fundamental problem in recognition systems is that the detailed timing of an utterance at recognition time will generally not be exactly the same as it was during the training phase. Not only will the two utterances have different durations, but the spacing between phonetic events will not be consistent. This means that time-dependent features may fail to match because the unknown and the reference word are out of time registration. In such a case, the correct pattern may seem as far different from the unknown as any incorrect pattern. This is a problem whether the word is to be compared as a whole with a template or is to be segmented and matched segment by segment. In fact, even between two training utterances the detailed timing may not agree, particularly if the various utterances have been recorded on different days. Clearly, averaging during the learning phase and comparison during the recognition phase are both meaningless unless the utterances are aligned in some way.

In many cases the accuracy of alignment depends on the accuracy of identifying the endpoints. Errors in recognizing beginnings and ends of words are particularly troublesome. Endpoint errors occur in words which begin or end in low-energy phonemes. Many speakers tend to end words with a gradual trailing-off of intensity or with a short burst of breath noise. A burst of breath noise at the end of a word may be mistaken for a phoneme and result in misidentification of a word.

In the laboratory, recognizing endpoints is usually relatively easy, because speech data are collected under controlled conditions and in some cases may be hand-edited to identify the endpoints. Furthermore, speakers recording data for laboratory work tend to speak with care. In the field, however, speech is not clean, the conditions are not controlled, and speakers may have no motivation to help the recognizer.

The principal feature for identifying endpoints is energy. The normal technique is to compare the energy with some threshold value and identify the start of the word as the point at which the energy first exceeds the threshold and the end as the point at which energy drops below the threshold.

Such a test requires a number of safeguards. First, the threshold itself may have to be normalized to general intensity; if the speech signal is weak, a lower threshold will have to be used. Alternatively, the intensity itself may be normalized. In one of the few published papers on endpoint detection, Lamel *et al.* (1981) set the energy level during silence to 0 dB and used fixed thresholds.

The process must also guard against false alarms; random noises may cause a momentary crossing of the threshold in the absence of speech, and these must not trigger the recognizer. Hence there is usually a length requirement: for example, if the intensity exceeds the threshold for (say) five analysis frames, then the first frame will be retroactively identified as the start of the word. Lamel *et al.* used two thresholds and accepted the point at which the lower threshold was passed, provided the higher threshold was also exceeded; they also required that the entire energy pulse representing the word last at least 75 ms.

Identifying the end of the word uses similar techniques. Final unvoiced plosives are an additional source of problems, because if the release of the plosive is delayed too long the recognizer may identify the beginning of the closure as the end of the word and thus miss the release. Hence most techniques require some frames of silence to elapse before the word is declared ended. (Rabiner, 1978, adjusted the endpoints to exclude plosive bursts at the ends of words, since they did not always occur and hence were not a reliable recognition feature.)

Sambur and Rabiner (1975) treated breath noise as a separate phonetic cate-

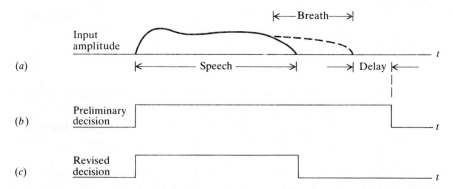

Figure 11-1 End-point determination. The actual end of the word is obscured by the presence of breath noise, shown as the dotted extension in (*a*). The preliminary decision (*b*) embraces the entire input and includes an extension; then the final decision (*c*) works backward to find the true word end.

gory and included means for recognizing it. The preliminary decision was made on amplitude and the final decision obtained by stripping off breath noise, as shown in Fig. 11-1.

Endpoint identification can also be done with the cooperation of subsequent stages in the recognition process (Lamel et al., 1981). In such systems, the endpoint detector provides a preliminary decision, or in some cases a list of candidates, and the final decision is made by the recognizer. If the recognizer uses time warping (described below), then the time-warping process can be used to determine the correct endpoints.

Time Normalization

By time normalization we mean the process whereby time-varying features within the words are brought into line. The classical technique was simply to stretch or compress the unknown uniformly until it was the same length as the reference. This process depended for its accuracy on accurate endpoint identification, which, as we have seen, is itself a problem; and it did not correct for time variation within the word. In any case, nearly every researcher has recognized that simple compression or expansion of the time scale is not enough to produce accurate alignment. Many investigators have tried to select recognizable landmarks from within the utterance itself. For example, Pruzansky (1963), in a talker-verification system, chose to line up the maximum-energy points in the utterance, and a large part of a similar system by Das and Mohn (1971) was given over to time-registration attempts.

Time normalization is now frequently done by a process known as "time warping" (Itakura, 1975; White and Neely, 1976; Sakoe and Chiba, 1978). In this process, the time axis of the unknown is nonuniformly distorted, or warped, to bring its features into line with those of the pattern. Normalization by means of time warping is an exceptionally powerful device and has contributed greatly to the accuracy of recognition systems.

An example of time warping is shown in Fig. 11-2. The contours to be matched are shown along the axes, and the wavy diagonal shows the mapping between them. If the mapping function passes through the point (i, j), then the ith sample of contour A is aligned with the jth sample of contour B. If no matching were done beyond a uniform expansion or compression, the line would be straight.

The inputs to the warping process are two time functions, typically amplitude or a formant or an LPC coefficient. If a formant is used, F_2 is usually chosen, because this formant shows the widest variation and is the most text-dependent formant. In some cases, each contour may be a bundle of features, e.g., a set of reflection coefficients as a function of time. This complicates the program but does not alter the basic way in which time warping is carried out. The outputs of the process are the warping function, the degree of mismatch remaining, and in some cases a new version of the unknown which has been brought into temporal alignment with the reference.

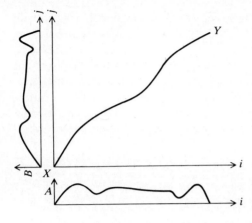

Figure 11-2 Dynamic time warping. The contours to be aligned are A and B; the mapping between the two is given by the wavy diagonal line, XY.

The contours to be matched are defined as sampled time functions,

$$A = a_1, a_2, \ldots, a_i, \ldots, a_M,$$
$$B = b_1, b_2, \ldots, b_j, \ldots, b_N.$$

The problem in time warping is to match up the a's and b's so as to minimize the discrepancy in each matched pair of samples. We can represent this by redrawing a portion of the previous figure, as shown in Fig. 11-3. Let the warping function be

$$C = c(1), c(2), \ldots, c(k), \ldots, c(K),$$

where each c is a pair of pointers to the samples being matched:

$$c(k) = [i(k), j(k)]$$

In the figure,

$$C = (1, 1), (2, 2), (3, 2), (4, 3), (5, 4), \ldots$$

and the dotted lines show the correspondence assigned between $a(5)$ and $b(4)$.

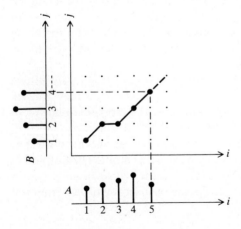

Figure 11-3 Detail of the time-warping process. The point at $(5, 4)$ aligns $a(5)$ with $b(4)$.

For each $c(k)$ we have a cost function
$$d[c(k)] = \delta(a_{i(k)}, b_{j(k)})$$
which reflects the discrepancy between the paired samples. A typical cost function is the square of the difference between the samples,
$$d[c(k)] = (a_{i(k)} - b_{j(k)})^2$$
If the contours are bundles of predictor coefficients, then the distance is frequently the Itakura residual.

The warping function is required to minimize the overall cost function
$$D(C) = \sum_{k=1}^{K} d[c(k)] \tag{11-1}$$
subject to the following constraints:

1. The function must be monotonic:
$$i(k) \geq i(k-1) \quad \text{and} \quad j(k) \geq j(k-1)$$
2. The function must match the endpoints of A and B:
$$i(1) = k(1) = 1$$
$$i(K) = M$$
$$j(K) = N$$
3. The function must not skip any points:
$$i(k) - i(k-1) \leq 1 \quad \text{and} \quad j(k) - j(k-1) \leq 1$$
4. There is usually some kind of global limit on the maximum amount of warp. The simplest is probably
$$|i(k) - j(k)| < Q$$
where Q is termed the "window width." Alternatively, a global limit can be imposed on the slope of the warping function; this can be done by restricting the domain of the process to the parallelogram shown in Fig. 11-4. The parallelogram method is safe to use provided M and N are roughly equal; if $M = 2N$ or $N = 2M$, the parallelogram collapses into a straight line and no warping can be done.

Computing the warping function can be viewed as the process of finding a minimum-cost path, through the lattice of points in Fig. 11-3, from point (1, 1) to point (M, N), where the cost is a function of the discrepancy between corresponding points of the two contours. This is a problem in *dynamic programming* (DP), and time-warping algorithms are normally implemented by means of dynamic programming techniques. (Warping is in fact also known variously as "DP normalization" or "dynamic time warping.")

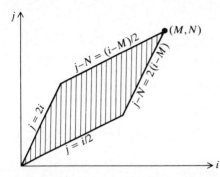

Figure 11-4 Parallelogram defined by slope limits in time warping.

At first glance, it would seem as if $D(C)$ would have to be evaluated and compared for a prohibitively large number of possible paths. Dynamic programming brings this problem under control by noting that the best path from (1, 1) to any given point is independent of what happens beyond that point. Hence the total cost of $[i(k), j(k)]$ is the cost of that point itself plus the cost of the cheapest path to it:

$$D(C_k) = d[c(k)] + \underset{\text{legal } c(k-1)}{\text{MIN}} [D(C_{k-1})] \qquad (11\text{-}2)$$

By the subscript "legal $c(k-1)$" we mean the minimum over all permissible predecessors of $c(k)$. However, by constraints 1 and 3 above, there are only three legal predecessors: if $c(k) = (i, j)$, these are $(i, j-1)$, $(i-1, j)$, and $(i-1, j-1)$. Hence we need consider only three possibilities per point.

Dynamic programming proceeds in stages. In the case of time warping, each stage corresponds to a point on the i axis and its corresponding column in the lattice. For each value of i, it considers all possible points (i.e., all points within the permitted domain) along the ordinate through the current i. We thus have a set of points to be considered and, for each point, a number of possible predecessors whose least-cost paths are already known. Using (3-1), we find the best predecessor for each of the new possible points and compute the corresponding cost. The predecessors can be kept in an M by N array. Since we need to consider only the accumulated costs of the immediate predecessors, the accumulated costs can be kept in a 2 by N array, where the columns correspond to the immediately preceding column in the lattice and the current column.

As the process continues, the paths tend to ramify and the number of possibilities tend to grow; but this growth is kept in check by two factors:

1. Constraint 4 terminates some paths prematurely when they wander outside the permitted domain.
2. There is usually a maximum permissible $D(C)$; badly fitting paths exceed the limit early on and are terminated.

The candidates thus typically form a bundle of paths, as shown in Fig. 11-5. Notice that at any point along the way there are rarely more than a dozen paths

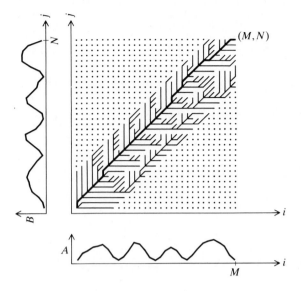

Figure 11-5 Tree of paths produced by time warping. Only one path reaches the point (M, N); this path is identified by the heavy line.

to be considered. At the termination of the process, the correct path is found by starting at (M, N) and backtracking until the original is reached; in Fig. 11-5, the path is the dark line.

Figure 11-5 was generated by the program WARP given in Appendix B. This represents the simplest, bare-bones time-warping algorithm. The array PRED contains predecessors found for points in the lattice. The program is somewhat simpler to implement if the predecessor coordinates are compressed into a single integer, and that has been done here. It also helps to border the PRED array with elements for $i = 0$ and $j = 0$, since this simplifies handling the cases where $i = 1$ or $j = 1$. Otherwise, the program is a direct implementation of the procedure outlined above.

If left to its own devices, the warping process will frequently tend to settle on an intermediate value for one or the other of the two contours and match a large portion of the other contour to that point. This results in paths which run horizontally or vertically, as can be seen in Fig. 11-5. Excessively long horizontal or vertical paths represent an unreasonable compression or expansion of the time axis, and hence are to be discouraged. In order to encourage the process to follow diagonal paths, a local slope constraint is frequently incorporated in the program. A number of such constraints have been considered by Sakoe and Chiba (1978), Rabiner et al. (1978), and Myers et al. (1980).

The common element in these constraints is a limit on the number of consecutive horizontal or vertical steps. Itakura conceived the warping contour to be a function of i, and so no vertical steps are allowed at all; he included a constraint that prevented two or more consecutive horizontal steps. The constraints investigated by Sakoe and Chiba require the contour to make no more than m vertical or horizontal steps without first making n diagonal steps. They considered values for n/m of 0, $\frac{1}{2}$, 1, and 2, as shown in Fig. 11-6a to d. Myers et al.

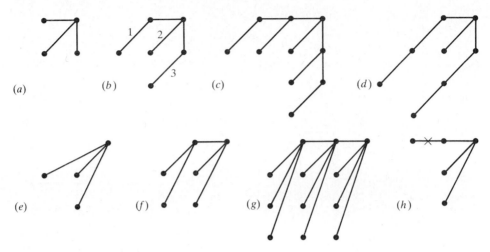

Figure 11-6 Sets of legal predecessor points and path segments considered by (*a*) to (*d*) Sakoe and Chiba, (*h*) Itakura, and (*b*) and (*e*) to (*h*) Myers *et al.* The × in (*h*) indicates a forbidden path.

investigated a total of five sets of constraints, including those of Sakoe and Chiba and Itakura; these are also shown in Fig. 11-6.

The cost of each step can also be weighted. Weighting influences the choice of steps by making some steps less expensive than others; it may also offset the cost differential between a path of two arcs (e.g., paths 1 and 3 in Fig. 11-6*b*) and a path of one arc. The weighting also enters into the computation of total path length, which is defined as the sum of the weights along the individual steps in the path. Sakoe and Chiba investigated asymmetric and symmetric weightings; Myers *et al.* investigated a variety of possible weights.

Both Sakoe and Chiba and Myers *et al.* evaluated the various possibilities by using them in a word recognizer and comparing recognition accuracies. Sakoe and Chiba obtained the best performance for the constraint of Fig. 11-6*a* with symmetric weighting. Myers *et al.* found little to choose between the various constraints, except that type (*d*) performed significantly worse. They found, however, that the best performance was obtained when the two contours were first normalized to equal lengths before time warping was applied.

Researchers have developed many different variations of the time-warping process. In particular, ways of relaxing the endpoint constraints have been given a lot of study, because, as we have seen, there is usually some uncertainty in identifying endpoints and we would prefer the performance of the time-warping process to be made independent of endpoint decisions. In fact, the time-warping process is frequently used to choose among a set of possible endpoint candidates. This type of warping is commonly known as unrestricted-endpoint (UE) warping. Relaxing the endpoint constraints can be done by opening out the ends of the parallelogram, as shown in Fig. 11-7*a*; in the UE warping techniques used by Rabiner *et al.*, the permitted domain is in a band which adaptively follows the path, as shown in Fig. 11-7*b*. Since the ultimate path is not actually known, the

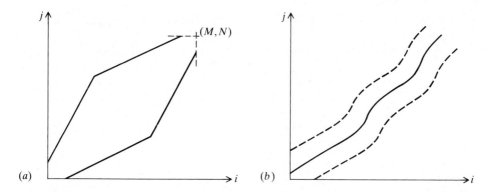

Figure 11-7 (*a*) Parallelogram method with relaxation of endpoint constraints. (*b*) Permitted domain following local cost minimum.

band follows the choice which represents the local minimum cost. Rabiner *et al.* refer to this as the unrestricted-endpoint/local-minimum (UELM) method.

Brown and Rabiner (1982) were able to reduce the computational cost of time warping further, using a method based on a graph-searching algorithm of Nilsson (1972). This method reduces the number of points for which cost calculations must be made, although the resulting program has a more complicated control structure than that of the classical dynamic programming technique. In applications where the distance calculations constitute a large part of the computational burden, this method may be an attractive one.

An important byproduct of the warping process is the total cost of the optimum path. In many cases, this is of greater interest than the warping function itself, because it can be used directly as a distance measure. In this case, it is important to compensate for the length of the warping function, since otherwise the recognition process will be biased in favor of those patterns yielding the shortest paths. The length of the path is given by the number of steps, K, in the warping function. If a weighting function $w(k)$ is applied to the steps, then the length is given by

$$L = \sum_{k=1}^{K} w(k)$$

Talker Independence

In a talker-independent system, we must find a way of desensitizing the recognizer to differences in talker characteristics without degrading its sensitivity to differences in words. If the vocabulary is small enough, it may be possible to select features which are stable between talkers and yet provide good discrimination between words. Otherwise, multiple patterns can be found for each word, so that each pattern reflects the word as spoken by one particular talker. For this approach to work, it is necessary to find some way of grouping the patterns in order to avoid a prohibitively large pattern library. A third possibility is to provide a way of correcting for differences among talkers by normalizing formant frequencies.

As an example of feature selection to minimize talker sensitivity, we instance a talker-independent digit recognizer by Sambur and Rabiner (1975). Since the size of the vocabulary is small, relatively broad phonetic categorization is sufficient to distinguish among the recognition classes. Sambur and Rabiner used six categories:

Vowels:
  Front
  Middle
  Back
Consonants:
  Vowel-like
  Noiselike, voiced
  Noiselike, unvoiced

The precision required to distinguish sounds on such a basis is much less than that required for a finer categorization; hence the recognizer has a relatively large amount of leeway and can accommodate talker-to-talker differences relatively easily. The features used to separate these categories were zero crossings, energy, and the LPC residual. They also used a gross spectral-shape measure, provided by a two-pole linear predictor, on the grounds that such a measure retained enough information to characterize the digits while wiping out talker-dependent information. The vowel classification was done on the basis of this measure.

Another problem in talker-independent recognition is that the decision thresholds, against which features are compared in order to make phonetic identifications, tend to be talker dependent. Rabiner and Sambur addressed this problem by using "self-normalization;" i.e., the decision thresholds were derived from statistical analysis of the utterance itself.

Each utterance was divided into three regions. The initial region was bounded by the beginning of the word and the point where the energy first reached 10 percent of its maximum value, and the end region was bounded by the point where the energy finally dropped below 10 percent of the maximum value; the rest of the word was the middle region. A preliminary classification was made by a sequence of tests on the phonetic characterizations of the three regions, after which a final decision selected the most likely digit. Using a data base of 1000 utterances (10 speakers, 10 digits, 10 repetitions per speaker), they obtained an error rate of 2.7 percent.

In a recognition system using multiple templates, Gupta *et al.* (1978) used as many as 14 templates for a word. Each word was divided into 50 overlapping, equal-length frames and the template consisted of the predictor coefficients for each frame. The initial learning set consisted of utterances by 25 talkers. Using a 40-word vocabulary, they obtained a recognition rate of 90.3 percent; in a second test using 105 speakers, the recognition rate was 89.2 percent.

Rabiner (1978) used a small number of templates obtained by clustering the templates obtained during training and representing each cluster by its average. Clustering and averaging were combined as follows. The initial cluster comprised all repetitions of the word, and this cluster was initially represented by that template whose length was closest to the average length of the templates in the cluster. The templates were then time-warped to match this reference and averaged, and this average was made the new reference. This process was repeated until the change between consecutive references was negligible, at which point the reference was taken as the centroid of cluster 1. All patterns within a distance δ of the reference were then removed from the data base, and the process was repeated to find cluster 2. In principle, this process could be repeated to find any desired number of clusters; Rabiner stopped after two clusters were found. Using a 54-word vocabulary, eight speakers, and telephone-quality speech, the recognition rate was 85 percent.

Formant Frequency Normalization

A speaker-dependent system is trained to respond to the formant frequencies habitually produced by the talker who is to use it. In a speaker-independent recognizer, performance tends to be degraded by the fact that different speakers have differing formant frequencies for the same vowels, as we saw in Chapter 5. One solution to this problem is to enable the recognizer to adapt to each speaker's formant frequencies without further training. Hence the problem of normalizing formant frequencies has received some attention. We cite three attempts to minimize scatter of vowel loci in formant space:

1. Gerstman (1968) found the upper and lower limits for each speaker's F_1 and F_2 frequencies and normalized the talker's frequencies with respect to these limits by a simple linear scaling. He also included the sum and difference of the normalized formants as recognition features. Analytically, this is of considerable interest. The use of $F_1 + F_2$ and $F_1 - F_2$ as features is equivalent to a 45° rotation of the F_1/F_2 coordinate system; inspection of the Peterson-Barney formant plots will show that such a rotation will align the (roughly) elliptical vowel loci with the new coordinate axes. This selection of features therefore represents a cheap and ingenious Karhunen-Loève transformation of the data.
2. Wakita (1977) normalized formant frequencies to estimated vocal tract length, assuming that the main source of interspeaker scatter is the scale of the vocal organs. It is not difficult to show that if the shape of the vocal tract is held constant, the formant frequencies are inversely proportional to the vocal tract length. Hence if the length for any speaker can be found, the observed formant frequencies can be converted to equivalent values for a vocal tract of some standard length.

   The success of this technique depends on getting a good estimate of the taker's vocal tract length. Wakita estimates the length in a roundabout way, as follows. Since a formant corresponds to a pole in the vocal tract transfer function, we can estimate these poles from measured formant data. The poles, in turn, will give us predictor coefficients and, ultimately, reflection coefficients. From the reflection coefficients, the shape of the corresponding acoustic tube can be computed. However, the relation between formants and pole locations depends on the assumed length of the vocal tract. From (7-5), we had

$$F_i = \frac{\theta_i}{2\pi T_s}, \qquad B_i = -\frac{\ln |z_i|}{\pi T_s}$$

Hence the corresponding pole is at

$$z_i = x_i + jy_i = \exp\left[-\pi T_s(B_i - j2F_i)\right]$$

When we related the order of the predictor, the sampling rate, and the length of the acoustic tube model in Sec. 6-9, we saw that $T_s = 2l/pc$, so

$$z_i = \exp\left[-\frac{2\pi l}{pc(B_i - j2F_i)}\right] \tag{11-3}$$

Thus different assumed lengths result in different pole locations, different predictor coefficients, and, ultimately, a different-shaped acoustic tube. Wakita, following Paige and Zue (1970), assumes that the best estimate is that which results in the most nearly uniform tube shape. Wakita points out there is no theoretical reason why this should be so, but this assumption leads to satisfactory experimental results. Formant frequencies and bandwidths are obtained from LPC data; then vocal tract shapes are computed from (11-3) for various assumed lengths until the most nearly uniform shape is found. (Readers interested in this problem should also see Kirlin, 1978.)

Using this procedure, Wakita ran vowel-recognition experiments using 14 male and 12 female speakers. When the formant frequencies were normalized to a standard vocal tract length, they showed less scatter than the unnormalized frequencies, but the overlap between formant regions was not greatly reduced. Normalization reduced the error rate of the vowel recognizer from 21 to 15.6 percent.

3. Neuburg (1980) normalized formant frequencies by transforming the frequency scale of each formant so as to line up speakers' formant frequency distributions. This process is similar to time normalization, except that the contours to be matched are the estimated probability densities of formant frequencies. He considered a number of different possible warpings. The simplest was scaling all frequencies by a multiplicative constant; Neuburg points out that this is equivalent to Wakita's technique, discussed above. Other techniques were more general linear transformations, in some cases tailored to each individual formant's distribution. The most successful procedure was a nonlinear warping, similar to time warping, applied to each formant separately. The warping function is a piecewise-linear curve which matches the percentile points of the corresponding formant distributions.

This technique has the advantage that it is not necessary to know what is being spoken. It is necessary only to be able to identify the first three formants reliably. This means that normalization can be done "live," as opposed to being done as part of a training session. Neuburg found that analysis of one minute of speech was sufficient to obtain representative distributions of the speakers' formant frequencies.

Hidden Markov Modeling

An alternative recognition strategy makes use of a stochastic model of speech production, known as the hidden Markov model (HMM). This model has been found to offer performance comparable to time warping in many applications at a fraction of the computational cost. The HMM has been explored by many researchers, including Baker (1975a, b), Bahl et al. (1975), and Levinson et al. (1983). The pair of papers by Levinson et al. and by Rabiner et al. (1983) together represent a classic "how-to" document; much of what we shall say here is drawn from these papers, and our notation will, for the most part, follow theirs. The Markov model was not initially applied to isolated-word recognition and its significance goes far beyond isolated-word recognition, but since this represents our first, and probably simplest, application, we will discuss it here.

With this technique, we take as a model of speech generation a system which is capable of being in only a finite number of different states. Each state is capable of generating a finite number of possible outputs. In generating a word, the system passes from one state to another, each state emitting an output, until the entire word is out. Such a model is illustrated in Fig. 11-8, where each state is represented by a circle and the transitions between states are represented by arrows. The transitions between states are random, as are the outputs associated with each state, as will be explained presently; by allowing random transitions and outputs, we enable the model to cope with subtle variations in pronunciation and timing.

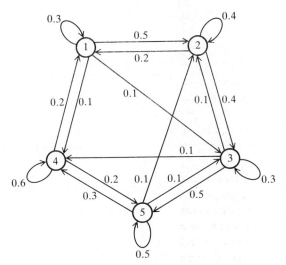

Figure 11-8 State diagram of a Markov process. The arrows indicate permitted state-to-state transitions; the numbers next to the arrows give the transition probability.

Each word in the recognition vocabulary is represented by a model of this sort. All the recognizer has to work with are the outputs, and its task is to decide which model gave rise to them. It is because the model itself is not visible to the recognizer, but must be inferred from the available data, that it is said to be *hidden*.

The motivation of this model is not as clear as that of other speech-processing techniques we have studied. It is perhaps intuitively easiest to think of the mechanism as the vocal tract, of the states as different positions of the vocal organs, and of the outputs as the acoustical observables associated with each articulatory position (Levinson et al., 1983). It should be emphasized, however, that the HMM does not require this correspondence, that normally no attempt is made to identify states with articulatory gestures, and that in isolated-word recognition the number of states in the model may have no bearing on the expected phonetic content of the word.

We assume that the transitions from state to state occur at discrete times and that each transition from state q_i to state q_j has a probability which depends only on state q_i. In Fig. 11-8, these probabilities are written as numbers next to the arrows representing the transitions. If there are N states, we can represent the transition probabilities compactly by an N by N matrix $\mathbf{A}$, where $a_{ij} = P\{\text{transition from } q_i \text{ to } q_j\}$. For example, the transition matrix for Fig. 11-8 is as follows:

$$\mathbf{A} = \begin{bmatrix} 0.3 & 0.5 & 0.1 & 0 & 0.1 \\ 0.2 & 0.4 & 0.4 & 0 & 0 \\ 0 & 0.1 & 0.3 & 0.5 & 0.1 \\ 0 & 0.1 & 0.1 & 0.5 & 0.3 \\ 0.2 & 0 & 0 & 0.2 & 0.6 \end{bmatrix}$$

Notice that, since the probabilities of the outgoing transitions from any state must sum to 1, each row of $\mathbf{A}$ must likewise sum to 1. By making the transitions nondeterministic, we enable the model to handle omissions or repetitions of states; in view of the known variability in pronunciation, this is a desirable capability. Finally, we allow the system to have more than one starting state; we will represent the initial state probabilities by the vector $\mathbf{p}(1)$, where $p_i(1) = P\{\text{initial state is } q_i\}$.

If there is a finite set (or alphabet) of M possible outputs $\{z_i\}$, then with each state q_i we associate an M vector $\mathbf{b}_i$ where $b_{ij} = P\{\text{output} = z_j | \text{state} = q_i\}$. The outputs of all the states can then be represented by the N by M matrix $\mathbf{B}$, whose ith row vector is $\mathbf{b}_i^T$. Since the output probabilities for each state must sum to 1, each row of $\mathbf{B}$ must also sum to 1.

Notice that this model assumes a finite number of discrete outputs; hence for a continuous signal like speech some way has to be found to select reasonable prototype outputs for $\{z_i\}$. Rabiner et al. solved this problem by using vector quantization, since this process automatically results in a desirable clustering; each cluster is then associated with an output z_i. Other investigators (e.g., Baker,

1975b; and Jelinek, 1976) have used HMMs capable of a continuum of outputs; we will not take these up here.

Not all HMMs are as complicated as the one in Fig. 11-8. The simpler the model, the easier it is to estimate and to use. One frequently used version is the left-to-right model, a common form of which is shown in Fig. 11-9. In a left-to-right model, there is a single starting state and a single final state, and once the process enters a new state it can never return to an earlier state again. The transition matrix for a left-to-right model is thus upper-triangular, and the bottom row, corresponding to the final state, is all zero, except for the final element, since there are no transitions away from the final state. Since there is only one starting state, $\mathbf{p}(1) = (1, 0, 0, \ldots)^T$. In the form shown in Fig. 11-9, the forward transitions are further restricted: the model can repeat the current state, advance one state, or advance two states. Rabiner et al. (1983) found that recognition performance with this restricted model was in fact superior to that of less-constrained forms.

Readers with a background in automata theory will see in Figs. 11-8 and 11-9 nondeterministic finite-state automata. With these probabilities, however, we now have a discrete-time, discrete-state Markov process (Papoulis, 1984). At any time t, the probability of entering q_j from q_i is equal to the probability of having been in q_i at time $t - 1$, times the probability of the transition. To find the overall probability of being in q_j, we sum these products over all possible antecedent states:

$$p_j(t) = \sum_{i=1}^{N} a_{ij} p_i(t - 1) \tag{11-4a}$$

If $\mathbf{p}(t)$ is a vector whose ith element is $p_i(t)$, then we can represent the probabilities of all the states at time t compactly by means of matrix notation:

$$\mathbf{p}(t) = \mathbf{A}\mathbf{p}(t - 1)$$
$$= \mathbf{A}^{t-1}\mathbf{p}(1) \tag{11-4b}$$

Similarly, to find the probability of any output z_k at time t, we must consider all the states that might give rise to it and sum the probabilities associated with each state; this gives us

$$p\{z_k \text{ at time } t\} = \sum_{i=1}^{N} b_{ik} p_i(t)$$
$$= \mathbf{b}_k^T \mathbf{p}(t)$$
$$= \mathbf{b}_k^T \mathbf{A}^{t-1}\mathbf{p}(1) \tag{11-5}$$

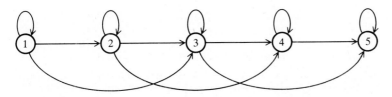

Figure 11-9 A left-to-right hidden Markov model. The starting state is 1; the final state is 5.

The model of any word is thus a set of parameters, $\mathbf{M} = \{N, \mathbf{p}(1), \mathbf{A}, \mathbf{B}\}$. To train the recognizer, we must construct a library of models for all of the words in the vocabulary. That is, for each word we must determine the number of states, the transition matrix $\mathbf{A}$, the initial-state probabilities $\mathbf{p}(1)$, and the output probabilities $\mathbf{B}$. (In some cases, for example the digit recognizer of Rabiner et al., 1983, the number of states is constant for all words in the vocabulary.) At recognition time, the system is given a sequence of observed outputs $\mathbf{O}$; the unknown is identified as that word whose model has the highest probability of generating the observed outputs. For each model $\mathbf{M}_i$ the system determines $P\{\mathbf{O}|\mathbf{M}_i\}$, the probability that $\mathbf{M}_i$ gave rise to $\mathbf{O}$, and the unknown is identified as that word j for which $P\{\mathbf{O}|\mathbf{M}_j\}$ is the maximum.

It is helpful to walk through one of these models in order to see what it does. Suppose, in generating a word, the model of Fig. 11-9 happens to pass through states 1, 2, 2, 3, 4, 4, and 5, in that order. We can illustrate this by the "history" shown in Fig. 11-10a. Here the passage of time is indicated left to right in the figure, and we have assumed various outputs for each state. Since the outputs themselves are nondeterministic, there is no one-to-one association of any particular z_k with any particular state, and the outputs in Fig. 11-10a are intended to illustrate this.

This sequence of outputs might well have been generated in other ways, however, and at recognition time we do not know what sequence actually led to the outputs. To show all these possibilities, we redraw this history embedded in a

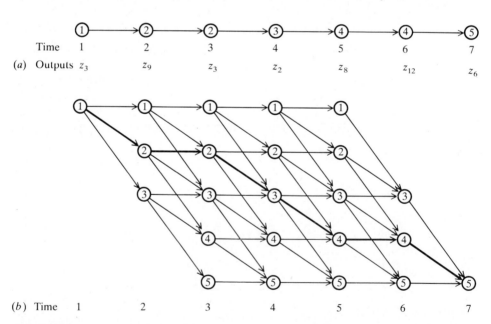

Figure 11-10 (a) Sequence of states ("history") in generating a hypothetical word. (b) Trellis diagram showing all possible seven-state paths from state 1 to state 5; the heavy line corresponds to the history in (a).

trellis diagram showing all possible histories, taking the model from state 1 to state 5 in seven steps; this is shown in Fig. 11-10b. Any one of these paths is a possible trajectory through the model; the one shown by the dark line is the one from Fig. 11-10a.

Recognition The probability $P\{\mathbf{O}|\mathbf{M}_j\}$ can be estimated in two ways. We can consider all the paths through the trellis, as in Fig. 11-10b, and compute the probability that any of these paths could have generated the observations; or we can consider only the most likely path and find its probability. For either of these methods, we must have an expression for the probability of arriving at a given state at time t, given that a particular sequence of outputs has occurred. We will start by considering the probabilities of all paths; in doing so we will obtain recursive relations among the probabilities which will also be important when we consider the training problem.

For the first method, suppose that at some time t, presumably in mid-word, the model has reached a state q_i, having emitted a series of observed outputs $\mathbf{O}(t) = (O_0, O_1, \ldots, O_t)$, where each observation O_i is some output symbol z_k. This event is known as a *partial sequence* of states and observations. The trellis in Fig. 11-11 shows a specific example for a four-state model; at $t + 1$ we see the transitions converging on a particular state q_j. We wish to compute the probability of this event. Suppose we knew the probability of arriving at q_i at time t with an observation vector $\mathbf{O}(t)$. Let this probability be $\alpha_t(i)$:

$$\alpha_t(i) = P\{\mathbf{O}(t) \text{ and } q_i \text{ at } t\}$$

We will show that if we know $\alpha_t(i)$, it is a relatively simple matter to find $\alpha_{t+1}(j)$.

If q_j were reachable only from q_i, then this new probability would be

$$\alpha_t(i) \, P\{\text{transition from } q_i \text{ to } q_j\} \cdot P\{O_{t+1} = z_k | \text{state is } q_j\}$$

The transition probability is a_{ij}. The final probability can be obtained from the **B** matrix; if O_{t+1} is z_k, then this probability is b_{jk}. [Levinson et al. write this as

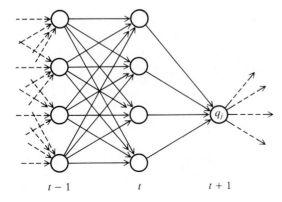

Figure 11-11 Portion of a lattice showing paths passing through state q_j at time $t + 1$.

$b_j(O_{t+1})$, but for notational simplicity we will stay with b_{jk} in the following discussion, with the understanding that this means $b_j(O_{t+1})$.]

Then if we consider only transitions from q_i, the probability is $\alpha_t(i)a_{ij}b_{jk}$. Since we can get to q_j from more than one antecedent state, however, we must consider them all; hence

$$\alpha_{t+1}(j) = \sum_{i=1}^{N} \alpha_t(i)a_{ij}b_{jk} \tag{11-6}$$

This is the recursion we are after; to start it, we set $\alpha_1(j) = p_j(1)b_{jk}$ for all j.

A similar backward recursion can be derived. Here we consider partial sequences of outputs starting in mid-word and ending at time $= T$; let $\beta_t(i)$ be the probability of producing the observed output $(O_{t+1}, O_{t+2}, \ldots, O_T)$ starting from q_i at time t. Then by reasoning as we did above, we find that

$$\beta_t(i) = \sum_{j=1}^{N} \beta_{t+1}(i)a_{ij}b_{jk} \tag{11-7}$$

To start this recursion, we set $\beta_T(i) = 1$ for all permitted final states. In the general model, this is for all i; for the left-right models in which state N is the only final state, $\beta_T(i) = 1$ for $i = N$ and 0 otherwise.

To see what these recursions can do for us, consider the model at any time t. It has emitted outputs which we see as the observations $O(t)$ and has landed in some state q_i. The probability of this partial sequence is $\alpha_t(i)$. This same state, q_i, is the beginning of another partial sequence which will take it to a final state and complete the word; the probability of this partial sequence is $\beta_t(i)$. These two events together constitute the event that model $\mathbf{M}_j$ gave rise to output $\mathbf{O}$, passing through state q_i at time t, and the probability of these two events together is the product of their individual probabilities:

$$P\{\mathbf{O} \text{ and } (q_i \text{ at } t) | \mathbf{M}_j\} = \alpha_t(i)\beta_t(i)$$

However, the model must pass through *some* state at t; hence the probability of $\mathbf{O}$ given some model $\mathbf{M}_j$ is just the sum of these probabilities over the states:

$$P\{\mathbf{O}|\mathbf{M}_j\} = \sum_{i=1}^{N} \alpha_t(i)\beta_t(i), \quad t = 1, \ldots, T \tag{11-8}$$

We can arrive at this probability using the forward recursion alone. The event that model $\mathbf{M}_j$ gave rise to the entire word is the event that $\mathbf{M}$ arrived at some final state with an output sequence $\mathbf{O}$. For any one final state q_i, this is clearly $\alpha_T(i)$, and therefore the probability that the word was produced by model $\mathbf{M}_j$ is the summation of this probability over all final states:

$$P(\mathbf{O}|\mathbf{M}_j) = \sum_{i=1}^{N} \alpha_T(i) \tag{11-9}$$

[Note that we obtain the same result by evaluating (11-8) at $t = T$.] For the left-right model with a single final state q_N, this reduces to $P(\mathbf{O}|\mathbf{M}_j) = \alpha_T(N)$. We can compute this probability by considering the observations one at a time and computing the new alphas from the most recent set using (11-6).

If the probability is determined considering only the most likely path, then instead of summing over all transitions to q_j, we find the transition with the maximum probability. The principles of dynamic programming lead to a recursion very similar in form to (11-6). Where we used $\alpha_t(i)$ above for the probability of a partial sequence by *any* path, we will write $\phi_t(i)$ for the probability of a partial sequence by the *most likely* path. Then we have the recursion

$$\phi_{t+1}(j) = \underset{i}{\text{MAX}}\ \phi_t(i) a_{ij} b_{jk}, \qquad t = 0, \ldots, T \qquad (11\text{-}10)$$

That is, we consider all possible predecessors of q_j; for each predecessor we find the probability of a transition to q_j based on the predecessor's phi and the transition probability; then the new state's phi, assuming that particular predecessor, is this transition probability times the probability of the new state giving rise to the observed output O_k. The phi finally associated with q_j is the maximum over all possible antecedent states. To start this recursion, $\phi_1(i) = p_i(1) b_i(O_1)$, where $b_i(O_1) = b_{ik}$ if $O_1 = z_k$.

If there are many final states, then the probability that the model gave rise to the word is the maximum over the states at time T:

$$p(\mathbf{O}|\mathbf{M}_j) = \underset{i}{\text{MAX}}\ \phi_T(i)$$

If the model is left-right with a single final state q_N, then this reduces to $P(\mathbf{O}|\mathbf{M}_j) = \phi_T(N)$, as before.

This latter process is known as the Viterbi algorithm (Viterbi, 1967; Forney, 1973); it was developed originally as a procedure for decoding convolutional codes, but has found a variety of other applications. A Viterbi program typically consists of three nested loops. The process proceeds by stepping through the observed outputs z_t; hence the outermost loop in the program is on t. For each pass through this loop, the program evaluates $\phi_t(j)$ for all states q_j. The innermost loop is on the possible predecessors of q_j, as described above. The output of the process is the most likely sequence of states and probability associated with that sequence. To do recognition, we apply this program to all possible models in the library and find the model with the highest probability.

Recognizers based on these estimates are simple and fast, a fact that accounts for much of the attractiveness of the HMM. In comparing HMM recognizers against DP time-warping recognizers, Rabiner *et al.* found that the HMM recognizer typically required one-tenth as much storage and one-seventeenth as much computation. The heavy computational load appears in the training phase, where the models themselves are estimated from the training data. Since training is normally done only once, while recognition is done repeatedly and in circumstances which require a fast response time, this is an advantageous tradeoff.

Training Training methods are iterative: initial values are assumed for **A**, **B**, and **p**(1), after which these estimates are refined in some way, using the observations found from utterances of the word in question. The refined estimates are then further refined, and this process is repeated until no further improvement is noted. The problem with all such methods currently in use is that the optimum which they reach may be only a local optimum: if a different starting estimate had been used, the process might have converged to a different, and possibly better, optimum. For this reason, it is customary to try several different starting estimates and select the best result. We will describe training based on the forward and backward recursions of Eqs. (11-6) and (11-7).

Consider the **A** matrix first. The element a_{ij} is the probability of a transition from q_i to q_j. If we can estimate this probability from an existing model, then we can replace the original a_{ij} with this estimate. Let $n(i, j | \mathbf{O}, \mathbf{M})$ be the expected number of transitions from q_i to q_j, given a known sequence of observations **O** and the model **M**, and let $n(i | \mathbf{O}, \mathbf{M})$ be the expected number of transitions from q_i anywhere under the same conditions. Then we can reestimate the transition probability as

$$\hat{a}_{ij} = \frac{n(i, j | \mathbf{O}, \mathbf{M})}{n(i | \mathbf{O}, \mathbf{M})} \tag{11-11}$$

where the hat indicates the new estimate. Clearly, $n(i | \mathbf{O}, \mathbf{M})$ can be found from $n(i, j | \mathbf{O}, \mathbf{M})$:

$$n(i | \mathbf{O}, \mathbf{M}) = \sum_{j=1}^{N} n(i, j | \mathbf{O}, \mathbf{M}) \tag{11-12}$$

[and note that (11-12) guarantees that each row of the new **A** matrix will sum to 1, as required]. Furthermore, if $n(i, j, t | \mathbf{O}, \mathbf{M})$ is the expected number of transitions from q_i to q_j at time t, then

$$n(i, j | \mathbf{O}, \mathbf{M}) = \sum_{t=1}^{T-1} n(i, j, t | \mathbf{O}, \mathbf{M}) \tag{11-13}$$

However, $n(i, j, t | \mathbf{O}, \mathbf{M})$ can be found with the aid of the forward and backward recursions given above. This expected value depends on the probability of such a transition and the total number of transitions, which for any given **O** is always the same and is thus ignored in what follows. If the probability is $p\{i, j, t | \mathbf{O}, \mathbf{M}\}$, then

$$p\{i, j, t | \mathbf{O}, \mathbf{M}\} = \frac{p\{i, j, t, \mathbf{O} | \mathbf{M}\}}{p\{\mathbf{O} | \mathbf{M}\}} \tag{11-14}$$

To find the numerator of (11-14), consider the probability of a transition from q_i to q_j at time t with a set of observations **O**. At any time t, this is

$P\{\text{partial sequence ending in } q_i \text{ at time } t\}$
 $\cdot P\{\text{transition from } q_i \text{ to } q_j \text{ with output } O_t = z_k\}$
 $\cdot P\{\text{partial sequence starting from } q_j \text{ at time } t + 1\}$

The first factor is $\alpha_t(i)$, the second factor is $a_{ij}b_{jk}$, and the third factor is $\beta_{t+1}(j)$. Abbreviating $p\{O|M\}$ as P, we have the result

$$n(i, j, t | O, M) = \frac{1}{P} \alpha_t(i) a_{ij} b_{jk} \beta_{t+1}(j) \qquad (11\text{-}15)$$

We can now work backwards to get our reestimates. The numerator of (11-11) is

$$n(i, j | O, M) = \frac{1}{P} \sum_{t=1}^{T-1} \alpha_t(i) a_{ij} b_{jk} \beta_{t+1}(j) \qquad (11\text{-}16)$$

and the denominator is

$$n(i | O, M) = \frac{1}{P} \sum_{t=1}^{T-1} \alpha_t(i) \sum_{j=1}^{N} a_{ij} b_{jk} \beta_{t+1}(j)$$

$$= \frac{1}{P} \sum_{t=1}^{T-1} \alpha_t(i) \beta_t(i) \qquad (11\text{-}17)$$

by substitution from (11-7).

It may appear to the reader that we have reasoned in a circle: we have gone from the given **A** and **B** matrices and massaged these values, together with the observed data, to obtain an estimated **A** matrix. Surely we will merely end up where we started, if everything is consistent. Baum (1972) has shown, however, that this will happen only at a local maximum of $P\{O|M\}$; anywhere else, the new estimate will result in a model with a higher $P\{O|M\}$.

To reestimate the **B** matrix, let $m(j, k | O, M)$ be the expected number of times state j emits z_k, given the observations **O**, and let $m(j | O, M)$ be the expected number of times state j produces any output at all. Then

$$\hat{b}_{jk} = \frac{m(j, k | O, M)}{m(j | O, M)} \qquad (11\text{-}18)$$

The reader should confirm that $m(j | O, M)$ is the same as $n(i | O, M)$. The numerator is the same sum taken over only those times when the output O_t is z_k:

$$m(j, k | O, M) = \frac{1}{P} \sum_{t:\, O_t = z_k} \alpha_t(i) \beta_t(i) \qquad (11\text{-}19)$$

If a left-right model is used, the initial probabilities are fixed; otherwise, the initial probabilities can be reestimated as follows:

$$\hat{p}(1) = \frac{1}{P} \alpha_1(i) \beta_1(i) \qquad (11\text{-}20)$$

To train the model on a given word, we go through the trellis, column by column, and evaluate (11-15) from the observed data. From these results, the numerators and denominators of (11-11) and (11-18) can be found. (Notice that the $1/P$ factors cancel and hence can be ignored.) Normally, one would use a number of utterances of each word of the training set. Since these numerators and denominators represent expected numbers of transitions, they can be accumulated over all the utterances.

The training process presents a number of serious difficulties. First, in the computations of the alphas and betas using real observations, underflow is likely. It can be seen that the iterations required in computing $\alpha_T(i)$ and $\beta_1(i)$ involve repeated multiplication by small probabilities; the accumulated effect of these multiplications is to drive α and β toward zero. Levinson et al. avoided this problem by rescaling $\alpha_t(i)$ and $\beta_t(i)$ as needed during computation. On the iteration for time t, a scale factor c_t was included such that

$$\sum_{i=1}^{N} c_t \alpha_t(i) = 1$$

These scale factors cancel between the numerator and denominator of (11-11) and (11-12), so the new estimates are unaffected. In the Viterbi algorithm, where no addition is done, it is convenient to work with logs rather than with the values themselves; clearly it is just as easy to find the maximum log as it is to find the maximum probability itself.

A second problem is that we need to estimate a large number of parameters, namely all the nonzero elements of **A** and all the elements of **B**. For a five-state model, **A** has 25 elements, of which 15 are nonzero if we assume a left-right model. A typical output alphabet may have as many as 64 symbols; hence **B** has 320 elements and we have 335 parameters to determine for each word in the recognition vocabulary. The amount of data required to form reliable estimates of recognition parameters grows roughly exponentially with the number of parameters (Duda and Hart, 1973), which implies that long training sessions will be necessary to obtain reliable models. The chief weakness of HMM recognizers is that there is, practically, never enough data to derive really good models. Levinson et al. discuss techniques for training by reestimation when the number of observations is limited.

In spite of these problems, Rabiner et al. report performance comparable to that of DP time warping in a talker-independent digit-recognition test. On a test using 100 talkers, a five-state, 64-element HMM showed a recognition accuracy of 96.3 percent; a DP time-warping recognizer using the same vector quantizer yielded an accuracy of 96.5 percent. A DP time-warping recognizer which did not use vector quantization showed an accuracy of 98.5 percent. Hence, although the amount of data available for training the HMM was, in the authors' words, "woefully inadequate," these comparisons suggest that the failings of the HMM recognizer may have been associated with vector quantization problems rather than with training problems.

Comparison with time warping There are a few similarities between the HMM and time-warping procedures. Clearly both operate in stages, and the Viterbi HMM recognizer uses essentially the same dynamic programming algorithm used by time warping. On the other hand, while the HMM uses relatively few states, time warping uses many. A single state in time warping corresponds to one frame of speech, but there is no exact temporal equivalent to an HMM state: the HMM remains in a given state as long as is necessary, but typically for more than one frame. For any given word, the time-warping algorithm assigns only one output to each state, while the HMM, as we have seen, associates many possible outputs with each state. Nevertheless, time warping can be viewed as a special case of the HMM algorithm.

11-2 WORD SPOTTING

As its name implies, word spotting is the detection of occurrences of a given word in continuous speech. Most successful published efforts are built around DP time warping. Every word to be spotted is represented by a template; as the input samples stream by, the time-warping program tries to find paths which align these samples with the template. Most of the time the paths (i.e., the possible warping functions) do not make it to the end of the template before being terminated because of excessive costs (as in Fig. 11-12). When a successful match is made, the system reports the presence of the word in the input stream.

It is clearly important to make the warping process independent of the endpoints, since these are known only for the template. The process must regard every sample of the incoming speech stream as a potential starting point and attempt to grow a path from it. If we are to terminate a path early because of excessive cost, however, we must have some way of compensating for the path length. Since the final point is not known, there is some uncertainty as to how to do this: a good match which happens to produce a longer path may lose to a poorer match which has produced a shorter path. Bridle (1973) uses a leaky integrator instead of a strict sum, so that the current and recent values contribute the

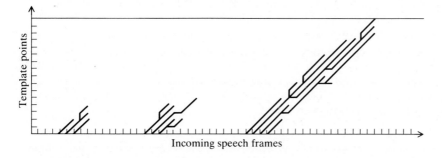

Figure 11-12 Application of time warping to word spotting. The process continually tries to find a path to the end of the template. Only those paths which can do so at a reasonable cost survive; successful completion of a path marks detection of the target word. *(Adapted from Bridle, 1973.)*

most to the cost function. In the limit, as the path becomes very long, the cost function is independent of the length; hence as the various paths grow, the differences in their lengths become steadily less important.

Christiansen and Rushforth (1977) use this same process, with a cost function based on the Itakura minimum prediction residual. Their process accommodates multiple templates, allowing corrections for multiple speakers or for variations in pronunciation which might arise from contextual effects or coarticulation. They match the input against a composite template formed from the collection of templates as follows. On each input sample, a match is attempted to the corresponding sample from each template in the collection. The template yielding the greatest similarity contributes that sample to the composite template. Thus the composite is not a weighted sum, but rather a concatenation of samples drawn from the various alternatives in the set. Detection accuracies were generally very high, in the neighborhood of 99 percent, except in the case of noisy speech, where the accuracy (after preprocessing to reduce the noise level) was approximately 95 percent for an initial 11-dB S/N ratio.

Bridle does not specify the features used in his word spotter; Christiansen and Rushforth, as mentioned, use the Itakura prediction residual. Wohlford *et al.* (1980) investigated five possible feature sets, all based on linear prediction: (1) normalized autocorrelation coefficients; (2) predictor coefficients; (3) cepstral coefficients; (4) area functions; (5) pseudoformants. Telephone-quality speech was used, with wideband noise added to test the systems' performance on noisy speech. They found that pseudoformants gave the best detection probability at almost every noise level and were a close second in the remaining cases.

Baker (1975*a*) describes a modification of the HMM recognizer for word spotting. The technique uses a modified left-to-right model with an extra state which corresponds to all acoustical events between occurrences of the desired word. Ideally, the model stays in the extra state most of the time, although occasional false starts may occur, as they do with time-warping spotters. These false starts will presumably terminate spontaneously if the Viterbi algorithm is used. Once a word is spotted, the system works through the model and then loops back to the extra state to await the next occurrence of the target word. Another application of the HMM is given in Bahl and Jelinek (1975).

11-3 CONTINUOUS-SPEECH RECOGNITION

The continuous-speech recognizer has two important problems which the isolated-word recognizer does not have:

1. Segmentation. It is obviously impractical to do recognition of whole phrases because the number of possible phrases is too vast. Hence the process must break the input stream into constituent parts, as people do. This means the system must be able to recognize word boundaries. This is in general

extremely difficult to do, since there is no consistent clue to their location. Energy minima are occasionally acceptable, but they usually need to be backed up by phonetic information.
2. Phonetic variability. Pronunciation in connected speech is sloppier than in isolated words, and coarticulation effects are more severe. Short words are especially affected: "the" can be reduced to [ə] and "and" to [n]. Hence just when segmentation forces us to lean more heavily on phonetic information, that information becomes less reliable.

We will describe two general approaches to continuous speech recognition. One is an extension of the DP time-warping techniques used in word spotting; the other is based on phonemic analysis and segmentation of the input, followed by a word-matching phase. In the former, the word is the unit of recognition and this process is often called connected-word recognition; in the latter, the phoneme is the object of interest, and words are assembled from the phonemes as they are identified.

Extensions of DP Time-Warping Techniques

Connected-word recognition can be implemented as an extension of word spotting or it can be done by a more general extension of the time-warping algorithm.

Word spotting Clearly, if we have a reliable technique for detecting the occurrence of a given word in continuous speech, then we should be able to make a continuous-speech recognizer simply by enlarging the set of words to be spotted until it comprises the entire vocabulary to be recognized. The principal drawback to this approach is the size of the vocabulary; hence applications of this approach are normally limited to tasks like connected-digit recognition or other limited-vocabulary tasks. The nature of the digit-recognition problem affords other convenient simplifications besides the vocabulary limit. Digit groups are normally spoken in bursts, so the length of signal to be analyzed is limited. In a burst, digits can be searched for from left to right.

Level building Myers and Rabiner (1981*a*, *b*) describe a level-by-level time-warping algorithm which drastically reduces the number of possible paths to be evaluated over the digit group. A level is defined by the duration of a possible template as matched to the incoming signal. The operation of this process is illustrated in Fig. 11-13. The levels are the horizontal bands in the figure; for the sake of simplicity, we have assumed here that all templates are of equal length.

A time-warping program normally proceeds from frame to frame of the unknown word; for each frame it then goes through all relevant frames of the template. Hence we can envision the process as proceeding up a series of vertical strips, as shown in Fig. 11-4. In the Myers-Rabiner level-building (LB) procedure, the vertical axis contains a sequence of concatenated templates, and the progress

320 APPLICATIONS

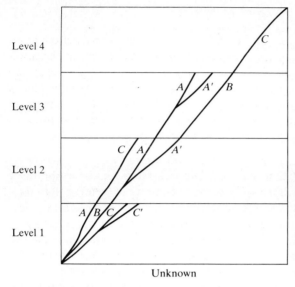

Figure 11-13 Connected-word recognition using level-building time warping. Each level corresponds to a new word in the input stream; its length is determined by the length of the word. Within each level, time warping is used to identify probable words. For this illustration, all templates are assumed to be of equal length. *(Adapted from Myers and Rabiner, 1981a; original © 1981, IEEE.)*

up each vertical strip terminates when the end of the current template has been reached.

For any given level, the templates for all possible words are considered. Where a single-word time-warping recognizer would end up with the most probable word, we will retain the paths, endpoints, and costs for all possible words.

In the example of Fig. 11-13, three possibilities have been tried at level 1. A time-warping program has found the paths labeled *A*, *B*, and *C*. For level 2, the various endpoints of these paths are taken as possible starting points for the templates to be matched at this level. Another set of paths is found through level 2. Notice that every possible endpoint at level 1 does not yield a path that makes it through level 2; this is because excessively expensive paths are eliminated along the way. Ultimately, at level 4, exactly one path makes it to the endpoint. Then we backtrack through the various levels to find the correct path. In the process, we will also select the words which have been matched to the unknown data.

We suggested, at the conclusion of our discussion of the HMM model, that DP warping could be viewed as a special case of the Viterbi HMM algorithm. It could be argued that the LB algorithm represents two recursive applications of the Viterbi algorithm. First, it is used from point to point of the unknown pattern to find the most probable paths through the current level. Then the algorithm is used from level to level to find the most probable path through the entire diagram.

The use of levels means that the matching process does not have to consider every sample as a possible starting point for a new template, but only points near a level boundary. In a test with six talkers and 80 digit groups, Myers and Rabiner achieved word error rates of less than 1 percent and string error rates of less than 5 percent in speaker-independent recognition.

Phoneme-Based Recognizers

An alternative strategy for continuous-speech recognition is to analyze the input stream into its constituent phonemes and then to identify the words in the utterance from their phonemes. Analysis tends to run from left to right, since the beginning of the first word at least is not in doubt. Systems generally pursue several alternative interpretations, frequently in parallel if the hardware can do so in a reasonable amount of time. These systems can usually be described in terms of two principal parts, the front end and the word matcher.

The front end This includes segmentation and preliminary phonetic or phonemic decisions. A segment at this level normally corresponds to a phoneme rather than a word or syllable. Features for segmentation are normally amplitude, voicing, zero-crossing rate, pitch, and changes in phonetic or spectral type. Of these, amplitude is the most important, but it is not sufficient by itself, and practical segmenters use it in combination with other cues. When changes in phonetic type are used as indicators of segment boundaries, segmentation and phonetic classification may proceed more or less in parallel; some systems work backward from phonetic decisions and infer segment boundaries from them.

Paul and Rabinowitz (1974) use amplitude to identify closures and silences and to determine stress level; they use spectrum data obtained from Fourier transformation and assign the most likely phone type to each 25.6-ms frame by comparison with patterns in a library. Medress et al. (1976) use a variety of features, most notably fundamental frequency, energy in various bands, and formant frequencies, to make phonetic decisions. Dixon and Silverman (1977) make general classifications of phonetic types (e.g., vowels, glides, fricatives, nasals), starting with the most easily identified types and using these as contexts for the more elusive ones, and identify segment boundaries from these decisions.

Recognition of segment boundaries is itself a pattern-recognition problem and like all such problems has two types of errors—false alarms (i.e., spurious boundaries) and missed boundaries. Decision thresholds are frequently set to favor false alarms, since for many systems, recovering from errors caused by missed boundaries is more troublesome than recovery from spurious boundaries.

The phonetic classifications from the front end are uncertain, because any given acoustical event typically has several possible phonetic interpretations. Hence the front end produces more than one conjecture for each segment; indeed, since segment decisions may rest on phonetic decisions, the front end will come up with alternative phonetic and segmentation decisions. In many systems the front end is guided by the word matcher in selecting from among the alternatives. Otherwise, the possible identifications are frequently represented by a lattice structure, as in Fig. 11-14. Here each state is associated with a number of possible phonetic events, as suggested by the clusters of circles; this should be compared with the isolated-word HMM described previously. It is then up to the word matcher to derive a plausible sequence of words from the information in the lattice.

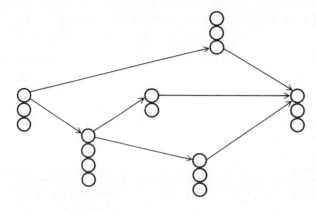

Figure 11-14 Part of a lattice showing possible phonetic identifications and sequences between them. Each cluster of circles corresponds to a state; each individual circle corresponds to a possible output from that state.

The word matcher; models of language The word matcher takes the phonetic data from the front end and tries to make words out of them on the basis of stored phonetic rules, vocabularly, and syntax rules. The syntax rules specify the allowable sequences of phonemes and of words; the syntax rules thus must provide a model of the language to be recognized.

The most commonly used language model is the generative model. This model views a language as a set of strings generated by a grammar. A grammar consists of a vocabulary, a set of syntactic categories (or types), and a set of generating rules, called *productions*, which lead from a designated starting category to the final string. A grossly oversimplified example will help make this clear. Suppose the list of syntactic types is

$$\langle \text{sentence} \rangle \langle \text{noun} \rangle \langle \text{verb} \rangle \langle \text{article} \rangle \langle \text{noun phrase} \rangle \langle \text{verb phrase} \rangle$$

and that the set of generating rules is

⟨sentence⟩ → ⟨noun phrase⟩⟨verb phrase⟩
⟨noun phrase⟩ → ⟨article⟩⟨noun⟩
⟨verb phrase⟩ → ⟨verb⟩⟨noun phrase⟩
⟨noun⟩ → man, woman, house, boy, dog, computer, pizza, . . . (or, ultimately, any noun in the vocabulary)
⟨verb⟩ → sees, is, has, walks, knows, buys, derives, . . . (or, ultimately, any verb in the vocabulary)
⟨article⟩ → the, a

In this example, syntactic types are enclosed in angle brackets to distinguish them from ordinary words; the designated starting type is ⟨sentence⟩. Each production says that the symbol on the left-hand side of the arrow may be replaced with the things on the right. When two syntactic types follow one another, as in ⟨article⟩ ⟨noun⟩, this indicates concatenation. For example, the second production says that wherever we have a noun phrase, we can replace it with an article followed by a noun. These productions permit us to expand ⟨verb phrase⟩ successively into ⟨verb⟩ ⟨noun phrase⟩ and then into ⟨verb⟩ ⟨article⟩ ⟨noun⟩. We can use this grammar to analyze a sentence such as "The man walks the dog" as follows:

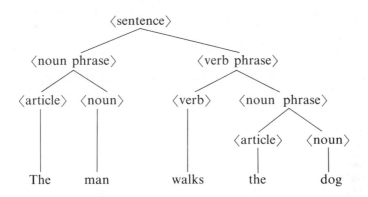

Doing such a structural analysis is known as *parsing* the sentence, and the diagram above is known as a *parse tree*. Notice that such a grammar determines structure but not meaning: it cannot generate an ungrammatical sentence like "Knows dog a the sees," but it can generate nonsense like "The house derives a pizza." Note also that a meaningful sentence like "The woman selects her computer carefully" is beyond the scope of this particular grammar, because we have not provided it with the syntactic types ⟨pronoun⟩ and ⟨adverb⟩ and the generating rules needed to handle them.

The type of language produced by a grammar is profoundly affected by the form of the generating rules. Chomsky (1959) distinguishes among four types of grammar. For our purposes, the most important types are context-dependent grammars, context-free grammars, and regular grammars. A context-dependent grammar is one in which a production can be applied only in a specified context. A context-free (or phrase-structure) grammar is one in which the generating rules can be applied anywhere, regardless of context. Our sample grammar above is a phrase-structure grammar. Regular grammars restrict the form of the right-hand side of the generating rules; these grammars correspond to finite-state models of language.

The finite-state model is of considerable historic interest. The work of Shannon (1948) suggested that natural languages could be represented by a model in which every new word was chosen at random, but where the probability of any particular choice was dependent on the preceding words. This model can be represented by a system containing a finite (but large) number of states; each state corresponds to a set of previously chosen words, and the transition to a new state represents the appending of a new word. The transition probabilities correspond to the probabilities of selection mentioned above.

It appeared from Shannon's examples that as the probabilities were made to depend on more and more preceding words, this finite-state model would converge to a natural language. In a classic paper, however, Chomsky (1956) showed that the finite-state model was inadequate to represent natural languages. Briefly, natural languages are capable of nested structures, and nesting cannot be managed without the aid of a pushdown stack to keep track of the levels of nesting. Finite-state models do not have pushdown stacks and hence cannot handle nesting.

In spite of Chomsky's finding, most grammatical models used in continuous speech recognizers are regular grammars rather than phrase-structure grammars. There are several reasons for this. First, if the grammar is used to model the generation of phonemes rather than words, then a regular grammar may be sufficient. Second, if the number of levels of nesting is limited, then the pushdown stack does not have to have an unlimited capacity. Pushdown stacks of limited size can be simulated by finite-state machines, however. Since most continuous-speech recognizers are designed around specialized applications, with a limited vocabulary and a limited variety of sentence structures, it is easy to keep such things as the level of nesting within bounds, or even to avoid nested structures altogether. Hence we do not need a more elaborate grammar. Third, the programming problems associated with using a phrase-structure grammar to control the recognition process can be very difficult and result in a large, complex, expensive, and slow system. Hence we do not want a more elaborate grammar. Finally, the finite-state grammar takes us back to the hidden Markov model, which is now well understood, has been shown to be computationally cheap, and lends itself to extension beyond the word-recognition level.

Word matching built around a finite-state model is known as stochastic matching. The process uses the recursions of (11-6) or (11-10) to compute the best match to the given possibilities and to estimate its probability. There is usually a considerable amount of intercommunication between the word matcher and the front end, since the word matcher is able to improve the front end's performance by ruling out certain possibilities or suggesting others.

Grammatical constraints have been used for connected-word recognition as well as for continuous speech. Levinson and Rosenberg (1978) investigated the use of a finite-state grammar in conjunction with time warping; the grammar fed the time warper a likely word and starting point, and the warper gave the grammar an endpoint and the cost of the optimal path. Myers and Levinson (1982) used the level-building algorithm of Myers and Rabiner (1981a, b) and included provision for investigating more than one possible transition out of each state.

Rabiner and Levinson (1985) have combined a finite-state grammar with the level-building algorithm and the HMM to produce a connected-word recognition system. The level-building algorithm is essentially the same as described above, with two important differences. First, the processing of each level is done using HMMs rather than templates. In cases where all models have the same number of states, this simplifies the level-building algorithm considerably. Second, the allowed sequence of words is governed by a second state diagram which represents the finite-state grammar. Where a level in, for example, a digit recognizer was identified with the position of a digit in the input speech stream, it is now identified with a state of the grammar.

When a phrase-structure grammar is used for matching, the grammar tends to be the controlling element. It is used to model processes that might have given rise to observed features. This is done because mappings from grammars to phonemes to speech sounds are well understood, while mappings in the reverse direction are extremely difficult to formulate. Hence it is easiest to have the word matcher formulate a set of alternative hypotheses and use these hypotheses to control the front end. (This also reduces the number of possibilities the front end must consider.) Matching by this technique is known as analysis by synthesis.

Front-end errors may take the form of omissions, spurious phonemes, and incorrect identifications. The word matcher must be able to identify and correct these three types of error. A system by Levinson (1983) using a finite-state grammar does word matching by finding the least-cost path through the state diagram, using a Viterbi-type algorithm by Dijkstra (1959). The error-handling technique is based on a substitution-insertion-deletion model due originally to Bahl and Jelinek (1975). The errors are actually incorporated in the state diagram in order to enable the system to handle them. Such a model might take the form shown in Fig. 11-15. The state diagram in Fig. 11-15a corresponds to the normal occurrence of a phoneme z: that is, recognition of z takes the system from state 1 to state 2. The additional state transitions in Fig. 11-15b model the three types of error: the transitions to and from the new state represent an inserted phoneme y, and the alternate paths to state 2 represent substitution of y for z and omission of z altogether (ε represents the "null phoneme"—i.e., no phoneme at all). In Levinson's system, error handling is built in by transforming every three states in the

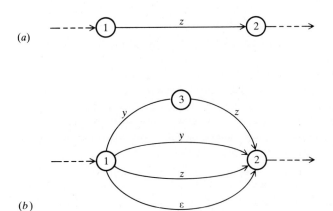

Figure 11-15 (a) Normal transition producing phoneme z. (b) Modified state set with provision for insertion, substitution, or omission of phonemes.

state diagram into a form which represents the three types of error. Each error transition has a cost assigned to it to discourage the system from taking it unnecessarily; however, when errors occur, the fact that they are a part of the model permits the system to proceed through the state diagram without mishap.

11-4 SPEECH-UNDERSTANDING SYSTEMS

This term was made popular by a large research effort in continuous speech recognition funded by the Advanced Research Projects Agency (ARPA) (Klatt, 1977), in which the goal was called a speech-understanding system. The rationale is this: human phonetic recognition is known to be only fair and is made workable by individual's extensive knowledge of speech and by the predictability of what is being said. Our perceptual and analytic powers are therefore backed up by an extensive knowledge of the language and, usually, of the matter being talked about; or, briefly, we do not so much perceive speech as understand it. Hence it is unrealistic to expect machines to outperform human phonetic recognition; it is better to enable them to "understand" speech also and make use of this understanding as humans do. This approach was no doubt further encouraged by an increased interest, among artificial-intelligence circles, in the use and representation of knowledge.

Using this "understanding," these systems are expected (1) to reject noise or babble (i.e., mumbles or irrelevant speech); (2) to be able to understand context and use it to correct errors and resolve ambiguities; and (3) to be able to handle utterances which are ungrammatical or not complete sentences. We would rather have the system get the gist of what is being said than have it recognize each word in detail.

It should be clear from this summary that the principal problems in speech-understanding systems are problems of knowledge representation and system organization. More than any other aspect of speech processing, speech-understanding systems draw heavily on artificial-intelligence research. We will only summarize some of the main problems here and sketch some of the efforts toward solutions.

Speech-understanding systems still have a phonetic identification and segmentation front end, as do continuous-speech recognizers, and they still have a back end which uses this information to identify words. The difference lies in the capabilities required of the back end and in the general system organization. The system must not only coordinate the operation of the front and back ends, but must also enable these to draw on the various types of general information, or "knowledge," which enables the system to understand speech.

There are a number of types of general knowledge which must be provided for the process. These include (Reddy, 1976) what phonemes the language possesses and how these phonemes go together to make words (phonetic knowledge, including both permissible sequences and allophonic variations resulting from these sequences); how the words go together in the language being spoken to make sentences (syntactic rules); the vocabulary used in the particular application (lexical knowledge); and a description of the universe of discourse (semantic knowledge). For example, a travel-reservation system must "know" such elementary facts as that planes have arrival and departure times, that there are twenty-four hours to a day, that motels do not fly.

The other important body of knowledge that must be accommodated and exploited consists of the various pieces of information about the utterance currently being analyzed. The system must have an organization that facilitates communications among all these sources, since we never know when some level of the system will uncover a fact that will be useful to some other level. Hearsay II (CMU) pools all information in a global data base called the "blackboard." The various processes in the system are regarded as sources and users of knowledge; every time a knowledge source finds out (or conjectures) something about the utterance, it enters the item on the blackboard, where it is available to any other knowledge source which may find it useful. The terminal characteristics of the various processes, where they interface with the blackboard, are made uniform, so they can be revised or replaced (or even removed) without disturbing the rest of the system.

The system has to be able to live with errors. One technique for doing this, used in the HWIM system of Bolt, Beranek, and Newman (Woods *et al.*, 1976) and the CMU Hearsay system (Reddy *et al.*, 1977) is to avoid absolute yes or no decisions and instead rate identifications or hypotheses by a score corresponding to the strength of the supporting evidence or some other estimated probability of their being correct. Another important protection against errors is to pursue several possibilities in parallel in order to have alternatives to fall back on if the first hypothesis turns out to be based on faulty data. This parallelism occurs at every level of the process; it significantly increases the computational burden and slows the recognition process.

Error resistance also means that speech-understanding systems do not generally depend on a simple left-to-right analysis, because if the leftmost word is wrong, then a left-to-right system will fail. Instead, the syntactic component of the system tends to choose high-scoring possible words and attempt to work outwards from them. This is sometimes called the "best-first search" (Jelinek, 1976). This search is done with the aid of knowledge sources from which it can determine which words are likely to precede and follow the portion already identified. It then uses this information to evaluate phonetic possibilities provided for these regions by the front end; it may also relay to the front end suggestions of other possible phonetic events to look for in the input stream.

The most successful system in the ARPA project, and the only one to meet the stated goals, was the "Harpy" system at Carnegie-Mellon University (CMU) (Lowerre, 1976). This system used a finite-state model of language to verify and control front-end phonetic decisions. The error rate for a 1011-word vocabulary and five talkers was 5 percent.

It appears that in the future these systems will also have to draw on an improved understanding of how human listeners perceive speech; some of the most recent research on perception (Pisoni, 1985) clearly has potential applications in this area: how humans use and organize their knowledge sources, what the elementary units of perception are, how listeners represent the speech input internally, and how the listener's attention is divided among different levels of the input stream.

REFERENCES

Collected Papers

Dixon, N. R., and T. B. Martin (Eds.): *Automatic Speech and Speaker Recognition*, IEEE Press, New York, 1979. Papers marked with asterisks [*] in the References below are reprinted in this volume.

Lea, W. A. (Ed.): *Trends in Speech Recognition*, Prentice-Hall, Englewood Cliffs, 1980.

Reddy, D. R. (Ed.): *Speech Recognition: Invited Papers Presented at the 1974 IEEE Symposium*, Academic Press, New York, 1975.

Surveys

Beek, B., et al.: An assessment of the technology of automatic speech recognition for military applications, *IEEE Trans.*, vol. ASSP-25, no. 4, pp. 310–322, August, 1977. [*]

Hyde, S. R.: Automatic speech recognition: a critical survey and discussion of the literature, in E. E. David and P. B. Denes (Eds.), *Human Communication: A Unified View*, McGraw-Hill, New York, 1972. [*]

Klatt, D. H.: Review of the ARPA speech understanding project, *JASA*, vol. 62, no. 6, pp. 1345–1366, December, 1977. [*]

Martin, T. B.: Practical applications of voice input to machines, *Proc. IEEE*, vol. 64, no. 4, pp. 487–501, April, 1976. [*]

Reddy, D. R.: Speech recognition by machine: a review, *Proc. IEEE*, vol. 64, no. 4, pp. 501–531, April, 1976. [*]

White, G. M.: Speech recognition: a tutorial overview, *Computer*, vol. 9, pp. 40–53, May, 1976. [*]

Individual Papers

Bahl, L. R., and F. Jelinek: Decoding for channels with insertions, deletions, and substitutions, with applications to speech recognition, *IEEE Trans.*, vol. IT-21, pp. 404–411, July, 1975.

———, et al.: Automatic recognition of continuously spoken sentences from a finite-state grammar, *ICASSP-78*, pp. 418–421, 1975.

Baker, J. K.: Stochastic modeling for automatic speech understanding, in D. R. Reddy (Ed.), *Speech Recognition*, pp. 521–542, 1975(a).

———: The DRAGON system—an overview, *IEEE Trans.*, vol. ASSP-23, no. 1, pp. 24–29, February, 1975(b). [*]

Baum, L. E.: An inequality and associated maximization technique in statistical estimation for probabilistic functions of a Markov process, *Inequalities*, vol. 3, pp. 1–8, 1972.

Bridle, J. S.: An efficient elastic-template method for detecting given words in running speech, *British Acoust. Society Meeting*, pp. 1–4, April, 1973.

Brown, M. K., and L. R. Rabiner: An adaptive, ordered, graph search technique for dynamic time warping for isolated word recognition, *IEEE Trans.*, vol. ASSP-30, no. 4, pp. 535–544, August, 1982.

Burton, D. K., J. E. Shore and J. T. Buck: A generalization of isolated word recognition using vector quantization, *ICASSP-83*, pp. 1021–1024, April, 1983.

Chomsky, N.: Three models for the description of language, *IRE Trans.*, vol. IT-2, pp. 113–124, 1956.

———: On certain formal properties of grammars, *Inf. Contr.*, vol. 2, no. 2, pp. 137–167, June, 1959.

Christiansen, R. W., and C. K. Rushforth: Detecting and locating key words in continuous speech using linear predictive coding, *IEEE Trans.*, vol. ASSP-25, no. 5, pp. 361–367, October, 1977. [*]

Das, S. K., and W. S. Mohn: A scheme for speech processing in automatic speaker verification, *IEEE Trans.*, vol. AU-19, no. 1, pp. 32–43, March, 1971.

Dautrich, B. A., et al.: On the effects of varying filter bank parameters on isolated word recognition, *IEEE Trans.*, vol. ASSP-31, no. 4, pp. 793–807, August, 1983.

Dijkstra, E. W.: A note on two problems in connection with graphs, *Numer. Math.*, no. 1, pp. 269–271, 1959.

Dixon, N. R., and H. F. Silverman: The 1976 modular acoustic processor (MAP), *IEEE Trans.*, vol. ASSP-25, no. 5, pp. 367–379, October, 1977.

Duda, R. O., and P. E. Hart: *Pattern Classification and Scene Analysis*, Wiley-Interscience, New York, 1973.

Forney, Jr., G. D.: The Viterbi algorithm, *Proc. IEEE*, vol. 61, no. 3, pp. 268–278, March, 1973.

Gerstman, L. J.: Classification of self-normalized vowels, *IEEE Trans.*, vol. AU-16, no. 1, pp. 78-80, March, 1968.

Gupta, V. N., et al.: A speaker-independent speech-recognition system based on linear prediction, *IEEE Trans.*, vol. ASSP-26, no. 1, pp. 27–33, February, 1978.

Itakura, F.: Minimum prediction residual principle applied to speech recognition, *IEEE Trans.*, vol. ASSP-23, no. 1, pp. 67–72, February, 1975. [*]

Jelinek, F.: Continuous speech recognition by statistical methods, *Proc. IEEE*, vol. 64, no. 4, pp. 532–556, April, 1976.

Kaneko, T., and N. R. Dixon: A hierarchical decision approach to large-vocabulary discrete utterance recognition, *IEEE Trans.*, vol. ASSP-31, no. 5, pp. 1061–1066, October, 1983.

Kang, G. S., and D. C. Coulter: 600 bits/second voice digitizer (linear predictive formant vocoder), Naval Res. Lab., 1976.

Kirkpatric, S., et al.: Optimization by simulated annealing, *Science*, vol. 220, no. 4598, pp. 671–680, May, 1983.

Kirlin, R. L.: *A posteriori* estimation of vocal tract length, *IEEE Trans.*, vol. ASSP-26, no. 6, pp. 571–574, December, 1978.

Lamel, L. F., et al.: An improved endpoint detector for isolated word recognition, *IEEE Trans.*, vol. ASSP-29, pp. 777–785, August, 1981.

Levinson, S. E.: Some experiments with a linguistic processor for continuous speech recognition, *IEEE Trans.*, vol. ASSP-31, no. 6, pp. 1549–1556, December, 1983.

——— and A. E. Rosenberg: Some experiments with a syntax-directed speech recognition system, *ICASSP-78*, pp. 409–412, 1978.

———, et al.: An introduction to the application of the theory of probabilistic functions of a Markov process to automatic speech recognition, *BSTJ*, vol. 62, no. 4, pp. 1035–1074, April, 1983.

Lowerre, B. T.: The Harpy speech recognition system, Ph.D. Thesis, Carnegie-Mellon University, 1976.

———: Dynamic speaker adaptation in the Harpy speech recognition system, *ICASSP-77*, pp. 788–790, 1977.

Martinez, H. G., et al.: Discrete utterance recognition based upon source coding techniques, *ICASSP-82*, pp. 539–542, May, 1982.

Medress, M. F., et al.: A system for the recognition of spoken connected word sequences, *ICASSP-76*, pp. 434–437, 1976.

Myers, C. S., et al.: Performance tradeoffs in dynamic time warping algorithms for isolated word recognition, *IEEE Trans.*, vol. ASSP-28, pp. 622–635, December, 1980.

———, et al.: On the use of dynamic time warping for word spotting and connected word recognition, *BSTJ*, vol. 60, no. 3, pp. 303–325, March, 1981.

——— and S. E. Levinson: Speaker independent connected word recognition using a syntax-directed dynamic programming procedure, *IEEE Trans.*, vol. ASSP-30, no. 4, pp. 561–565, August, 1982.

——— and L. R. Rabiner: A level building dynamic time warping algorithm for connected word recognition, *IEEE Trans.*, vol. ASSP-29, pp. 284–297, April, 1981(*a*).

——— and ———: Connected digit recognition using a level-building DTW algorithm, *IEEE Trans.*, vol. ASSP-29, pp. 351–363, June, 1981(*b*).

Neuburg, E. P.: Frequency-axis warping to improve automatic word recognition, *Proc. ICASSP-80*, IEEE Press, New York, pp. 166–168, 1980.

Nilsson, N. J.: *Problem-Solving Methods in Artificial Intelligence*, McGraw-Hill, New York, 1972.

Paige, A., and W. V. Zue: Calculation of vocal tract length, *IEEE Trans.*, vol. AU-18, pp. 268–270, September, 1970.

Papoulis, A.: *Probability, Random Variables, and Stochastic Processes*, McGraw-Hill, New York, 1984.

Paul, D. B.: Training of HMM recognizers by simulated annealing, *ICASSP-85*, pp. 13–16, 1985.

Paul, Jr., J. E., and A. S. Rabinowitz: An acoustically based continuous speech recognition system, *IEEE Symposium on Speech Recognition*, pp. 63–67, 1974.

Pierce, J. R.: Whither speech recognition?, *JASA*, vol. 46, no. 4(2), pp. 1049–1051, October, 1969. A view which has (fortunately) proved unduly pessimistic.

Pisoni, D. B.: Speech perception: some new directions in research and theory, *JASA*, vol. 78, no. 1, pt. 2, pp. 381–388, July, 1985.

Pols, L. C. W.: Real-time recognition of spoken words, *IEEE Trans.*, vol. C-20, no. 9, pp. 972–978, September, 1971. [*]

Pruzansky, S.: Pattern-matching procedure for automatic talker recognition, *JASA*, vol. 35, no. 3, pp. 354-358, March, 1963.

Rabiner, L. R.: On creating reference templates for speaker independent recognition of isolated words, *IEEE Trans.*, vol. ASSP-26, no. 1, pp. 34–42, February, 1978.

——— and S. E. Levinson: A speaker-independent, syntax-directed, connected word recognition system based on hidden Markov models and level building, *IEEE Trans.*, vol. ASSP-33, no. 3, pp. 561–573, June, 1985.

——— and M. R. Sambur: Some preliminary experiments in the recognition of connected digits, *IEEE Trans.*, vol. ASSP-24, no. 2, pp. 170–182, April, 1976. [*]

——— and C. E. Schmidt: Application of dynamic time warping to connected digit recognition, *IEEE Trans.*, vol. ASSP-28, no. 4, pp. 377–388, August, 1980.

——— and J. G. Wilpon: Speaker-independent isolated word recognition for a moderate size (54 word) vocabulary, *IEEE Trans.*, vol. ASSP-27, no. 6, pp. 583–587, December, 1979.

———, *et al.*: Considerations in dynamic time warping algorithms for discrete word recognition, *IEEE Trans.*, vol. ASSP-26, no. 6, pp. 575–582, December, 1978.

———, *et al.*: On the application of vector quantization and hidden Markov models to speaker-independent, isolated word recognition, *BSTJ*, vol. 62, no. 4, pp. 1075–1105, April, 1983.

Reddy, D. R., *et al.*: Speech understanding systems, Final Report, Computer Science Dept., Carnegie-Mellon University, 1977.

Regel, P.: A module for acoustic-phonetic transcription of fluently spoken German speech, *IEEE Trans.*, vol. ASSP-30, no. 3, pp. 440–450, June, 1982.

Sakoe, H., and C. Chiba: Dynamic programming algorithm optimization for spoken word recognition, *IEEE Trans.*, vol. ASSP-26, no. 1, pp. 43–49, February, 1978. [*]

Sambur, M. R., and L. R. Rabiner: A speaker-independent digit-recognition system, *BSTJ*, vol. 54, pp. 81–102, January, 1975. [*]

Shannon, C. E.: A mathematical theory of communication, *BSTJ*, vol. 27, pp. 379–423, 1948.

Shore, J. E., and D. Burton: Discrete utterance speech recognition without time normalization, *ICASSP-82*, pp. 907–910, May, 1982.

Viterbi, A. J.: Error bounds for convolutional codes and an asymptotically optimal decoding algorithm, *IEEE Trans.*, vol. IT-13, pp. 260–269, April, 1967.

Wakita, H.: Normalization of vowels by vocal-tract length and its application to vowel identification, *IEEE Trans.*, vol. ASSP-25, no. 2, pp. 183–192, April, 1977.

White, G. M., and R. B. Neely: Speech recognition experiments with linear prediction, bandpass filtering, and dynamic programming, *IEEE Trans.*, vol. ASSP-24, no. 2, pp. 183–188, April, 1976. [*]

Wohlford, R. E., *et al.*: The enhancement of wordspotting techniques, *ICASSP-80*, pp. 209–212, 1980.

Woods, W. A., *et al.*: Speech understanding systems: final technical progress report, Bolt, Beranek, and Newman, Inc., Report No. 3438, 1976.

Zelinski, R., and F. Class: A segmentation algorithm for connected word recognition based on estimation principles, *IEEE Trans.*, vol. ASSP-31, no. 4, pp. 818–827, August, 1983.

CHAPTER
TWELVE

SPEAKER RECOGNITION

The problem of speaker recognition can be divided into two main subproblems: speaker identification and speaker authentication (or verification). The identification problem asks, "Which talker (out of a group known to us) is this?"; the authentication problem asks, "Is this talker the person he claims to be?" A possible identification problem may be to name the probable source of a telephoned bomb threat; a possible authentication problem is the use of spoken passwords to screen people seeking access to a restricted area or service.

We have observed that any utterance carries at least two types of information: the message itself and the identity of the talker. These two problems have as their main element in common the fact that feature selection will usually jettison the message content and retain the information which identifies the talker; the only exception to this is the case in which the message is always the same, as in a spoken password or account number. Beyond this fact, the two problems differ considerably in their operational contexts, as the following comparison makes clear:

Identification	Verification
Talker may be reluctant	Talker is cooperative
Voice disguise a problem	Mimicry a problem
Must test many patterns	Need compare to only one pattern
System response can be slow	System response must be fast
Vocabulary may be different	Vocabulary can be restricted to standard test phrase
Channels may be poor or differing	Can frequently control channel characteristics
Signal-to-noise ratio may be poor	Can usually control signal-to-noise ratio

The reasons for most of these differences are self-evident. In the identification problem, talkers may not wish to be identified and hence may be uncooperative if recordings are made later for evaluation purposes; they may also try to disguise their voices, either when making the original utterance (if they suspect that their voices are being recorded) or when making test recordings. Such disguises may easily fool a machine, since pitch and formant frequencies are relatively easy to displace (Endres *et al.*, 1971). It is probably less easy to disguise unconscious prosodic habits, such as pitch contours or timing, but many recognizers do not use these features. In the authentication problem, true talkers will be cooperative, since they wish to gain access and are willing to put themselves to some trouble to get it. An impostor who is a good mimic may also be able to fool the system. Research using mimics has yielded various results; professional mimics who have undergone intensive training have occasionally been alarmingly successful (Rosenberg and Sambur, 1975).

An identification program used to select the true speaker from among (say) 50 possibilities has to test 50 prototypes; hence response time may be slow, especially since most recognizers perform best on long sample segments of speech. On the other hand, in forensic applications quick response time is seldom called for. In authentication, fast response time is desirable but is also easier to achieve, since the program is required to test only the prototype corresponding to the talker's claimed identity.

Authentication errors can be classified into two categories: false rejections and false acceptances. In a false rejection, a genuine talker is rejected as an impostor; in a false acceptance, as the name implies, an impostor is accepted as genuine. Like most recognizers, an authenticator will compute a distance measure from the talker's template in the pattern library and will compare this distance against a predetermined threshold. The probabilities of false acceptances and rejections will typically look like Fig. 12-1. Usually the decision threshold is placed at the point where the two probabilities are equal.

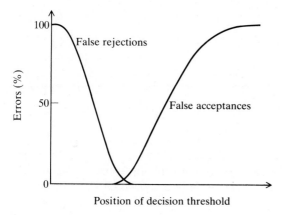

Figure 12-1 False rejections and false acceptances as a function of the decision threshold.

Experimental Methods

The test population should generally be as large as can be managed. Many studies have used test populations of only 10 to 20 talkers. A practical system, on the other hand, may have to work with populations in the hundreds of thousands. Small populations are sometimes a practical necessity: a graduate student, for example, may have limited resources and be unable to round up a larger body of talkers. Even in industry, recording sessions for particular talkers may be preempted by trips, conferences, or the like. The problem of data gathering is aggravated by the fact that the recording sessions should be spaced out in time, since a body of 20 utterances by a single speaker will show much less variation if they are recorded in a single session than if they are recorded at intervals of, say, a month. Getting each of a large number of volunteers to show up at a series of weekly recording sessions can sometimes be a major logistical problem. The smallness of these populations is one important reason why gaussian statistics are so often assumed: there may not be enough data to justify any other assumption.

For these reasons, a good-sized data base usually represents a considerable investment in time and money. Hence, in gathering data for recognition purposes, it is prudent to look beyond the current research goals and design the acquisition phase so the data can be reused later in other projects. This means, for example, that the text to be spoken should be kept as general as possible, even if the current project concentrates on a limited set of phonetic observables. Use of phonetically balanced material, e.g., the Harvard sentences (IEEE, 1969), is recommended, especially if the duration of the recordings is short. Another frequently used text is the "rainbow passage" (Fairbanks, 1960). Some researchers have simply had the subject talk at random for 15 minutes. It is usually safe to assume that 15 minutes' worth of talk represents a balanced sample of an individual's speech.

Archival copies of the original recordings and the original digitized version should be kept. One reason for this is to be able to compare the performance of different techniques on the identical material; another reason is simply that the digitized data usually represent a considerable investment in time and effort which it is best not to have to repeat. Some researchers have difficulty gaining access to digitization facilities, although with A/D and D/A conversion hardware and software now available, even for personal computers, this may become less of a problem in the future. The researcher with such problems frequently has to take whatever is available, but wherever practical the A/D conversion should be done using the longest word length and the highest sampling rate available. The data can always be rounded off to shorter word lengths, and digitally filtered and down-sampled, later, if this is deemed desirable.

Another consequence of using small populations is that the researcher, in evaluating the system, may be tempted to take the unknown data from the learning set for reasons of economy. This nearly always results in spuriously high performance, since the unknown data consist of utterances which the system has heard already. It is much more realistic, if more expensive, to try the system on fresh data.

12-1 SELECTION OF FEATURES

Many features have been explored as indicators of talker identity. Most feature selections indicate an attempt to focus either on individual differences in vocal tract anatomy or on individual speaking habits. Surveys evaluating a large variety of features have been published by Wolf (1972) and Sambur (1975).

Wolf's data consisted of a set of six standard test sentences recorded 10 times over by a group of 21 male talkers. Spectral data were obtained by means of a filter bank, and pitch was measured by low-pass filtering and measuring time between zero crossings. (This could be done because the recording bandwidth included the fundamental frequency, the talkers covered a limited pitch range, and the signal-to-noise ratio was high.) Pitch and spectral observables were measured for selected phonetic events. The parameters considered were: (1) pitch at selected points in words; (2) spectral characteristics of nasal consonants; (3) spectral characteristics of selected vowels; (4) estimated slope of the excitation spectrum; (5) spectral characteristics of fricatives; (6) duration of a selected vowel; and (7) presence of prevoicing in a selected context. Each feature was evaluated by means of its F ratio, and correlations between features were estimated. In a recognition experiment using a selection of nine features having high F ratios and low intercorrelations, recognition error rates of 1.5 percent were obtained; when the number of features was increased to 17, the error rate decreased to 0.

Sambur used the same test sentences as Wolf, recorded in a series of five sessions spanning $3\frac{1}{2}$ years. The features considered were: (1) vowel formant frequencies and bandwidths and glottal source poles, computed from twelfth-order linear-predictions analysis; (2) location of pole frequencies in nasal consonants; (3) location of poles in sibilants /s/ and /ʃ/; (4) pitch contours over a selected sentence; and (5) timing characteristics, specifically the rate of change of formant 2 over a diphthong and the duration of closure for the phoneme /k/. These choices yielded a total of 92 features, which were ranked by means of the "knock-out" technique described in Chapter 7. Sambur tabulates the ranking of the 38 best features. From this tabulation it appeared that timing characteristics, pitch, and low-order formants were the most important features. Using the best five features in a recognition experiment, Sambur obtained an error rate of 3 percent.

12-2 EXAMPLES OF USE OF VARIOUS FEATURES

In this section, we briefly summarize examples of the wide variety of features used in talker recognition and verification experiments. We have chosen to arrange these examples by the type of feature used for recognition, but the reader should bear in mind that many researchers have used more than one type of feature, and that in any case these lists are not exhaustive.

Frequency-Band Analysis

A number of researchers have used filter banks to obtain spectral information. A typical system is shown in Fig. 12-2; note the similarity to the transmitting end of a channel vocoder. The outputs are sampled at some appropriate rate (typically

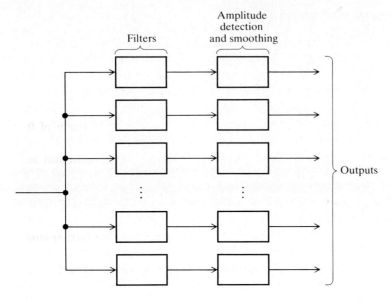

Figure 12-2 Filter bank used for analysis of input data. The number of filters varies from approximately 10 to 20; bandwidths may be equal, logarithmic, or may correspond to critical bands or equal intervals on the mel scale.

100 Hz) and used as the feature vector for recognition. The library pattern will then consist of an approximate ensemble average obtained by averaging the pattern vectors from a number of utterances made during the training session.

Filter banks were historically the first source of spectral information. Pruzansky (1963) and Pruzansky and Mathews (1964) used a filter bank covering the range from 100 Hz to 10 kHz and sampled the outputs at 10-ms intervals. Features were (1) individual time/frequency samples and (2) averages over more than one frequency channel or more than one time sample, or both. The unknown and reference patterns were time-registered by aligning points of maximum energy. Features were evaluated by F ratio; no allowance was made for possible correlations among features.

Das and Mohn (1971) also used averaged filter-bank outputs but supplemented these features with formant data, timing information, and pitch. Their process incorporated techniques for automatic temporal alignment by locating particular landmarks in the patterns being compared. Formants were estimated from the filter-bank outputs. Features were evaluated by F ratio, as with Pruzanzky and Mathews.

Li and Hughes (1974) formed a correlation matrix from the filter-bank outputs: the (i, j) element of the matrix was the correlation, over time, between the outputs of filter i and filter j. The correlation process removes the time information, and thus there is no alignment problem. Using 30 male talkers reading a 30-s passage from the rainbow text, they estimated the authentication accuracy using the normalized euclidean distance, the correlation, and the average absolute difference as distance measures. Using the full 30-s length of the passage, they obtained error rates in the neighborhood of 1 percent.

Formant Frequencies

Formant frequencies have been used by many researchers, usually in combination with other features. Goldstein (1976) made an extensive study of formants in individual vowel sounds as recognition features. A set of three vowels, four diphthongs, and three syllables containing [r] were recorded in test sentences spoken by 10 American males. Formant frequencies were obtained by finding the complex roots of the transfer function as estimated by a twelfth-order covariance linear predictor. Formants were evaluated at various points in each of the vowels studied. Then 199 features were measured and initially screened by F ratio; those features with F ratios greater than 60 were retained for further study. The "add-on" method described in Chapter 7 was used to rank the features. The predicted error rate using the five highest-ranking features was estimated at 0.24 percent.

As in the case of speech recognition, simple compression or expansion of the time scale is not enough to produce accurate alignment, and many investigators have tried to select recognizable landmarks from within the utterance itself. Thus Pruzansky (1963) lined up the maximum-energy points in the utterance, and time registration was a major component of the system of Das and Mohn (1971). Doddington (1970) used formant frequencies in a very important study in speaker verification. Doddington's solution to the alignment problem was to use dynamic time warping, described in Chapter 11. The warping was controlled so as to minimize the discrepancy in formant 2 frequencies between the unknown and the reference pattern. Doddington claimed that it was the power of this time-warping procedure which enabled his process to achieve its low (1.5 percent) error rate. As a result of Doddington's research, time-axis warping has become a standard technique in talker verification.

Doddington chose formant 2 for the warping criterion because of its range and its sensitivity to phonetic content. Formant estimation is a time-consuming process, however, and it would be desirable to use other parameters as features, in which case it would also be desirable to be able to dispense with formant 2 as the warping criterion. In order to determine whether a suitable alternative to formant 2 could be found, Lummis (1973) used essentially the same set of features but did time warping on the amplitude function instead. The error rate, using the same data base as Doddington's, was in the neighborhood of 1 percent.

Pitch Contours

Atal (1972) used samples from pitch contours as a recognition feature. Ten speakers made six recordings of a test sentence; the recordings were normalized to 2 seconds' duration and the pitch contour was determined for each utterance and divided into 40 contiguous segments, each 50 ms long. A pitch value was assigned to each segment by averaging the measured pitch over its length. The raw recognition features consisted of the average pitches of the 40 segments. To obtain features from these pitch values, Atal orthogonalized them by means of the KL transformation described in Chapter 7. In one version of the system, the 10 features having the largest eigenvalues were used; in a second version, the top 20 were used. Because maximum variance does not necessarily correspond to maximum ability to separate talkers, Atal ranked the transformed features by variance and tested each quartile for ability to discriminate by means of the J_1 ($=\text{tr } W^{-1}B$) measure described in Chapter 7. He found that the top quartile accounted for 98.5 percent of the total variance and 89.1 percent of the variance between speakers. Recognition was done by transforming the selected features again using the $W^{-1}B$ transformation of Chapter 7 and using the squared euclidean distance between transformed vectors. Recognition accuracy with the 10 best features was 93 percent; with the 20 best features it was 97 percent.

Features Derived from Linear Prediction

The various parameters derivable from linear prediction are now probably the most popular source of recognition features. We instance a few of the more prominent recognition efforts based on these parameters.

Wakita (1976) used the residual energy as a distance measure in the recognition of vowel sounds. (The application to speaker recognition comes about because the results showed considerable speaker dependence.) In the learning phase, a predictor filter was computed for each talker/vowel combination. In the recognition phase, a filter was computed for the unknown utterance. Prediction errors were found (1) for the unknown vowel and the reference filter in the pattern library and (2) for the unknown vowel and its optimum filter. The ratio of these errors, (1)/(2), was found for all reference vowels and the vowel giving the smallest ratio was selected. In a test with nine male speakers and seven females, the correct vowel was selected in 99 percent of the utterances. Speaker dependency suggested that the same technique could select the correct speaker with 100 percent accuracy. No doubt because of the small number of speakers used in this study, Wakita claimed no more than that the technique might be used to screen out a subset of likely candidates for closer examination by other methods.

Li and Wrench (1983) extended Wakita's technique by comparing all the vowels in the unknown utterance with all the vowels in each reference set. Each speaker-vowel combination forms a cluster in a multidimensional feature space. The clustering technique is that version of the K-means algorithm in which each feature which is farther than some threshold distance from all existing clusters is made the nucleus of a new cluster. Using unconstrained conversation from 11 male speakers, they obtained recognition accuracies ranging from 79 percent for 3-s unknown samples to 96 percent for 10-s unknown samples.

When predictor coefficients are plotted against time, they show a great deal of redundancy. As can be seen from Fig. 12-3, consecutive coefficients tend to

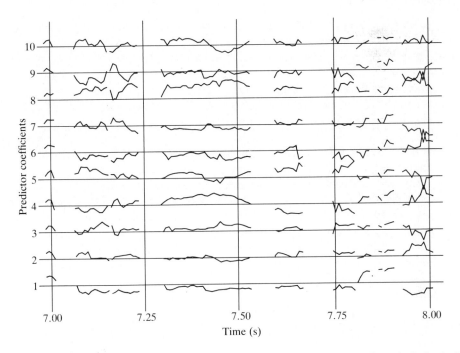

Figure 12-3 Autocorrelation predictor coefficients plotted against time. The phrase is the beginning of "ten above in the suburbs."

move in opposite directions. Sambur (1976) found the covariance matrix of predictor coefficients for each frame of speech and obtained a covariance matrix for the utterance as a whole by averaging. When the coefficients were orthogonalized by diagonalizing the averaged matrix, he observed that only a small number of the orthogonalized parameters were text-dependent, while the rest were essentially constant over the utterance. When this process was repeated with other talkers, the constant parameters took on different values. This suggested that the constant parameters were talker-dependent and could be used for talker recognition. The fact that these features were constant over the duration of the utterance meant that no time normalization would be required.

Sambur used six repetitions of a single sentence spoken by each of 21 male speakers on six different days covering a period of three weeks. The coefficients were obtained from a twelfth-order autocorrelation predictor with speech sampled at 10 kHz. Various numbers of orthogonalized parameters were selected for use as features, starting in all cases with the least-significant (i.e., least text-dependent) parameters, since these were the ones which had been found to be most talker-dependent. The parameters examined in this way were the predictor coefficients, the reflection coefficients, and the log-data ratios. The most effective features were the orthogonalized reflection coefficients (ORCs) and the orthogonalized log-area ratios (OLARs). Including the five least-significant ORCs, this gave a recognition accuracy of 99.2 percent; the same accuracy was obtained using the seven least-significant OLARs.

The experiment was then expanded to eliminate text dependence. A set of six test sentences were recorded; when the recognizer was trained on one sentence and recognition was done on the other five, the accuracies ranged from 52 to 73 percent. When the recognizer was trained on five of the six sentences and recognition done on the sixth, an average accuracy of 94 percent was obtained.

Cheung and Eisenstein (1978) compared Sambur's knock-out strategy with the dynamic programming technique discussed in Chapter 7. Their initial feature set consisted of 10 normalized autocorrelation coefficients, 10 reflection coefficients, 10 cepstral coefficients, and time-averaged prediction-error energy, pitch, and log energy. Subsets of features were selected by the knock-out method and by dynamic programming. There was a fair amount of overlap between the sets chosen by the two methods; e.g., the two subsets of 10 features have seven features in common. The performance of the two methods was also very close; when the recognition accuracies of the two subsets of 10 features were compared, the dynamic programming subset enjoyed an advantage of approximately 2 percent, but this advantage began to disappear when the number of voiced frames used approached 40.

Shridhar *et al.* (1981) investigated the performance of Sambur's orthogonal linear-prediction method on longer sections of speech. They determined experimentally that it took approximately 100 s of speech to get a stable estimate of the LPC covariance matrix. Using Sambur's method and parameters from varying amounts of speech, however, they found relatively small differences in performance between experiments using 20 and 100 s of speech. To test Sambur's conjecture that the higher-order orthogonalized parameters were the best indicators of talker identity, they used Cheung and Eisenstein's dynamic programming technique to select the best subsets of 6 and 8 parameters. They found that the subsets selected varied from talker to talker and that the dynamic programming technique did not show any significant tendency to select the high-order parameters.

Markel *et al.* (1977) examined the long-term averages of 10 reflection coefficients, taken from the speech of four talkers who were recorded during interviews which yielded approximately 15 to 18 min of speech for each talker. These long samples permitted the evaluation of long-term-averaged parameters as recognition features. In addition to the reflection coefficients, pitch, standard deviation of pitch, and relative standard deviation of pitch were considered.

Long-term averages were taken over various numbers of frames of voiced speech, ranging from 10 to 1000 frames. As the number of frames increased from 10 to 1000 frames, the standard deviation of pitch decreased by a factor of 3; the other pitch-related features showed very little change as a function of the number of frames included. The standard deviation of the reflection coefficients showed a steady decrease proportional to approximately the cube root of the number of frames included. It should be borne in mind, however, that the data for each speaker were taken from a single recording session, and therefore the effects of long-term intraspeaker variation could not be included.

The features were further evaluated by means of discriminant analysis. Since there were 13 features and only four talkers, only four nonzero eigenvalues were obtained. The variance ratio of the first three of these eigenvalues increased with increasing numbers of frames, and the first two eigenvalues gave extremely good separation of the talkers when 1000 frames were used. (It should be noted that 1000 frames of voiced speech came to about 70 s.)

In a later study of time-averaged parameters, Markel and Davis (1979) used a data base of approximately 36 h of speech, taken from interviews similar to those in the previous study from 17 speakers, recorded over a period in excess of three months. The features used were pitch, amplitude, and 10 reflection coefficients; means and standard deviations for all these parameters were computed for varying numbers of voiced frames. Features were evaluated using F ratios, but no consistent pattern emerged. The best recognition results were obtained using means and standard deviations of all features except amplitude, taken over approximately 39 s of speech. For this case, the recognition accuracy was 98 percent and the authentication error was 4.25 percent.

A similar technique was examined by Pfeifer (1977). In this method, decisions are made on each frame of the unknown speech, and the final identification is made on the basis of a majority decision. Wrench (1981) implemented both the Markel and Pfeifer systems, using a high-speed processor for the LPC and distance computations. Testing the system with speech of 30 talkers, recorded from commercial television, he found that Markel's method yielded superior results. He also tried various combinations of the two methods and concluded that averaging should be done before any decisions are made.

Schwartz et al. (1982) and Wolf et al. (1983) used log-area ratios as features and investigated four recognition methods. The methods were the Mahalanobis distance, two bayesian classifiers assuming a gaussian probability density, and a nonparametric classifier based on the k-nearest-neighbor technique. In the earlier study, these methods were used with a data base consisting of clean speech and speech to which noise had been added to simulate speech transmitted through a noisy channel. It was found that the bayesian and nonparametric classifiers outperformed the minimum-distance classifier. The later study used actual noisy channel data obtained from radio transmissions. The speech is degraded by noise and distortion and at times is barely intelligible; the levels of both noise and distortion vary widely and rapidly. The accuracies obtained in the later study were significantly poorer than the earlier ones, but the bayesian and nonparametric classifiers were still better than the minimum-distance ones.

Use of Coarticulation

Coarticulation is the process in which the speech organs prepare to produce the following speech sound, or retain vestiges of the previous sound, while they are in the process of producing the current sound. Since coarticulation effects are not phonemic, they are subject to considerable variation and tend to be speaker-dependent.

Su et al. (1974) take advantage of this fact to do speaker identification by measuring a specific coarticulation effect. If the nasal /m/ is followed by a vowel, then the tongue, while its position is masked by the lip closure, can begin to move into position for the following vowel. Variations in the tongue position will cause variation in the frequency content of the /m/ being produced; these variations are not generally noticed in conversation, but they can be measured spectrographically. A weaker coarticulation effect can be obtained with /n/. Using a population of 14 male talkers, Su had them record the utterances /həmVd/ and /hənVd/, where the vowel, V, was any of /i, ɪ, e, u, o, a/. Spectra were estimated by a bank of 25 filters. The spectral data were orthogonalized for each speaker and the dependence on both vowel and speaker of the first two eigenvectors was noted. Using this feature alone, a recognition accuracy of 100 percent was obtained; in a larger experiment using 33 talkers, the accuracy was 85 percent.

Identification from Spectrograms

Kersta (1962) reported an experiment in which a group of eight high-school girls were taught to identify speakers by visual examination of spectrograms. The training lasted for one week and the girls worked in teams of two. A number of tests were made of identification accuracy, the number of unknown talkers varying from 5 to 15. In one test involving 2000 identification attempts, the error rate was 1.0 percent. Comparable accuracies were reported for other tests.

This work caught the attention of law-enforcement agencies, and under the name of "voiceprints," spectrograms came to be used for talker identification in forensic applications.

Young and Campbell (1967) attempted to duplicate Kersta's results. They trained a group of graduate students and faculty members. Kersta's paper provides no information on how his subjects were trained; Young and Campbell taught their subjects to observe frequency, amplitude, and bandwidth of formants with particular attention to beginnings and ends of formant tracks and to formant spacing and translations. Features also included pitch fluctuations and the durations of utterances. Recognition accuracies obtained were 78.4 percent for isolated words and 37.3 percent for words in context. Stevens et al. (1968) carried out a similar experiment and obtained recognition accuracies averaging 75 percent.

Bolt et al. (1970) published a lengthy critique of the spectrographic method, in which the following conclusions were stated:

1. It is possible to identify voices from spectrograms.
2. Spectrograms do not facilitate distinguishing between speaker-dependent and message-dependent features.
3. Similarities and differences in spectrogram patterns can arise from any different sources and can be misleading.
4. Spectrograms are not the same as fingerprints, since speech patterns change over time, while fingerprints do not.

5. Research has yielded highly inconsistent results, depending on details of the methods used.
6. Success in a criminal trial depends on many factors and does not imply validity of spectrographic identification techniques.
7. Rigorous experiments simulating the conditions found in law-enforcement applications have not been made.

With this, the battle was joined. Tosi *et al.* (1972) reported an experiment in which examiners were screened and then trained for a month. Error rates ranged from 0.2 to 18 percent, but when examiners were permitted a "don't know" response, there was a false-alarm rate of 2 percent and a miss rate of 5 per cent. Black *et al.* (1973) published a rebuttal to Bolt, and Bolt *et al.* (1973) presented more arguments based on recent research.

At this writing, identification by visual inspection of spectrograms is regarded with suspicion by a large segment of the speech community, although the technique is still in use in some jurisdictions.

REFERENCES

Atal, B. S.: Automatic speaker recognition based on pitch contours, *JASA*, vol. 52, no. 6, pp. 1687–1697, December, 1972.

―――: Effectiveness of linear prediction characteristics of the speech wave for automatic speaker identification and verification, *JASA*, vol. 55, no. 6, pp. 1034–1312, June, 1974.

―――: Automatic recognition of speakers from their voices, *Proc. IEEE*, vol. 64, no. 4, pp. 460–475, April, 1976.

Black, J. W., *et al.*: Reply to "Speaker identification by speech spectrograms: a scientists' view of its reliability for legal purposes," *JASA*, vol. 54, no. 2, pp. 535–537, August, 1973.

Bolt, R. H., *et al.*: Speaker identification by speech spectrograms: a scientists' view of its reliability for legal purposes, *JASA*, vol. 47, no. 2, pp. 597–612, February, 1970.

―――, *et al.*: Speaker identification by speech spectrograms: some further observations, *JASA*, vol. 54, no. 2, pp. 531–534, August, 1973.

Cheung, R. S., and B. A. Eisenstein: Feature selection via dynamic programming for text-independent speaker identification, *IEEE Trans.*, vol. ASSP-26, no. 5, pp. 397–403, October, 1978.

Coleman, R. O.: Speaker identification in the absence of inter-subject differences in glottal source characteristics, *JASA*, vol. 53, no. 6, pp. 1741–1743, June, 1973.

Compton, A. J.: Effects of filtering and vocal duration upon the identification of speakers, aurally, *JASA*, vol. 35, no. 11, pp. 1748–1752, November, 1963.

Das, S. K., and W. S. Mohn: A scheme for speech processing in automatic speaker verification, *IEEE Trans.*, vol. AU-19, no. 1, pp. 32–43, March, 1971.

Doddington, G. R.: A computer method of speaker verification, Ph.D. Dissertation, Department of Electrical Engineering, University of Wisconsin, Madison, 1970.

Endres, W., *et al.*: Voice spectrograms as a function of age, voice disguise, and voice imitation, *IEEE Trans.*, vol. c-20, no. 9, pp. 972–978, September, 1971.

Fairbanks, G.: *Voice and Articulation Drillbook*, 2d ed., Harper and Row, New York, 1960.

Goldstein, U. G.: Speaker-identifying features based on formant tracks, *JASA*, vol. 59, no. 1, pp. 176–182, January, 1976.

Hazen, B.: Effects of differing phonetic contexts in spectrographic speaker identification, *JASA*, vol. 54, no. 3, pp. 650–660, September, 1973.

Hecker, M. H. L.: *Speaker Recognition: An Interpretive Survey of the Literature*, Am. Speech and Hearing Assoc. Monograph No. 6, 1971.

Hollien, H.: Peculiar case of "voiceprints," *JASA*, vol. 50, no. 1, pp. 210–213, July, 1974.

IEEE Subcommittee on Subjective Measurements: IEEE recommended practice for speech quality measurements, *IEEE Trans.*, vol. AU-17, no. 3, pp. 225–246, September, 1969.

Kersta, L. G.: Voiceprint identification, *Nature*, vol. 196, no. 4861, pp. 1253–1257, Dec. 29, 1962.

Li, K.-P., et al.: Experimental studies in speaker verification using an adaptive system, *JASA*, vol. 40, no. 5, pp. 966–978, May, 1966.

——— and G. W. Hughes: Talker differences as they appear in correlation matrices of continuous speech spectra, *JASA*, vol. 55, no. 4, pp. 833–837, April, 1974.

——— and E. H. Wrench, Jr.: An approach to text-independent speaker recognition with short utterances, *ICASSP-83*, pp. 555–558, 1983.

Luck, J. E.: Automatic speaker verification using cepstral measurements, *JASA*, vol. 46, pp. 1026–1032, 1969.

Lummis, R. C.: Speaker verification by computer using speech intensity for temporal registration, *IEEE Trans.*, vol. AU-21, no. 2, pp. 80–89, April, 1973.

Markel, J. D., et al.: Long-term feature averaging for speaker recognition, *IEEE Trans.*, vol. ASSP-25, no. 4, pp. 330-337, August, 1977.

——— and S. B. Davis: Text-independent speaker recognition from a large linguistically unconstrained time-spaced data base, *IEEE Trans.*, vol. ASSP-27, no. 1, pp. 74–82, February, 1979.

Pollack, I., et al.: On the identification of speakers by voice, *JASA*, vol. 26, no. 3, pp. 403–406, May, 1954.

Pfeifer, L. L.: Feature analysis for speaker identification, RADC-TR-77-277, Rome Air Development Center, August, 1977.

Pruzanzky, S.: Pattern-matching procedure for automatic talker recognition, *JASA*, vol. 35, no. 3, pp. 354–358, March, 1963.

——— and M. V. Mathews: Talker-recognition based on analysis of vairance, *JASA*, vol. 36, no. 11, pp. 2041–2047, November, 1964.

Rosenberg, A. E.: Listener performance in speaker verification tasks, *IEEE Trans.*, vol. AU-21, no. 3, pp. 221–225, June, 1973.

———: Automatic speaker verification: a review, *Proc. IEEE*, vol. 64, no. 4, pp. 475–487, April, 1976.

——— and M. R. Sambur: New techniques for automatic speaker verification, *IEEE Trans.*, vol. ASSP-23, no. 2, pp. 169–176, April, 1975.

Sambur, M. R.: Selection of acoustic features for speaker identification, *IEEE Trans.*, vol. ASSP-23, no. 2, pp. 176–182, April, 1975.

———: Speaker recognition using orthogonal linear prediction, *IEEE Trans.*, vol. ASSP-24, no. 4, pp. 283–289, August, 1976.

Schwartz, R., et al.: The application of probability density estimation to text-independent speaker identification, *ICASSP-82*, pp. 1649–1652, 1982.

Shridhar, M., et al.: Text-independent speaker recognition using orthogonal linear prediction, *ICASSP-81*, pp. 197–200, 1981.

———, et al.: A comparison of distance measures for text-independent speaker identification, *ICASSP-83*, pp. 559–562, 1983.

Stevens, K. N., et al.: Speaker authentication: a comparison of spectrographic and auditory presentations of speech material, *JASA*, vol. 44, no. 6, pp. 1596–1607, December, 1968.

Su, L.-S., et al.: Identification of speakers by use of nasal coarticulation, *JASA*, vol. 56, no. 6, pp. 1876–1882, December, 1974.

Tosi, O., et al.: Experiment on voice identification, *JASA*, vol. 51, no. 6, pp. 2030–2043, June, 1972.

Wakita, H.: Residual energy of linear prediction applied to vowel and speaker recognition, *IEEE Trans.*, vol. ASSP-24, no. 3, pp. 270–271, June, 1976.

Wolf, J. J.: Efficient acoustic parameters for speaker recognition, *JASA*, vol. 51, no. 6, pp. 2044–2056, June, 1972.

———, et al.: Further investigation of probabilistic methods for text-independent speaker identification, *ICASSP-83*, pp. 551–554, 1983.

Wrench, Jr., E. H.: A real time implementation of a text independent speaker recognition system, *ICASSP-81*, pp. 193–196, 1981.

Young, M. A., and R. A. Campbell: Effects of context on talker identification, *JASA*, vol. 42, no. 6, pp. 1250–1254, December, 1967.

CHAPTER THIRTEEN

ENHANCING NOISY SPEECH

The theory and applications we have explored in the preceding chapters have been developed, for the most part, using speech data acquired under near-ideal conditions. By far the majority of recognition and encoding schemes have been developed initially using speech recorded on high-fidelity equipment and, in particular, read in a quiet environment.

As long as speech research was "pure" research, these conditions, which greatly simplify most of our problems, were acceptable. As speech processing has moved from the laboratory to the field, however, it has become increasingly important to face the problems imposed by the presence of ambient noise. These problems can be formidable. It is a particularly unfortunate irony that linear prediction, probably the most powerful tool in the speech-processor's armamentarium, is especially susceptible to the degrading effects of noise (see, for example, Sambur and Jayant, 1976). If linear prediction is interpreted as a spectrum-matching process, then it can be seen that when significant amounts of noise distort the spectrum, the predictor will try to match the distorted spectrum rather than that of the underlying speech. When the same predictor is used at the receiving end of a vocoder system, the intelligibility of the synthesized speech is seriously degraded.

The types of noise of concern to us can be classified roughly as follows: (1) periodic noise; (2) impulsive noise; (3) wideband noise; (4) interfering speech. Periodic noise is characterized by a (possibly large) number of discrete, narrow spectral peaks. It arises most often from rotating machinery—e.g., automotive and aircraft engines—and from electrical interference, particularly 50- or 60-Hz hum. Impulses are usually the result of electrical discharges such as ignition noise. They can sometimes simply be removed from the time function by interpolation from adjacent samples, provided they are not too closely spaced. Wideband noise is usually assumed to be gaussian and white. Sources of wideband noise include wind, breath noise, and random sources in general, including, sometimes, jamming. Quantization noise can frequently be treated as white noise. After identifiable periodic components have been removed from the input signal, there is usually a residue that is treated as wideband noise. Interfering speech may arise from other voices picked up by the microphone or from crosstalk during transmission.

All of these noise sources are difficult to handle. Periodic components probably pose the fewest problems: they can be located by inspection of the power spectrum and can be removed by filtering or by transform techniques. The hum problem can be particularly severe, however, since the interfering components are almost never the fundamental itself, which is below the usual frequency range of voice signals, but rather its harmonics, which can overlay the entire audible spectrum with a picket fence of narrow spectral spikes. Wideband noise is a much more difficult problem. The most successful techniques developed so far make use of some form of nonlinear processing. Removal of interfering speech is probably the most difficult problem of all. Dramatic results have been demonstrated which process certain simplified cases, but the techniques used have not yet been successfully applied to the general multitalker problem, or even to the removal of unrestricted speech.

The principal application areas of speech enhancement are noise reduction for human listening, preprocessing for recognition systems, and preprocessing for linear predictive coding. In most cases, processing for one of these applications has also been used for the others, and we will not distinguish among these applications except as necessary.

13-1 PERIODIC NOISE

Periodic noise components can be removed by filtering, provided they can be estimated accurately and provided a filter can be devised which will remove the interference without producing side-effects which themselves interfere with speech intelligibility. We will consider three kinds of filtering: stationary filters, adaptive filters, and filtering by means of Fourier transform techniques.

Stationary Filters

These are usable only when the interfering components are also stationary. The most frequent case is that of 50- or 60-Hz hum. High-pass filtering to remove the 60-Hz component is of little use; the interference arises from the odd-order harmonics, especially the third through the seventh. (The famous Watergate buzz was a particularly severe 60-Hz hum, rich in harmonics, probably caused by an ungrounded connection to a microphone-level input jack.) Stationary filters can be used to remove these components, although when processing tape-recorded speech it may be necessary to control the playback speed to correct for any frequency errors caused by errors in the recording speed. Hollien and Fitzgerald (1977) give a good summary of the use of filtering for speech enhancement in general.

Banks of analog notch filters (such as the twin-T filter) can be used, but feedback techniques must be employed to make the notches narrow so that the spectral balance of the remaining signal is not disturbed. The performance of twin-T filters depends critically on balancing the components to produce a deep notch; it is usually necessary to include provision for adjustments, and the filters must be checked and rebalanced periodically. Such systems are cheap, however, and have been used successfully in forensic applications.

Notch filters can also be implemented using sampled-data techniques. Indeed, by a suitable choice of the delay length, a comb filter can be produced where the notches lie on all the harmonics of the hum. Such a system is shown in Fig. 13-1a. The delay element consists of T unit delays; hence the transfer function is

$$A(z) = 1 - z^{-T} \qquad (13\text{-}1)$$

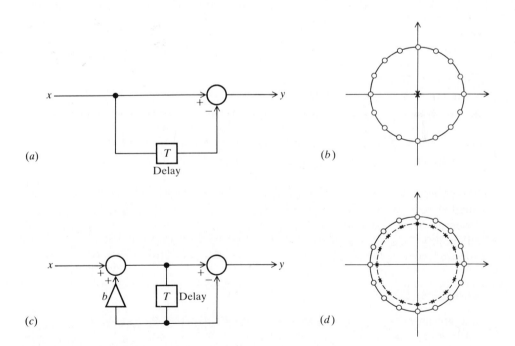

Figure 13-1 (a) A comb filter made from a delay and a subtractor. The delay time is made equal to the reciprocal of f_0, the spacing between the notches of the filter. (b) Poles and zeros of the filter in (a). (c) A comb filter with narrower notches obtained by means of feedback. (d) Poles and zeros of the filter in (c).

This results in T zeros equally spaced about the unit circle, as shown in Fig. 13-1b; there is also a pole of multiplicity T at the origin. By a suitable choice of T and sampling rate, the zeros can be made to coincide with the harmonics of the hum. If a feedback path is now added, as in Fig. 13-1c, the transfer function becomes

$$A(z) = \frac{1 - z^{-T}}{1 - bz^{-T}} \tag{13-2}$$

The feedback causes the poles to move out from the origin and approach the zeros as shown in Fig. 13-1d. When the poles are very close to the zeros, partial cancellation results everywhere about the unit circle except in a small neighborhood about each zero; hence the teeth of the comb can be made very narrow with a relatively flat response between them. If such a filter is implemented digitally, it can be made to track the hum frequency by phase-locking a subharmonic of the system clock to one of the hum components. This is useful if the speech has been tape-recorded on battery-operated equipment, which is often subject to speed fluctuations.

Adaptive Filtering

Adaptive filters work by automatically identifying the components they are supposed to remove. One way to do this (Sambur, 1979) is to recall that predictor coefficients form a filter whose frequency response approximates the inverse power spectrum of the input signal. Then if we apply the prediction algorithm to noise with strong periodic components, we will get a filter with transmission minima located at the frequencies of the periodic components. Thus the predictor is, in a sense, matched to the noise. If noisy speech is now passed through this predictor, the filtering action will attenuate the noise components. If the noise is stationary, or changes slowly, estimates can be obtained during nonspeech intervals and used to update the filter. The main problem with this technique is that the resulting filter frequently has a general spectral imbalance that colors the recovered speech and may interfere with the operation of a linear-prediction vocoder. Narrowing the notches by partial pole-zero cancellation, as described above, does not materially improve the performance of the system; some experiments have suggested that we can get improved rejection and less coloring by using a predictor of significantly higher order than that ordinarily used by LPC.

Transform Techniques

It is also possible to remove periodic components by direct manipulation of the spectrum (Weiss et al., 1974a). A block diagram of a transform filter is shown in Fig. 13-2a. The signal is applied to a DFT in order to provide access to the frequency domain. The input and output transformations are usually done using the overlapping-window technique described in Sec. 1-6, using either Hamming or Hanning weighting. In the frequency domain, peaks due to periodic signals are

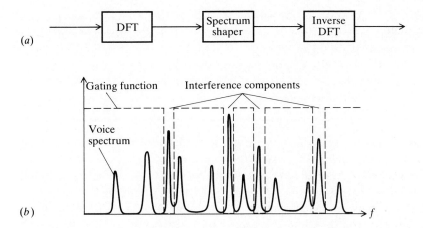

Figure 13-2 Removal of periodic interference by spectrum shaping. (*a*) Block diagram; (*b*) placement of rejection gates to remove interference components. (*Adapted from Weiss et al., 1974a; original © 1974, IEEE.*)

identified either by inspection or automatically. The spectrum shaper can be as simple as a series of gates, as shown in Fig. 13-2*b*. If the transform points corresponding to the interference components are set to zero, then the inverse transformation will yield a signal from which the periodic interference components are removed. Because of the burden of computing the Fourier transforms, these systems tend to be expensive, especially if they are to perform in real time.

13-2 WIDEBAND NOISE

When the interfering noise is white, the noise components appear throughout the spectrum and the filtering and spectrum-gating techniques of the preceding section are not applicable. The principal methods for reducing wideband noise fall into three categories: nonlinear processing, spectrum subtraction, and adaptive canceling.

Nonlinear Processing

The principal nonlinear processes involve clipping of the waveform or its transform. A number of researchers have used peak clipping as a way of better using the dynamic range of the transmission equipment; if large peaks are relatively infrequent, then they can be clipped without too great an impact on the quality of the resulting speech, and the general signal amplitude can be made larger without overload. Peak-clipped speech has been investigated by Hawley and Meeker (1955), Pollack and Pickett (1959), Ewing and Huddy (1966), and Fawe (1966, 1967). Thomas and Niederjohn (1968, 1970) used peak clipping in combination with filters designed to enhance the formant 2 frequency range. These investigations were all centered on getting the most out of limited-power transmitting equipment operating over a noisy channel, and hence do not constitute speech enhancement as we mean it here; however, Thomas and Ravindran (1974) tried using the Thomas-Niederjohn filtering and clipping process to enhance noisy speech and reported a 5 to 7 percent increase in the number of phonetically balanced words correctly recognized in signal-to-noise ratios ranging from 0 to 10 dB.

Several researchers have investigated center clipping as a speech-enhancement technique. If the noise is of lower amplitude than the speech, then removal of all low-amplitude material should remove the noise. We saw in Chapter 3 that center clipping of the time waveform is destructive to intelligibility; hence center clipping must be done in the frequency domain.

In an early example of this approach, Mitchell and Berkley (1970) used center clipping to reduce reverberation in speech; they employed a filter bank and center-clipped the output of each filter, then removed distortion products resulting from the clipping by passing the outputs through an identical filter bank before combining them.

Weiss et al. (1974a) applied center clipping to the Fourier transform. This technique was implemented using a system essentially the same as that in Fig. 13-2 in which the spectrum shaper was replaced by a center clipper. The time function was recovered by inverse transformation of the clipped signal. Spectrum clipping was also done by Jackson and Olinski (1974) using a nonlinear system based on parametric excitation of vibrational modes in a yttrium-iron-garnet crystal. Each vibrational mode acts as a narrowband filter, so that the crystal and its associated electronics function as a filter bank. The spacing of the modes is determined by the physical size of the crystal; if the spacing is close enough, the bandwidths of the modes overlap and the behavior of the system approaches that of the Fourier transform system of Weiss et al. The signal was applied as modulation of a 60-MHz carrier and the center clipping was provided by the nonlinear operation of the system, which passes high-amplitude components but not low-amplitude ones.

Spectrum Subtraction

Most current techniques for handling wideband noise are variants of an approach based on subtracting an estimate of the spectrum of the noise from that of the noisy speech (see, for example, Boll, 1979, and Berouti et al., 1979). If we assume that speech is a stationary signal and that the noise is additive and uncorrelated, then we can represent the noisy speech signal as

$$y(t) = s(t) + n(t) \qquad (13\text{-}3)$$

where s and n are the speech and noise components, respectively. If we represent the corresponding Fourier transforms by $Y(\omega)$, $S(\omega)$, and $N(\omega)$, then clearly the transforms are related by

$$Y(\omega) = S(\omega) + N(\omega) \qquad (13\text{-}4a)$$

and the power spectra by

$$|Y(\omega)|^2 = |S(\omega)|^2 + |N(\omega)|^2 \qquad (13\text{-}4b)$$

(Since the noise is assumed uncorrelated, there are no crossproducts.) If we can obtain a satisfactory estimate of $|N(\omega)|^2$, then $|S(\omega)|^2$ can be recovered simply by subtracting the N from Y. In practice, the noise is estimated by observing the signal at times when speech is known to be absent.

Speech is not stationary, however, and in practice we must work with short, windowed segments of signal. In this case, we can only write,

$$|Y_w(\omega)|^2 = |S_w(\omega)|^2 + |N_w(\omega)|^2 + S_w(\omega)N_w^*(\omega) + S_w^*(\omega)N_w(\omega) \qquad (13\text{-}5)$$

where the w subscripts indicate the windowed signal and the asterisks represent complex conjugates. We can estimate $|Y_w(\omega)|^2$ from the observed data; the remaining terms must be approximated by their expected values. If $n(t)$ and $s(t)$ are uncorrelated, then the expected values of the cross-spectra are zero and we are left with

$$|\hat{S}_w(\omega)|^2 = |Y_w(\omega)|^2 - \langle |N_w(\omega)|^2 \rangle \qquad (13\text{-}6)$$

where the hat, as usual, represents an estimate.

Since we are dealing with estimates, it will occasionally happen in practice that this difference goes negative. (Recall that a power spectrum must be everywhere nonnegative.) This problem is generally dealt with either by forcing negative values to zero or by changing their signs.

The power spectra are obtained by squaring the Fourier transforms of the signals. In order to recover the speech by inverse Fourier transformation, however, we also need the phase of $S_w(\omega)$. (We will write this as Ph $[S_w(\omega)]$.) This is customarily approximated by the phase of $Y_w(\omega)$. If we have

$$S_w(\omega) = |S_w(\omega)| \exp(j \text{ Ph } [Y_w(\omega)]) \qquad (13\text{-}7)$$

then the recovered speech is just the inverse Fourier transform of this estimate.

We can illustrate this process with the block diagram of Fig. 13-3. Here $\mathscr{F}$ and $\mathscr{F}^{-1}$ represent direct and inverse Fourier transformations, respectively, and $|\cdot|^2$ and $\sqrt{}$ represent taking the square and square root of the absolute value. If the noise is assumed white, then the estimated spectrum to be subtracted can be

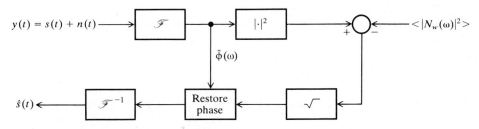

Figure 13-3 Attenuation of wideband noise by subtraction.

approximated by a constant. In this case, it is not difficult to show that spectral subtraction, where negative-going portions of the difference are forced to zero, is functionally the same as the center-clipping method of Weiss et al. (1974a).

Boll subtracted the magnitude spectra themselves instead of the power spectra, setting the output to zero whenever the magnitude difference went negative. This process can be viewed as a filtering operation; if the incoming spectrum is $Y(\omega)$ and the output is $S(\omega)$, then the filter transfer function is $S(\omega)/Y(\omega)$; this is

$$H(\omega) = \left(1 - \frac{\langle|N(\omega)|\rangle}{|Y(\omega)|}\right) - [1 + \text{sgn}\,(|Y(\omega)| - \langle|N(\omega)|\rangle)]$$

(Note that $0 \le H(\omega) \le 1$.) In an extension of this method, Boll (1979) modified $H(\omega)$ further as follows. In the absence of speech, $H(\omega)$ should be zero except for those (presumably infrequent) points where $N(\omega) > \langle|N(\omega)|\rangle$. These spikes give rise to residual noise in the recovered signal. From the statistics of $N(\omega)$, Boll showed that these spikes in $H(\omega)$ will have amplitudes less than 0.6 for 99 percent of the time; if such spikes are zeroed, then the residual noise will be removed 99 percent of the time. It would be desirable to extend this to speech as well, but unless special provisions are made, low-amplitude speech components will be removed as well. If $H(\omega)$ is examined during speech, however, low-amplitude frequency regions can be identified, over which the nonzero portions of H can be assumed to be due only to noise. Hence the 0.6 threshold can be used to eliminate noise spikes over these stretches, leaving the other regions of $H(\omega)$ undisturbed. Boll applied this technique to all such stretches of $H(\omega)$ above 800 Hz only, on the grounds that below this frequency narrow harmonics might also be lost, leading to degraded pitch detection. He also chose to attenuate the suspected spikes by 20 dB, rather than removing them altogether.

These subtraction techniques were shown by Lim and Oppenheim (1979) to be special cases of a technique developed by Weiss et al. (1974b). Their system is shown in Fig. 13-4. There are two features of interest here; first, the squaring operation is replaced by taking the nth root of the absolute value of the transform, where n is not necessarily an integer. Second, another transform is applied before subtracting the noise estimate. If the noise is white, then in the second transform it will appear as an impulse function at the origin. It should then be

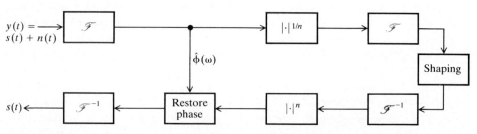

Figure 13-4 The noise-attenuation system of Weiss et al. (*Adapted from Weiss et al., 1974b.*)

sufficient to remove this impulse. Since the actual impulse corresponds to the mean of the rooted first transform, it will not do to remove the entire impulse; otherwise the first transform, on the return trip through the process, would go negative. Presumably the amplitude of the noise component could be estimated during nonspeech intervals, but Weiss et al. chose instead to remove the sidelobes of the impulse and, in a later modification, a fixed fraction of the impulse itself.

The value of n was chosen empirically. It can be shown (Weiss et al., 1974b) that, in the limit for large n, the mean of the noise samples in the first spectrum approaches 1 and the variance approaches 0. In practice, values of n ranging from 3 to 4 were found to yield improvements in the signal-to-noise ratio of the order of 6 dB.

There is indeed a perceptible increase in the S/N ratio and the speech sounds clearer, but detailed measurements by Lim (1978) have shown that the process actually degrades intelligibility as measured by recognition scores with human listeners. The same techniques, however, applied to noisy speech before LPC encoding, show an improvement in intelligibility. The use of spectral subtraction ameliorates the spectral distortion and hence helps the predictor to match the desired speech spectrum more closely.

Autocorrelation Subtraction

We saw in Chapter 2 that the power spectrum of a signal is the Fourier transform of its autocorrelation function; hence any process applied to the power spectrum should be applicable to the autocorrelation as well. This observation is the basis of enhancement by autocorrelation subtraction (Magill and Un, 1976; Un and Choi, 1981). The reasoning parallels that of spectral subtraction almost exactly: if the noisy speech signal is $y(t) = s(t) + n(t)$, then the autocorrelation function will be

$$R_{yy}(\tau) = R_{ss}(\tau) + R_{nn}(\tau) \tag{13-8}$$

As in the case of the power spectrum, the assumption that speech and noise are uncorrelated means that there are no crossproducts. If the noise is assumed white, then $R_{nn}(\tau)$ is an impulse function, and we have

$$R_{yy}(\tau) = R_{ss}(\tau) + \sigma_n^2 \delta(\tau) \tag{13-9}$$

Then the autocorrelation of the speech can be estimated by subtracting an estimate of the noise power from $R_{yy}(0)$. This approach is attractive because it does not require the expense of Fourier transform computation. Further, if the speech is to be encoded by linear prediction, the autocorrelation function is going to have to be computed in any case, so the added cost of using this technique is negligible.

The main problem with autocorrelation subtraction is that the estimate of σ_n^2 is uncertain, and subtracting the wrong amount may give a result which is no longer an autocorrelation function. It is not nearly as simple to detect this problem in the autocorrelation domain, where the test is nothing so simple as the nonnegativity requirement in spectral subtraction. Burg (1975) shows that a sequence r can be the beginning of an autocorrelation function if and only if the matrix $[r_{|i-j|}]$ is nonnegative-definite. It is also not apparent how the difference should be treated to correct this problem. One solution is to use an iterative technique in which increasing amounts are subtracted from $r_{yy}(0)$ and to use the largest estimate for which the autocorrelation matrix is still nonnegative-definite.

Adaptive Cancelation

In most speech-enhancement problems, only a single input is available for processing. If a separate estimate of the noise can be obtained, however, then this can be used to attenuate interference by means of a technique described by Widrow et al. (1975) and illustrated in Fig. 13-5. We assume that in addition to the noisy signal $x = s + n$, known as the primary signal, we have a second signal r, known as the reference signal, which is uncorrelated with s but correlated with n. For example, r may be a representation of n obtained through a channel which excludes s. Widrow's system attempts to remove n by filtering r to make it match n. The filter is an adaptive filter, and the idea is to enable the system to control the filter until y is as close an approximation to n as possible. To see how this can be done, consider the mean square output of the system:

$$\langle z^2 \rangle = \langle (s + n - y)^2 \rangle \tag{13-10}$$

Because n are r are uncorrelated with s, we can write this as

$$\langle z^2 \rangle = \langle s^2 \rangle + \langle (n - y)^2 \rangle \tag{13-11}$$

Note that $\langle s^2 \rangle$ is independent of the filter and that $\langle s^2 \rangle$ and $\langle (n-y)^2 \rangle$ are additive. The best approximation between y and n will be marked by a minimum in $\langle (n-y)^2 \rangle$ and hence in $\langle z^2 \rangle$. Hence we arrive at the surprisingly simple result: to get the best cancellation of the noise, adjust the filter so that $\langle z^2 \rangle$ is a minimum.

The filter can be determined as follows. Clearly, its output y is the convolution of the filter's impulse function with the input r:

$$y(n) = h(n) * r(n) \tag{13-12}$$

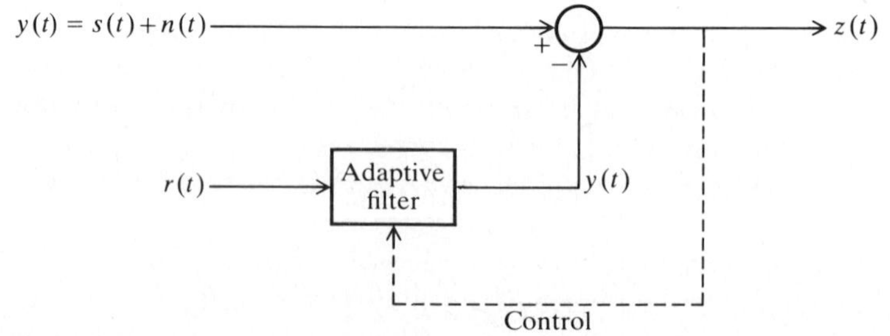

Figure 13-5 Adaptive noise cancellation. The adaptive filter attempts to match $y(t)$ and $n(t)$.

We wish to minimize $\langle z^2 \rangle = \langle (x - y)^2 \rangle$. Let us consider z to be the error in estimating x by means of r. Then by the orthogonality principle, the h which minimizes the error is that which makes the error orthogonal to all of r:

$$\langle z(n) r(n - k) \rangle = 0 \quad \text{for all } n$$

This is

$$\langle [x(n) - h(n) * r(n) r(n - k)] \rangle = 0$$

Expanding and interchanging the operations of convolution and expected value, we get

$$\langle x(n) r(n - k) \rangle - h(n) * \langle r(n) r(n - k) \rangle = 0$$

The first term is the cross-correlation of r and x; the second term is the autocorrelation of r; hence we have

$$h(k) * R_{rr}(k) = R_{rx}(k) \tag{13-13}$$

The required filter may turn out to be non-causal—i.e., to have an impulse response that is nonzero for negative t. The impulse response of these filters typically decays rapidly with increasing time, and hence it is practical to approximate them by filters whose impulse response is truncated beyond some limit and then delayed to render the filter realizable, as shown in Fig. 13-6.

This equation can be solved in a number of ways. Widrow et al. (1975) show that the error is a quadratic form over the filter weights. Then the filter can be adjusted by the method of steepest descent: i.e., by determining the derivative of the error with respect to each filter weight and adjusting the individual weights so that the new error will be smaller than the previous error. In time, the weights

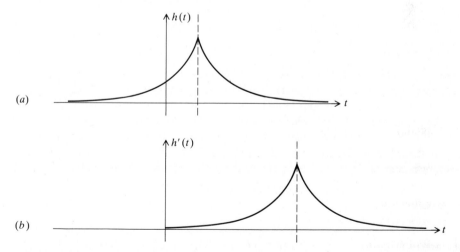

Figure 13-6 Noncausal impulse response in an adaptive filter. (a) Computed impulse response; (b) impulse response made realizable by delaying and truncating.

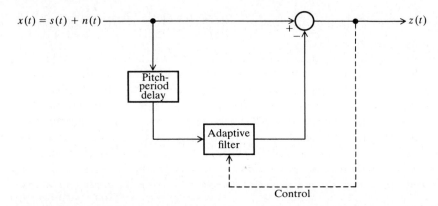

Figure 13-7 Adaptive filter for enhancing speech. Here the reference signal is the input speech delayed by one pitch period.

will converge to the optimum values. The computational requirements for this process increase linearly with the size of the filter, and in some cases (Boll and Pulsipher, 1980) the filter size may run to 1000 points or more. Boll (1980) addresses this problem by Fourier transform techniques. If we transform (13-13), we can obtain

$$H(n) = \frac{S_{rx}(n)}{S_{rr}(n)} \qquad (13\text{-}14)$$

These transforms are easy to obtain. If the transforms of $x(k)$ and $r(k)$ are $X(n)$ and $R(n)$, respectively, then $S_{rr}(n) = R(n)R^*(n)$, and $S_{rx}(n) = R(n)X^*(n)$, where the asterisks denote complex conjugates. Since the time functions must be windowed for Fourier transformation, special precautions are required to avoid errors introduced by the windowing process. This can be done using an extension of the overlapping-window technique outlined in Chapter 1; details are in Boll (1980) and Rabiner and Allen (1979).

This method clearly depends on having the reference signal, but in most speech-enhancement applications no such signal is available. Sambur (1978) attacked the problem by interchanging the roles of the speech and noise signals. He took advantage of the fact that the waveforms of successive pitch periods of voiced speech are highly correlated, while the noise in these two periods can be assumed to be uncorrelated. Hence if noisy speech is taken as the primary signal and the same signal delayed by one pitch period is taken as the reference signal, then the adaptive filter can be used to find the best estimate of the noise-free speech by minimizing the noise output, as shown in Fig. 13-7.

Other Adaptive Techniques

No one enhancement technique appears optimal for all kinds of speech. This consideration has led investigators on at least two occasions (Drucker, 1968; Boll and Wohlford, 1983) to consider adaptive systems which examine the incoming signal and select the appropriate processing technique according to the form of signal currently being received.

Drucker originally conceived of a set of five switchable filters, for stops, fricatives, glides, vowels, and nasals. The incoming speech would be segmented into phonemes by a preprocessor, and a decision device would examine each phoneme, determine its type, and direct the speech signal to the appropriate filter. The filters were to be designed to minimize the likelihood of confusion among the various types of speech sound. A set of intelligibility tests was used to determine which type of confusion was actually most likely; from these, Drucker found that the greatest intelligibility loss was due to confusion among fricatives and stops. Further tests indicated the /s/ phoneme produced the worst confusion among fricatives. On the strength of these results, the system as ultimately realized had three filters, one for stops, which operated in the time domain by reinserting the pause that marks the stop, a high-pass filter for enhancing the /s/ phoneme, and an 8-kHz low-pass filter for all other speech sounds. In the research, segmentation and decision were done by hand by a human operator; intelligibility, measured by the number of correct word identifications by a listener, was improved dramatically for low signal-to-noise levels.

Boll and Wohlford used three noise-removal techniques: plain spectral subtraction, spectral subtraction with residual noise removal (i.e., the modified technique described earlier), and adaptive comb filtering. Adaptive comb filtering and spectral subtraction were intended for vowels, and spectral subtraction with residual noise removal for nonvowel speech, comb filtering being reserved for vocalic speech with relatively high S/N ratios. Comb filtering was done in the Fourier transform domain, as in Weiss *et al.* (1974a), using pitch data obtained from a cepstrum. Performance was measured by the degree of phonemic separability in the processed speech as compared with noisy speech; in the processed speech the number of false acceptances was reduced from 75 to 25 percent.

Perceptual Techniques

A few investigators have explored techniques which enlist the aid of some aspect of the human perceptual apparatus. These techniques are for the most part empirical—none of them has produced striking enhancement—and yet the idea of enlisting the aid of the brain's own processing powers is very attractive.

Reynolds *et al.* (1961) attempted to enhance speech received from AM radio by separately demodulating the two sidebands and applying the two sidebands binaurally. They evaluated this process by recording the errors in recognizing phonetically balanced words and various signal-to-noise ratios. Their results suggested that the technique enhances speech, but only at S/N levels already above 10 dB; at low levels, it tended to degrade intelligibility.

Feldman (1963) investigated speech perception in the presence of a reference signal similar to that used by Widrow. Specifically, he found that intelligibility of noisy speech was improved if it was applied to one ear while the same noise, without speech, was applied to the other ear. The effect was enhanced if either the speech or the reference noise was delayed by a small amount, but no improvement at all was observed if the reference noise and the interfering noise were incoherent.

Feldman's observation that delaying the signal between the two ears improves intelligibility has been confirmed elsewhere. Gasaway (1972) also investigated binaural time delay as an enhancement technique. This paper describes apparatus with which the delay can be varied between 0 and 1500 ms; he reports improvement in intelligibility when one ear receives a delayed version of the noisy speech applied to the other ear.

Cox and Malah (1981) reported a system which used the masking behavior of the ear to reduce the perceived noise in speech. This system was based on compression and expansion of the spectrum of the noisy speech. By means of decimation and interpolation of the time signal, they were able to scale the spectrum; they found that when this was done with noisy periodic speech, successive compression and expansion of the spectrum moved the noise components closer to the pitch harmonics and hence improved the ability of the harmonics to mask the interfering noise.

Petersen and Boll (1981a, b) carried the spectrum subtraction process into the domain of human perception of sound. The resulting technique resembles conventional spectral subtraction, but differs from it in two important respects. First, instead of a conventional Fourier transform, they simulated the perception of the ear by a bank of bandpass filters shaped to reflect the response of the ear to masking tones. The bandwidths of these filters correspond to the critical bands found in studies of the phenomenon of masking and mentioned in Chapter 3. The other difference is that the noise component is not subtracted linearly. Instead, a computation is used which simulates, in each critical band, the masking function of the brain. The goal is, in effect, to do the masking for the brain and so relieve it of the necessity of doing so itself. In their process, the noisy speech is analyzed into critical bands, and then in each critical band the masking function of the brain is simulated. The processed outputs of the bands are then recombined to obtain the output speech signal. Finally, some researchers have found it helpful, in spectrum shaping or clipping techniques, to apply unprocessed speech to one ear while applying processed speech to the other.

13-3 INTERFERING SPEECH

Resolution of two or more voices in a conversation is done by human listeners as a matter of course; it is one of the perceptual powers built into the human speech-understanding mechanism. The ability to separate voices in this way is commonly known as the "cocktail-party effect," since it is the way in which we are able to concentrate on one voice to the exclusion of all others in a crowded room, as at a cocktail party. How the mind does this is not well understood, although it is easy to show that the process depends on having binaural input;

the reader need only cover one ear in a cocktail-party situation to hear all the voices merge into one unintelligible babble. Sayers and Cherry (1957) have found evidence that the process depends in part on cross-correlation of the binaural inputs. Artificial processing of speech to remove interfering speech becomes necessary chiefly when the voices are transmitted over a single channel in which binaural information is merged and lost.

The enhancement techniques outlined so far, with the exception of those which are based on perceptual phenomena, all depend on an inherent difference between the speech and the interference. In the case of interference from a competing voice, the differences are too subtle to be of any use; for practical purposes, there is no difference. Instead, voice-separation techniques depend mainly on differences in the pitch of voiced speech. If the two pitches can be determined, then the components belonging to either speaker can be identified and selected. This attack will succeed except when the speakers' pitches are either equal or are integer multiples; in normal speech such moments are rare. A more difficult problem is that this approach is usable only when both speakers are uttering periodic sounds—i.e., vocoids. Since such sounds constitute a large part of the acoustical speech signal, and since, as we have seen in Chapter 4, they also furnish important perceptual information about adjacent consonants, this restriction is not, in principle, a serious one.

The desired speaker's harmonics can be recovered in a number of ways. Shields (1970) and Frazier *et al.* (1976) used variable comb filters which passed the harmonics of the desired speaker's voice. They assumed that pitch information was already known and slaved the comb filters to the pitch measurements. Everton (1975) also assumed that pitch information was known; the process extracted formant information from the combined speech and used pitch and formant information to control a synthesizer which produced the output speech.

Another possible way to identify the harmonics is by inspection of the Fourier transform itself (Parsons, 1976). If a speaker's fundamental frequency is known, then it should, in principle, be possible to step through the spectrum from harmonic to harmonic and select only those belonging to the desired speaker. Then a new Fourier transform can be synthesized, containing only the desired components; when this is inverted, the output will be the desired voice. Overlapping, Hanning-weighted windows will yield a smooth, generally high-quality output.

The difficulty with this line of attack is that some harmonics from one speaker will inevitably overlap with those of the other, even if the fundamentals are different, and in these cases it is difficult to recover the parameters of the desired harmonic component. If the harmonic peaks do not overlap exactly, however, they can be separated provided a good estimate of one of the peaks can be subtracted from the composite. An estimate can be found by recognizing that the peak shape is the Fourier transform of the time window used and by assuming that the amplitude of each voice is essentially constant over the duration of the time window. This assumption is a good one if the separation process is applied to all-vocalic speech (i.e., speech consisting only of vocoids, e.g., "We were away a year ago"). The output of this peak-separation process is a set of peak tables; pitches of both speakers can be found from these tables quite reliably by an adaptation of Schroeder's histogram method.

With vocalic utterances, this technique yields dramatic results; the clarity is excellent and when the reconstructed speech is played back slowly (e.g., at one-eighth speed), individual pulses of the glottis can be discerned. When the process was applied to unrestricted speech, however, it fell apart. Peak separation by these means proved impossible, because the continual interruption of phonation by consonants and the often abrupt pitch changes invalidated the assumptions on which the separation technique was based. This in turn affected the pitch-extraction process, and the reconstructed speech was unacceptable and at times barely intelligible. This process involves a heavy computational burden as well, because of the repeated transforms and the detailed inspection of each transform, although if the peak-separation problem could be solved for unrestricted speech, the quality of the output might well justify the expense.

13-4 MEASURES OF INTELLIGIBILITY

As research in speech enhancement has advanced, it has become more important to provide an objective measure of the improvement obtained. Tests of speech intelligibility are based on the performance of human listeners and are in most cases descended from tests used by audiologists to measure hearing performance.

Most intelligibility measures are based on the responses of a jury of listeners. Typically, a list of words is transmitted through the channel under test and the output is played for the jury; the intelligibility measure is based on the number of correct identifications by the jury. Egan (1948) is a veritable "how-to" manual, containing the classic description of the design of tests of this sort; the word list must contain all the phonemes of the language in proportions close to their natural frequency of occurrence in speech. Monosyllabic nonsense words are the most sensitive indicators of the number of phonemes actually perceived correctly, since the listener cannot extrapolate from understood sounds to those not understood, but they may be difficult to pronounce and, unless a standard recording is used, may not be pronounced uniformly from experiment to experiment unless they are written phonetically.

The Articulation Index

This technique, introduced by French and Steinberg (1947), is of interest because it uses measurements of channel performance instead of a jury. It assumes that, in the absence of masking by high-energy speech components, every frequency band makes a contribution to intelligibility which is independent of all other bands, and that the S/N ratios over all bands can be summed to obtain an indication of intelligibility. French and Steinberg used 20 frequency bands, selected on the basis of tests, so that each band made an equal contribution of intelligibility. The bands were chosen empirically, but it can be no accident that they are most closely spaced over approximately the upper two-thirds of the formant 2 frequency range.

The procedure for computing the articulation index is given in detail in Kryter (1962a). Briefly, it consists of measuring the speech and noise spectra, and determining the S/N ratio for each band, making corrections for the masking effects of the noise and, where applicable, for reverberation. The resulting figures are summed over all the bands to obtain the index. Kryter also (1962b) reported a series of investigations of the masking effects of noise, using the articulation index; the results suggested that articulation index values could reproducibly be converted to equivalent scores based on methods similar to that of Egan.

Diagnostic Tests

If a communications system yields poor results in an intelligibility test, the designer's first concern is naturally to know why it failed. Hence tests which can shed light on this question are particularly useful, and there has long been an interest in designing tests which focus separately on different aspects of system performance.

One of the first tests of this sort is reported by Fairbanks (1958). This test concentrated on the ability to distinguish among consonants. Each test item was drawn from a list of five possible words, differing only in the initial consonants. For example, one such set was

$$\text{male} \quad \text{tale} \quad \text{sale} \quad \text{pale} \quad \text{bale}$$

In the test, one item from each set is read and the listener is asked to enter the correct first letter on a scoring sheet; thus, for the above set, the sheet would be marked, _ale. The test comprised 18 consonants, all the common ones in English except /ŋ/ and /ʒ/, which do not occur initially. The test does not appear to have been devised with a specific diagnostic purpose, but rather to focus on consonants generally as the principal information-bearing elements in speech, but in a final paragraph Fairbanks alludes to the possibility of diagnostic use of versions of the test using selected combinations of features.

Voiers's (1977) Diagnostic Rhyme Test (DRT) builds on the work of Fairbanks. The DRT uses pairs of words; each pair differs only in the initial consonant, and each consonant differs in only one parameter. Thus, for example, one DRT pair is bond/pond; the two vary in manner of articulation only, where the Fairbanks words sale/bale differ in point of articulation, manner of articulation, and voicing. The reader will recognize these as minimal pairs, but the difference goes beyond this. Each pair of parameters is intended to represent some minimal feature that can distinguish one consonant from another, and they are intended to measure the ability of the system under test (which, in clinical applications, may be a human being) to distinguish that feature.

For his features, Voiers went to the distinctive-feature sets of Jakobson *et al.* (1952) and of Miller and Nicely (1955). The DRT uses the following subset of distinctive features:

Voicing
Nasality
Sustention
Sibilance
Graveness
Compactness
Vowel-likeness

(Most of these terms will be recognized from the list given in Chapter 2. Sustention is generally equivalent to the discontinuous/continuant feature listed there, and sibilance to the strident/mellow feature; the glides and liquids /w/, /j/, /r/, and /l/ are vowel-like.) It will be recalled that the distinctive features were drawn up with acoustical observables in mind; hence they are particularly appropriate for a test intended to diagnose failings in preserving perceptually meaningful acoustical features. These features are represented by a total of 22 consonants, and for each item a consonant pair is chosen which differs only in a single feature; thus the consonants in the item bond/pond differ only in voicing.

Each test item consists of one word selected from each pair. The test is usually administered by recording the words and playing the recording to the listener, who has a list of the word-pairs at hand and is asked to identify which member of each pair has actually been uttered. In tests of speech communication systems (e.g., vocoders), the test items are passed through the system and the output played for a jury of eight to ten listeners. The results are corrected for guessing by subtracting the number of errors from the number of correct answers, and the results provide percentage scores for each of the features as well as an overall score obtained by averaging the individual feature scores. Since the test is based on the ability of the jury to recognize the consonants correctly, it has a direct bearing on intelligibility, and the designers of the system can use the diagnostic results to identify those parts of the process most in need of improvement.

REFERENCES

Berouti, M., *et al.*: Enhancement of speech corrupted by acoustic noise, *ICASSP-79*, pp. 208–211, 1979.

Boll, S. F.: Suppression of acoustic noise in speech using spectral subtraction, *IEEE Trans.*, vol. ASSP-27, no. 2, pp. 113–120, April, 1979.

———: Adaptive noise cancelling in speech using the short-time transform, *ICASSP-80*, pp. 692–695, 1980.

——— and D. C. Pulsipher: Suppression of acoustic noise in speech using two microphone adaptive noise cancellation, *IEEE Trans.*, vol. ASSP-29, no. 6, pp. 752–753, December, 1980.

——— and R. E. Wohlford: Event-driven speech enhancement, *ICASSP-83*, pp. 1152–1155, 1983.

Burg, J. P.: Maximum entropy spectral analysis, Ph.D. Dissertation, Stanford University, 1975.
Cox, R. V., and D. Malah: A technique for perceptually reducing periodically structured noise in speech, *ICASSP-81*, pp. 1089–1092, 1981.
Drucker, H.: Speech processing in a high ambient noise environment, *Trans. IEEE*, vol. AU-16, no. 2, pp. 165–168, June, 1968.
Egan, J. P.: Articulation testing methods, *Laryngoscope*, vol. 58, no. 9, pp. 955–981, 1948.
Everton, Sr., J. K.: The separation of the voice signals of simultaneous speakers, Ph.D. Thesis, Department of Computer Science, University of Utah, 1975.
Ewing, G. D., and N. W. Huddy, Jr.: RF clipping and filtering to improve the intelligibility of speech in noise, *IEEE Trans.*, vol. AU-14, no. 4, pp. 184–186, December, 1966.
Fairbanks, G.: Test of phonemic differentiation: the rhyme test, *JASA*, vol. 30, no. 7, pp. 596–600, 1958.
Fawe, A. L.: Interpretation of infinitely clipped speech properties, *IEEE Trans.*, vol. AU-14, no. 4, pp. 178–183, December, 1966.
———: A new approach to speech bandwidth reduction, *IEEE Trans.*, vol. AU-15, no. 1, pp. 37–39, March, 1967.
Feldman, H.: Untersuchungen uber das binaurale Horen unter Einwirkung von Storgerausch, *Arch. Ohren-usw. Heilkunde und Z. Hals-usw. Heilk.*, vol. 181, pp. 337–374, 1963; reprinted in *Translations of the Beltone Inst. for Hearing Research*, no. 18, July, 1965.
Frazier, R. H., et al.: Enhancement of speech by adaptive filtering, *ICASSP-76*, pp. 251–253, 1976.
French, N. R., and J. C. Steinberg: Factors governing the intelligibility of speech, *JASA*, vol. 19, no. 1, pp. 90–119, 1947.
Gasaway, D. C.: Development of binaural time-delay apparatus for improving intelligibility, *JASA*, vol. 51, no. 1, p. 120, January, 1972.
Greenwood, D. D.: Critical bandwidth and the frequency coordinates of the basilar membrane, *JASA*, vol. 33, pp. 1344–1356, 1961.
Hawley, M. E., and W. F. Meeker: Experiments in peak clipping a mixture of speech and noise, *JASA*, vol. 27, no. 5, p. 1000, 1955.
Hollien, H., and J. T. Fitzgerald: Speech enhancement techniques for crime lab use, *Proc. 1977 Int. Conf. on Crime Countermeasures, Science and Engineering*, pp. 21–29, July, 1977.
Jackson, D. R., and P. J. Olinski: Spectrum clipping, *IEEE Trans.*, vol. COM-22, no. 1, pp. 38–45, January, 1974.
Jakobson, R. C., et al.: *Preliminaries to Speech Analysis*, MIT Press, Cambridge, 1952.
Kryter, K. D.: Methods for the calculation and use of the articulation index, *JASA*, vol. 34, no. 11, pp. 1689–1697, November, 1962(a).
———: Validation of the articulation index, *JASA*, vol. 34, no. 11, pp. 1698–1702, November, 1962(b).
Lim, J. S.: Evaluation of a correlation subtraction method for enhancing speech degraded by additive white noise, *IEEE Trans.*, vol. ASSP-26, no. 5, pp. 471–472, October, 1978.
——— and A. V. Oppenheim: Enhancement and bandwidth compression of noisy speech, *Proc. IEEE*, vol. 67, no. 12, pp. 1586–1604, December, 1979.
Magill, D. T., and C. K. Un: Wide-band noise reduction of noisy speech, *JASA*, vol. 60, suppl. 1, p. s107, Fall, 1976.
Miller, G. A., and P. Nicely: An analysis of perceptual confusions among some English consonants, *JASA*, vol. 27, pp. 338–352, 1955.
Mitchell, O. M. M., and D. A. Berkley: Reduction of long-time reverberation by a center-clipping process, *JASA*, vol. 47, no. 1, p. 84, 1970.
Parsons, T. W.: Separation of simultaneous vocalic utterances of two talkers, Ph.D. Thesis, Department of Electrical Engineering, Polytech. Inst. of New York, 1975.
———: Separation of speech from interfering speech by means of harmonic selection, *JASA*, vol. 60, no. 4, pp. 911–918, October, 1976.
Petersen, T. L., and S. F. Boll: Acoustic noise suppression in the context of a perceptual model, *ICASSP-81*, pp. 1086–1088, 1981(a).
——— and ———: Critical band analysis-synthesis, *ICASSP-81*, pp. 773–775, 1981(b).

Pollack, I., and J. M. Pickett: Intelligibility of peak-clipped speech at high noise levels, *JASA*, vol. 31, no. 1, pp. 14–16, January, 1959.

Rabiner, L. R., and J. B. Allen: Short-time Fourier analysis techniques for system identification and power spectrum estimation, *IEEE Trans.*, vol. ASSP-27, no. 2, pp. 182–192, April, 1979.

Reynolds, A. J., et al.: A technique for improving the intelligibility of speech transmitted by amplitude modulation over noisy channels, *IRE Trans.*, vol. CS-9, no. 3, pp. 222–225, September, 1961.

Sambur, M. R.: Adaptive noise cancelling for speech signals, *IEEE Trans.*, vol. ASSP-26, no. 5, pp. 419–423, October, 1978.

———: A preprocessing filter for enhancing LPC analysis/synthesis of speech, *ICASSP-79*, pp. 971–974, 1979.

——— and N. S. Jayant: LPC analysis/synthesis from speech inputs containing quantizing noise or additive white noise, *IEEE Trans.*, vol. ASSP-24, no. 6, pp. 488–494, December, 1976.

Sayers, B. McA., and E. C. Cherry: Mechanism of binaural fusion in the hearing of speech, *JASA*, vol. 29, no. 9, pp. 973–987, September, 1957.

Shields, Jr., V. C.: Separation of added speech signals by digital comb filtering, S.M. Thesis, Department of Electrical Engineering, MIT, 1970.

Thomas, I. B., and R. J. Niederjohn: Enhancement of speech intelligibility at high noise levels by filtering and clipping, *JAES*, vol. 16, p. 412, June, 1968.

——— and ———: The intelligibility of filtered-clipped speech in noise, *JAES*, vol. 18, no. 3, pp. 299–303, June, 1970.

——— and A. Ravindran: Intelligibility enhancement of already noisy speech signals, *JAES*, vol. 22, no. 4, pp. 234–236, May, 1974.

Un, C. K., and K. Y. Choi: Improving LPC analysis of noisy speech by autocorrelation subtraction method, *ICASSP-81*, pp. 1082–1085, 1981.

Voiers, W. D.: Diagnostic evaluation of speech intelligibility, in M. Hawley (Ed.), *Speech Intelligibility and Speaker Recognition*, Benchmark papers in Acoustics, vol. 11, Dowden, Hutchinson, & Ross, Stroudsburg, pp. 374–387, 1977.

Weiss, M. R., et al.: Processing speech signals to attenuate interference, *IEEE Symp. Speech Recognition*, pp. 292–293, April, 1974(a).

———, et al.: Study and development of the INTEL technique for improving speech intelligibility, Nicolet Scientific Corp., Report NSC-F/4023, December, 1974(b).

Widrow, B., et al.: Adaptive noise cancelling: principles and applications, *Proc. IEEE*, vol. 63, no. 12, pp. 1695–1716, December, 1975.

APPENDIX A

THE ORTHOGONALITY PRINCIPLE

Problem Given m observations of a variable y and of a k-vector $\mathbf{x}$, we wish to estimate each observed y as a weighted sum of the elements of the corresponding $\mathbf{x}$. Let the ith observation be y_i and $x_{i1}, x_{i2}, \ldots, x_{ik}$ and let the weights be $a_1, a_2, \ldots, a_k$. Then the estimate for the ith observation is

$$\hat{y}_i = \sum_{j=1}^{k} a_j x_{ij}, \qquad i = 1, 2, \ldots, m$$

We assume that $m > k$. Then the error for the ith observation is

$$e_i = y_i - \hat{y}_i = y_i - \sum_{j=1}^{k} a_j x_{ij}$$

and we wish to find the weights $\{a\}$ to minimize $\sum_i |e|_i^2$.

Define the vectors $\mathbf{e} = [e_1, e_2, \ldots, e_m]^t$, $\mathbf{a} = [a_1, a_2, \ldots, a_k]^t$, and $\mathbf{y} = [y_1, y_2, \ldots, y_m]^t$, and let $\mathbf{X}$ be the m by k matrix, $[x_{ij}]$. Then

$$\mathbf{e} = \mathbf{y} - \mathbf{X}\mathbf{a}$$

and we want to minimize

$$|\mathbf{e}|^2 = \mathbf{e}^*\mathbf{e}$$

(* denotes the conjugate transpose throughout). We will show that the optimum weighting vector is the one that makes each error orthogonal to the observations x_i.

Theorem (a) The value of **a** that minimizes $|\mathbf{e}|^2$ satisfies

$$\mathbf{X}^*\mathbf{e} = \mathbf{X}^*(\mathbf{y} - \mathbf{X}\mathbf{a}) = \mathbf{0} \qquad (A\text{-}1)$$

(b) The resultant minimum is given by

$$|\mathbf{e}_{min}|^2 = \mathbf{e}^*\mathbf{y} \qquad (A\text{-}2)$$

PROOF Let a be such as to satisfy (A-1). Consider any other weighting vector **b**, and let **f** be its error, $\mathbf{y} - \mathbf{X}\mathbf{b}$. Then

$$\mathbf{f} = \mathbf{e} + \mathbf{X}(\mathbf{a} - \mathbf{b})$$

and
$$\begin{aligned}|\mathbf{f}|^2 &= |\mathbf{e} + \mathbf{X}(\mathbf{a} - \mathbf{b})|^2 \\ &= [\mathbf{e} + \mathbf{X}(\mathbf{a} - \mathbf{b})]^*[\mathbf{e} + \mathbf{X}(\mathbf{a} - \mathbf{b})] \\ &= \mathbf{e}^*\mathbf{e} + \mathbf{e}^*\mathbf{X}(\mathbf{a} - \mathbf{b}) + (\mathbf{a} - \mathbf{b})^*\mathbf{X}^*\mathbf{e} + [\mathbf{X}(\mathbf{a} - \mathbf{b})]^*[\mathbf{X}(\mathbf{a} - \mathbf{b})]\end{aligned}$$

The first term is $|\mathbf{e}|^2$; the second and third terms are zero by virtue of (A-1); and the last term is $|\mathbf{X}(\mathbf{a} - \mathbf{b})|^2$. Hence

$$|\mathbf{f}|^2 = |\mathbf{e}|^2 + |\mathbf{X}(\mathbf{a} - \mathbf{b})|^2$$
$$\geq |\mathbf{e}|^2$$

with equality only for $\mathbf{b} = \mathbf{a}$. This proves part (a). The resultant error is

$$\begin{aligned}|\mathbf{e}|^2 &= \mathbf{e}^*\mathbf{e} \\ &= \mathbf{e}^*(\mathbf{y} - \mathbf{X}\mathbf{a}) \\ &= \mathbf{e}^*\mathbf{y} - \mathbf{e}^*\mathbf{X}\mathbf{a}\end{aligned}$$

but by (A-1), $\mathbf{e}^*\mathbf{X} = \mathbf{0}$; hence part (b) follows.

Corollary The normal equations for a are

$$\mathbf{X}^*\mathbf{X}\mathbf{a} = \mathbf{X}^*\mathbf{y}$$

This is just a rewriting of (A-1).

If the observations and the error are orthogonal, then there is no more information to be extracted from the observations. If there were some systematic relation between one of the observations and the error, we could use that fact to make the error smaller, and hence the existing estimate would not be optimal.

Application to Linear Prediction

In the prediction problem, we wish to estimate the nth sample of a signal s from the preceding p samples. If we note the following correspondences, we can use the results given above to set up our normal equations. For the ith observation,

$$y_i = s(i)$$
$$x_{ij} = s(i - j)$$

Then the (i, j) element of the product $\mathbf{X^*X}$ is

$$\phi_{ij} = \sum_k s(k-i)s(k-j)$$

and the ith element of the product $\mathbf{X^*y}$ is

$$\phi_{0j} = \sum_k s(k-i)s(k)$$

These sums are the same as those in Eqs. (6-5) and (6-6) in the LPC section of the text, and their limits depend on the considerations outlined there. Indeed, if we rewrite (A-1) above as follows:

$$\mathbf{X^*y} - \mathbf{X^*Xa} = 0$$

this leads directly to (6-6).

The papers on linear prediction by Morf et al. (1977a, 1977b) take a development similar to the one given here as a starting point.

REFERENCES

Morf, M., et al.: A classification of algorithms for ARMA models and ladder realizations, *ICASSP-77*, IEEE Press, New York, pp. 13–19, 1977(a).

———, et al.: Efficient solution of covariance equations for linear prediction, *IEEE Trans.*, vol. ASSP-25, no. 5, pp. 429–433, October, 1977(b).

APPENDIX
B

PROGRAM LISTINGS

```
              subroutine FFT (logn, x, table, isign)
c     Radix-2 fast Fourier transform
c     Uses "decimation-in-frequency" form of Cooley-Tukey algorithm.
c     Direct transform is defined as having negative exponent in W.
c     Fortran-77 version by T. Parsons, Dec., 1980
c     Calling usage: Calling program must contain
c         complex x(n), table (n/2)       ! note relative array sizes
c             .
c             .
c             .
c         table (1) = (0., 0.)            ! force creation of table
c             .
c             .
c             .
c         call fft (logn, x, table, isign)
c     Variables
c         x       vector to be transformed
c         n       length of x
c         logn    log (base 2) of n
c         table   array for sin/cos tables
c         isign   option control
c                    if isign < 0, direct transform
c                    if isign > , inverse transform
c                    if |isign| = 1, division by n on inverse
c                    if |isign| = 2, division by n on direct
c     Sin/cos tables are generated as needed. Program looks to see
```

```
c           whether tables have been generated & bypasses generation if
c           it has been done.
c        Subroutines called:
c              bitrev   maktbl   ishft
c              (ishft(i, j) shifts argument i left by j bit-positions,
c              filling vacated bits with ∅s.   (Shifts right if j < ∅.)
c              Used as fast alternative to doubling, halving, & finding
c              powers of 2.)
         complex x(1), table(1), hold, w
         integer bitrev
         n = ishft(1, logn)           ! = 2**logn
c     Fill sin/cos tables if not already done
         if (table(1) .ne. (1., ∅.)) call maktbl (n, table)
         nsub = 1
         lsub = ishft(n, −1)          ! = n/2
c     Loop on iterations
         do 400 iter = 1, logn
            lim1 = 1
            lim2 = lsub
c     Loop on subtransforms within iteration
            do 300 isub = 1, nsub
               w = table(isub)
               if (isign .lt. ∅) w = conjg(w)
c     Loop within subtransform
               do 200 ix = lim1, lim2
                  jx = ix + lsub
                  hold = w*x(jx)           ! This is
                  x(jx) = x(ix) − hold     ! butterfly
200               x(ix) = x(ix) + hold     ! operation
               lim1 = jx + 1
300            lim2 = jx + lsub
            nsub = ishft(nsub, 1)     ! = nsub*2
400         lsub = ishft(lsub, −1)    ! = lsub/2
c     Permute out of bit-reversed order
         jx = ∅
         do 500 ix = 1, n
         kx = jx + 1
         if (kx .lt. (ix) then
            hold = x(kx)
            x(kx) = x(ix)
            x(ix) = hold
         end if
```

```
500         jx = bitrev(jx, n)
c     Divide through by n if required
            if (isign .eq. 1 .or. isign .eq. -2) then
                recn = 1./n
                do 600 i = 1, n
600                 x(i) = x(i)*recn
            end if
            return
            end


            subroutine MAKTBL (n, table)
c           Forms sin/cos tables in bit-reversed order for use
c           by FFT & RFFT.
c           Fortran-77 version by T. Parsons, Dec., 1980
c           Calls integer function BITREV
            parameter (pi = 3.14159265359)
            real table(1)
            integer bitrev

            factor = pi/n
            jx = 0
            do 50 i = 1, n, 2
                angle = factor*jx
                table(i) = cos(angle)
                table(i + 1) = sin(angle)
50              jx = bitrev(jx, n)
            return
            end


            integer function BITREV(ix, n)
c           Does bit-reversed addition: adds n/2 to ix & propagates
c           carries to right. Used by FFT, RFFT, & MAKTBL.
c           Fortran-77 version by T. Parsons, Dec., 1980
c           For integer function ishft, see comments in FFT.
            k = n
            j = ishft(k, -1)          ! j = k/2
            bitrev = ix
            do 20 jj = 1, 32
                bitrev = bitrev + j
c     Test for carry
                if (bitrev .lt. k) return
```

```
c     If carry, undo addition & add carry
            bitrev = bitrev − k
            k = j
            j = ishft(k, −1)        !  j = k/2
            if (j .eq. 0) return
20       continue
         end


         subroutine RFFT (logn, x, table, isign)
c     Computes DFT of an all-real vector using algorithm of
c     Cooley et al (J. Sound Vib., v 12, pp 315–337, July, 1970).
c     Adapted from a program by R. Singleton (IEEE Trans., v AU-17,
c     pp 93–103, June, 1969).
c     On direct transform, replaces real vector x with first half
c     of DFT of x (corresponding to positive frequencies). On
c     inverse, replaces complex vector x with real transform.
c     (Note details of packing of complex vector as given under
c     VARIABLES, below.)
c     Fortran-77 version by T. Parsons, Dec., 1980
c     Calling usage: Calling program must contain
c           real x(n), table(n)        !  note relative
c           complex y(n/2)             !     array sizes
c           equivalence (x, y)
c              .
c              .
c              .
c           table(1) = 0.              !  force creation of table
c              .
c              .
c              .
c           call rfft (logn, x, table, isign)
c     Variables
c        x         vector to be transformed. In time domain, x
c                  contains n real elements; in frequency domain, x
c                  contains (n/2 + 1) complex elements packed as
c                  implied by equivalence above, EXCEPT that d-c
c                  term is in x(1) & half-frequency term in x(2).
c                  (This is done to fit transform into same space &
c                  takes advantage of fact that these 2 terms are
c                  pure real.)
c        table     array for storage of sin/cos tables
c        n         length of x & table arrays
c        logn      log (base 2) of n
```

```
c          isign    option control; functions as in fft (q.v.)
c          Subroutines called
c             fft      bitrev    maktbl
           real x(1), table(1), im
           integer bitrev
           n = ishft(1, logn)              ! = 2**logn
           nh = n/2
           nk = n + 2
           nkh = nk/2
c    Form sin/cos table if not already formed
           if (table(1) .ne. 1.) call maktbl (n, table)
c    If direct transform, call fft
           if (isign .lt. 0) call fft (logn − 1, x, table, isign)
c    Take care of d-c & half-freq. terms outside loop
           hold = x(1)
           x(1) = hold + x(2)
           x(2) = hold − x(2)
           if (isign .gt. 0) then
              x(1) = .5 * x(1)
              x(2) = .5 * x(2)
           end if
c    Main loop
           jb = bitrev(0, nh)
              do 100 j = 3, nkh, 2
              k = nk − j
              aa = x(j) + x(k)
              ab = x(k) − x(j)
              ba = x(j + 1) + x(k + 1)
              bb = x(j + 1) − x(k + 1)
              jx = jb + jb
              cs = table(jx + 1)
              sn = table(jx + 2)
              if (isign .gt. 0) cs = −cs
              re = cs * ba + sn * ab
              im = cs * ab − sn * ba
              x(j) = .5 * (aa + re)
              x(k) = .5 * (aa − re)
              x(j + 1) = .5 * (im + bb)
              x(k + 1) = .5 * (im − bb)
100           jb = bitrev(jb, nh)
c    If inverse transform, call fft
           if (isign .gt. 0) call fft (log − 1, x, table, isign)
           return
           end
```

```
          subroutine LPCA (x, n, iorder, rc, a, r0, ierr)
c         Computes predictor coefficients & reflection coefficients
c         for an input time series x by "autocorrelation" method.
c         Forms autocorrelation vector & then solves the normal
c         equations using Levinson (Durbin) recursion.
c         Maximum predictor order is 15 (limited by dimension of R).
c         Fortran-77 version by T. Parsons, Dec., 1980
c         Variables
c            Inputs
c               x      input time series
c               n      length of x
c               iorder order of predictor
c            Outputs
c               a      predictor coefficients
c               rc     reflection coefficients
c               r0     power in x
c               ierr   outcome code
c                         0 – normal
c                         1 – zero power in input
c                         2 – prediction error power <= 0
c            Internal
c               r      array of autocorrelations
c               pe     prediction error
c               akk    most recent reflection coefficient
          real x(n), a(0:n), rc(n), r(0:15)
c   A. Compute autocorrelations
          do 40 i = 0, iorder
             sum = 0.
             do 20 k = 1, n – i
20              sum = sum + x(k) * x(k + i)
40           r(i) = sum
          r0 = r(0)
          if (r0 .eq. 0.) go to 200
c   B. Compute reflection coefficients & predictor coefficients
          pe = r0
          a(0) = 1.
          do 100 k = 1, iorder
c            --New reflection coefficient
             sum = 0.
             do 60 i = 1, k
60              sum = sum – a(k – i) * r(i)
             akk = sum/pe
             rc(k) = akk
```

```
c               -- New predictor coefficients
                    a(k) = akk
                    do 80 i = 1, k/2
                        ai = a(i)
                        aj = a(k - i)
                        a(i) = ai + akk * aj
80                      a(k - i) = aj + akk * ai
c               -- New prediction error
                    pe = pe * (1. - akk**2)
                    if (pe .le. 0.) go to 300
100             continue
                ierr = 0                  ! Normal return
                return
200             ierr = 1                  ! Zero-power return
                return
300             ierr = 2                  ! Nonpositive-prediction-
                return                    !    error   return
                end


                subroutine LPCB (x, n, iorder, rc, a, r, ierr)
c       Computes predictor coefficients, reflection (PARCOR) coef-
c       ficients, & autocorrelations by means of Burg's algorithm.
c       Maximum length of time series is 256 (limited by size of
c       PER & PEF arrays).
c       Fortran-77 version by T. Parsons, Dec., 1980
c       Ref.: J. P. Burg, Maximum Entropy Spectral Analysis, PhD
c       Thesis, Stanford University, 1975
c       Variables
c           Inputs
c               x       input time series
c               n       length of x
c               iorder  order of predictor
c           Outputs
c               a       predictor coefficients
c               rc      reflection coefficients
c               r       autocorrelations
c               ierr    outcome code
c                       0 - normal
c                       1 - zero power in time series
c                       2 - prediction-error power zero or negative
c           Internal
c               k       order of current recursive step
```

```
c          akk    most recent reflection coefficient
c          pe     prediction-error power
c          pef    forward prediction error
c          per    reverse prediction error
      real x(n), rc(iorder), a(0:iorder), r(0:iorder), pef(256),
     1     per(256)
c  Preliminaries
      sum = 0.
      do 20 i = 1, n            ! Find signal power
20       sum = sum + x(i)**2
      if (sum .eq. 0.) go to 300
      pe = sum
      r(0) = sum
      a(0) = 1.
c             * *** M A I N  L O O P  * ***
      do 200 k = 1, iorder

         if (k .eq. 1) then
c           --compute initial prediction errors
            do 40 i = 2, n
               pef(i) = x(i)
40             per(i) = x(i − 1)
         else
c           --compute updated prediction errors
            do 60 i = n, k + 1, −1
               pef(i) = pef(i) + akk * per(i)
60             per(i) = per(i − 1) + akk * pef(i − 1)
         end if
c  Compute new reflection coefficient
         sn = 0.
         sd = 0.
         do 80 i = k + 1, n
            sn = sn − pef(i) * per(i)
80          sd = sd + pef(i)**2 + per(i)**2
         akk = 2. * sn/sd
         rc(k) = akk
c  Compute new predictor coefficients (Levinson recursion)
         a(k) = akk
         do 100 i = 1, k/2
            ai = a(i)
            aj = a(k − i)
            a(i) = ai + akk * aj
100         a(k − i) = aj + akk * ai
```

```
c       Compute new autocorrelation estimate
                sum = 0.
                do 120 i = 1, k
120                 sum = sum - a(i) * r(k - i)
                r(k) = sum
c       Update prediction-error power
                pe = pe * (1. - akk**2)
                if (pe .le. 0.) go to 400
200             continue
                ierr = 0                    ! Normal return
                return
300             ierr = 1                    ! Zero-power error
                return
400             ierr = 2                    ! Nonpositive error-power
                return                      !       return
                end


                subroutine LPCC (x, n, iorder, rc, a, r0, ierr)
c       Computes predictor coefficients & generalized reflection
c       coefficients by "covariance" method. Forms covariance
c       matrix (C) from input, then solves the normal equations using
c       in-place LU (Cholesky) decomposition of the covariance
c       matrix.
c       Predictor computation replaces contents of C with packed
c       LU values.
c       Maximum predictor order is 13 (limited by size of C).
c       Fortran-77 version by T. Parsons, Dec., 1980
c       Variables
c           Inputs
c               x         input time series
c               n         length of x
c               iorder    predictor order
c           Outputs
c               rc        vector of generalized reflection coefficients
c               a         vector of predictor coefficients
c               r0        power in x
c               ierr      outcome code
c                           0 - normal
c                           1 - zero power in input
c                           2 - zero divide in computation
c           Internal
c               c         covariance matrix (augmented: rhs of normal
c                         equations is taken from first column of C)
```

```
              real x(n + iorder), rc(iorder), a(∅:iorder), c(∅:13, ∅:13)
              a(∅) = 1.
c     A. Compute covariance matrix (lower half only)
              iorl = iorder + 1
              ntot = n + iorder
              ntl = ntot + 1
              do 8∅ j = ∅, iorder
                  if (j .eq. ∅) then
c                 --Form first column
                      do 4∅ i = ∅, iorder
                          sum = ∅.
                          do 2∅ k = iorl, ntot
2∅                            sum = sum + x(k − i) * x(k)
4∅                        c(i, j) = sum
                      r∅ = c(∅, ∅)
                      if (r∅ .eq. ∅.) go to 3∅∅
                  else
c                 --Form remaining columns recursively
                      do 6∅ i = j, iorder
6∅                        c(i, j) = c(i − 1, j − 1) + x(iorl − i) * x(iorl − j)
     1                              − x(ntl − i) * x(ntl − j)
                  end if
8∅            continue
c     B. Compute generalized reflection coefficients & predictor
c                      coefficients
c         1. Decompose C into LU & find grc's
              do 18∅ i = 1, iorder
                  do 14∅ j = 1, i
                      do 12∅ k = 1, j − 1
12∅                       c(i, j) = c(i, j) − c(i, k) * c(k, j)
                      if (j .lt. i) c(j, i) = c(i, j)/c(j, j)
14∅               continue
                  if (c(i, i) .eq. ∅.) go to 4∅∅
                  sum = −c(i, ∅)                    !  rhs is negative
                  do 16∅ k = 1, i − 1
16∅                   sum = sum − rc(k) * c(i, k)
18∅           rc(i) = sum/c(i, i)
c         2. Find A from U & grc's
              do 22∅ i = iorder, 1, −1
                  sum = rc(i)
                  do 2∅∅ j = i + 1, iorder
```

```
200             sum = sum − c(i, j) * a(j)
220           a(i) = sum
              ierr = 0                  ! Normal return
              return
300           ierr = 1                  ! Zero-power return
              return
400           ierr = 2                  ! Divide-by-zero
              return                    !    return
              end

              subroutine LPCS (x, n, iorder, rc, a, r0, ierr)
c       Computes predictor coefficients & reflection coefficients
c       for an input time series X by "autocorrelation" method.
c       Forms autocorrelation vector & then solves the normal
c       equations using Schur's algorithm.
c       Maximum predictor order is 15 (limited by size of S).
c       Fortran-77 version by T. Parsons, April, 1981
c       Variables
c          Inputs
c             x        input time series
c             n        length of x
c             iorder   order of predictor
c          Outputs
c             a        predictor coefficients
c             rc       reflection coefficients
c             r0       power in x
c             ierr     outcome code
c                      0 − normal
c                      1 − zero power in input
c                      2 − prediction error power < 0
c          Internal
c             s        array of Schur variables (initially contains
c                          autocorrelations)
c             pe       prediction error
c             akk      most recent reflection coefficient
              real x(n), a(0: n), rc(n), s(−15: 15)
c    A. Compute autocorrelations
              do 40 i = 0, iorder
              sum = 0.
                  do 20 k = 1, n − i
20                sum = sum + x(k) * x(k + i)
              if (i .eq. 0) then
```

```
                r0 = sum
                if (r0 .eq. 0) go to 200
            end if
c           --Normalize to r0
            s(i) = sum/r0
40          s(-i) = s(i)
            pe = 1.
            a(0) = 1.
c   B. Compute reflection coefficients & predictor coefficients
            do 100 k = 1, iorder
c           --New reflection coefficient
            akk = -s(k)/s(0)
            rc(k) = akk
            pe = pe * (1. - akk**2)
            if (pe .le. 0.) go to 300
c               --Update S-array
                do 60 i = (k + 1)/2, iorder
                ai = s(k - i)
                s(k - i) = ai + akk * s(i)
60              s(i) = s(i) + akk * ai
            a(k) = akk
c               --Update predictor coefficients
                do 80 i = 1, k/2
                ai = a(i)
                aj = a(k - i)
                a(i) = ai + akk * aj
80              a(k - i) = aj + akk * ai
100         continue
            ierr = 0                ! Normal return
            return
200         ierr = 1                ! Zero-power return
            return
300         ierr = 2                ! Nonpositive-prediction-error
            return                  !      return
            end


            subroutine WARP (a, m, b, n, tcost, path, k)
*           Time-warping program
*           Implements DP time-warping procedure to align two
*               patterns, A & B. Returns resultant minimum cost &
*               the warping function (here called PATH). Stages
*               in DP process are samples of pattern A.
```

```
*           Maximum template length is 50 (limited by COST &
*              PRED arrays).
*           Fortran-77 version by T. Parsons, Jan., 1983
*           References:
*              Sakoe & Chiba, IEEE Trans., v. ASSP-26, no. 1,
*                 Feb., 1978
*              Myers et al., IEEE Trans., v. ASSP-28, no. 6,
*                 Dec., 1980
*           Variables
*             Inputs
*                a        first pattern
*                m        number of points in A
*                b        second pattern
*                n        number of points in B
*             Outputs
*                tcost    cost of optimum path
*                path     encoded optimum path
*                k        length of optimum path
*             Internal
*                cost     array of recent accrued costs (vide infra)
*                pred     array of predecessor points
*           To minimize storage requirements:
*             (a) Accrued costs are retained for only two most
*                 recent rows of points; at the end of a row,
*                 costs for row 2 (current row) replace costs
*                 for row 1 (previous row), which are no longer
*                 needed.
*             (b) Paths & predecessor-point coordinates are com-
*                 pressed into a single 16-bit integer by means
*                 of the function, PFUNC.
            real a(m), b(n), cost(2, 50)
            integer path(m + n − 1), pred(0:50, 0:50), pfunc
            parameter (HUGE = 1.0e37)
*           -- Define cost function
               cfunc(x, y) = (x − y)**2
*           -- Define path-encoding function
               pfunc(i, j) = 256*i + j
*     Clean up predecessor array
            do 20 i = 0, 50
               do 20 j = 0, 50
   20             pred(i, j) = 0
*     Loop through A
            do 100 i = 1, m
```

```
*           liml = max∅(1, i − 7)
            lim2 = min∅(M, i + 7)
*       Loop through B
            do 6∅ j = liml, lim2
*           −−Cost for this point
            c = cfunc(a(i), b(j))
*           −−Cost for path to this point
            if (i .eq. 1 .and. j .eq. 1) then
*               ...no predecessors
                cost(2, j) = c
                pred(i, j) = pfunc(1, 1)
            else
*               ...must consider 3 predecessors
                c1 = HUGE
                if (pred(i − 1, j) .gt. ∅)
1                   c1 = cost(1, j) + c
                c2 = HUGE
                if (pred(i − 1, j − 1) .gt. ∅)
1                   c2 = cost(1, j − 1) + c
                c3 = HUGE
                if (pred(i, j − 1) .gt. ∅)
1                   c3 = cost(2, j − 1) + c
*               −−Find cheapest
                if (c1 .ge. HUGE .and. c2 .ge. HUGE .and. c3 .gt. HUGE) then
                    pred(i, j) = ∅
                else if (c1 .lt. c2 .and. c1 .lt. c3) then
                    cost(2, j) = c1
                    pred(i, j) = pfunc(i − 1, j)
                else if (c2 .le. c1 .and. c2 .le. c3) then
                    cost(2, j) = c2
                    pred(i, j) = pfunc(i − 1, j − 1)
                else if (c3 .lt. c1 .and. c3 .lt. c2) then
                    cost(2, j) = c3
                    pred(i, j) = pfunc(i, j − 1)
                end if
            end if
6∅      continue

*       −−Shift costs down
            do 9∅ j = lim1, lim2
9∅          cost(1, j) = cost(2, j)

1∅∅     continue

*       −−Note total cost
            tcost = cost(2, n)
```

```
*         --Work backward from final point to find path
          kk = pfunc(m, n)
          k = m + n - 1
          do 200 k = m + n - 1, 1, -1
              path(k) = kk
*             --Decode kk
              i = kk/256
              j = mod(kk, 256)
              if (i .eq. 1 .and. j .eq. 1) go to 210
*             --Find next predecessor
              kk = pred(i, j)
200       continue
*         --Shift path down to start of array
210       ii = k - 1
          k = m + n - k
          if (ii .gt. 0) then
              do 300 i = 1, k
300               path(i) = path(i + ii)
          end if
          return
          end
```

INDEX

Abdominal breathing, 60
Abdominal musculature, 60
Abate, J. E., 245, 260
Absolute magnitude-difference function (AMDF), 202f, 209
Abut, H., 269, 271, 274f, 288
Acoustic characteristics of nasals, 117ff
Acoustic characteristics of stops and fricatives, 119ff
Acoustic characteristics of vowels, 106ff
Acoustic ohms, 108
Acoustic phonetics, 59, 66, 84, 100f, 103
Acoustic reflex, 68
Acoustical analysis, 76
Acoustical filtering, 66
Acoustical variables, 291
Acoustics:
   of a cylindrical tube, 106ff
   of the vocal tract, 103ff
   of vocoids, 106ff
A/d and d/a conversion, 334
Adam's apple, 61
Adaptive cancellation, 354ff
Adaptive comb filtering, 357
Adaptive delta modulation, 245f
Adaptive filtering, 199ff, 348, 346
Adaptive prediction, 234ff
Adaptive quantization, 230, 234
Add-on method, 181, 188, 337
Admittance, 108

ADPCM, 234
Advanced research projects agency (ARPA), 86, 326
   (*See also* ARPA)
Affixation, 287
Affricate, 66, 87
Agglomeration, clustering by, 190f
Agrawala, A. K., 193
Ahmed, N., 258, 260
Ainsworth, W. A., 81
Aliasing, 5f, 256
All-pole filter, 153
All-pole model, 137
   stability of, 151f
All-zero model, 137
Allen, J., 286ff
Allen, J. B., 41, 356, 364
Allophones, 94, 117, 128, 281, 292
Alveolar ridge, 63
Alveolar/dental noise, 120
Ambiguity of acoustical variables, 291
AMDF, 202f, 209, 267f
   applied to LPC residual, 203
Analog-to-digital (a/d) conversion, 5, 225ff
Analysis:
   acoustical, 76
   articulatory, 76
   bottom-up, 77
   left-to-right, 77
Analysis bandwidth, 164

INDEX

Analysis by synthesis, 76, 211, 243, 325
Analysis of the cylindrical model of the vocal tract, 109ff
Anderson, T. W., 56
Andrews, D. R., 176, 192
Anti-aliasing filter, 6, 226, 264
Anvil, 67
Apicoalveolar, 87
Apicodental, 87
Apicodomal, 87
Apicogingival, 87
AR model, 137
ARMA model, 138
Area functions, 318
Arithmetic:
 fixed-point, 160f
 floating-point, 160f
ARPA, 86, 326
 speech-understanding project, 326
ARPAbet, 85f, 286
Articulation:
 manner of, 361
 point of, 361
Articulation index, 360f
Articulatory analysis, 76
Articulatory gestures, 308
Articulatory locus, 282f
Articulatory phonetics, 59, 66, 84
Artificial intelligence, 326
Arytenoid cartilages, 61, 64
Aschkenasy, E., 205f, 222
Aspirated, 87
Associativity, of convolution, 9
Atal, B. S., 134, 159, 166, 168, 192, 200, 202, 209, 222, 235, 238ff, 242f, 249, 260f, 263, 337, 343
Auditory cortex, 71
Auditory system, perception capabilities, 71f
Authentication errors, 333
Autocorrelation equations, 141ff, 149
Autocorrelation function, 197ff, 353
 of speech, 126f
Autocorrelation, long-term averaged estimates, 126, 128
Autocorrelation matching, 147ff, 152
Autocorrelation matrix, 271
 nonnegative-definite, 354
Autocorrelation method, 140f
 details, 165
Autocorrelation, modified, 199ff
Autocorrelation of speech samples, 234
Autocorrelation predictors, 213
Autocorrelation subtraction, 353f
Autocorrelation vocoder, 264f

Autocorrelations, 148
 Burg, 162
Automata, 309
Autoregressive model, 137
Autoregressive moving-average model, 138
Axioms of probability, 43

Babble, 326
Backward predictor, recurrence relations, 146
Bahl, L. R., 307, 318, 325, 328
Baker, J. K., 307f, 318, 328
Ball, G. H., 190, 192
Bands, critical, 358
Bandwidth:
 analysis, 164
 formant, 114, 213, 218f
 telephone, 226
Barney, H. L., 135, 305
Barnwell, T. P. III, 168, 267, 290
Baseband, 249, 265f
Baseband vocoder, 266
Basilar membrane, 68f
Baum, L. E., 315, 328
Bayes, T., 43, 172, 295, 341
Bayes' theorem, 43, 171
Bayesian classifiers, 341
Bayesian recognition, 295
Beddoes, M. P., 260
Beek, B., 328
Békésy, G. von, 68, 81
Bell, C. G., 211, 222
Beranek, L., 81
Berkley, D. A., 350
Bernoulli, D., 64
Bernoulli effect, 64
Bernstein, S. N., 253
Berouti, M., 238, 241, 261, 266, 289, 350, 362
Best-first search, 327
Bilabial, 87
Binaural inputs, 292
 cross-correlation of, 359
Binaural techniques, 357f
Binaural time delay as an enhancement technique, 358
Bit assignments, 255
 adaptive, 255
Bit rate, 225, 257, 267
Black box, 3
Black, J. W., 343
Blackboard, 327
Blade, 64
Blends, formant, 210, 214f
Block diagram, 7
Block-floating-point arithmetic, 267

Bloomfield, L., 99
Bogert, D. P., 203, 223
Boll, S. F., 350, 352, 356ff, 362f
Bolt, R. H., 342f
Bottom-up analysis, 77f
Boundaries:
  between phones, 128
  syllable, 65
Boxcar, 226
Bracewell, R., 41
Brain, left hemisphere of, 75
Brantingham, L., 289
Breath noise, 295f, 346
Breath-groups, 60
Breathing, 60
Bricker, P. D., 193
Bridle, J. S., 317, 328
Bronchi, 61
Brosnahan, L. F., 86, 96, 99
Brown Corpus, 287
Brown, M. K., 303, 328
Buck, J. T., 329
Burg, J. P., 142, 161ff, 168, 354, 362, 374
Burg's method, 161ff
Burton, D. K., 329, 330
Buzo, A. A., 174, 269, 271f, 274ff, 289

Call-interception systems, 225
Campanella, S. J., 258, 260
Campbell, R. A., 342, 344
Canal, external, 67
  resonant frequencies, 67
Cancellation, adaptive, 354ff
Cardinal vowels, 89
Carelessness in speaking, 291f
Cartilage, cricoid, 61
Cartilage, thyroid, 61
Cartilages, arytenoid, 61, 64
Categorical perception, 75f
Categories, syntactic, 322f
Cavity, nasal, 62f, 64
Cavity, oral, 62
Cell-centered, 25f, 30ff
Cent, 73
Center clipping, 80, 200ff, 209, 229, 350
Central limit theorem, 48f
Central processor, 75
Centro-domal, 87
Centroid, 271
Centroids, 294
Cepstral coefficients, 318, 340
Cepstrum, 203ff, 209, 211f, 357
  with additive noise, 204
  with noiseless speech, 204

Certain event, 43
Chandra, S., 168
Channel vocoder, 226, 246ff, 262, 336
Characteristic impedance, 107f
Characteristic roots, 183
Characteristic vectors, 183
Checked/unchecked distinctive feature, 95
Chen, W., 260
Cherry, E. C., 81, 123, 134, 359, 364
Chest tone, 65
Cheung, R. S., 182, 193, 340, 343
Chiba, C., 297, 301f, 330
Chien, Y. T., 193
Chirp-Z transform, 214f
Choi, K. Y., 353, 364
Cholesky decomposition, 156f, 235, 267, 376
Chomsky, N., 76, 82, 95, 99, 288, 323f, 329
Christensen, R. L., 218, 222f
Christiansen, R. W., 318, 329
Chu, T. K., 260
Churcher, B. G., 71, 81
Ciarcia, S., 280, 289
Class, F., 331
Classes, 171
Classifiers, bayesian, 341
Clipping, 79f, 349f
  center, 200ff, 350
  peak, 349f
Close phonetic transcription, 84
Clustering, 188ff, 271
  by agglomeration, 190f
  by farthest-neighbor rule, 190
  by k-means algorithm, 189f, 338
  by re-classification, 189
  templates, 305
Coarticulation, 92, 130, 284, 292f, 341f
Cochlea, 68
Cochlear nucleus, 71
Cocktail-party effect, 358
Codebook, 188, 269
Codebook entries, 294
Codebook formation, 274f
Codebook search time, 275ff
Codebook, tree-searched, 276f
Coders, waveform, 278
Coding, entropy, 241
Coding, transform, 257ff
Coefficients:
  filter, 154
  generalized reflection, 235
  PARCOR, 161f
  predictor, 137ff, 235, 264f, 304, 306, 348
  reflection, 144, 158f, 234f, 265, 280, 306
Coker, C. H., 282f, 289

Cole, R. A., 77, 81, 102
Coleman, R. O., 343
Colliculus, inferior, 71
Comb filters, 202f, 347, 359
  adaptive, 357
Commutativity, of convolution, 9
Compactness, 362
Compact/diffuse distinctive feature, 95
Compandor, 229
Complementary distribution, 94
Complex roots, finding, 151, 212f
Compression, 64, 66, 225, 280
Compton, A. J., 343
Computer simulation, 19f
Conditional probabilities, 43, 171
Connected-word recognition, 319
  grammatical constraints in, 324
Consonantal vocoids, 87
Consonantal/non-consonantal distinctive feature, 95
Consonants, 65f, 86, 106, 293
  nasal, 117ff
Constriction in the vocal tract, 87
Context, influence on perception, 76
Context-dependent grammars, 323
Context-free grammars, 323
Continuous Fourier transforms, 13
Continuous speech recognition, 318ff
  grammatical models in, 324f
Continuous system, 4f
Contoids, 86f, 106, 125
Contour, 214f
Conversion:
  a/d and d/a, 334
  analog-to-digital, 225ff
  digital-to-analog, 226, 278
Convolution, 9f, 37ff, 49, 138
  time-reversal property, 53
Cooley, J. W., 368
Cooper, F. S., 121, 134
Coordinate system,
  rotation of, 179, 183f
  scaling of, 179
Correlation, 48, 174
Correlation between speech samples, 231
Correlation coefficient, 48
Correlation matrix, 336
Correlations:
  among features, 181
  removal of, 182ff
Cortex, auditory, 71
Corti, A., organ of, 68f
Cosine transform, discrete, 258
Cost function, warping, 299

Coulter, D. C., 216ff, 222f, 329
Covariance, 48
Covariance equations, solution of, 156ff
Covariance linear predictor, 267
Covariance matrix, 50, 172ff, 178f, 257f, 268
  interclass, 178
  intraclass, 178
Covariance matrix of predictor coefficients, 339
Covariance method, 140f, 151
  details, 166f
Covariance predictors, 213
Cox, R. V., 258, 363
Cricoid cartilage, 61
Critical bands, 74, 358
Crochiere, R. E., 255, 256, 259ff, 290
Cross spectral density, 52
Cross-correlation, 52
  of binaural inputs, 359
Crosstalk, 346
Crout reduction, 156f
Cubing, 202
Cuperman, V., 289
CVSD, 245f
Cylindrical model of the vocal tract, 109ff
Cylindrical tube, acoustics of, 106ff

Dadson, R. S., 71, 82
Das, S. K., 297, 329, 336f, 343
Data links, 225
Data preparation, 34
Data-reduction pitch estimator, 208f
Dautrich, B. A., 294, 329
Davenport, W. B., 134
David, E. E., Jr, 249, 260
Davis, S. B., 341, 344
DCT, 258
Deaf, spectrograms as aid to, 102
Decision rule, 171
Decision thresholds, 187
Deconvolution, blind, 138
Deflation, 212
Degradation, resistance to, 225
Delattre, P. C., 81, 134
Delta modulation, 244ff
  continuously-variable-slope, 245f
  optimum step size, 245
Demisyllables, 284ff
Denes, P. B., 82, 99
Density function:
  gamma, 125f
  gaussian, 46, 125f, 182f
    multivariate, 172, 184
  laplacian, 125f
Detection, synchronous quadrature, 252f

Determinant, 184f
DFILT (program), 21
DFT, 163f, 258
DFT spectrum, 293
Diagnostic rhyme test, 96, 361f
Diagonalization, 183, 258
Diaphragm, 60
Difference equations, 7, 137
Differencing, 167
Differential PCM, 231ff
Differential quantization, 231ff
Digit recognition, talker-independent, 304f
Digital data links, 225
Digital filter, direct form, 269, 279
    FIR, 256
Digital-to-analog conversion, 5, 226, 278
Digitization, 5
    for linear prediction, 167
Dijkstra, E. W., 325, 329
Dimensionality reduction, 187
Diphones, 284ff
Diphthongs, 91, 337
Direct form, 20
    digital filter, 269, 279
Discontinuities, 221f
Discontinuous/continuous distinctive feature, 95
Discrete Fourier transform (DFT), 13, 21ff
    direct, 21
    inverse, 21
    domains, circularity, 22
    elementary properties, 26ff
    of elementary functions, 25f
Discrete random functions, 50
Discrete random variables, 44, 47
    joint moments of, 47f
Discrete cosine transform, 258
Discrete-time system, 4f
Discriminant analysis, 185ff, 341
Disruptions, effect on intelligibility, 81
Distance, 270
Distance measures, 172ff, 333
    characteristics, 173
    euclidean, 271
    LPC-based, 174f
    simplified, 173ff
Distance, euclidean, 173f, 270, 338
Distance, Mahalanobis, 173, 271, 341
Distance, normalized euclidean, 174, 337
Distance, weighted euclidean, 174
Distinction between speech and nonspeech sounds, 75
Distinctive features, 76, 90, 94ff, 283, 362
Distortion, 267
    effect on intelligibility, 78
    measure of, 270f
    slope overload, 245
Distortion of spectrum by noise, 345
Distributed-parameter system, 4
    vocal tract as, 109
Dither, 228f
Divergence, 180
Dixon, N. R., 284, 289, 295, 321, 328f
Doddington, G. R., 337, 343
Dorso-velar, 87
Down-sampling, 6
DP normalization, 299, 337
DPCM, 231ff
DPCM, adaptive, 234
DRT, 361f
Drucker, H., 356f, 363
Dubnowski, J. J., 201, 209, 223
Duda, R. O., 173, 188, 193, 316, 329
Dudley, H., 100, 134, 246, 260
Dunn, H. K., 134
Durbin, J., recursion, 142ff, 157, 373
Dyadic synthesizer, 284f
Dyads, 284ff
Dynamic programming, 181f, 188, 299f, 313, 316f
    feature selection by, 340
Dynamic time warping, 299, 337

Ear:
    inner, 67
    middle, 67
    outer, 67
Ear-training, 84
Eardrum, 67
Editing, interactive, 281
Egan, J. P., 360, 363
Eigenvalue problem, 183
Eigenvalues, 183, 338
Eigenvectors, 183, 258
Eisenstein, B. A., 182, 193, 340, 343
Electrical interference, 345
Electrical transmission line, 106
Elementary functions, discrete Fourier transforms of, 25f
Elovitz, H. S., 286f, 289
Encoded voice, quality, 248
Encoders:
    linear-prediction, 272ff
    multiple-rate, 248
    multiple-stage, 277
    multipulse, 243f
Encoding reflection coefficients, 159
Encoding speech, 159
Encoding, variable-rate, 267
Encryption, 225

Endpoint detection, 293, 295ff
Endpoint errors, 295
Endres, W., 333, 343
Energy loss within the vocal tract, 114
Enhancement, speech, 59, 345ff
  by binaural time delay, 358
Ensemble, 50
Ensemble average, 51, 336f
Entropy, 269
  maximum, 162
Entropy coding, 241
Envelope, spectrum, 203, 210
Epiglottis, 62f
Equations, autocorrelation, 149
Erf, 47
Ergodic process, 51
Error:
  endpoint, 295
  forward prediction, 147
  mean-squared, 139
  minimum, 139
  minimum prediction, 152
  omission, 325
  prediction, 157f
  recurrence relations among, 147
  reverse prediction, 147
  Z transforms of, 147
Error function, 47
Error measure, Itakura, 270
  Itakura-saito, 270
Esteban, D., 256, 260
Euclidean distance, 173f, 270f, 338
  normalized, 174
  weighted, 174
Eustachian tube, 67
Event, 42
  certain, 43
  impossible, 43
Events:
  independent, 43f
  mutually exclusive, 43
Everton, J. K., Sr, 359, 363
Ewing, G. D., 349
Excitation, 64ff, 263
Excitation and modulation, 262
Excitation source for speech, 62
Excitation, voice, 249f, 265f
Excitation-modulation model, 203ff
Expected value, 45
Expected-value operations, interchangeability with linear operations, 53
Experiment, 42
External auditory meatus, 67, 71
External canal, 67, 71

F-ratio, 177, 187, 335f
  generalization of, 178f
Fairbanks, G., 334, 343, 361, 363
False acceptances, 333
Falsetto, 65
Fant, C. G. M., 73, 76, 82, 94f, 99, 106, 124, 135
Fawe, A. L., 349, 363
Farthest-neighbor rule, 190
Fast Fourier transform, 25, 102
  pruning of, 164
Feature correlations, 181
Feature evaluation, 171, 176ff
Feature ranking, 181
Feature selection, 171, 175ff
  criteria, 175f
  for speaker recognition, 332, 335ff
  mechanization of, 176
Feature space, 171, 180
Feature statistics, 171
Feature vectors, 171f
Features:
  correlated, 181
  distinctive, 283, 362
  in speech recognition, 293f
  prosodic, 285, 287f
  recognition, 170
  uncorrelated, 173, 177
  variances of, 182f
Feedback, 19
Feedback techniques, 347
Feldman, H., 357, 363
Feller, W., 56
Feucht, D., 193
FFT, 25, 102
  pruning of, 164
Filter:
  all-pole, 153
  anti-aliasing, 6, 226, 264
  comb, 202f, 347
  IIR, 153
  inverse, 150
  lattice, 265, 278, 280
  non-causal, 355
  prediction error, 150
  predictor-coefficient-controlled, 152ff
  reflection-coefficient-controlled, 152ff
  twin-T, 347
  vocal-tract, 150
Filter banks, 294, 336f
  formant estimation from, 210f
Filter coefficients, 154
Filter structure, fir, 152ff
Filter structure, lattice, 152ff, 155

Filter structures, 152ff
 use for synthesis, 151
Filter-bank:
 analysis, 102
 coders, 246ff
 outputs, 293f
Filtering, 78f, 147ff
 adaptive, 197, 199ff
  comb, 357
 by Fourier transform techniques, 346
 high-pass, 346
 low-pass, 197
Filters:
 comb, 359
 FIR, 256
 quadrature mirror, 256
 stationary, 346ff
Finite-duration impulse-response (FIR) system, 11f, 273
Finite-state models, 323f, 327
FIR, 273
FIR digital filters, 256
Fischer-Jørgensen, E., 135
Fisher, R. A., discriminant, 176ff
Fitzgerald, J. T., 347, 363
Flanagan, J. L., 64, 82, 99, 211, 223, 250f, 253, 260, 289
Flat/plain distinctive feature, 95
Flattening, spectrum, 199ff
Fletcher, H., 71, 74, 82
Fletcher-munson curves, 71f
Formant bandwidths, 114, 213, 218f
Formant blends, 210
Formant contours, 282f
Formant estimations, analysis by synthesis, 211
Formant estimators, filter bank, 210f
Formant estimators, LPC envelope, 210
Formant frequencies, 198, 213, 279, 282f, 337
 Burg, 163
Formant frequency:
 normalization, 305ff
 probability densities, 306
 ranges, 104f
 estimation, 210ff
 nonlinear warping, 306
Formant loci, 122, 291
Formant peaks, 150
Formant peaks, spurious, 210
Formant poles, 116
Formant tracks, 342
Formant transitions, 75, 120ff, 130, 282ff, 293
Formant vocoder, 250
Formant-frequency transformation, 306

Formants, 66, 75, 103, 132f, 241f, 293, 359
 in time warping, 297
Forney, G. D., Jr, 313, 329
Forward predictor, recurrence relations, 146
Forward-backward algorithm, 314ff
Four types of grammar, 323
Fourier, J., transform, 13, 21, 52, 203, 321
 center clipping of, 350
 filtering by, 346
Frames, 34, 264f
Francis, W. N., 287, 289
Frazier, R. H., 359, 363
French, N. R., 78, 82, 360, 363
Frequencies, formant, 282f, 337
Frequency:
 formant, 104f, 198, 210ff, 305ff
 fundamental, estimation, 197ff
 sampling, 164
Frequency histogram, 206f
Frequency perception, 71
Frequency response, telephone channel, 197
Frequency theory, 69f
Frequency-band analysis, 335ff
Frequency-domain analysis, 108
Frication, 64, 66, 87
Fricative noise, 120f
 spectral content of, 120f
Fricatives, 66, 101, 293, 321
 spectral characteristics of, 335
Friedland, B., 41
Friedman, D. H., 207f, 223
Front end, 321, 324
Fu, K. S., 193
Fujimura, O., 117, 135, 284, 289
Fukunaga, K., 170, 178, 193
Function, gapped, 161
Fundamental frequency,
 estimation, 197ff
 perception of, 69f

Gain constant, 149
Galand, C., 256, 260
Gallagher, N. C., Jr, 223
Gamma density, 125f
Gapped function, 161
Gasaway, D. C., 358, 363
Gaussian density, 46, 125f, 182f
 multivariate, 172, 184
Gaussian random variables, 48
Geçkinli, N. C., 209, 223
Generalized reflection coefficients, 158f
Generating rules, 322f
Generative model, 322
Geniculate body, medial, 71

Gersho, A., 289
Gerstman, L. J., 305, 329
Gibson, J. D., 159, 168
Gleason, H., 93, 97, 99
Glisson, T. H., 126, 135, 229, 261
Glides, 321
Glottal, 87
Glottal excitation function, 164
Glottal excitation spectrum, 203f
Glottal pulse, 101
    onset of, 128
Glottal pulse-train, 103
Glottal source poles, 335
Glottal waveform, 115
Glottis, 62
    pulses of, 360
Gold, B., 5, 13, 41, 208f, 223, 246, 248, 260
Golden, R. M., 251, 253, 260
Goldstein, U. G., 181, 193, 337, 343
Gonzalez, R. C., 170, 193
Grammar, 322f
    phrase-structure, 325
    types of, 323
Grammars:
  context-dependent, 323
  context-free, 323
  phrase-structure, 323
  regular, 323
Grammatical constraints used for connected-word recognition, 324
Granular noise, 245
Grapheme, 281
Graphemic representation, 291
Grave/acute distinctive feature, 95
Graveness, 362
Gray, A. H., Jr, 152, 168f, 174, 236ff, 260f, 264f, 273, 277, 289,
Gray, R. M., 269, 271, 274f, 277, 288ff
Greefkes, J. A., 246, 260
Green, D. M., 193
Greenwood, D. D., 363
Guegen, C., 169
Gupta, V. N., 304, 329

Hadamard, J. S., 258
Hair cells, 68
Hall, D. J., 190, 193
Halle, M., 76, 82, 94f, 99, 120, 133, 135, 288
Hammer, 67
Hamming, R. W., weighting, 34, 131, 135, 165, 264, 348
Hanauer, S. L., 134, 168, 200, 222
Hanning weighting, 34, 135, 348

Hard palate, 63
Harmonic peaks, 205ff
Harmonic peaks, differences in, 205f
Harmonics, 346
  odd-order, 346
  perception of, 74
HARPY system, 327
Harris, C. M., 289
Harris, F. J., 32, 41
Hart, P. E., 173, 188, 193, 316, 329
Harvard sentences, 334
Haskins laboratories, 121
Hawley, M. E., 349
Hazen, B., 343
Head tone, 65
Headroom, 227f
Hearing, 59, 67ff
HEARSAY II, 327
Hecker, M. H. L., 343
Heffner, R.-M. S., 62, 82, 89, 99
Heinz, J. M., 120, 135
Helicotrema, 68
Hemisphere, left, 75
Hidden Markov model, 294, 307ff, 324f
  (*See also* HMM)
High-pass filtering, 346
HIPEX, 206f
Histogram:
  Schroeder, 360
  frequency, 206f
  period, 206f
HMM:
  algorithm, Viterbi, 320
  comparison with time-warping, 316f
  recognizer for word spotting, 318
  recursive relations, 311ff
  training, 310, 314ff
Ho, Y.-C., 193
Hockett, C., 86, 93, 96, 98f
Hollien, H., 343, 347, 363
Holmes, J. N., 289
Hotelling, 258
House, A. S., 75, 82
Huang, J. J. Y., 257, 260
Huddy, N. W., Jr, 349
Huffman, D., 241
Huggins, A. W. F., 81, 82
Hughes, G. W., 120, 133, 135, 206, 224, 236, 344
Hum removal, forensic applications, 347
Hum, 50 and 60-hz, 345f
HWIM system, 327
Hyde, S. R., 328
Hyperellipsoids, 184f
Hyperplanes, 173

I.i.d. samples, 51
Ignition noise, 345f
Impedance:
  characteristic, 107f
  input, 108f
  radiation, 114, 125
Impedance transformation by ossicles, 68
Impossible event, 43
Impostors, 333
Impulse response, 8, 53f
Impulsive noise, 345f
Incus, 67
Independent events, 43f
Independent random variables, 47
Independent, identically distributed samples, 51
Inferior colliculus, 71
Infinite clipping, 79f
Infinite-duration impulse-response (IIR) system, 11f
Infinite-order prediction error, 174
Information theory, 180
Information to be extracted from the observations, 366
Inner ear, 67
  estimated frequency sensitivity of, 211f
Input impedance, 108f
Integer-band sampling, 256
Integrator, leaky, 241, 317
Intelligibility, 225, 345ff, 353
  effects of disruption on, 81
  effects of distortion on, 78
  effects of interruption on, 81
  measures of, 360ff
  tests of, 360ff
Interactive editing, 281
Interception system, telephone, 278, 281
Interference, 292
Interfering noise, 264
Interfering speech, 292, 345f, 358ff
International phonetic alphabet, 85f
Interpolation, 154, 221
  removal of impulse noise by, 346
Interruptions, effect on intelligibility, 81
Inverse filter, 150, 199f
  unstable, 158
IPA, 85f
Isodata, 190
Itakura, F., 151, 155, 168, 174, 267, 270, 272, 295, 297, 299 301f, 318, 329
Itakura error measure, 270
Itakura likelihood measure, 267
Itakura minimum prediction residual, 294f, 299, 318
Itakura-Saito error measure, 270
Itakura-Saito lattice structure, 155

Jackson, D. R., 350, 363
Jackson, L. B., 165, 168
Jakimik, J., 77, 81
Jakobson, R. C., 76, 82, 94, 99, 362, 363
Jamming, 346
Jayant, N. S., 169, 228, 230, 245, 261, 345, 363
Jelinek, F., 309, 318, 325, 327ff
Joint probabilities, 44
Joint probability density, 47
Jones, D., 89, 99
Juang, B.-H., 277, 289
Juncture, 97f
Jury, E. I., 13, 41

K-means algorithm, 189f
K-means clustering technique, 338
K-nearest neighbor technique, 341
Kaneko, T., 295, 329
Kang, G. S., 216ff, 222f, 267, 289, 329
Kantner, C., 98f
Karhunen, K., 183, 258, 305
  -Loève transformation, 183, 185, 305, 338
Kay, S. M., 165, 168
Kelly, J. L., Jr, 113, 135
  -Lochbaum equations, 113
Kempelen, W. von, 100
Kersta, L. G., 342, 344
Kimme, E. G., 238, 241, 261
Kimura, D., 75, 82
King, A. J., 71, 81
Kirkpatrick, S., 329
Kirlin, R. L., 306, 329
Klatt, D. H., 326, 328
Knock-out method, 181, 188, 335, 340
Knowledge,
  lexical, 327
  phonetic, 326
  representation of, 326
  semantic, 327
Knowledge of language, 291
Koenig, W., 73, 82, 101, 104, 211
  approximation, 73, 104, 211
Kramer, H. P., 193
Kryter, K. D., 361, 363
Kucera, H., 287, 289
Kullback, S., 180, 193
Kuo, F. F., 238, 241, 261

Labial noise, 120
Labio-dental, 87
Ladefoged, P., 99
Lag, 52
Lagged products, 52
Lagrange, J. L., multiplier, 179

Lamel, L. F., 296f, 329
Lamino-alveolar, 87
Language, models of, 322ff
Laplace, P. S. de, transforms, 12
Laplacian density, 125f
Laryngeal pharynx, 62f
Larynx, 59
Lateral, 87
Lateral lemnisci, 71
Lattice filter, 152ff, 155, 265, 278, 280, 321f
LBG algorithm, 271
Le Roux, J., 160
Lea, W. A., 328
Leakage, 32ff
Leaky integrator, 54f
Learning phase, 171
Lee, F. F., 287, 289
Left-right model, 309
Left-to-right analysis, 77, 327
Lehiste, I., 99, 106, 135
Level building algorithm, 78, 319, 324
Levels of nesting, 324
Levine, M. D., 193
Levinson, N., 142, 151, 157, 159, 218, 235, 269
  recursion, 142ff, 151, 235f, 269
Levinson, S. E., 307, 316, 324f, 329f, 373
Lexical knowledge, 327
Li, K.-P., 336, 338, 344
Liberman, A. M., 75f, 82, 102, 289
Liberman, M. Y., 285, 289
Licklider, J. C. R., 79, 81f
Liftering, 203
Liftering, long-pass, 212
Likelihood measure, Itakura, 267
Likelihood ratios, 180
Likelihood, maximum, 151, 172, 174
Lim, J. S., 352f, 363
Limiting, by inner-ear muscles, 68
Lin, W. C., 168
Linde, Y., 271, 274, 289
Linear operations, interchangeability with
  expected-value operations, 53
Linear prediction, 109, 116, 136ff, 212, 233, 259,
  338ff, 366f
  applied to pitch estimation, 199f, 209
  effect of noise, 345
  frequency-domain properties, 151ff
  practical considerations, 163ff
  spectrum-matching function of, 345
  (*See also* LPC)
Linear prediction of noisy speech, 165
Linear predictive coding, 346
Linear predictor, covariance, 235, 267
Linear system, 4

Linear systems:
  autocorrelations of output and input, 53f
  power spectral densities of input and output, 54
  random signals in, 53ff
Linear-prediction encoder, 272ff
Linear-prediction equations, derivation, 138ff
  frequency-domain derivation, 149ff
Linear-prediction vocoder, 262, 348
Linearity, of convolution, 9
Lips, 63
  radiation of speech from, 115
  unrounded, 89
Lloyd, S. P., 271, 275, 289
  algorithm, 271, 275
Local maxima, 214f
Lochbaum, C. C., 113, 135
Loève, M., 183, 258, 305
Log area ratios, 268, 339, 341
Long-pass liftering, 212
Long-term averaged autocorrelation estimates,
  126, 128
Loudness, 71
Loudness level, 71
Loudness perception, 71
Low-pass filtering, 197
Lower jaw, 62
Lowerre, B. T., 328f
LPC, 209
LPC coefficient, 297
LPC encoding, 353
LPC envelope, 210
LPC parameters, 293
LPC residual, 304
LPC vocoder, 248
  (*See also* linear prediction)
LPC-10 algorithm, 267ff
LPC-based distance measures, 174f
LPCA (program), 144, 373
LPCB (program), 163, 374
LPCC (program), 157, 159, 376
LPCS (program), 160, 378
L-U decomposition, 156f
Luck, J. E., 344
Lummis, R. C., 337, 344
Lumped-parameter system, 4
  vocal tract as, 109
Lungs, 59f
  capacity, 60

Madariaga, S. de, 91, 99
Magill, D. T., 266f, 289f, 353, 363
Magnitude-difference function, 202f
Mahalanobis distance, 173, 271, 341

Makhoul, J. I., 149, 168, 210, 223, 237f, 241, 261, 266f, 289
Maksym, J. N., 200, 223
Malah, D., 358, 363
Malleus, 67
Malmberg, B., 86, 96, 99
Mandible, 63
Manner of articulation, 86ff
Marill, T., 193
Markel, J. D., 152, 164, 168f, 174, 199, 209, 223, 236ff, 260f, 264f, 273, 289, 340f, 344
Markov model, hidden, 307ff, 324
Markov process, 309
Marple, S. L., Jr, 168
Marple, L., 169
Martin, T. B., 328
Martinez, H. G., 294, 329
Masking, 74, 241f, 259, 358
Mathews, M. V., 193, 211, 223, 336, 344
Matrix:
  autocorrelation, 271
  covariance, 172ff, 178f, 257f, 268
  factorization of, 156f
  positive-definite, 156
  scattering, 110, 112f
  symmetric, 156
  Toeplitz, 142
  transformation, 112, 164
  wave transformation, 110
Maxey, H. D., 284, 289
Maximum-entropy method, 162
Maximum likelihood, 151, 172, 174
Maximum-likelihood measure, 295
  applied to pitch, 207f
McCandless, S. S., 215ff, 222f
McDonald, R. A., 125, 135
McGonegal, C. A., 209, 223
Mean-squared error, 139
Measures of separability, 176, 178ff
Meatus, external auditory, 67, 71
Medial geniculate body, 71
Median smoothing, 221f
Medress, M. F., 321, 329
Meeker, W. F., 76, 81f, 349, 362f
Mel, 73
Mel scale:
  Fant approximation, 73
  Koenig approximation, 73
Membrane,
  basilar, 68
  Reissner's, 68
  tectorial, 68
  tympanic, 67
Method of steepest descent, 355

Middle ear, 67
Miller, N. J., 208f, 223
Miller, R. L., 207, 223
Mimicry, 333
Minimal pairs, 93, 361
Minimum prediction error, 152
Minimum prediction residual, 175
Mirror filters, quadrature, 256
MITalk, 286ff
Mitchell, O. M. M., 350
Mixed pole-zero model, 138
Model of speech production, 124ff, 278
Model:
  all-pole, 137
  all-zero, 137
  autoregressive, 137
  autoregressive moving-average, 138
  autoregressive system, 148
  finite-state, 327
  left-right, 309
  mixed pole-zero, 138
  moving-average, 137
  stochastic, 307
  system, 3, 136f, 147f
  vocal-tract, 153
Modeling, 147ff
  hidden markov, 307ff
  system, 3, 136f, 147f
Models of language, 322ff
Models, finite-state, 323f
Models, grammatical, in continuous speech recognizers, 324f
Modified autocorrelation, 199ff
Modified gamma density function, 229
Modulation, 64ff
Mohn, W. S., 297, 329, 336f, 343
Moments, 45
Moorer, J. A., 202, 223
Morf, M., 169, 367
Morph dictionary, 287f
Morphs, 287f
Motor theory, 76
Moving-average model, 137
Mu-law compandor, 229f
Mu-law encoded speech, 239
Multi-talker problem, 346
Multiple patterns, 303
Multiple-rate encoders, 248
Multiplier, lagrangian, 179
Multipulse, 243f, 263
Multivariate gaussian probability density, 49f, 172, 184
Multivariate normal probability density, 49f, 172, 184

Munson, W. A., 71, 74, 82
Myers, C. S., 301f, 319, 324, 329, 380

Nagy, G., 193
Narrow-band spectrogram, 101
Nasal, 87
Nasal cavity, 62ff, 103
Nasal consonants, 117ff, 335
Nasal pharynx, 62f
Nasal/oral distinctive feature, 95
Nasalization, 91
Nasalized vowels, 117ff, 210
Nasals, 321
  acoustic characteristics of, 117ff
Natarajan, T., 258, 260
Nearest-neighbor rule, 270
Neely, R. B., 294, 297, 331
Nemhauser, G. L., 182, 193
Nested structures, 324
Nesting, levels of, 324
Neuburg, E. P., 306, 330
Neutral vowel, 90
Newton, I., 107, 212
  equation, 107
  -Raphson algorithm, 212f
Nicely, P., 362f
Niederjohn, R. J., 349, 364
Nilsson, N. J., 303, 330
Nodes, T. A., 223
Noise, 292, 345
  additive, 204f
  alveolar/dental, 120
  breath, 346
  degradation by, 225, 248
  distortion of spectrum by, 345
  fricative, 120f
  ignition, 345f
  labial, 120
  periodic, 346ff
  quantization, 227f, 232, 255, 346
  robustness, 208
  types of, 345f
  velar, 120
  wideband, 346, 349ff
  wind, 346
Noise shaping, 241f
Noisy channels, 225
Noisy speech, 318
  linear prediction of, 165
Noll, A. M., 203, 207, 223
Noll, P., 234, 241, 258f, 261
Non-stationary signals, 141
Non-uniform quantizers, 229f
Nonlinear processing, 200ff, 346, 349f

Nordmark, J. O., 69, 82
Normal density function, 46
Normalization, formant frequency, 304ff
Normalized euclidean distance, 337
Notch filters, analog, 347
NRL rules, 286f
Nucleus, syllable, 96
Number of phonemes, 93
Numerical errors, 151
Nyquist, H., 5f, 41, 164, 226, 244f
  rate, 5f, 164, 226, 244f

Octave errors, 207f
Olinski, P. J., 350, 363
Olivary complex, 71
Olive, J. P., 211, 223, 284f, 289
Oliver, B. M., 261
Open transition, 97
Oppenheim, A. V., 5, 13, 39, 41, 352, 363
Optimum warping path, total cost, 303
Oral cavity, 62
Oral pharynx. 62f
Order of predictor, 164
Organ of corti, 68
Organs of speech, anatomy of, 56ff
Orthogonality of observations and errors, 365
Orthogonality principle, 139, 355, 365ff
Orthogonalization, 183
Orthogonalized reflection coefficients, 339
Ossicles, 67f
Ossicles, functions, 67f
Outer ear, 67
Oval window, 67
Over-sampling, 6
Overlap-add, 38f
Overlap-save, 38f
Overlapping segments, 37
Overlapping-window technique, 348, 356

Paez, M. D., 126, 135, 229, 261
Paige, A., 306, 330
Palatal, 87
Palatalization, 87
Palate, 63
Papamichalis, P. E., 267, 290
Papoulis, A., 41, 47, 49, 56, 139, 152, 163, 169, 229, 253, 261, 290, 309
Parallel processing, 208f
Parametric excitation, 350
PARCOR coefficients, 144, 154ff, 161f, 293
Parse tree, 323
Parseval, A. von, 149
Parsing, 323

Parsons, T. W., 123, 135, 359, 363
Partial sequence, 311ff
Partial-correlation coefficients, 144, 154ff, 161f, 293
Partial-fraction expansion, 14
Particle velocity, 107
Pattern library, 171
  updating, 292
  searching, 295
  reference, 170f
  test, 170
Pattern playback, 121f
Pattern recognition, 170ff, 271
Patterns, 294
Paul, A. P., 211, 223
Paul, D. B., 330
Paul, J. E., Jr, 321, 330
Peak clipping, 349f
Peak picking, 212, 214f, 219
Peak-difference pitch estimators, 205f
Perception, 59, 67, 210
  categorical, 75
  elementary units of, 328
  influenced by context, 76
  speech, 244, 328
  use of knowledge in, 77
Perception of fundamental frequency, 69f
Perceptual techniques, 357f
Performance, effect of vocabulary, 293
Period histogram, 206f
Periodic functions, 165
Periodic noise, 345ff
Peripheral processor, 75
Petersen, T. L., 358, 363
Peterson, G. E., 104, 135, 284, 290, 305
Pfeifer, L. L., 341, 344
Pharyngeal, 87
Pharynx, 63
  laryngeal, 62f
  nasal, 62f
  oral, 62f
Phase locking, 348
Phase vocoder, 251ff
Phon, 71
Phonation, 64
  detecting, 198
Phoneme-based recognizers, 321ff
Phonemes, 92ff, 284, 357
  conversion to speech, 281ff
  notation, 86
  number of, 93
Phonemic, 91
Phonemic representation, 278, 281
Phonemics, 84, 92ff

Phones, 281
  boundaries between, 128
Phonetic alphabets, 85f
Phonetic knowledge, 326
Phonetic transcription, 291
Phonetic variability, 319
Phonetically-balanced words, 350
Phonetics, acoustic, 59, 66, 100f
Phonetics, articulatory, 59, 66
Phrase-structure grammar, 323, 325
Picket-fence effect, 31
Pickett, J. M., 82, 349, 363
Pickles, J. O., 82
Piecewise-cylindrical model, 106
Pierce, J. R., 330
Pike, K., 86, 99
Pinna, 67
Pinson, E. N., 82, 99, 211, 223
Pisoni, D. B., 82, 212, 223, 328, 330
Pitch, 65, 73, 98, 101, 264, 281, 321
Pitch and formant frequencies, altering, 333
Pitch contours, 337f
Pitch estimation, 197ff, 249, 265
  from LPC residual, 199f, 209
  histogram methods, 206f
  maximum-likelihood, 207f
  time-domain, 208f
Pitch estimator, data reduction, 208f
Pitch estimators, peak-difference, 205f
Pitch extraction, 197ff
Pitch frequency, 198
Pitch harmonics, 132
Pitch of interfering voice, 359
Pitch periods, correlation of, 356
Pitch range, 197
Pitch tracking, 198
Pitch-period predictor, 238f
Place theory, 69f, 74
Pleura, 60
Plosives, 66, 87
Point of articulation, 86f, 120
Poles, 17, 137
  and zeroes, 109
Pollack, I., 82, 344, 349, 363
POLRT, 212
Pols, L. C. W., 330
Polynomials, finding roots of, 151
Position, vowel, 88
Positive-definite quadratic form, 48, 270
Potter, R. K., 99, 135
Power:
  signal, 52
  prediction-error, 272
Power series, 13f

Power spectral density, 52
Power spectrum, 52
Power spectrum, logged, second derivative, 218f
Pre-emphasis, 264
   high-frequency, 131
Pre-processing of speech, 81
Prediction, adaptive, 234ff
Prediction error, 142f, 157f, 174f
   infinite-order, 174
Prediction-error filter, 150
Prediction-error power, 272
Prediction errors:
   forward, 147
   reverse, 147
Prediction residual:
   center clipping of, 239
   compression, 239ff
   minimum, 175
   peak clipping of, 239
   quantization, 239ff
Predictor, 137
   autocorrelation, 213
   covariance, 213
   order of, 164
   pitch-period, 238f
Predictor coefficients, 137ff, 235, 264f, 293, 304, 306, 348
   correlations among, 338ff
Predictor-coefficient-controlled filter, 152ff
Predictor parameters, vector quantization of, 272ff
Predistortion, 229
Pressure waves, 107
Principal cycles, 208
Probability, conditional, 43, 171
Probability density:
   gaussian, 46
   joint, 47
   multivariate gaussian, 184
   uniform, 46
   of speech, 125f
Process:
   ergodic, 51
   stationary, 51
   stochastic, 50
Product codes, 275
Product spectrum, 206f
Product-code quantizers, 277
Productions, 322f
Propagation constant, 108
Propagation velocity, 107
Properties of vowel waveforms, 114ff
Prosodic habits, 333
Prosodics, 98, 285, 287f

Pruning of FFT, 164
Pruzansky, S., 297, 330, 336f, 344
Pseudoformants, 216, 318
Pseudorandom numbers, 268
Pulmonary tract, 61
Pulsipher, D. C., 356, 362
Pushdown stacks, 324

Quadratic form, 48, 355
   positive-definite, 48, 270
Quality, 225
Quantization, 5
   adaptive, 234
   vector, 174
Quantization error, probability density of, 227
Quantization errors, 5
Quantization noise, 227f, 232, 255, 346
   frequency distribution of, 259
   masking, 241f, 259
   power, 227
   variance of, 227
Quantized speech, signal-to-noise ratio of, 227
Quantizers, product-code, 277
Quefrency, 203

Rabiner, L. R., 5, 13, 41, 169, 188, 193, 202, 208f, 211, 214, 221, 223f, 228, 254, 261, 282, 290, 294, 296, 301, 303ff, 307ff, 313, 316, 319, 324, 328, 330, 356, 364
Rabinowitz, A. S., 321, 330
Rader, C. M., 41, 246, 260
Radiation impedance, 114, 125
Radiation of speech from the lips, 115
Rahmonics, 203, 212
Rainbow passage, 334, 336
Random function, 50ff
   mean and autocorrelation of, 51f
   statistics of, 51f
Random signals in linear systems, 53ff
Random variables, 44ff
   gaussian, 48
   independent, 47
   joint second central moment, 48
   jointly gaussian, 48
   mean of, 45
   probability density, 44
   probability distribution, 44
   standard deviation, 45
   statistics, 45
   variance, 45
Range of pitch, 197
Rao, K. R., 258, 260
Raphson, 212
Ravindran, A., 350, 364

Real function, DFT of, 28
Realization of stochastic process, 50
Rebolledo, G., 269, 271, 275, 288
Recognition:
　connected-word, 318
　isolated-word, 293ff, 307
　pattern, 170ff
　speech, problems in, 291f
　word, 188
Recognition errors, living with, 327
Recognition parameters, reliable estimates, 316
Recognition phase, 171
Recognition strategy, bayesian, 295
Recognizer, speech, types of, 292f
Recognizers, speech:
　continuous, grammatical models in, 324f
　talker-dependent, 293
　talker-independent, 293
Recording sessions, spacing of, 334
Rectangular weighting, 32
Recurrence relations, LPC, 145ff
　among prediction errors, 147
Recursion:
　Levinson/Durbin, 142ff
　Schur, 159ff
Recursive relations, in HMM, 311ff
Reddy, D. R., 326ff, 330
Redundancy, 257
Reference pattern, 170f
Reflection coefficients, 111, 144, 154f, 158f, 216, 234, 265, 280, 306
　bit allocation, 236ff
　Burg's method, 161ff
　encoding, 159
　generalized, 158f, 235
　long-term averages of, 340
　obtaining from LU decomposition, 159
　orthogonalized, 339
　probability densities, 238
　quantizing, 236ff
　Schur's recursion for, 159ff
　standard deviation, 237
　(*See also* PARCOR)
Reflection-coefficient-controlled filter, 152ff
Regel, P., 330
Regular grammars, 323
Reissner, E.'s membrane, 68
Rejections, 333
RELP, 266
Remde, J. R., 239, 243, 249, 260, 263
Repiod, 203
Residual, 263
　LPC, AMDF of, 203
Residual excitation, 266

Residue theorem, 13
Retroflex, 87
Reverberation, 350, 361
Reverse predictor, 145ff
Reynolds, A. J., 357, 364
Rhode, W. S., 69, 82
Rhythm, 281
Ribs, 60
Robinson, D. W., 71, 82
Robinson, E. A., 161, 169
Robinson, G. S., 258, 260
Robustness, 248
Robustness in the presence of noise, 208
Roots, characteristic, 183
Rosenberg, A. E., 324, 329, 333, 344
Rosenblatt, M., 223
Ross, M. J., 202, 209, 224
Rouché's theorem, 151
Round window, 67
Rules:
　generating, 322f
　syntactic, 327
Rushforth, C. K., 318, 329

Sabin, M. J., 277, 290
Saito, S., 151, 155, 168, 174, 270, 272
Sakoe, H., 297, 301f, 330, 380
Sambur, M. R., 169, 181, 193, 213, 224, 294, 296, 304, 330, 333, 335, 339f, 344f, 348, 356, 364
Sampled-data system, 4f
Sampled-data techniques for removing periodic noise, 347f
Samples, independent, identically distributed, 51
Sampling frequency, 164
Sampling, integer-band, 256
Sampling rate, 226
Sampling theorem, 5
Sayers, B. McA., 359, 364
Scala tympani, 68
Scala vestibuli, 68
Scattering matrix, 110, 112f
Schafer, R. W., 41, 169, 209, 211, 214, 224, 254, 261
Scharf, B., 74, 82
Schmidt, C. E., 330
Schroeder, M. R., 67, 82, 159, 168, 206, 208, 220, 224, 235, 238ff, 246, 248, 250, 260f, 360
Schroeder histogram method, 360
Schultheiss, P. M., 257, 260
Schur, J., 159ff, 166, 169, 378
　recursion, 159ff
Schwa, 90, 286

Schwartz, H. A., 160
  inequality, 160
Schwartz, M., 41
Schwartz, R., 284, 290, 341, 344
Schwarz, R. J., 41
Search time, codebook, 270
Second-order statistics, 50
Segment boundaries, recognition, 321
Segmentation, 318f
Selection algorithms:
  add-on, 181, 188
  knock-out, 181, 188
Self-normalization, of decision thresholds, 304
Semantic knowledge, 327
Semi-pitch-synchronous, 268
Semicircular canals, 68
Semitone, 73
Semivowel, 87
Seneff, S., 206, 224
Separability:
  maximizing, 185ff
  measures of, 176, 178ff, 185ff
Separability requirement, 182
Shannon, C. E., 5, 41, 261, 269, 275, 290, 323, 330
Shape-gain quantizers, 277
Sharp/plain distinctive feature, 95
Shaw, G. B., 90, 99
Shaw, L., 41
Shields, V. C., Jr, 359, 364
Shift-invariant system, 3
Shore, J. E., 294, 329f
Shridhar, M., 340, 344
Sibilants, 66, 87, 293, 335
Side information, 234
Sidelobes, 32ff, 165
SIFT, 199f, 209, 265
Signal power, 52
Signals, 3
Signals, non-stationary, 141
Silverman, H. F., 321, 329
Simplified distance measures, 173ff
Simplified inverse filter tracking, 199f, 209, 265
Singleton, R. C., 371
Slepian, D., 207
Slew rate, 244f
Slope overload, 245
Small populations, use of, 334
Smith, B., 229, 261
Smoothing, 219ff
  median, 221f
Snow, T. B., 206, 224
Soft palate, 63
Sondhi, M. M., 199f, 206, 224
Sone, 71

Sonorants, 106
Sound spectrograms, 121
Sound spectrograph, 100ff, 121
Sounds:
  mute, 65
  unvoiced, 65
  voiced, 65
Source impedance at the glottis, 114
Souza, P. de, 193
Space, feature, 171
Speaker authentication, 332f
Speaker characteristics, changes in, 188
Speaker identification, 332f
Speaker recognition, 332ff
  feature selection for, 332, 335ff
  forensic applications, 333, 342f
Speaker verification, 332f
Speaker-recognition system, 175
Speakers, uncooperative, 332f
Speaking habits, 335
Specific heats of air, 107
Spectral characteristics of fricatives, 335
Spectral content of fricative noise, 120f
Spectral subtraction, 357
Spectrogram, 101f
  narrow-band, 101
  wide-band, 101
Spectrograms, 282f
  as aid to deaf, 102
  speaker recognition by, 342f
Spectrum analysis, 21
  by basilar membrane, 69
Spectrum envelope, 116, 150, 163ff, 203, 210, 246ff, 259
  from cepstrum, 211f
  local maxima in, 212
Spectrum flattening, 151, 199ff, 248f
Spectrum manipulation, 37f
Spectrum matching, 147, 149ff, 165
Spectrum shaper, 349
Spectrum subtraction, 350ff
Spectrum weighting, 226
Spectrum re-scaling, 206f
Speech:
  autocorrelation function of, 126f
  automatic recognition of, 59
  high-pitched, 210
  probability density of, 125f, 229f
  redundancy in, 231
  sample spectra of, 130ff
  telephone-bandwidth, 200
Speech analysis, 150
Speech and nonspeech sounds, distinction between, 75

Speech encoding, 159, 195, 203
Speech enhancement, 59
  application areas of, 346
Speech generation, 56
  excitation-modulation model, 203ff
Speech intelligibility, 225, 247f
Speech perception, 56, 74ff, 210, 328
Speech production, model of, 124ff, 262, 278
Speech pre-processing, 81
Speech quality, 225, 257
Speech recognition, 195, 291ff
  connected, 292
  continuous, 318ff
  isolated-word, 292
Speech recognizers, continuous, grammatical models in, 324f
Speech signals, statistics of, 125ff
Speech synthesis, 59, 195, 209, 262, 277ff
Speech synthesizer, 247
Speech understanding, 292
Speech understanding systems, 326ff
Spickenagel, N., 284, 289
Spirants, 87
Splitting, 274f
Spurious phonemes, 325
Stability, 17f
Stability of the all-pole model, 151f
Stability of vocal-tract filter, 151f
Staircase, 244
Stapedius muscle, 68
Stapes, 67
States, transitions between, 307
Stationarity, input signal, 163
Stationary filters, 346ff
Stationary process, 51
Statistics of a random function, 51f
Statistics of speech signals, 125ff
Steepest descent, method of, 355
Steinberg, J. C., 78, 82, 360, 363
Step size, 226f, 240
Stevens, K. M., 76
Stevens, K. N., 82, 120, 135, 342, 344
Stevens, S. S., 73, 82
Stirrup, 67
Stochastic matching, 324
Stochastic model, 307
Stochastic process, 50
  realization of, 50
Stops, 66, 87
Stops and fricatives, acoustic characteristics of, 119ff
Stress, 98, 281
Strevens, P., 120, 135
Strident/mellow distinctive feature, 95

Su, L.-S., 342, 344
Sub-band vocoder, 248, 255f
Submultiples, 206f
Subset selection, 180ff
Substitution-insertion-deletion model, 325f
Sum of two independent random variables, variance of, 49
Sums of random variables, 48f
Superposition principle, 4, 8
Sustention, 362
Syllable boundaries, 65
Syllable peak, 96
Syllables, 96ff
Synchronous quadrature detection, 252f
Syntactic categories, 322f
Syntactic rules, 327
Syntax rules, 322
Synthesis, 265
  pitch-synchronous, 265
  speech, 59, 209, 277ff
Synthesis by rule, 278, 281ff
Synthesis hardware, 278ff
Synthesized speech, 94, 123
Synthesizer:
  dyadic, 284f
  formant controlled, 279
  LPC controlled, 280
  terminal-analog, 125, 250, 262, 278ff
System, 3
  continuous, 4f
  discrete-time, 4f
  distributed-parameter, 4
  finite-duration impulse-response (FIR), 11f, 273
  infinite-duration impulse-response (IIR), 11f
  lumped, 4
  sampled-data, 4f
  shift-invariant, 3
  time-invariant, 3
  voice response, 278
System function, 3
System model, 136
  types, 137ff
System modeling, 147f

Talker independence, 303ff
Tap, 88
Tape recorders, speed fluctuations, 348
Tape-recorded speech, processing, 347
Tarnoczy, T. H., 100, 134
Tectorial membrane, 68
Teeth, 63
Telephone bandwidth, 226, 246
Telephone speech, 294

Telephone system, transmission, 74
Telephone-bandwidth speech, 200
Template clustering, 305
Templates, 170, 188, 294
  multiple, 304f
Temporal alignment, 336f
Temporal misalignments, 292
Temporal theory, 69f
Temporal variations, 292
Tendency to quantize, 93
Tense and lax vowels, 90
Terminal-analog synthesizer, 125, 250, 262, 278ff
Tense/lax distinctive feature, 95
Test pattern, 170
Test populations, size of, 334
Tests, diagnostic, 361f
Text-to-speech, conversion, unrestricted, 286ff
Thomas, I. B., 349f, 364
Thomson, P. J., 193
Thoracic breathing, 60
Thresholds, decision, 187
Thyroid cartilage, 61
Thyroid cartilage, 61
Tierney, J., 169
Tilde (~) as indication of nasalization, 91
Timbre, 74
Time average, 51
Time normalization, 297ff
Time registration, 336
Time warping, 295, 297ff, 307, 317, 319ff, 337
  constraints, 300ff
Time weighting, 32ff, 34, 208
Time-domain pitch estimation, 208f
Time-invariant system, 3
Time-reversal, 53
  in convolution, 9
Time-warping endpoint constraints, relaxing, 302f
Tip, 64
Tobias, J. V., 83
Toeplitz matrix, 142
Tone quality, 74
Tongue, 63f
  blade, 89
  middle, 64, 89
  root, 64
  back, 64
Tosi, O., 343f
Tou, J. T., 170, 193
Trace, 50, 184f, 189, 187
Trachea, 59f, 61
Tracking, 219ff
Tracks, formant, 342
Training phase, 171

Training set, 271
Training, of hmm, 314ff
Transcription, phonetic, 291
Transfer function, 16f, 19, 106
  inverse, 19
  vocal-tract, 138, 199, 203f, 263, 278, 305f
Transform:
  chirp-Z, 214f
  discrete cosine, 258
  filter, 348f
  Fourier, 203
  Hotelling, 258
  Walsh-Hadamard, 258
Transform coding, 257ff
Transform techniques, 348f
Transformation matrix, 112, 164
Transformation, Karhunen-Loève, 185, 258, 305, 338
Transformations, 182ff
Transforms, 12ff
  continuous Fourier, 13
  discrete Fourier, 13
  Laplace, 12
  Z, 13ff
Transition matrix, 308ff
Transition probabilities, 308ff
Transitions:
  formant, 120, 282f, 284
  state, 307
Treitel, S., 161, 169
Trellis diagram, 310f
Tremain, T. E. 267f, 290
Trial, 42
Triangle equality, 273
Triangle inequality, 173
Tribolet, J. M., 259, 261, 290
Trill, 87
  dental, 87f
  labial, 87
  laryngeal, 87
  uvular, 87f
Tube, eustachian, 67
Tukey, J. W., 203, 221, 224, 368
Twin-T filter, 347
Two random variables, 47f
Two-port, 110
Tympanic membrane, 67

UE warping, 302
UELM warping, 302
Umeda, N., 283, 290
Un, C. K., 203, 224, 266, 290, 353, 363f
Undersampling, 5, 256
Understanding, use of context in, 326

Uniform density, 46
Unit circle, 212f
Unit impulse function, 8, 14f
Unit step, 15
Units of perception, elementary, 328
Unrestricted-endpoint (UE) warping, 302
Unrestricted-endpoint/local-minimum (UELM) warping, 302f
Unstable inverse filter, 158
Unvoiced, 88
Unvoiced plosives, 296
Utterance currently being analyzed, information about, 327
Uvula, 63

Van Trees, H. L., 56
Variability, phonetic, 319
Variable-rate encoding, 267
Variation:
　between-talker, 291
　phonetic, 292
　power, 294
　within-talker, 291f
Vector quantization, 174, 188, 190, 269ff, 294, 308
　of predictor parameters, 272ff
Vectors, characteristic, 183
Vectors of features, 171f
Velar noise, 120
Velocity of propagation, 107
Velocity particle, 107
Velocity, volume, 107
VELP, 265f
Velum, 63, 103, 117
Vestibular apparatus, 68
Vibration, 66
Viswanathan, R., 237, 261, 267, 290
Viterbi, A. J., 313, 316, 318, 320
　algorithm, 313, 316, 318
Vocal cords, 61f
　functions of, 62
　oscillation, 64
　vibration, 64
Vocal fry, 65
Vocal organs, 59ff
Vocal registers, 65
Vocal tract, 59, 62f, 164, 308
　acoustics of, 103ff
　anatomy, 335
　as distributed-parameter system, 103, 109
　as lumped-parameter system, 109
　cylindrical model of, 109ff
　functions of, 64
　losses in, 114

Vocal tract filter, 150, 212
　stability of, 151f, 235
Vocal tract length, 64, 305f
Vocal tract model, 153
Vocal tract resonances, 64
Vocal tract transfer function, 103, 138, 199, 203f, 263, 278, 305f
　as all-pole function, 117
　poles of, 103
Vocalic r, 86
Vocalic/nonvocalic distinctive feature, 95
Vocoder:
　autocorrelation, 264f
　channel, 246ff, 262
　formant, 250
　linear-prediction, 262, 348
　LPC, 248
　phase, 251ff
　residual-excited, 262
　sub-band, 248, 255f
　voice-excited, 262
Vocoders, 225, 362
　excitation of, 248
Vocoids, 86, 101, 125
　acoustics of, 106ff
　consonantal, 87
　in interfering speech, 359
Voice bar, 130
Voice compression, 280
Voice disguise, 332f
Voice excitation, 249f, 265f
Voice response systems, 262, 278, 280f
Voice quality, 247f
Voiced/voiceless distinctive feature, 95
Voicing, 86, 88, 120, 264, 321, 361
　determination, 249f
　detecting, 198
Voiers, W. D., 96, 99, 361, 364
Volkmann, J., 73, 82
Volume velocity, 107
Von Kempelen, W., 100
Vowel diagrams, 89ff, 105
Vowel waveforms, frequency domain characteristics, 115f
　properties of, 114ff
　time domain characteristics, 115
Vowel-cloud, 91
Vowel-space, 89ff
Vowels, 66, 86, 293, 321
　back, 88
　cardinal, 89
　close, 88
　front, 88
　high, 88

Vowels, (*continued*)
    lax, 90
    low, 88
    nasalized, 117ff, 210
    open, 88
    tense, 90

Warping path, length, 303
Wakita, H., 109, 135, 169, 305f, 330, 338, 344
Walsh, J. L., transform, 258
Warping, time, 295, 297ff, 307, 317, 319ff, 337
    unrestricted-endpoint (UE), 302
    unrestricted-endpoint/local-minimum (UELM), 302f
Watanabe, S., 193
Watergate buzz, 346
Wave equation, 106ff
Wave transformation matrix, 110
Waveform encoding, 225, 278
Weighting:
    Hamming, 34, 36, 131, 264, 348
    Hanning, 34f, 348
    raised-cosine, 34f
    rectangular, 32
    spectrum, 226
    triangular, 32f
Weinstein, C. J., 265, 290
Weiss, M. R., 81, 83, 123, 135, 348, 350, 352f, 357, 364
West, R., 98f
Whispering, 65f
White, G. M., 294, 297, 328, 331
White noise, 53, 75
    effect on linear prediction, 165
Whitening, 186
Wide-band spectrogram, 101
Wideband noise, 119, 345f, 349ff
Widrow, B., 354f, 357, 364
Wiley, R., 81, 123, 134
Wilpon, J. G., 330
Wind noise, 346

Window:
    oval, 67
    round, 67
Window shape, 165
Window width, time-warping, 299
Windowing, 29ff, 140, 351
Windows, overlapping, 37f
Windpipe, 61
Wintz, P. A., 258, 261
Wise, G. L., 223
Wise, J. D., 207, 224
Wohlford, R. E., 318, 331, 356f, 362
Wolf, J. J., 149, 168, 335, 341, 344
Wong, D. Y., 168
Woods, W. A., 327, 331
Word boundaries, 130, 318f
Word matcher, 321ff, 324
Word recognition, 188
Word spotting, 292, 317ff, 319
    HMM recognizer for, 318
Word-length limitations, 5
Wraparound, 22
Wrench, E. H., Jr, 338, 341, 344

Yang, S.-C., 203, 224
Yavuz, D., 209, 223
Young, M. A., 342, 344

Z transform:
    direct, 13
    elementary properties, 15f
    inverse, 13
Z transforms, 13ff, 112, 146f
    of errors, 147
Zelinski, R., 258f, 261, 331
Zero crossing locations, 208f
Zero crossings, 208f, 293, 304, 321
Zero padding, 31f, 131
Zeroes, 17, 137
Zue, W. V., 306, 330
Zwislocki, J. J., 83